2011
The Supreme Court Review

2011
The

"Judges as persons, or courts as institutions, are entitled to no greater
immunity from criticism than other persons or institutions . . .
[J]udges must be kept mindful of their limitations and
of their ultimate public responsibility by a vigorous
stream of criticism expressed with candor however blunt."
—*Felix Frankfurter*

". . . while it is proper that people should find fault when
their judges fail, it is only reasonable that they should recognize the
difficulties. . . . Let them be severely brought to book,
when they go wrong, but by those who will take the trouble
to understand them."
—*Learned Hand*

THE LAW SCHOOL

THE UNIVERSITY OF CHICAGO

Supreme Court Review

EDITED BY

DENNIS J. HUTCHINSON

DAVID A. STRAUSS

AND GEOFFREY R. STONE

 THE UNIVERSITY OF CHICAGO PRESS

CHICAGO AND LONDON

CONTENTS

HOGS GET SLAUGHTERED AT THE SUPREME COURT   1
    Suzanna Sherry

ARIZONA FREE ENTERPRISE V BENNETT AND THE
    PROBLEM OF CAMPAIGN FINANCE   39
    Stephen Ansolabehere

HARM(S) AND THE FIRST AMENDMENT   81
    Frederick Schauer

THE NEW PURPOSIVISM   113
    John F. Manning

FORMALISM WITHOUT A FOUNDATION: STERN V
    MARSHALL   183
    Erwin Chemerinsky

NOT A *WINN*-WIN: MISCONSTRUING STANDING AND THE
    ESTABLISHMENT CLAUSE   215
    William P. Marshall and Gene R. Nichol

"THE ORDINARY DIET OF THE LAW": THE PRESUMPTION
    AGAINST PREEMPTION IN THE ROBERTS COURT   253
    Ernest A. Young

THE SIGNIFICANCE OF THE FRONTIER IN AMERICAN
    CONSTITUTIONAL LAW   345
    Justin Driver

SUZANNA SHERRY

HOGS GET SLAUGHTERED AT THE SUPREME COURT

Class action plaintiffs lost two major five-to-four cases last Term. Both will potentially have a significant negative impact on future litigation. The tragedy is that the impact of each of these cases might well have been avoided had the plaintiffs' lawyers, the lower courts, and the dissenting Justices not overreached. In this article, I show that the losing side insisted on broad and untenable positions and thereby set itself up for an equally broad defeat. Whether described in the poker vernacular of this essay's title[1] or, in a more cultured phrasing, as hubris—in its original meaning of tempting the gods—the losing side got greedy and suffered the inevitable consequences. Unfortunately, in these cases, the consequences will redound to the detriment of many other potential litigants.

And these two cases are not isolated tragedies; they provide a window into a larger problem. Rule 23 turns class counsel into

Suzanna Sherry is Herman O. Loewenstein Professor of Law, Vanderbilt University Law School.

Author's note: I thank Lisa Bressman, Brian Fitzpatrick, Maria Glover, and Jay Tidmarsh for their helpful comments. Matt Meltzer provided excellent research assistance. This article was inspired by my late colleague, Richard Nagareda, from whom I learned so much. He will be missed.

[1] In poker, the expression is used to describe players with potentially winning hands who get too greedy and take risks that ultimately cause them to lose. Although the idiom has broader currency than at the poker table, it is a common sentiment there and is especially apt for a game in which players have a choice about exactly how much to risk at any given time. See Larry W. Phillips, *The Tao of Poker: 285 Rules to Transform Your Game and Your Life* 118 (Adams Media, 2003) (Rule 162, attributing it to a poker-room saying).

able.[7] If (but only if) the waiver provision was unconscionable, then the courts had to decide whether the Federal Arbitration Act (FAA) preempts state-law doctrines of unconscionability.

The relevant substantive provision of the FAA is § 2, which provides:

> A written provision in any . . . [commercial] contract . . . to settle by arbitration a controversy thereafter arising out of such contract . . . shall be valid, irrevocable, and enforceable, save upon such grounds as exist at law or in equity for the revocation of any contract.[8]

Section 2 effectively embodies an implied preemption directive and an explicit savings clause wrapped into one. The Court has frequently reiterated that the FAA manifests a "liberal federal policy favoring arbitration."[9] To the extent that state law stands as an obstacle to this federal goal, it is preempted. But state laws that are generally applicable to all contracts—that is, grounds that "exist in law or equity for the revocation of *any* contract"—are saved from preemption.

Unconscionability, of course, is a general doctrine applicable to all contracts. The clear language of § 2 therefore suggests that the FAA does *not* preempt the invalidation of an arbitration clause found to be unconscionable, because the invalidation rests on grounds that exist for "the revocation of any contract." If contracts without arbitration clauses are sometimes found to be unconscionable—as of course they are—then unconscionability should fall within the savings clause. And, indeed, both the district court and the Ninth Circuit, after concluding that the class-arbitration waiver was unconscionable under California law, found no preemption.

A majority of the Supreme Court disagreed. To be fair, the Court was in something of a bind. If ATTM's carefully constructed ar-

---

[7] The contract also contained a "blow-up" clause, declaring that if the class-arbitration ban were to be found unenforceable, the entire arbitration clause would be "null and void" and any class action would be litigated in court. Invalidation of the class-arbitration waiver thus effectively invalidated the arbitration clause. Brief for Respondent, *AT&T Mobility LLC v Concepcion*, Civil Action No 109-893, *3 (S Ct file, Sept 29, 2010) ("Respondent's Brief").

[8] 9 USC § 2.

[9] *Moses H. Cone Memorial Hospital v Mercury Construction Corp.*, 460 US 1, 24 (1983); see also *Buckeye Check Cashing, Inc. v Cardegna*, 546 US 440, 443 (2006) (noting that FAA embodies "national policy favoring arbitration").

bitration clause is invalid,[10] then *no* waiver of classwide arbitration will ever be valid. Given the strong pro-arbitration policy of the FAA—aggressively enforced by the Court in recent years[11]—as well as the legitimate reasons for a company to prefer one-on-one arbitration even if it is not trying to escape liability,[12] invalidating *all* waivers of classwide arbitration no matter the circumstances is probably not the right result. The majority, however, did more than simply uphold the particular arbitration clause. Adopting a breathtakingly broad view of implied preemption, the Court held that "requiring the availability of classwide arbitration interferes with the fundamental attributes of arbitration and thus creates a scheme inconsistent with the FAA."[13]

The Court's analysis is vulnerable to several criticisms. First, the Court's reading of § 2 turns preemption doctrine on its head. In determining whether a federal statute preempts state law, the touchstone is always congressional intent. Moreover, federalism concerns dictate a presumption against preemption: "In all preemption cases, and particularly in those in which Congress has 'legislated . . . in a field which the States have traditionally occupied,' we 'start with the assumption that the historic police powers of the States were not to be superseded by the Federal Act unless that was the clear and manifest purpose of Congress.'"[14]

In the absence of either an express statutory statement preempting state law or unequivocal evidence that Congress intended to preempt state law, the Court looks at whether the state law in question would interfere with the purposes and objectives of the federal statute. That is a questionable endeavor, as several Justices have noted, because it is "potentially boundless."[15] This type of

---

[10] See text accompanying notes 42–46 for an analysis of the special features of ATTM's arbitration clause.

[11] For a discussion of this trend, see Gilles, 104 Mich L Rev at 393–96 (cited in note 3). The trend has continued. See, for example, *Stolt-Nielsen SA v AnimalFeeds International Corp.*, 130 S Ct 1758 (2010); *Rent-a-Center West v Jackson*, 130 S Ct 2772 (2010).

[12] See text accompanying notes 55–68 for a discussion of these reasons.

[13] 131 S Ct at 1748.

[14] *Medtronic Inc. v Lohr*, 518 US 470, 485 (1996) (citation omitted), quoting *Rice v Santa Fe Elevator Corp.*, 331 US 218, 230 (1947). See also *Wyeth v Levine*, 129 S Ct 1187, 1195 n 3 (2009); *Altria Group, Inc. v Good*, 555 US 70, 76 (2008); *Bates v Dow Agrosciences LLC*, 544 US 431, 449 (2005).

[15] *Geier v American Honda Motor Co.*, 529 US 861, 907 (2000) (Stevens, J, dissenting); see also *Wyeth v Levine*, 129 S Ct at 1207 (Thomas, J, concurring in judgment); *Pharmaceutical Research & Manufacturers of America v Walsh*, 538 US 644, 678 (2003) (Thomas,

implied preemption should therefore be cabined—and rare—even for statutes that contain no savings clause. But the *AT&T Mobility* majority went even further than ordinary purposes-and-objectives implied preemption: It found such preemption in the face of an express savings clause. Only once before—and in a much narrower context—has the Court ever overridden an express savings clause by finding implied preemption.[16] Doing so is inconsistent with both the presumption against preemption and the goal of implementing congressional intent.

Second, the Court read into the FAA a particular approach to implied preemption that is inconsistent with the statutory language. The FAA saves from preemption "such grounds as exist . . . for the revocation of any contract." The *AT&T Mobility* majority recognized that California unconscionability law applies equally to waivers of class arbitration and waivers of class litigation, and is thus "a doctrine normally thought to be generally applicable."[17] It nevertheless concluded that even a generally applicable state-law doctrine is preempted if it is "applied in a fashion that disfavors arbitration."[18]

The majority gave as examples of laws "applied in a fashion that disfavors arbitration" hypothetical state laws conditioning enforceability of arbitration clauses on the availability of judicially monitored discovery or on the application of the Federal Rules of Evidence, and found the availability of classwide arbitration to be similar.[19] These examples—as well as the Court's analysis of how a requirement of class arbitration interferes with the purposes of arbitration[20]—suggest that the majority did *not* mean to focus on instances in which state (or federal) courts apply the same doctrines differentially in cases that involve arbitration clauses and cases that do not, because all of the examples supplied by the majority (including the classwide arbitration at issue in *AT&T Mobility*) seem to assume that the doctrine will be applied equally in all cases.

Instead, the majority seems to have had in mind a concept anal-

---

J, concurring in judgment); *Crosby v National Foreign Trade Council*, 530 US 363, 388–91 (2000) (Scalia, J, concurring in judgment).

[16] See *Geier*, 529 US at 861 (2000).

[17] 131 S Ct at 1747.

[18] Id.

[19] Id at 1747–48.

[20] Id at 1751–52. For further discussion of that analysis, see text accompanying notes 21–25.

ogous to disparate impact. Although unconscionability applies identically in all cases to invalidate certain limitations on classwide dispute resolution, it disproportionately invalidates arbitration contracts because they are inherently more likely to run afoul of the requirements. Similarly, a requirement that all enforceable contracts provide for the use of discovery or evidence rules will disproportionately invalidate arbitration contracts. Another way to put it is to suggest that these sorts of requirements will have a disparate impact on arbitration generally, by influencing contracting parties to prefer litigation.

But neither the language nor the purpose of the FAA justifies importing a disparate impact principle into the savings clause. The unconscionability principle is a "ground[] . . . for the revocation of any contract"; its application is not limited, in principle or in fact, to agreements to arbitrate. As for purposes, the FAA was enacted primarily to counter state (and federal) hostility to arbitration: "the basic purpose of the Federal Arbitration Act is to overcome courts' refusal to enforce agreements to arbitrate."[21] It therefore should not be read to preempt a neutral state doctrine—like unconscionability—unless the purpose of that doctrine was to diminish the enforceability of arbitration clauses. The Court was mistaken to compare unconscionability to hypothetical state law requirements that juries be used, that judicially supervised discovery be allowed, or that the Federal Rules of Evidence be followed, because those requirements would be obvious pretexts, designed to prevent arbitration. But there is no evidence that California's doctrine of unconscionability was in any way motivated by hostility toward arbitration.

In fact, the first case in which a California court found the unavailability of classwide dispute resolution unconscionable was *America Online, Inc. v Superior Court*,[22] which involved class *actions* rather than class *arbitration*. The court found the "unavailability of class action relief . . . in and by itself sufficient to preclude enforcement" of a consumer contract.[23] Four years later, the Cal-

---

[21] *Allied-Bruce Terminix Companies v Dobson*, 513 US 265, 270 (1995).

[22] 90 Cal App 4th 1, 108 Cal Rptr 2d 699 (Cal Ct App 2001).

[23] 90 Cal App 4th at 18, 108 Cal Rptr 2d at 713. The contractual provision at issue was a forum-selection clause, but because the forum specified by the contract did not permit consumer class actions, the court found it to be the "functional equivalent" of a class-action waiver. 90 Cal App 4th at 5, 108 Cal Rptr 2d at 702.

ifornia Supreme Court relied in part on *America Online* when it
held, in *Discover Bank v Superior Court*, that exculpatory waivers
of either class actions or class arbitration are unconscionable.[24]
Other California courts have also applied the *Discover Bank* doctrine to class-action waivers in contracts without arbitration
clauses.[25] In light of the absence of any deliberate attempt to disadvantage or limit *arbitration* contracts, the majority's holding that
the FAA preempts neutral, generally applicable California unconscionability doctrines because of their effect on arbitration
clauses is a misreading of the federal statute.

Finally, the majority turns its back on a recent, directly relevant
case, without so much as a citation to it. In the course of its
purposes-and-objectives analysis, the majority suggested that classwide arbitration interferes with the goals of the FAA because of
the "fundamental" differences between classwide and bilateral arbitration.[26] In particular, the Court reasoned, "class arbitration
greatly increases the risks to defendants" because the "higher
stakes of class litigation" will cause defendants to be "pressured
into settling questionable claims."[27] But just the previous Term,
in *Shady Grove Orthopedic Associates v Allstate Insurance Co.*,[28] a
majority that included three members of the *AT&T Mobility* majority held that class litigation *did not* fundamentally differ from
bilateral litigation. Rejecting the defendant's argument that allowing class litigation "transform[s] the dispute over a *five hundred*
dollar penalty into a dispute over a *five million* dollar penalty," the
Court in *Shady Grove* described the threat of greater liability as
just an "incidental effect" of the availability of a class action.[29] The

---

[24] 113 P3d 1100, 1106–07, 1108 (2005). The Ninth Circuit ruling reversed by *AT&T
Mobility* also relied on *Discover Bank*.

[25] See, for example, *In re Yahoo! Litigation*, 251 FRD 459 (CD Cal 2008); *Elhilu v Quiznos
Franchise Co., LLC*, No 06-CV-07855 (CD Cal April 3, 2008). Courts in other states have
also refused to enforce class-action waivers (or forum-selection clauses with the same
effect) in nonarbitration cases. See, for example, *Dix v ICT Group, Inc.*, 161 P3d 1016
(Wash 2007); *America Online, Inc. v Pasieka*, 870 S2d 170 (Fla Ct App 2004).

[26] 131 S Ct at 1750, quoting *Stolt-Nielsen*, 130 S Ct at 1776.

[27] 131 S Ct at 1752. The Court also pointed to the fact that class arbitration might
slow down the dispute-resolution process and the fact that class arbitration requires procedural formality. Id at 1751. As the dissent points out, the Court has previously upheld
state-law requirements that have each of these effects. See id at 1761 (Breyer, J, dissenting).

[28] 130 S Ct 1431 (2010).

[29] Id at 1443. The *Shady Grove* plurality—which largely overlapped the *AT&T Mobility*
majority, with both opinions written by Justice Scalia—may have been concerned about
a possible tension with the Rules Enabling Act, 28 USC § 2072. If bringing claims as a

class action in *Shady Grove* and class arbitration in *AT&T Mobility* both increased the stakes for the defendant in the same way, creating what the latter case labeled a "risk of 'in terrorem' settlements."[30] One would therefore expect the *AT&T Mobility* Court to follow, or at least to distinguish explicitly, *Shady Grove* in its analysis of whether classwide and bilateral dispute resolution are so fundamentally different that class arbitration interferes with the purposes of arbitration.[31] It did not do so.

B. THE ROAD NOT TAKEN

On the *preemption* question, then, the dissent has the better of the argument: The FAA should not be interpreted to preempt California's neutral, generally applicable unconscionability doctrine. But that does not necessarily mean that the class-arbitration waiver in this case should have been invalidated. Indeed, given pragmatic concerns that I will address shortly, AT&T Mobility's waiver (but not all such waivers) *should* be enforceable. The problem is that once the issue was joined on preemption rather than enforceability vel non, the majority seemed unable to refrain from issuing broad pronouncements on preemption in general, and preemption of unconscionability doctrines in particular. But while the majority might have been a bit more restrained, more of the fault lies with the other side. The majority would not have addressed preemption at all, but for the insistence of the plaintiffs' lawyers, the lower federal courts, and the dissenting Justices that the class-arbitration waiver was unconscionable.[32] It is that insistence, I

---

class action has more than an incidental effect on substantive rights, then Rule 23 might be invalid. Regardless, the difference between class litigation and individual litigation should be analyzed the same way in *Shady Grove* and *Concepcion*. For further discussion of the limits on procedural rules, see note 68.

[30] 131 S Ct at 1752.

[31] The late Professor Richard Nagareda suggested that *Shady Grove* supported reversal of the Ninth Circuit. See Richard Nagareda, *The Litigation-Arbitration Dichotomy Meets the Class Action*, 86 Notre Dame L Rev 1069 (2011). His analysis, however, turns on his assumption that California unconscionability law is based on a state law policy that seeks to "confron[t] . . . the defendant with the full force of class-wide deterrence." Id at 1121. In Section IB, I take issue with that assumption.

[32] Indeed, the plaintiffs explicitly urged the Supreme Court to "decline AT&T's invitation" to decide the case on the basis of state law. Respondent's Brief at *12. Although ATTM did not explicitly ask the Supreme Court to rule on the state-law question, its brief repeatedly denigrated the Ninth Circuit's interpretation of California unconscionability law as "a new rule," a "wildly idiosyncratic interpretation," "novel," and a "plainly discriminatory application of California's unconscionability principles." See Brief for Petitioner, *AT&T Mobility LLC v Concepcion*, No 09-893, 19, 36, 43 (S Ct, filed Aug 2, 2010)

contend, that constitutes the hubris (or the greediness for a big win) that ultimately led to the majority's broad ruling. We can blame the majority for its poor legal analysis and the unnecessary breadth of the opinion. But given the lawyers' arguments, the disastrous consequences of invalidating this class-arbitration waiver clause (one of the most consumer-friendly such clauses imaginable), and the Court's previous strong support for arbitration generally, it was the dissenters who had the last clear chance to rescue the situation.

Arguments about the preemptive effect of the FAA are only relevant if the contract is in fact unconscionable under state law. The plaintiffs claimed that it was, and both the district court and the Court of Appeals explicitly agreed. The Supreme Court—including the dissenters—took those courts' word for it without comment. Had they not, the result might have been very different, because if the contract was not unconscionable there was no need to decide any preemption questions. And an examination of the context of the California Supreme Court decision in *Discover Bank*, on which the lower courts relied, demonstrates that those courts misapplied California law when they concluded that the ATTM contract was unconscionable. The whole mess might have been avoided if this issue and not the big win were the focus of the case.

How should the issue have been more modestly framed and resolved? Let us begin with basic unconscionability doctrine. Courts considering previous generations of class-arbitration waivers had invalidated them as unconscionable because they were exculpatory—they placed such onerous burdens on complaining consumers that no individual consumer would ever seek arbitration, and thus the corporate defendants could engage in unlawful conduct with impunity. The first generation of class-arbitration waivers were truly unconscionable, as "avaricious drafters included terms that excluded punitive damages and incidental or conse-

---

("Petitioner's Brief"). Perhaps ATTM failed to make the state-law argument more explicit because it, too, was greedily hoping for a broad federal-law win rather than a narrow state-law one. But the potential downside for ATTM was much lower: Had the Court rejected the preemption argument, ATTM could still have argued to other courts (both state and federal) that its particular contract was *not* unconscionable; only in the Ninth Circuit would that argument have been foreclosed. And, of course, California state courts would not be bound by the Ninth Circuit's interpretation of California law, so ATTM might have been able to undo even that damage. ATTM was therefore not risking as much as the plaintiffs were by downplaying the state-law grounds for reversal.

quential damages, prohibited attorneys fees, required the arbitration to proceed in a location far from the consumer's home, required the consumer to pay half or sometimes all of the arbitration fees, imposed mandatory confidentiality clauses, or gave the drafter the sole capability of selecting the arbitrator."[33]

Responding to multiple courts' invalidation of such contractual terms as unconscionable,[34] the second generation of class-arbitration waivers omitted all these punitive provisions and allowed consumers to bring individual claims at a relatively low cost. The problem, however, was that imposing *any* monetary cost (in addition to the expenditure of the consumer's time and energy) served as a disincentive for consumers—or attorneys, even if their fees would be paid—with very small claims. Recall that the Concepcions' claim was for $30: No individual would be willing to take that individual claim to arbitration if the only pay-out was $30; and the award of attorney's fees to a prevailing party, without some premium for the risk of losing, would be insufficient to motivate most attorneys. Some courts therefore held these second-generation waivers unconscionable as well.[35]

The California Supreme Court's decision in *Discover Bank* addressed one of these second-generation waivers. The court explained the problem with such waivers, quoting *Szetela v Discover Bank*:[36]

> Fully aware that few customers will go to the time and trouble of suing in small claims court, Discover has instead sought to create for itself virtual immunity from class or representative actions despite their potential merit, while suffering no similar detriment to its own rights. . . . The clause is not only harsh and unfair to Discover customers who

---

[33] Ramona L. Lampley, *Is Arbitration Under Attack? Exploring the Recent Judicial Skepticism of the Class Arbitration Waiver and Innovative Solutions to the Unsettled Legal Landscape*, 18 Cornell J L & Pub Pol 477, 503–04 (2009). Professor Lampley's excellent article canvasses the three generations of class arbitration waivers. For a history of the development of the first generation of waivers, see Gilles, 104 Mich L Rev at 396–99 (cited in note 3).

[34] See Lampley, 18 Cornell J L & Pub Pol at 504 n 131 (cited in note 33); Gilles, 104 Mich L Rev at 399–400 & n 136 (cited in note 3); Paul Carrington, *Unconscionable Laywers*, 19 Ga St U L Rev 361, 373–80 (2002).

[35] In addition to *Discover Bank*, see, for example, *Kristian v Comcast Corp.*, 446 F3d 25 (1st Cir 2006); *Scott v Cingular Wireless*, 161 P3d 1000 (Wash 2007); *Kinkel v Cingular Wireless LLC*, 857 NE2d 250 (Ill 2006). See also Jean R. Sternlight, *As Mandatory Binding Arbitration Meets the Class Action, Will the Class Action Survive?* 42 Wm & Mary L Rev 1, 80 (2000) ("no one has seriously suggested that arbitration ensures an economically viable forum for persons with claims of five dollars, ten dollars, or even two hundred dollars . . . [because] the minimum filing fee will exceed the size of a small claim").

[36] 97 Cal App 4th 1094, 1101, 118 Cal Rptr 2d 862, 867–68 (Cal App 2002).

might be owed a relatively small sum of money, but it also serves as a disincentive for Discover to avoid the type of conduct that might lead to class action litigation in the first place. . . . The potential for millions of customers to be overcharged small amounts without an effective method of redress cannot be ignored.[37]

This passage illustrates the problem with second-generation class arbitration waivers: Very small claims, however meritorious, are unlikely to be brought, and the bank is therefore free to engage in unlawful conduct that makes millions of dollars for the bank but that costs each consumer very little. As one commentator put it, a class arbitration waiver of this kind allows businesses "to engage in unchecked market misbehavior that results in small and seemingly insignificant consequences upon individuals, but which leads to sizeable windfalls for the particular corporation in the aggregate."[38]

The *Discover Bank* court, however, was careful to limit its holding: "We do not hold that all class action waivers are necessarily unconscionable." It invalidated only "waiver[s] . . . found in a consumer contract of adhesion in a setting in which disputes between the contracting parties predictably involve small amounts of damages . . . when it is alleged that the party with the superior bargaining power has carried out a scheme to deliberately cheat large numbers of consumers out of individually small sums of money."[39]

Discover Bank, like the other cases invalidating second-generation waivers, also found no preemption.[40] Because the unconscionability doctrine applied to *all* exculpatory contracts, not just to arbitration clauses, the FAA savings clause protected it from preemption. The fact that the Supreme Court did not grant certiorari in any of these earlier cases[41] suggests that it was content to allow the unconscionability doctrine and the FAA to coexist.

AT&T Mobility's contract, however, was different. It contained a third-generation arbitration clause. This clause did more than simply require arbitration and waive classwide arbitration: It set

---

[37] 113 P3d at 1107–08.

[38] J. Maria Glover, Note, *Beyond Unconscionability: Class Action Waivers and Mandatory Arbitration Agreements*, 59 Vand L Rev 1735, 1747 (2006).

[39] 113 P3d at 1110.

[40] Id at 1110–17.

[41] See Nagareda, 86 Notre Dame L Rev at 1106 (cited in note 31).

up a complicated structure that was designed both to enable small claims and to channel them into bilateral arbitration. Responding to some of the problems with first-generation waiver clauses, the ATTM contract provided that ATTM would pay the cost of arbitration unless an arbitrator determined that the claim was frivolous; allowed consumers to choose arbitration in person (in the consumer's home county), by telephone, or through documentary evidence; and allowed the arbitrator to award any remedy including injunctive relief, punitive damages, and attorneys' fees.[42]

More importantly, the ATTM contract also rectified the problems with second-generation waivers by offering premiums to successful consumers and their attorneys. It provided that if the arbitrator awarded more than ATTM's last written settlement offer, ATTM would pay the jurisdictional maximum of the small claims court in the consumer's jurisdiction—which in California is $7,500—if that amount was larger than the arbitrator's award.[43] It also provided that if the arbitral award was larger than ATTM's last settlement offer, ATTM would pay double the attorneys' fees.[44] Finally, it provided for streamlined procedures, with relevant information and documents available on ATTM's website.[45] The district court concluded that the contractually mandated arbitration process was "quick, easy to use, and prompts full or, as described by Plaintiffs, even excess payment to the customer *without* the need to arbitrate or litigate."[46]

Such a clause is not exculpatory and therefore should not be unconscionable under *Discover Bank*. The incentive structure gives consumers a reason to pursue small individual claims and ATTM a reason to settle such claims fairly. Even an individual consumer with a small claim has an incentive to mail in the one-page Notice of Dispute form that is posted on the ATTM website[47] (which is surely no more onerous than consulting an attorney to initiate a class action). By filing such a claim, the consumer can anticipate

---

[42] See *Laster v T-Mobile USA, Inc.*, 2008 WL 5216255 at *2–3 & n 2 (SD Cal Aug 11, 2008), aff'd, *Laster v AT&T Mobility LLC*, 584 F3d 849 (9th Cir 2009), rev'd, *AT&T Mobility v Concepcion*, 131 S Ct 1740 (2011).

[43] Id at *2.

[44] Id.

[45] Id at *3.

[46] Id at *11.

[47] Id at *3.

either a prompt and reasonable settlement offer or a windfall if an arbitrator ultimately finds the settlement offer inadequate. And ATTM has every incentive to offer an appropriate amount in settlement, rather than insist on arbitration, in order to avoid the penalties that attach if an arbitrator ultimately awards more than the settlement offer.[48] The waiver clause is thus not exculpatory because it does not allow ATTM to "cheat large numbers of consumers out of individually small sums of money."[49]

The Ninth Circuit essentially conceded that ATTM had an incentive to settle all disputes for reasonable amounts. The problem, according to that court, was somewhat different:

> The provision does essentially guarantee that the company will make any aggrieved customer whole who files a claim. Although this is, in and of itself, a good thing, the problem with it under California law—as we read that law—is that not every aggrieved customer will file a claim.[50]

Similarly, the district court was troubled by the premium provisions because they "prompt[ed] ATTM to *accept liability*, rather than 'escape liability,' for small dollar claims."[51] In other words, the problem was not that the contract created "a disincentive for [defendant] to avoid the type of conduct that might lead to class action litigation in the first place," but that it did not create *sufficient* incentive to avoid that conduct because some aggrieved consumers might not file claims.

But think about the most likely reasons a consumer would not file a claim: Either she concludes that the burden of filing a claim outweighs the harm she has suffered, or she is unaware that she has suffered any harm at all. Given the ease of claim filing under the AT&T Mobility contract, the first possibility seems unlikely. Resting a finding of unconscionability on the second possibility requires a conclusion that we ought to deter conduct that is not

---

[48] Not only does ATTM have an incentive to offer an adequate settlement, but one study suggests that a party making a written settlement offer is less likely to err in its calculation of the ultimate worth of a claim as found by a court or an arbitrator. See Randall L. Kiser, Martin A. Asher, and Blakely B. McShane, *Let's Not Make a Deal: An Empirical Study of Decision Making in Unsuccessful Settlement Negotiations*, 5 J Empirical Leg Stud 551, 572–74 (2008).

[49] *Discover Bank*, 113 P3d at 1110. Professor Lampley offered a similar analysis prior to the *AT&T Mobility* litigation. See Lampley, 18 Cornell J L & Pub Pol at 513–17 (cited in note 33).

[50] *Laster*, 584 F3d at 856 n 9.

[51] *Laster*, 2008 WL 5216255 at *10.

perceived as harmful by the person it supposedly harms. While that conclusion may be warranted in rare cases—perhaps where the target is especially vulnerable—it seems a poor basis on which to invalidate a broad range of consumer contracts. And under either possibility, it seems contrary to our underlying principle of litigant autonomy to argue that legal doctrines should entice people into litigation rather than simply removing any barriers that inhibit them from suing.[52]

The AT&T Mobility contract is thus a far cry from the second-generation waivers found exculpatory in *Discover Bank* on the basis that it would not be worthwhile for *any* aggrieved consumer to pursue arbitration.[53] The lower courts' assumption that the availability of classwide resolution provides significantly more deterrence thus ends up resting on the most likely monetary difference between classwide and bilateral dispute resolution: the ratcheting up of attorneys' fees as a percentage of the settlement.[54]

But if a third-generation arbitration clause like that in the ATTM contract is not exculpatory, why would a company include one, and why would plaintiffs—or their lawyers—object? Understanding the answers to those questions might help explain why the plaintiffs overreached. The key lies in the effect of aggregating multiple individual claims into a single classwide suit or arbitration proceeding.

There is great dispute about whether a "hydraulic pressure . . . to settle"[55] actually causes defendants to settle class actions for more than they are worth on their merits.[56] The most persuasive

---

[52] This question also implicates the relationship between substance and procedure, which is beyond the scope of this article. See note 68.

[53] Professor Nagareda identified the crux of the difference as that between exculpation and suboptimal deterrence, 86 Notre Dame L Rev at 1118–19 (cited in note 31). He suggested that the lower courts in *AT&T Mobility* were implementing a state-law policy in favor of "confronting . . . a defendant with the full force of class-wide deterrence," and that such a policy cannot trump federal law. Id at 1121. My argument is that state-law policy, as enunciated in *Discover Bank*, does not in fact embody a preference for full-force deterrence; the federal courts were mistaken in thinking that it did.

[54] See text accompanying notes 67–68.

[55] *Newton v Merrill Lynch*, 259 F3d 154, 164 (3d Cir 2011).

[56] Compare Henry Friendly, *Federal Jurisdiction: A General View* 119–20 (Columbia, 1973) (aggregation "blackmails" defendants into settling); Richard A. Epstein, *Class Actions: Aggregation, Amplification, and Distortion*, 2003 U Chi Legal F 457 (examining distortion effect of class actions); Alan S. Kaplinsky and Mark J. Levin, *Excuse Me, but Who's the Predator: Banks Can Use Arbitration Clauses as a Defense*, 7 Bus L Today 24 (May–June 1998) ("companies often feel pressured to pay substantial amounts in settlement for reasons having nothing to do with the actual merits of the dispute"), with Charles Silver, *"We're*

argument that aggregation distorts settlement values is that it increases the variance, leading risk-averse defendants[57] to settle even
low-probability or unmeritorious claims. Consider the situation
in *In re Rhone-Poulenc Rorer Inc.*,[58] probably the most famous example of a judge declining to certify a class because of the likely
settlement pressure exerted by certification. In *Rhone-Poulenc*,
Judge Posner estimated—based on prior individual trials—that
plaintiffs had approximately an 8 percent chance of prevailing.[59]
He noted a concern with "forcing these defendants to stake their
companies on the outcome of a single jury trial."[60] As Professor
Richard Nagareda has explained, Judge Posner was concerned
about the variance, or "amplification effect" of aggregation.[61] If
liability determinations were spread out over one thousand individual trials, the great likelihood was that the defendants would
indeed lose about 8 percent of the cases, and pay out 8 percent
of the claimed damages. Perhaps they would lose 5 percent or 15
percent, but the variance would still be small. If, instead, liability
was determined in a single class action, the defendants faced a 92
percent chance of paying nothing and an 8 percent chance of
having to pay *100 percent of the claimed damages*. Although the
expected value is the same under both scenarios, the variance has
increased dramatically, and—given risk aversion—so has the pres-

---

Scared to Death": Class Certification and Blackmail, 78 NYU L Rev 1357 (2003) (suggesting
that class actions are rarely if ever inappropriately threatening); Bruce Hay and David
Rosenberg, *"Sweetheart" and "Blackmail" Settlements in Class Actions: Reality and Remedy*,
75 Notre Dame L Rev 1377 (2000) (suggesting that few class actions are blackmail). See
also William B. Rubenstein, *Why Enable Litigation? A Positive Externalities Theory of the
Small Claims Class Action*, 74 UMKC L Rev 709 (2006) (arguing aggregation and the
resulting settlement pressure causes positive externalities).

[57] Defendants as a group tend to be more risk-seeking than risk-averse, see Jeffrey J.
Rachlinski, *Gains, Losses, and the Psychology of Litigation*, 70 S Cal L Rev 113 (1996), but
the typical aggregation scenario makes them more risk-averse in two ways. First, the
uncertainty caused by a large variance induces defendants to behave in risk-averse fashion.
See Joseph A. Grundfest and Peter H. Huang, *The Unexpected Value of Litigation: A Real
Options Perspective*, 58 Stan L Rev 1267 (2006). Second, risk-seeking defendants and risk-
averse plaintiffs switch attitudes when confronting low-probability claims. See Chris Guth-
rie, *Framing Frivolous Litigation: A Psychological Theory*, 67 U Chi L Rev 163 (2000). As
one scholar put it, "[r]isk aversion comes naturally to defendants facing mass litigation."
Howard M. Erichson, *Uncertainty and the Advantage of Collective Settlement*, 60 DePaul L
Rev 627, 636 (2011).

[58] 51 F3d 1293 (7th Cir 1995).

[59] Id at 1298.

[60] Id at 1299.

[61] Richard A. Nagareda, *Aggregation and Its Discontents: Class Settlement Pressure, Class-
Wide Arbitration, and CAFA*, 106 Colum L Rev 1873, 1881–82 (2006).

sure to settle.[62] Aggregation, by increasing the risk to defendants, increases their incentive to "offload" that risk by offering a settlement that includes a premium.[63]

If aggregation (whether in litigation or arbitration) has this effect, we can understand why defendants would favor, and plaintiffs would disfavor, waivers of classwide arbitration. But a waiver by itself (that is, a typical second-generation arbitration clause) also has the effect of excusing liability altogether. A second-generation waiver, therefore, does not tell us whether the defendant is trying to avoid liability altogether or simply to avoid being put in a position where it might have to overcompensate plaintiffs for conceded liability.

That is where the third-generation arbitration clause comes in. An arbitration clause like ATTM's is designed—as the district court noted—to cause the defendant to "accept liability" by making it easy for consumers to make claims and expensive for the defendant to refuse to adequately compensate meritorious claimants. But at the same time, the clause precludes plaintiffs from using the pressure of a class action to demand *excessive* compensation. The third-generation clause, especially as a development after the invalidation of second-generation clauses, removes the ambiguity about the defendant's motives: Rather than trying to avoid liability altogether, the defendant is simply trying to ensure that plaintiffs will obtain only the compensation for which ATTM is liable and not the overcompensation that might be extracted based on the increase in variance.[64]

Another aspect of the distortive effect of aggregation provides

---

[62] A second reason that aggregation increases the pressure to settle is that it simply increases the likely number of claims. As several scholars have suggested, this is not a valid argument against class treatment—if the claims are meritorious, we ought to encourage them and remove any barriers to filing them. See, for example, Nagareda, 106 Colum L Rev at 1882–85 (cited in note 61); Silver, 78 NYU L Rev at 1365–69 (cited in note 56). But see Andrew T. Berry, *Comments on Aggregation: Some Unintended Consequences of Aggregative Disposition Procedures*, 31 Seton Hall L Rev 920, 921–22 (2001) (suggesting that defendants are likely to settle large class actions for accounting reasons rather than because of their likely liability).

[63] See Richard Nagareda, *1938 All Over Again? Pretrial as Trial in Complex Litigation*, 60 DePaul L Rev 647, 668–69 (2011); see also Jonathan T. Molot, *A Market in Litigation Risk*, 76 U Chi L Rev 367 (2009).

[64] Moreover, to the extent that showing unconscionability under *Discover Bank* requires "a scheme to *deliberately* cheat large numbers of consumers," 113 P3d at 1110, the Concepcion class seems particularly ill-suited to claim unconscionability. After all, the tax money that was collected on the "free" phone went straight to the state.

a second insight into the ATTM arbitration clause. The conventional justification for class actions for damages under Rule 23(b)(3)—as opposed to "limited fund" class actions under Rule 23(b)(1) or suits seeking injunctive or declaratory relief under Rule 23(b)(2)—is that it removes barriers to suit that would otherwise exist for small, unmarketable claims.[65] This justification diminishes or backfires when small claims are marketable. For example, when the legislature has provided for minimum statutory damages in order to ensure that plaintiffs with small actual damages will still be likely to bring suit, a class action may be described as overkill. One court described the issue as

> aris[ing] from the effects of combining a statutory scheme that imposes minimum statutory damages awards on a per-consumer basis—usually in order to encourage the filing of individual lawsuits as a means of private enforcement of consumer protection laws—with the class action mechanism that aggregates many claims—often because there would otherwise be no incentive to bring an individual claim. Such a combination may expand the potential statutory damages so far beyond the actual damages suffered that the statutory damages come to resemble punitive damages—yet ones that are awarded as a matter of strict liability, rather than for the egregious conduct typically necessary to support a punitive damages award. It may be that the aggregation in a class action of large numbers of statutory damages claims potentially distorts the purpose of both statutory damages and class actions. If so, such a distortion could create a potentially enormous aggregate recovery for plaintiffs, and thus an *in terrorem* effect on defendants, which may induce unfair settlements.[66]

The ATTM premium provisions—which give plaintiffs and their attorneys incentives to file small claims—operate similarly to statutory damages provisions. And, analogously, the availability of

---

[65] See, for example, *Eisen v Carlisle & Jacquelin*, 417 US 156, 161 (1974) ("Economic reality dictates that [a suit involving a $70 claim] proceed as a class action or not at all."); *Phillips Petroleum Co. v Shutts*, 472 US 797, 809 (1985) ("Class actions . . . may permit the plaintiffs to pool claims which would be uneconomical to litigate individually."); *Amchem Prods, Inc. v Windsor*, 521 US 591, 617 (1997) ("The policy at the very core of the class action mechanism is to overcome the problem that small recoveries do not provide the incentive for any individual to bring a solo action prosecuting his or her rights.").

[66] *Parker v Time Warner Entertainment Co.*, 331 F3d 13, 22 (2d Cir 2003). See also J. Maria Glover, *The Structural Role of Private Enforcement in Public Law*, 53 Wm & Mary L Rev 1137 (forthcoming 2012) (calling the combination of statutory damages and class actions "remedial overkill"). As Professor Stephen Burbank put it in a posting on the Civil Procedure Listserv, "most of the pain that opponents of the modern class action have felt has been where, from the perspective of private enforcement, Rule 23 acts as a wild-card, trans-substantively raising the stakes without regard to congruence with the goals of substantive law."

class arbitration magnifies the effect of the premiums. Thus a third-generation arbitration clause, offering premiums but waiving class arbitration, serves as choice between two alternative methods of removing barriers for low-value claims. While consumers might prefer one method over the other, inclusion of the premium provisions strongly suggests that the corporation is not attempting to avoid liability.

Finally, even if the classwide nature of the dispute-resolution process does not itself cause defendants to settle unmeritorious claims, or to settle meritorious claims for more than their objective worth, another aspect of class arbitration might. It is well known that class actions—especially those involving small claims—are driven less by the class members (even the named class representative) and more by entrepreneurial lawyers.[67] Those lawyers, however, may reap significantly greater fees from class actions than they might from a series of individual suits, at least where the claims are small. One scholar has suggested that in a large percentage of damages class actions, "attorneys [are] effectively the *sole* beneficiaries."[68] It is therefore reasonable for a potential de-

---

[67] For a classic description of this regime, see John C. Coffee, Jr., *Understanding the Plaintiff's Attorney: The Implications of Economic Theory for Private Enforcement of Law Through Class and Derivative Actions*, 86 Colum L Rev 669 (1986); see also John C. Coffee, Jr., *The Regulation of Entrepreneurial Litigation: Balancing Fairness and Efficiency in the Large Class Action*, 54 U Chi L Rev 877 (1987); Jonathan R. Macey and Geoffrey P. Miller, *The Plaintiffs' Attorney's Role in Class Action and Derivative Litigation: Economic Analysis and Recommendations for Reform*, 58 U Chi L Rev 1 (1991); Martin H. Redish, *Class Actions, Litigation Autonomy, and the Foundations of Procedural Due Process*, 95 Cal L Rev 1573 (2007).

[68] Martin H. Redish, *Wholesale Justice: Constitutional Democracy and the Problem of the Class Action Lawsuit* 15 (Stanford, 2009). See also John H. Beisner, Matthew Shors, and Jessica D. Miller, *Class Action "Cops": Public Servants or Private Entrepreneurs?* 57 Stan L Rev 1441 (2005); Jill E. Fisch, *Class Action Reform, Qui Tam, and the Role of the Plaintiff*, 60 L & Contemp Probs 167 (1997); Susan P. Koniak and George M. Cohen, *Under Cloak of Settlement*, 82 Va L Rev 1051 (1996); Jay Tidmarsh, *Pound's Century, and Ours*, 81 Notre Dame L Rev 513 (2006); Charles Wolfram, *Mass Torts—Messy Ethics*, 80 Cornell L Rev 1228 (1995).
Some scholars have argued that despite the absence of benefit to class members, class actions are socially beneficial because they "caus[e] the defendant-wrongdoer to internalize the social costs of its actions." Myriam Gilles and Gary B. Friedman, *Exploding the Class Action Agency Costs Myth: The Social Utility of Entrepreneurial Lawyers*, 155 U Pa L Rev 103, 105 (2006); see also Brian Fitzpatrick, *Do Class Action Lawyers Make Too Little?* 158 U Pa L Rev 2043 (2010) (suggesting that the deterrence value of class actions justifies higher fees for lawyers, especially when the class benefits little). The problem with this argument is the same one that underlies the Ninth Circuit's misapplication of *Discover Bank*: it assumes, controversially, that the measure of the validity of a *procedural* rule is its deterrence value. See Stephen B. Burbank, *Aggregation on the Couch: The Strategic Uses of Ambiguity and Hypocrisy*, 106 Colum L Rev 1924, 1929 (2006) ("where is the authority to promulgate a rule with the purpose . . . of enabling vigorous enforcement . . . ?"); Beisner, Shors, and Miller, 57 Stan L Rev at 1442 (cited in note 68) ("if the true purpose of the

fendant to wish to avoid classwide actions—including class arbitration—in order to avoid the large additional expense of attorneys' fees. The ATTM contract, typical of third-generation clauses, thus attempted to provide sufficient incentive to attorneys (by paying twice their fees) even in the absence of the more substantial class-action payoff.

In summary, the ATTM clause was almost certainly not exculpatory, and therefore should not have been found unconscionable. By insisting that it was, the plaintiffs, the lower courts, and the dissenting Justices forced the majority to confront the preemption question. The result was a disastrously broad opinion that abrogated *Discover Bank* (and its equivalents) even for the *second*-generation clauses (and their equivalents). *AT&T Mobility* may even be read by some courts to make harsh *first*-generation clauses enforceable, because the invalidity of such contracts rests on the same general doctrine of unconscionability that the Court found preempted by the FAA. The majority opinion thus serves as an invitation for corporations to go back to contracts of adhesion that are much less consumer friendly than the ATTM contract.

Was there any way to avoid this fiasco? If my analysis was correct, then there was a way at every stage in the litigation. The simplest solution, of course, would have been for the plaintiffs' lawyers to refrain from challenging ATTM's class waiver—focusing instead on more exculpatory contracts—or for the lower federal courts to have found the waiver valid. But even at the Supreme Court, the damage could have been minimized. The dissenting Justices should have conceded that the Ninth Circuit erred in its application of California law,[69] rather than insisting that the clause was invalid. That would have set up a reversal on narrow grounds, and they might have attracted at least one more vote. We can't be sure, of course. But in other cases last Term, several Justices in the *AT&T Mobility* majority refused to sign on to broad pro-

---

class concept were to facilitate private law enforcement" it would violate the Rules Enabling Act, which "authorizes the federal judicial branch to create nothing more than purely procedural mechanisms"). Even if we cannot sharply distinguish between substance and procedure, we should place *some* limits on the substantive effects of rules of procedure. See John Hart Ely, *The Irrepressible Myth of Erie*, 87 Harv L Rev 693 (1974). A full discussion is beyond the scope of this article, but wherever we draw the line, maximizing deterrence seems to be on the substantive side. In any event, in most class actions, the primary motivation of class counsel is to maximize fees, not achieve optimal deterrence. See Jay Tidmarsh, *Rethinking Adequacy of Representation*, 87 Tex L Rev 1137, 1170 (2009).

[69] See *Salve Regina College v Russell*, 499 US 225 (1991) (holding appellate courts should decide questions of state law *de novo*, with no deference to district court determination).

nouncements, concurring only in the judgment because they preferred to rely on narrower grounds.[70] Perhaps a similar approach
would have been attractive in this case—and, if the dissenting
Justices had been the ones proposing it, they would have put together a majority. In particular, Justice Thomas, who takes a very
dim view of what he calls "purposes-and-objectives" preemption,[71]
might have joined an opinion reversing the Ninth Circuit without
reaching the preemption question. It would then have been the
Justices urging broad preemption who would have been reduced
to writing nonprecedential concurrences.

The lawyers and judges who would settle for nothing short of
the invalidation of all arbitration waivers ended up with a decision
that arguably creates a regime prohibiting the invalidation of any.
Through their obduracy, they squandered the opportunity to cabin
the damage done by the majority's broad preemption holding. *That*
was unconscionable.

II. WAL-MART V DUKES

Wal-Mart differs from *AT&T Mobility* in a number of ways,
but it ultimately illustrates the same dangers of overreaching. The
Court was again correct in rejecting certification of the *Wal-Mart*
class, but this time the majority's reasoning was sound. In this
section, therefore, I begin not by criticizing the majority's reasoning but by defending it, showing that the plaintiffs tried to
stretch existing doctrine too far. However, the majority opinion
contained some broad language and other potentially troublesome
aspects that may bear harmful fruit in future cases. And the dissenting opinion, by highlighting some of that language, increases
the probability that the case will be read broadly in the future. As
in *AT&T Mobility*, the plaintiffs and their sympathizers might have

---

[70] See, for example, *J. McIntyre Machinery, Ltd. v Nicastro*, 131 S Ct 2780, 2793 (2011)
(Breyer, J, joined by Alito, J, concurring in judgment) ("this [case] is an unsuitable vehicle
for making broad pronouncements that refashion basic jurisdictional rules"); *Ortiz v Jordan*,
131 S Ct 884, 893 (2011) (Thomas, J, joined by Scalia, J, and Kennedy, J, concurring in
judgment) ("I would limit our decision to the question presented and remand for consideration of any additional issues.").

[71] See *Wyeth*, 129 S Ct at 1205, 1211–18 (Thomas, J, concurring in judgment); see also
AT&T Mobility, 131 S Ct at 1754 (Thomas, J, concurring). See also Gregory M. Dickinson,
An Empirical Study of Obstacle Preemption in the Supreme Court, 89 Neb L Rev 682 (2011)
(documenting Justice Thomas's aversion to obstacle preemption).

limited the damage done by the decision if they had not been greedy.

A. REACHING TOO HIGH: UNCONSCIOUS DISCRIMINATION

The *Wal-Mart* plaintiffs were more sympathetic, but the over-reaching by lawyers and judges had similar consequences. The plaintiffs alleged that their employer, Wal-Mart, had violated Title VII by discriminating against them on the basis of their gender in salary and promotion decisions. Based on the affidavits sub-mitted in the case, it seems very likely that some female employees were indeed discriminated against and could have prevailed in individual suits against the company.

The overreaching in the case started at its very inception: Rather than suing individually, Betty Dukes and several other Wal-Mart employees brought a nationwide class action on behalf of 1.5 mil-lion current and former female employees. They alleged that the company intentionally discriminated on the basis of gender. It did so, they argued, by granting complete discretion to individual store managers to make salary and promotion decisions and simulta-neously creating a "corporate culture" of gender bias.

No class action of this magnitude had ever been certified. The class consisted of a million and a half members, working at 3,400 stores, alleging discrimination by what the Court characterized as "a kaleidoscope of supervisors (male and female), subject to a va-riety of regional policies that all differed."[72]

Rule 23(a)(2) requires at least one "question[] of law or fact common to the class" in order for certification to be appropriate. As both the majority and the dissent recognized, this requirement really focuses on the common *resolution* of questions:

> What matters to class certification . . . is not the raising of common "questions"—even in droves—but, rather the capacity of a classwide proceeding to generate common *answers* apt to drive the resolution of the litigation.[73]

---

[72] *Wal-Mart Stores, Inc. v Dukes*, 131 S Ct 2541, 2557 (2011), quoting *Dukes v Wal-Mart Stores, Inc.*, 603 F3d 571, 652 (9th Cir 2010) (Kozinski dissenting).

[73] 131 S Ct at 2551, quoting Richard Nagareda, *Class Certification in the Age of Aggregate Proof*, 84 NYU L Rev 97, 132 (2009) (emphasis in original). See also id at 2567 (Ginsburg, J, dissenting): "Thus, a 'question' 'common to the class' must be a dispute, either of fact or of law, *the resolution of which will advance the determination of the class members' claims*" (emphasis added).

Because of the decentralized decision making by Wal-Mart managers, claims by members of the class would not share any common answers to the question "why was I disfavored?"[74] unless the plaintiffs could "provide a nexus between the subjective decision-making and discrimination."[75]

The plaintiffs argued that the required nexus was a company-wide policy of discrimination. But Wal-Mart had an official policy against discrimination, imposed penalties for EEO violations, and had won national diversity awards.[76] Plaintiffs therefore had to rely on a claim that despite Wal-Mart's announced anti-discrimination policies, a "corporate culture" of gender bias existed, providing the glue that linked the disparate individual claims together.

The most significant problem with the plaintiffs' theory is that there was insufficient evidence that such a corporate culture—if it existed—caused the discrimination against all, or even most, of the members of the class. Without a common cause for the individual discriminatory acts, the plaintiff class lacked a common question (or common answers).[77] Plaintiffs attempted to show causation through the testimony of Dr. William Bielby, their sociological expert. Relying on the concept of "social frameworks," Dr. Bielby testified that Wal-Mart was "vulnerable" to gender bias[78] and that gender stereotyping likely influenced many promotion and salary decisions made by individual Wal-Mart managers.[79]

But Dr. Bielby's testimony was insufficient to show causation, for two reasons. First, he conceded that gender stereotyping might

---

[74] 131 S Ct at 2552.

[75] *Dukes v Wal-Mart Stores, Inc.*, 222 FRD 137, 150 (ND Cal 2004), aff'd in part and rem'd in part, 603 F3d 571 (9th Cir 2010), rev'd *Wal-Mart Stores Inc. v Dukes*, 131 S Ct 2541 (2011).

[76] See *Wal-Mart*, 131 S Ct at 2553 (policy, penalties); *Dukes*, 222 FRD at 154 (penalties, awards).

[77] Note that requiring plaintiffs to show causation is not equivalent to requiring them to prove their case on the merits. To obtain class certification, plaintiffs must "affirmatively demonstrate" compliance with Rule 23's requirements, *Wal-Mart*, 131 S Ct at 2551, including the existence of a common question. Plaintiffs were relying on the theory of corporate culture to weave together the individual acts of discrimination into a single classwide common question. At the certification stage, then, they did not need to prove the *existence* of the corporate culture, but they did need to prove that the individual acts alleged to be discriminatory arose from some common source, whether corporate culture or something else. In other words, they had to show that corporate culture really was the causative glue.

[78] *Dukes*, 222 FRD at 154.

[79] Id at 153.

have influenced as few as half a percent of employment decisions at Wal-Mart.[80] The possibility that corporate culture motivated such a small number of decisions deprived that culture of its status as the link among the disparate individual acts of discrimination; Dr. Bielby's testimony therefore could not establish the existence of a common question.

Dr. Bielby also misused the concept of social frameworks by using general research findings to draw conclusions about a specific case.[81] As described by one group of prominent social-framework scholars, Dr. Bielby "utilized no standardized cultural assessment tool, no employee surveys or interviews, nor any causal testing" to conclude that "gender was a causal factor in some unspecified percentage of all personnel decisions at all Wal-Mart facilities across the USA."[82] Because his testimony was based on general research rather than on an examination of Wal-Mart or its employees, it could not demonstrate a causal link between corporate culture and any individual employment decision. Such a link cannot be assumed: There is research suggesting that implicit bias (in other words, individual internalization of a discriminatory corporate culture) does not predict discriminatory behavior.[83]

Once we strip away Dr. Bielby's testimony, the *Wal-Mart* plaintiffs are left with anecdotal evidence of individual instances of discrimination, and statistics that arguably demonstrate that women were paid less and promoted less frequently than men. Neither suffices to demonstrate the "common question" required for class certification.

As the majority noted, the anecdotal evidence was "too weak to raise any inference that all the individual, discretionary personnel

---

[80] *Dukes v Wal-Mart*, 222 FRD 189, 192 (ND Cal 2004) (ruling on motion to strike expert testimony).

[81] See John Monahan, Laurens Walker, and Gregory Mitchell, *Contextual Evidence of Gender Discrimination: The Ascendance of "Social Frameworks,"* 94 Va L Rev 1715 (2008). This essay, two of whose authors were the only sources relied on by Bielby in his analysis, specifically criticizes his testimony in this case. See id at 1716. The same authors in a later article assert that "expert opinions" that rely on "general scientific evidence to make case-specific descriptive and causal claims . . . lack legal or scientific justifications." John Monahan, Laurens Walker, and Gregory Mitchell, *The Limits of Social Framework Evidence*, 8 L Prob & Risk 307, 309 (2009).

[82] Monahan, Walker, and Mitchell, 8 L Prob & Risk at 312 (cited in note 81).

[83] See Gregory Mitchell and Philip E. Tetlock, *Antidiscrimination Law and the Perils of Mindreading*, 67 Ohio St L J 1023, 1033–34, 1065–72; Amy L. Wax, *The Discriminating Mind: Define It, Prove It*, 40 Conn L Rev 979, 984–85 (2008); Amy Wax, *Discrimination as Accident*, 74 Ind L J 1129, 1139–42 (1999).

decisions are discriminatory."[84] The dissent's contrary view of the anecdotal evidence suffered from one of the same problems that plagued Dr. Bielby's testimony. The dissenting Justices asserted that the anecdotal evidence "suggest[ed] that gender bias suffused Wal-Mart's company culture."[85] But even if that is true, there was no evidence that a discriminatory culture caused all—or even any—of the allegedly discriminatory employment decisions. The whole notion of a discriminatory company culture depends on an unjustified assumption that anyone immersed in a particular cultural milieu will necessarily respond to it in the same discriminatory manner. Without that unjustified assumption, there is no question common to all class members: Each class member is alleging an individual act of discrimination that might have occurred with or without a biased corporate culture.

Plaintiffs also introduced statistical evidence in the form of regression analyses. Holding other variables constant, plaintiffs' expert found statistically significant differences between men and women in both salary and promotion levels.[86] If there were nothing else to explain those differences, it might be plausible to conclude that company-wide gender discrimination caused them.[87] But there was something else, something much more likely than intentional discrimination by Wal-Mart. The disparities at Wal-Mart closely mirrored nationwide salary and promotion disparities.[88] As one commentator put it:

> One might say that if Wal-Mart were indeed discriminating . . . then its execution of that enterprise was startlingly inept. If a highly organized, national employer really intended to keep down its female hourly

---

[84] 131 S Ct at 2556.

[85] Id at 2563 (Ginsburg, J, dissenting). The dissent also accused the majority of requiring a specified number of anecdotes. Id at 2564 n 4. To be fair, while the majority mentions the lack of a causal link, it focuses on the number of anecdotes and also asserts that "a few anecdotes selected from literally millions of employment decisions prove nothing at all." 131 S Ct at 2556 & n 9.

[86] See id at 2555; see also id at 2564 (Ginsburg, J, dissenting).

[87] There are still some problems with that conclusion. The majority and the dissent disagreed about whether the statistical analyses demonstrated disparities within stores. See 131 S Ct at 2555 (majority); id at 2564 n 5 (dissent) (labeling it an "arcane disagreement about statistical method"). More fundamentally, regression analysis is a flawed technique—despite its almost universal judicial acceptance—for demonstrating intentional discrimination, because it shows only a correlation between a chosen set of variables rather than whether changes in one variable cause changes in the other. See D. James Greiner, *Causal Inference in Civil Rights Litigation*, 122 Harv L Rev 534 (2008).

[88] See Nagareda, 84 NYU L Rev at 154–55 (cited in note 73).

employees, then one would think that it could manage to become more than just a "conduit" for broader labor-market characteristics.[89]

The statistical evidence shows only that Wal-Mart behaved no differently than most American employers. There was no showing that the disparities were caused by a unique corporate culture at Wal-Mart rather than by whatever caused the broad labor-market disparities in general. Again, this is not to say that Wal-Mart supervisors did not discriminate, but only that the statistical evidence is not enough to demonstrate the company-wide policy of discrimination that is the necessary predicate for the court to find a common question.

It is important to remember that, as in *AT&T Mobility*, the plaintiffs in *Wal-Mart* had an economically and legally viable alternative to a class action suit. With strong evidence that individuals were the victims of intentional discrimination, significant back-pay awards at stake, and attorneys' fees available in all except frivolous cases, individual suits under Title VII were marketable. Some plaintiffs might also have been able to bring smaller class actions focused on particular regions or particular employment opportunities.[90] Instead, they tried to combine all possible claims into a single class action.

Why might they have taken that risky approach? I suggest that just as the insistence on unconscionability in *AT&T Mobility* rested (at least in part) on a desire to insert deterrence concerns into Rule 23, the seemingly incomprehensible decision to proceed as a class action in *Wal-Mart* can be explained as a desire to change the substantive law of employment discrimination. The allegation of a culture of discrimination was essentially an attempt to write into Title VII the concepts of structural discrimination and implicit bias.[91] Some scholars have been urging this approach for over two decades, beginning with Charles Lawrence's seminal article in 1987.[92] These scholars argue that even as overt, conscious

---

[89] Id at 155.

[90] Indeed, plaintiffs' attorneys recently filed a much smaller class action in California federal court on behalf of about 90,000 women in four regions in California and neighboring states. See Andrew Martin, *Female Wal-Mart Employees File New Bias Case*, New York Times (Oct 27, 2011), available at http://www.nytimes.com/2011/10/28/business/women-file-new-class-action-bias-case-against-wal-mart.html?scp=1&sq=&st=nyt.

[91] See Nagareda, 84 NYU L Rev at 152–62 (cited in note 73).

[92] Charles R. Lawrence III, *The Id, the Ego, and Equal Protection: Reckoning with Unconscious Racism*, 39 Stan L Rev 317 (1987).

discrimination is fading, implicit bias continues unabated. Unconscious discrimination is so pervasive that it is woven into the structure of institutions, the theory goes, and if we do not restructure discrimination law to make it legally actionable we will make no progress against the persistence of discrimination.[93] One commentator describes this scholarship in language that almost mirrors the *Wal-Mart* plaintiffs' claims: Disparities in wages and promotions continue to exist "because workplace structures facilitate conduct—often driven by subtle or unconscious bias—that operates as a drag on the achievements" of women and minorities.[94]

But such a theory distorts Title VII beyond recognition. It is one thing to allege that a particular individual has unconsciously discriminated (that is, that he has acted out of an unrecognized prejudice), but quite another to argue—as the *Wal-Mart* plaintiffs' theory does—that the entire workplace culture is infected with unrecognized bias. Such an argument moves Title VII from a prohibition against intentional discrimination to a prohibition against a workforce that does not "look like America."[95]

The idea of implicit bias has remained controversial within the academy and has never made any headway outside it. Indeed, there is no credible scientific evidence to support the existence of the alleged widespread unconscious discrimination that purportedly

---

[93] See, for example, Virginia Valian, *Why So Slow? The Advancement of Women* (MIT, 1998); Patrick S. Shin, *Liability for Unconscious Discrimination? A Thought Experiment in the Theory of Employment Discrimination Law*, 62 Hastings L J 67 (2010); Ivan E. Bodensteiner, *The Implications of Psychological Research Related to Unconscious Discrimination and Implicit Bias in Proving Intentional Discrimination*, 73 Mo L Rev 83 (2008); Tristin K. Green, *A Structural Approach as Antidiscrimination Mandate: Locating Employer Wrong*, 60 Vand L Rev 849 (2007); Audrey J. Lee, Note, *Unconscious Bias Theory in Employment Discrimination Litigation*, 40 Harv CR-CL L Rev 481 (2005); Susan Sturm, *Second Generation Employment Discrimination: A Structural Approach*, 101 Colum L Rev 458 (2001); Linda Hamilton Krieger, *The Content of Our Categories: A Cognitive Bias Approach to Discrimination and Equal Employment Opportunity*, 47 Stan L Rev 1161 (1995).

[94] Samuel R. Bagenstos, *The Structural Turn and the Limits of Antidiscrimination Law*, 94 Cal L Rev 1, 2 (2006). Compare this to the "basic theory" of the plaintiffs' case in *Wal-Mart*: "a strong and uniform 'corporate culture' permits bias against women to infect, perhaps subconsciously, the discretionary decisionmaking of each one of Wal-Mart's thousands of managers." 131 S Ct at 2548.

[95] Even scholars who support the concept of structural discrimination find it inconsistent with current law. Professor Samuel Bagenstos, who believes that there is implicit bias and "find[s] the case for a structural approach to employment discrimination law . . . compelling" nevertheless recognizes that remedying the structural inequalities that result from implicit bias is inconsistent with "the generally accepted normative underpinnings of antidiscrimination law." Bagenstos, 94 Cal L Rev at 3 (cited in note 94); see also Wax, 74 Ind L J at 1146–52 (cited in note 83).

results in structural discrimination.[96] The *Wal-Mart* class action can nevertheless be seen as an attempt to turn implicit bias theory into explicit law. Bringing a class action in order to rewrite the substantive law of employment discrimination to include implicit bias and structural discrimination was thus overreaching at its worst.

B. THE HARM OF OVERREACHING AND OVERWRITING

As in *AT&T Mobility*, the strategy backfired. Overreaching by the plaintiffs and the dissenters led to a majority opinion that was broader and more harmful than a simple rejection of class certification would have been. Had the majority crafted a narrower opinion, the repercussions for future class actions would have been less significant. In short, if a lower court or a unanimous Supreme Court had held that class certification was inappropriate under Rule 23(a),[97] the accompanying opinion might have been quite different. Four aspects of the majority opinion are particularly noteworthy.

First, the majority opinion can be interpreted as ratcheting up the requirements for class certification. The *Wal-Mart* suit was brought under Rule 23(b)(2), which meant that it—like all class actions—had to satisfy the requirements of Rule 23(a), but not the more demanding requirements of Rule 23(b)(3). While Rule 23(a)(2) requires only a single common question, Rule 23(b)(3) requires that the common questions predominate over individual ones. The dissent accused the majority of conflating the commonality requirement of Rule 23(a)(2) with the predominance requirement of Rule 23(b)(3).[98] By blending the two, the dissent charged, the majority "elevate[d] the (a)(2) inquiry so that it is no longer 'easily satisfied.'"[99]

---

[96] For a thorough discrediting of the purported "evidence" for the pervasiveness of unconscious discrimination, see Mitchell and Tetlock, 67 Ohio St L J (cited in note 83); Hal R. Arkes and Philip E. Tetlock, *Attributions of Implicit Prejudice, or "Would Jesse Jackson 'Fail' the Implicit Association Test?"* 15 Psychol Inquiry 257 (2004).

[97] In *Wal-Mart*, the majority and the dissent agreed that the class was improperly certified under Rule 23(b)(2) for reasons irrelevant to my arguments. See 131 S Ct at 2557–61 (majority); id at 2561–62 (dissent). They disagreed over whether the suit met the commonality requirements of Rule 23(a).

[98] Id at 2561–62, 2565–66 (Ginsburg, J, dissenting).

[99] Id at 2565 (Ginsburg, J, dissenting), quoting John W. Moore, et al, 5 *Moore's Federal Practice* § 23.23[2] at 23–72 (Matthew Bender, 3d ed 2011).

The dissenters were both right and wrong. They were wrong in contending that the majority conflated the requirements of 23(a)(2) and 23(b)(3)—as the majority concluded, there was simply not enough evidence of even a single common question. But the intuition that the majority might be performing some kind of alchemy on the 23(a)(2) commonality requirement, "elevat[ing]" it beyond previous incarnations, is supported by language in the majority opinion. Most troubling is the majority's assertion that the plaintiffs failed to establish the existence of a common question because they provided "no *convincing proof*" of a company-wide discriminatory policy.[100] Similarly, the majority rejected the statistical evidence as "insufficient to *establish* that respondents' theory can be *proved* on a classwide basis."[101] These statements might be read to suggest that plaintiffs seeking class certification must come very close to proving their case on the merits.[102]

The majority rightly asserted that the precedents require a "rigorous analysis" to determine whether a plaintiff seeking class certification has demonstrated actual compliance with the requirements of Rule 23.[103] As the majority also noted, "[f]requently, that 'rigorous analysis' will entail some overlap with the merits of the plaintiff's underlying claim."[104] But there is a line, however fine, between that "rigorous analysis" and actual proof of the merits of the case. The language about "convincing proof" creates some ambiguity about where that line lies. Lower courts—or the Supreme Court in a future case—might use the language to impose a higher burden and deny certification even in cases with stronger

---

[100] 131 S Ct at 2556 (emphasis added).

[101] Id at 2555 (emphasis added).

[102] Lower courts had already recognized—and the Court in *Wal-Mart* confirmed—that a plaintiff seeking certification must demonstrate satisfaction of the relevant Rule 23 requirements, even if that necessitates some review of the merits. See, for example, *In re: Hydrogen Peroxide Antitrust Litigation*, 552 F3d 305 (3d Cir 2008); *In re Initial Public Offerings Securities Litigation*, 471 F3d 24 (2d Cir 2006). But the Court's language in *Wal-Mart* seems to raise the standard even higher.

[103] 131 S Ct at 2551. The dissent does not appear to disagree.

[104] Id. Again, the dissent makes no comment. Despite some confounding language in *Eisen v Carlisle and Jacquelin*, 417 US 156, 177 (1974), which the *Wal-Mart* Court labeled as "the purest dictum," 131 S Ct at 2552 n 6, lower courts had already reached this conclusion. See *Wal-Mart*, 603 F3d at 581–86; *Hydrogen Peroxide*, 552 F3d at 309; *Oscar Private Equity Investments v Allegiance Telecom, Inc.*, 487 F3d 261, 268 (5th Cir 2007); *In re Initial Public Offerings Securities Litigation*, 471 F3d 24, 33 (2d Cir 2006); *Gariety v Grant Thornton, LLP*, 368 F3d 356, 366 (4th Cir 2004); *Szabo v Bridgeport Machines, Inc.*, 249 F3d 672, 676 (7th Cir 2001).

evidence than the *Wal-Mart* plaintiffs provided. The dissent's claim that the majority elevated the burden might become a self-fulfilling prophecy, even though the dissent misidentified the source of the problem.

The second troubling aspect of the majority opinion is its treatment of the anecdotal evidence. As I noted earlier, the majority found the anecdotal evidence too weak to create a causal inference. But in support of that conclusion, the majority focused not on the absence of any linkage between the allegedly discriminatory culture and the individual employment decisions, but instead on the small number of anecdotes and the fact that they were from stores in a small number of states.[105] Again, then, the dissenters had some justification for their accusation that the majority created a "numerical floor before anecdotal evidence can be taken into account."[106] And both the majority's focus on the number of anecdotes and the dissent's accusation might lead to later decisions citing *Wal-Mart* for the proposition that there is a numerical floor.

Two final issues arise in Part III of the majority opinion, in which all nine Justices joined and which concluded that this particular lawsuit should not have been certified under Rule 23(b)(2). Here, too, the analysis is broader than it needs to be, again suggesting that the plaintiffs' overreaching produced disastrous results.

The Court first suggested that the "procedural protections" of Rule 23(b)(3)—including the right to opt out—are constitutionally required by the Due Process Clause under *Phillips Petroleum Co. v Shutts*,[107] at least in suits predominantly seeking damages.[108] But that is not the holding of *Shutts*, which involved complicated personal-jurisdiction issues intertwined with the class certification question. As a number of commentators have noted, reading the opt-out provision as constitutionally required is an "extreme reading" of *Shutts*.[109] In reading *Shutts* to constitutionalize the opt-out

---

[105] See text accompanying notes 84–85.

[106] 131 S Ct at 2563 n 4 (Ginsburg, J, dissenting).

[107] 472 US 797 (1985).

[108] See 131 S Ct at 2559: "In the context of a class action predominantly for money damages we have held that absence of notice and opt-out violates due process. See [*Shutts*]."

[109] Diane P. Wood, *Adjudicatory Jurisdiction and Class Actions*, 62 Ind L J 597, 605–06 (1987). See also Redish, *Wholesale Justice* at 158 (cited in note 68); Tobias Barrington Wolff, *Federal Jurisdiction and Due Process in the Era of the Nationwide Class Action*, 156 U Pa L Rev 2035, 2076–109 (2008); David L. Shapiro, *Class Actions: The Class as Party and*

requirement, the *Wal-Mart* Court elided the difference between constitutional requirements and those derived from rules or statutes, a form of "intellectual slippage" that narrows the authority of the legislature.[110] Should Congress at some time in the future wish to expand the reach of mandatory class actions, *Wal-Mart*'s interpretation of *Shutts* will stand in the way.

Finally, in addressing the inappropriateness of certification under Rule 23(b)(2), the Court considered the Ninth Circuit's solution to the problem that *Wal-Mart* might have individual defenses to claims by some class members. Even if plaintiffs could establish a pattern or practice of discrimination, the Court noted, not every class member would be entitled to damages—*Wal-Mart* might be able to "show that it took an adverse employment action against an employee for [a] reason other than discrimination."[111] The Court of Appeals, recognizing this possibility, suggested that the district court could allow *Wal-Mart* "to present individual defenses in . . . randomly selected 'sample cases,' thus revealing the approximate percentage of class members whose unequal pay or nonpromotion was due to something other than gender discrimination."[112] The court could then "extrapolat[e] the validity and value of the untested claims from the sample set."[113]

In one short paragraph, the Supreme Court "disapprove[d] that novel project," calling it "Trial by Formula."[114] But such statistical sampling is not as novel as the Court would have it, nor is it necessarily inappropriate. Statistical sampling of various sorts, including both survey evidence and bellwether trials, has been used

---

Client, 73 Notre Dame L Rev 913, 954–55 (1998); Arthur R. Miller and David J. Crump, *Jurisdiction and Choice of Law in Multistate Class Actions After Phillips Petroleum Co. v. Shutts*, 96 Yale L J 1, 31–32 (1986). Cf. Henry Paul Monaghan, *Antisuit Injunctions and Preclusion Against Absent Nonresident Class Members*, 98 Colum L Rev 1148, 1166 (1998) ("*Shutts* is about due process limitations on state court *in personam jurisdiction* over absent, nonresident class 'plaintiffs'") (emphasis added); Patrick Woolley, *Collateral Attack and the Role of Adequate Representation in Class Suits for Money Damages*, 58 U Kan L Rev 918, 971–75 (2010) (agreeing with Monaghan).

[110] The notion of "intellectual slippage" of this sort was first suggested in David E. Engdahl, *The Classic Rule of Faith and Credit*, 118 Yale L J 1584, 1589 (2009).

[111] 131 S Ct at 2560–61. It is ironic that the dissenting Justices joined this portion of the opinion. By suggesting that not every pay or promotion decision was tainted by discrimination, the Court is essentially reiterating that plaintiffs have shown an insufficient causal link between a hypothetical company-wide policy and the harms to class members.

[112] 603 F3d at 627 n 56, quoted in 131 S Ct at 2550.

[113] 131 S Ct 2550.

[114] Id at 2561.

in a few legal contexts.[115] A number of commentators have explained its value (in allowing the accurate resolution of cases that could not otherwise be resolved because of scarcity of judicial resources) and demonstrated how it can be consistent with the Constitution and with our litigation regime.[116] Indeed, to the extent that statistical sampling is problematic at all, it is problematic for *plaintiffs*: While it produces an amount of damages that is accurate overall, it may distribute those damages in a less than perfect fashion.[117] No commentator has suggested that *defendants* have any ground to object to sampling. In addition, the question of the validity of statistical sampling as a technique for resolving large-scale disputes necessarily prompts a comparison to other techniques; at least in some contexts, empirical research has shown that traditional trials often do not provide the benefits thought to flow from individualized adjudication.[118] In a world of increasingly globalized harm and limited judicial resources, sampling might ultimately serve the interests of both plaintiffs and defendants.

The Court considered none of this information in concluding that statistical sampling violated the Rules Enabling Act. Nor did it consider whether such a ruling might be premature. The use of statistical sampling in the context of class actions is still in its infancy. In the scientific context, it took decades for statistical

---

[115] See *In re Estate of Marcos Human Rights Litigation*, 910 F Supp 1460 (D Hawaii 1995), aff'd, *Hilao v Estate of Marcos*, 103 F3d 767 (9th Cir 1996); *Cimino v Raymark Industries, Inc.*, 751 F Supp 649 (ED Tex 1990), rev'd, 151 F3d 297 (5th Cir 1998). See also Laurens Walker and John Monahan, *Sampling Damages*, 83 Iowa L Rev 545, 559–60 (1998) (documenting uncontroversial use of surveys—a form of sampling—in trademark cases since 1963).

[116] See, for example, Alexandra D. Lahav, *The Case for "Trial by Formula,"* 90 Tex L Rev (forthcoming 2012), available at http://ssrn.com/abstract=1945514; Alexandra D. Lahav, *Bellwether Trials*, 76 Geo Wash L Rev 576 (2008); Laurens Walker and John Monahan, *Sampling Evidence at the Crossroads*, 80 S Cal L Rev 969 (2007); Laurens Walker and John Monahan, *Sampling Liability*, 85 Va L Rev 329 (1999); Walker and Monahan, 83 Iowa L Rev 545 (cited in note 115); Michael J. Saks and Peter David Blanck, *Justice Improved: The Unrecognized Benefits of Aggregation and Sampling in the Trial of Mass Torts*, 44 Stan L Rev 815 (1992); Christopher J. Roche, Note, *A Litigation Association Model to Aggregate Mass Tort Claims for Adjudication*, 91 Va L Rev 1463 (2005). The dispute about statistical sampling and bellwether trials may be viewed as one facet of the larger argument between those who insist on individual autonomy and those who favor collective justice. See generally David Shapiro, *Class Actions: The Class as Party and Client*, 73 Notre Dame L Rev 913 (1998). The authorities cited in this note argue, however, that statistical sampling *also* serves the interests of individual plaintiffs.

[117] See Robert G. Bone, *Statistical Adjudication: Rights, Justice, and Utility in a World of Process Scarcity*, 46 Vand L Rev 561, 572–73 (1993).

[118] See Deborah Hensler, *Resolving Mass Toxic Torts: Myths and Realities*, 1989 U Ill L Rev 89 (1989).

sampling to move from "early controversy" to "decisive acceptance."[119] Had statistical sampling in the law survived beyond *Wal-Mart*, it might have proven similarly enduring—but the majority's "disapproval" ensured that we will never know.

Wal-Mart and *AT&T Mobility* are thus similar in that the majority opinions may well have detrimental effects in the future. They differ, however, in the extent to which different choices by the dissent might have changed the jurisprudential landscape. Of course, in both cases the majority opinion would not have been written had the plaintiffs' lawyers not brought the class action in the first place, or had the lower courts rejected the plaintiffs' arguments. In *AT&T Mobility*, it also seems quite likely that if the dissenting Justices had urged reversal on the ground that the Ninth Circuit misapplied California law, that view would have attracted a majority and the Court—or at least the majority opinion—would never have reached the preemption question.

As to *Wal-Mart*, however, my argument is that the dissenting Justices should have *agreed* with the majority's reasoning. How might that have cabined the troubling aspects of the majority opinion? For the two final issues, which arose in the context of the Rule 23(b)(2) requirements, the answer is straightforward. A court should first determine that the general requirements of Rule 23(a) are met, before moving on to the more specific requirements of the various subsections of Rule 23(b). The discussion of 23(b)(2) was therefore technically unnecessary, but in the circumstances of the actual case it was hard to avoid because the failure to satisfy (b)(2) was the reason that the dissenting Justices concurred in the judgment. Had the dissenting Justices instead agreed that the lower court should be reversed because of the lack of the common question required by Rule 23(a)(2), the Court would have been much less likely to go out of its way to reach the (b)(2) issue. In particular, as I noted with regard to *AT&T Mobility*, some of the Justices in the majority are inclined to rule narrowly.[120] While Justice Scalia might have convinced them that addressing the (b)(2) question was appropriate given actual Justices' votes, it seems likely that if there had been unanimity with regard to Rule 23(a), some-

---

[119] Walker and Monahan, 80 S Cal L Rev at 971 (cited in note 116).

[120] See note 70.

one would have raised the question of whether it was appropriate to go beyond that issue.

For the troublesome language regarding "proof" and the creation of ambiguity regarding a numerical floor for anecdotes, I suggest that had the dissenting Justices not been so eager to discredit the majority's reasoning, they might have been better able to focus on the particular language. And that focus might have produced either of two results. First, Justice Scalia, as author of the opinion, might have been willing to tweak the language of the opinion at the request of Justices joining it, especially if doing so would allow the Court to issue a unanimous or nearly unanimous opinion.[121] Second, even had the language remained in the opinion, the Justices who objected to it could have written a *concurring* opinion stressing the narrowness of the majority's holding instead of a *dissenting* opinion highlighting its potential breadth. Later interpreters—including both lower court judges and the Court itself in subsequent cases—looking for help in parsing the majority's language would be led to interpret it narrowly rather than broadly.

Language matters. There is a danger that future cases building on the *Wal-Mart* precedent will engage in the same kind of expansive interpretation as occurred between *Bell Atlantic Corp. v Twombly*[122] and *Ashcroft v Iqbal*.[123] The "plausibility" language of *Twombly*[124]—arguably appropriate in the circumstances of that case, but not well thought out—took on a life of its own in *Iqbal*. Dismissing the complaint in *Twombly* could be justified on the ground that an inference that defendants had acted unlawfully was not only not "plausible," but decidedly implausible.[125] But in *Iqbal*,

---

[121] The Court benefits from—and therefore is likely to try to achieve—unanimity or near-unanimity, especially in controversial cases. See, for example, Howard Gillman, *The Court as an Idea, Not a Building (or a Game): Interpretive Institutionalism and the Analysis of Supreme Court Decision-Making*, in Cornell W. Clayton and Howard Gillman, eds, *Supreme Court Decision-Making: New Institutionalist Approaches* 65, 81 (Chicago 1999); Frank H. Easterbrook, *Ways of Criticizing the Court*, 95 Harv L Rev 802, 804 (1982); Kent Greenawalt, *The Enduring Significance of Neutral Principles*, 78 Colum L Rev 982, 1007 (1978).

[122] 550 US 544 (2007).

[123] 129 S Ct 1937 (2009).

[124] In *Twombly*, the majority opinion used "plausible," "plausibly," or "plausibility" sixteen times to describe the standard for withstanding a motion to dismiss. See 550 US at 556 & n 4, 557 & n 5, 558, 559, 560, 564, 566, 569 & n 14, 570.

[125] See Suzanna Sherry, *Foundational Facts and Doctrinal Change*, 2011 Ill L Rev 145, 176 (2011); Robert G. Bone, *Twombly, Pleading Rules, and the Regulation of Court Access*, 94 Iowa L Rev 873, 900–09 (2009); Richard A. Epstein, *Bell Atlantic v Twombly: How*

the Court moved from requiring plaintiffs to show that an inference of illegality is not implausible to requiring them to show that an inference of illegality is more likely than not. It seems clear from the fact that Justice Souter, the author of *Twombly*, was in dissent in *Iqbal* that this was not what (at least some members) of the Court meant by invoking a plausibility standard. But "more likely than not" is one reasonable interpretation of "plausible."[126] Had Justice Souter chosen his language more carefully in *Twombly*, the Court might have had a more difficult time concluding that Iqbal's complaint should have been dismissed.

The majority's language in *Wal-Mart* has the potential to work the same mischief. As in *Twombly*, the application of that language to the facts of the particular case is not problematic. But there is a danger that the language of "convincing proof" and "a few anecdotes selected from literally millions" might preclude certification in a case in which there is *some* (but not "convincing") evidence of a common question or *a few more* anecdotes. Such a consequence—potentially avoidable had the dissenting Justices agreed with the majority, focused on the language, and either exerted pressure to change it or written a concurrence minimizing its significance—is made even more likely by the fact that the dissent characterized it as making certification harder to obtain.

As in *AT&T Mobility*, then, the lawyers and judges who wanted to have it all ended up with nothing. And in the process, they opened the door to a potential contraction of liability in future cases.

III. THE NEED FOR JUDICIAL VIGILANCE

Two dangers inhere in Rule 23, one recognized and one hidden. The recognized danger is that plaintiffs' counsel—especially in class actions and other aggregated cases—often have both the opportunity and the incentive to favor their own interests at the expense of their clients' interests; various scholars have identified that danger and proposed solutions.[127]

Motions to Dismiss Become (Disguised) Summary Judgments, 25 Wash U J L & Pol 61, 84–90 (2007).

[126] One definition of "plausible" is: "Of an argument, an idea, a statement, etc.: seeming reasonable, probable, or truthful; convincing, believable." Oxford English Dictionary, online at http://www.oed.com/view/Entry/145466?redirectedFrom=plausible#eid (definition 4a).

[127] See, for example, Tidmarsh, 87 Tex L Rev 1137 (2009) (cited in note 68); Howard

But as *Wal-Mart* and *AT&T Mobility* illustrate, the problem goes much deeper than the relationship between lawyers and clients. The further danger hidden in Rule 23 is that in class actions, much more than in individual cases, the ability of plaintiffs' counsel to frame the legal issues puts tremendous power into the hands of private attorneys general who owe no duty to the general public or to subsequent plaintiffs. Class actions, both because of their scope and because they are so often high profile, offer repeat-player plaintiffs' lawyers a tempting opportunity to try to shape the law rather than simply to win a judgment. If class-action lawyers cannot always be counted on to put their own clients' interests first, how can we expect them to worry about the interests of those who are not even clients? Lawyers in this situation thus have an enormous incentive to overframe (and overargue) the legal issues and go for the big win—for both themselves and their existing clients. Ultimately, though, when the hogs get slaughtered, it is future plaintiffs who pay the price. The biggest losers in *AT&T Mobility* and *Wal-Mart* were not the class members, who deserved to lose on their particular claims, but consumers and employees who might wish to bring class actions in the future.

The real tragedy of *AT&T Mobility* and *Wal-Mart* is not that the plaintiffs' lawyers overreached, it is that the Ninth Circuit and the dissenting Justices took the bait and bought into the over-framing of the issues. Had they been more focused on the narrow procedural questions and less dazzled by the lawyers' grandiose claims, they might have reached different conclusions.

These two cases also suggest a solution to this inherent danger of Rule 23, one that does not require rewriting the rule or tin-kering with doctrine. Instead, judges need only be alert to the danger and take steps to avert it.[128] The courts should serve as a safeguard against lawyers' short-sighted strategic decisions, not act in complicity with them. Just as courts are vigilant in moni-

---

M. Erichson and Benjamin C. Zipursky, *Consent versus Closure*, 96 Cornell L Rev 265 (2011). The core problem is that the development of an entrepreneurial plaintiffs' bar ends up replicating, as between lawyer and client (or potential client), the conflicts between repeat-player "haves" and one-shot "have-nots" that Professor Marc Galanter identified a generation ago. Marc Galanter, *Why the "Haves" Come Out Ahead: Speculations on the Limits of Legal Change*, 9 L & Soc Rev 95 (1974). On the replication at the lawyer-client level, see John Fabian Witt, *Bureaucratic Legalism, American Style: Private Bureaucratic Legalism and the Governance of the Tort System*, 56 DePaul L Rev 261 (2007).

[128] It would help if Supreme Court Justices—and court of appeals judges—had more litigation experience as lawyers or trial judges. See Suzanna Sherry, *Logic Without Experience: The Problem of Federal Appellate Courts*, 82 Notre Dame L Rev 97 (2006).

toring legislative or administrative aggrandizement, they should protect the system as a whole from overreaching by lawyers whose loyalties lie elsewhere.

IV. CONCLUSION

More than a decade ago, Professor William Rubenstein warned of the potential conflicts arising out of simultaneous civil rights litigation by "professional public interest litigators" and "occasional pro bono attorneys."[129] The problem is that the latter—unaware of or indifferent to the big picture—might bring weak or badly timed cases that establish bad precedent for other similarly situated litigants. In *AT&T Mobility* and *Wal-Mart*, we see this scenario writ large. Rather than a conflict between two sets of litigators, it is a conflict between a powerful plaintiffs' bar and the mass of ordinary consumers and employees.

But the real culprits in these cases were the lower court judges and dissenting Justices. In a context in which both parties had incentives to distort the issues, these judges abdicated their responsibility to frame the issues objectively. Accepting the plaintiffs' claims at face value, they backed a player who was overplaying his hand—and consequently failed to notice the powerhouse across the table. Faced with weak arguments in novel cases with obviously far-reaching consequences, they should have folded instead of betting someone else's ranch.

---

[129] William B. Rubenstein, *Divided We Litigate: Addressing Disputes Among Group Members and Lawyers in Civil Rights Campaigns*, 106 Yale L J 1623, 1632 (1997).

STEPHEN ANSOLABEHERE

ARIZONA FREE ENTERPRISE v BENNETT AND THE PROBLEM OF CAMPAIGN FINANCE

Electoral activities of candidates and political organizations are the lifeblood of the democratic process in the United States. Political campaigns educate the electorate about the choices it faces. The fanfare, debates, and advertising over the course of the year leading up to an election excite people to pay attention to the election, to vote, and to participate in other ways. Such an atmosphere encourages people to speak out about their beliefs and use their judgment in determining what people and ideas ought to govern. Out of the din of political campaigns comes a collective decision about who should govern and peaceful transitions of government. It is here that the Supreme Court finds the justification for the First Amendment: healthy democratic elections require free, open, and robust public discourse.[1] That is the air in which democracy thrives.

How our society—or any democracy—pays to sustain that robust exchange in the electoral arena is the central problem of campaign finance law. Most Western democracies limit expenditures on campaigns and regulate how candidates use the media.[2] Most other

Stephen Ansolabehere is Professor, Department of Government, Harvard University.

AUTHOR'S NOTE: The author thanks Richard Pildes and Geof Stone for their commentary and critical reading and Randall Johnston for her assistance.

[1] *New York Times Company v Sullivan*, 364 US 254, 270 (1964).

[2] Mijeong Baek, *A Comparative Analysis of Political Communication Systems and Voter Turnout*, 53 Am J Pol Sci 376–93, esp. 388–89 (2009).

democracies set forth campaign finance systems that favor parties over candidates and provide large public subsidies to the parties to wage their election campaigns.[3] In 1971, the United States started down a similar path. The Federal Election Campaign Act (FECA) provided for public funding of presidential general elections; it continued the ban on corporate and union direct contributions, allowing them to give only through their political action committees (or PACs); it further limited the size of individuals' and PACs' contributions to candidates and parties; and it limited the amounts that candidates, parties, and groups could spend in federal elections.[4]

The constitutionality of the Federal Election Campaign Act was challenged in 1976, and the Supreme Court's decision in that case fundamentally rewrote the laws governing campaign finance. In its groundbreaking decision in *Buckey v Valeo*,[5] the Court struck down limitations on campaign spending by candidates and organizations. The only real exceptions were the spending limits in presidential elections, which were tied to public funding and entered into voluntarily. The Court let stand limitations on contributions from individuals and organizations, resulting in a system of regulated supply of money but unrestricted demand.

Central to the Court's view of campaign finance is the contention that money is speech, and not just any speech, but speech in the electoral setting. It is therefore subject to the closest scrutiny under the First Amendment. Government limits on spending by candidates, parties, or groups are generally unacceptable. Contributions are also a form of speech, but a compelling government interest in preventing "real or apparent corruption" justifies limits on contributions. Contributions express support for a candidate, much like public endorsements, but contributions may be used to buy political favors or subvert the legislative process in other ways. A compelling government interest in preventing "real or apparent corruption," the Court reasoned, may justify reasonable limits on contributions. On this matter the Justices drew a fundamental distinction between contributions and expenditures. Limitations on contributions have a much more modest effect on the ability of individuals to use their resources in the political process because what they cannot con-

---

[3] David M. Farrell and Paul Webb, *Political Parties as Campaign Organizations*, in Russell Dalton and Martin P. Wattenberg, eds, *Parties without Partisans* 102 (Oxford, 2000).

[4] 2 USC § 431 (1971).

[5] 424 US 1 (1976).

tribute they can still spend to express their ideas. Campaign contributions, on the other hand, may render political discourse during
elections less effective by making legislators beholden not to the
wishes of those who voted but to the desires of those who provided
the funds. Preventing corruption of the political process, then, is
essential for preserving the effectiveness of political speech. That
understanding of the First Amendment led the Court to allow limitations on campaign contributions, but not expenditures.

Likewise, the problem of campaign finance shapes the meaning
of the First Amendment and its application. Electoral politics since
1976 offer something of a proving ground for the notion that aggressive assertion of the First Amendment is indeed the best way
to provide for healthy discourse in a democracy. Is the marketplace
of ideas working properly? Or has the system created by *Buckley*
distorted the electoral arena or allowed one voice to monopolize
over others?

Emerging from the *Buckley* decision come two distinct strains of
thought about campaign finance and political discourse. In line with
the governing opinion in *Buckley*, there is the view that the best
assurance of adequate political discourse is unfettered and unreg-
ulated campaign spending. There is certainly much to recommend
that view. Campaign spending has grown appreciably relative to
inflation (consumer prices) over the past four decades, and we have
seen the rise of independent expenditures by groups and parties
trying to influence election outcomes.[6] An alternative view finds
expression in Justice White's dissent in *Buckley*. Just as there is a
compelling government interest in capping contributions to limit
corruption, so too is there a compelling government interest in
stemming the excessive expenditures of funds. Expenditure limits,
White reasoned, "reinforce contribution limits"[7] and "ease the candidate's understandable obsession with fundraising, and so free him
and his staff to communicate in more places and in more ways
unconnected with the fundraising function."[8] The ultimate consequence of limits, White concluded, would be to "restore and
maintain public confidence in federal elections . . . to dispel the
impression that federal elections are purely and simply a function

---

[6] Stephen Ansolabehere, *The Scope of Corruption: Lessons from Comparative Campaign Finance*, 6 Election L J 163 (2007).

[7] *Buckley*, 424 US at 264 (White, J, dissenting).

[8] Id at 265.

of money, that federal offices are bought and sold, or that political races are reserved for those who [can] . . . bring together . . . large fortunes in order to prevail at the polls."[9] Justice White went still further, arguing that reasonable expenditure limits in fact help maintain the objective of the First Amendment. A limitation on expenditures would keep elections open to those who do not have ready access to money and ensure that competing candidates and perspectives could have a reasonable chance of putting forth their views in the public domain.[10] In this view, monopolization of political speech by one side could be as destructive of robust political discourse as government regulation of expenditures.[11] It was important, then, not only to keep speech free, but to encourage competition between electoral adversaries.

These two views of campaign finance and free speech do not differ in their objectives. Both seek a healthy marketplace of ideas. Rather, they differ in their understanding of what such a marketplace looks like and how to ensure it.

The majority view in *Buckley* embraces a pluralistic notion of the marketplace in which many different voices—candidates, parties, groups, and individuals—can and will express themselves. No one way of organizing political discourse is favored. Indeed, it is a view deeply distrustful of legislation that regulates campaign speech, as such laws are written by and for those already in power.

White's dissenting opinion embraces an adversarial view of the marketplace and of electoral competition, which, in the American context, is centered on debate between competing political candidates. In a single-member district, first-past-the-post system, voters hold government accountable not by picking one group or idea, but by choosing one of the competing candidates. While it would be nice to live in the pluralistic world imagined in the per curiam decision in *Buckley*, the reality is that elections are contests between competing candidates, usually two. The essential objective of the First Amendment is to preserve electoral choice for the public and the electoral accountability of government, and that objective would

---

[9] Id.

[10] Id at 266.

[11] For a discussion of the problem of monopolization of speech by incumbents and electoral competition in the context of contemporary election law, see Richard Pildes, *The Constitutionalization of Democratic Politics*, 118 Harv L Rev 29–154, esp. 42–54 (2004).

allow government regulation of campaign spending so long as it furthers electoral competition.[12]

The Court has repeatedly upheld the framework constructed in *Buckley*, but White's dissenting opinion increasingly found voice, and even gained majority support, such as in *McConnell v Federal Election Commission*.[13] Justice Stevens, originally a critic of White's view,[14] later embraced the same perspective in his opinions in *Randall v Sorrell*.[15] The time had come, Stevens concluded, to end the "pernicious effects of endless fundraising" and to overturn the limit on expenditures.[16] In a series of separate opinions, Justices Scalia and Thomas, finding the distinction between contributions and expenditures untenable, have repeatedly sounded the call to end contribution limits.[17] Justice Kennedy, troubled by the problems created by the rise of soft money expenditures of party organizations and independent expenditures of groups, has called for a substantial rethinking of the principles governing campaign finance.[18] Might there be a different constitutionally defensible approach to campaign finance?

The Justices are not the only ones troubled by fund-raising and campaign practices at the state and federal levels. Over the years, state legislatures and state electorates have enacted various laws to take on the challenge of ensuring political competition and limiting corruption. Most states now have some form of limitation on contributions, and half employ some form of public finance.[19] In 2002, Congress passed the most sweeping campaign finance legislation in

---

[12] For a fuller discussion of the relationship between the electoral laws and competition, see Samuel Issacharoff and Richard Pildes, *Politics as Markets: Partisan Lockups of the Democratic Process*, 50 Stan L Rev 50 643–717 (1998).

[13] 540 US 93 (2003).

[14] 548 US 230, 276 (2006) (Stevens, J, dissenting).

[15] Id at 273–81.

[16] Id at 274.

[17] See, for example, *Randall*, 548 US at 238, 265–73 (2006) (Thomas, J, concurring); *Federal Election Commission v Colorado Republican Federal Campaign Committee*, 533 US 431, 465–66 (2001) (Thomas, J, dissenting); *Nixon v Shrink Missouri Government PAC*, 528 US 377, 410–18 (2000) (same); *Colorado Republican Federal Campaign Committee v Federal Election Commission*, 518 US 604, 635–644 (1996) (Thomas, J, concurring in judgment and dissenting in part).

[18] See *Nixon*, 528 US at 405–09 (Kennedy, J, dissenting).

[19] For a list of states with public financing laws and their text, see Common Cause, *Public Financing in the States* (June 2007), online at http://www.commoncause.org/site/pp.asp?c=dkLNK1MQIwG&b=4773825.

a quarter century. The Bipartisan Campaign Reform Act[20] (BCRA) kept FECA as the central organization of campaign finance, but made some important adjustments to the law, including indexing contribution limits to inflation, but it also put in place restrictions on party spending and independent advertising. In a decision surprising to some experts working on the issue, the Court in *McConnell* deemed those regulations constitutionally acceptable.[21] By 2005, then, the Court had embarked on exactly the sort of rethinking of the legal principles governing campaign finance of which Justice Kennedy spoke. The many state experiments in campaign finance law as well as the Bipartisan Campaign Reform Act provided ample grist for the mill.

Over the past five years, under Chief Justice Roberts's stewardship, the Court has decided five important campaign finance cases. These are *Wisconsin Right to Life, Inc. v FEC (I and II)*,[22] *Randall v Sorrell*,[23] *Citizens United v Federal Election Commission*,[24] *Davis v Federal Election Commission*,[25] and *Arizona Free Enterprise Club's Freedom PAC v Bennett*.[26] Some observers see in this line of cases an "unsettling of campaign finance law."[27] These cases certainly upended other recent decisions, such as parts of *McConnell* and *Austin v Michigan*.[28] Both the *McConnell* decision and the *Austin* decision opened questions about *Buckley*, as the governing decisions of the Court in each case tolerated regulations of party spending and other regulations that leveled the playing field for the purpose of improving the overall level and quality of political discourse. The string of decisions issued by the Roberts Court has strengthened the approach developed in *Buckley* and hardened the First Amendment principle applied to the regulation of campaign finance. Re-

---

[20] Pub L No 107-155, 116 Stat 81 (2006), codified as amended in scattered sections of 2 USC.

[21] On the surprising nature of the decision, see Stephen Ansolabehere, James M. Snyder, Jr., and Michiko Ueda, *Did Firms Profit from Soft Money?* 3 Election L J 193 (2004).

[22] 546 US 410 (2006) and 551 US 449 (2007).

[23] 548 US 230.

[24] 130 S Ct 876 (2010).

[25] 554 US 724 (2008).

[26] 131 S Ct 2806 (2011).

[27] Richard Briffault, *WRTL and Randall: The Roberts Court and the Unsettling of Campaign Finance Law*, 68 Ohio St L J 807 (2007).

[28] *McConnell v Federal Election Commission*, 540 US 93 (2003); *Austin v Michigan Chamber of Commerce*, 494 US 652 (1990).

peatedly in recent years the same five-Justice majority has asserted the overriding importance of its understanding of the First Amendment and the proposition that free speech means the government cannot restrict campaign spending. Other considerations, such as electoral competition, whether there is a governmental interest in corruption that extends to fund-raising, and even empirical evidence concerning the actual amount of speech resulting from different regulatory frameworks, have failed to sway the Court.[29] In this regard, the Roberts Court appears to have put the *Buckley* precedent back on a solid footing. This article views the shifting legal ground in the field of campaign finance through the lens of the most recent of these cases, *Arizona Free Enterprise v Bennett*, and what it may mean for election law and electoral politics in the United States.

I. PUBLIC OR PRIVATE?

At issue in all campaign finance cases is a basic question of the law of democracy. How do we pay for elections? Although the courts often focus on free speech issues, this is not the central concern of the legislators. They focus on the practicalities of creating workable campaign finance laws.

Western democracies finance electoral politics through two different methods: publicly granted and privately raised funds. Typically, campaign finance laws provide for a mix of private and public resources.[30] In this regard, the U.S. system of campaign finance is distinctive. Campaign finance in the United States relies almost entirely on contributions from private citizens and organizations, channeled chiefly to candidates and their campaign committees and secondarily to political parties. Of the estimated $4 billion spent on political campaigns at the federal level in 2008, nine of every ten dollars came ultimately from individuals, either donated directly to politicians or political parties' campaign committees or indirectly through an organization such as a corporate or labor political action committee. Groups can engage in their own independent spending campaigns, but in 2008 that came to roughly $280 million of the nearly $4 billion, and most of this money came through PACs, and thus ultimately from individual donations.[31] The United States also

---

[29] 131 S Ct at 2820–22.

[30] See Frank Sorauf, *Inside Campaign Finance* ch 5 (Yale, 1994).

[31] Federal Election Commission, *Growth in PAC Activity Slows* (April 24, 2009), online at http://fec.gov/press/press2009/20090415PAC/20090424PAC.shtml.

uses public funds for presidential elections, national party conventions, and in many states' elections. However, only $242 million of federal campaign spending, about 6 percent, came from public sources.[32] The lion's share of money in U.S. elections comes in the form of voluntary contributions from individuals.[33]

Most democracies provide extensive public subsidies to their political parties. One study concluded that 53 of 74 democracies in the world provide public subsidies to parties, and half put further limitations on candidates' expenditures. Of 24 long-standing Western-style democracies, 19 provide public funding for parties, and 13 limit campaign spending by parties and candidates.[34] These grants and subventions to parties pay for general election expenditures, and in some countries day-to-day operations of party organizations between elections. Many democracies regulate the mode and manner of political communication, especially bans or limitations on the use of television advertising.[35] These rules have the effect of favoring parties over candidates in most democracies. Parties are subsidized by the government; candidates receive public funds only indirectly through their parties. One caveat: party organizations are usually allowed to raise funds from private sources as well, often without any limitations for their day-to-day operations between general elections. In some countries, such as Italy, parties even own property and derive rents from those to finance the day-to-day operation of the organization. Exactly how much is usually unclear, as disclosure of party resources is typically weak or entirely absent.[36] The category of independent group expenditures is also

---

[32] Federal Election Commission, *2008 Presidential Campaign Finance Summarized* (June 8, 2009), online at http://fec.gov/press/press2009/20090608PresStat.shtml.

[33] For a general accounting of private financing in the United States, see Stephen Ansolabehere, Jon de Figueiredo, and James M. Snyder, Jr., *Why Is There So Little Money in U.S. Politics?* 17 J Econ Perspectives 105 (2003).

[34] These are the United States, United Kingdom, Germany, France, Italy, Spain, Canada, Japan, Korea, Australia, Austria, Belgium, Denmark, Sweden, Norway, Finland, the Netherlands, New Zealand, Israel, India, Ireland, Portugal, and Switzerland. See Thomas Grant, ed, *Lobbying, Government Relations, and Campaign Finance Worldwide* (Oceana, 2005).

[35] Baek, *Political Communication Systems* at 376–93, esp. pp 388–89 (cited in note 2). Baek further shows that access to television corresponds with higher turnout in countries, and campaign funding limits with lower turnout. Id at 385. See also Library of Congress, *Campaign Finance: An Overview* (2011), online at http://www.loc.gov/law/help/campaign-finance/index.php.

[36] See Farrell and Webb, *Political Parties* (cited in note 3), on the weakness of disclosure and the dominance of party spending over candidate spending. See also Baek, *Political Communication Systems* at 390 (cited in note 2). Eric Booth and Joseph Robbins, *Assessing the Impact of Campaign Finance on Party System Institutionalization*, 16 Party Politics 629

ambiguous or absent in many other systems. Independent expenditures are a term created by the U.S. system, and the extent of independent spending by unions, media firms, and other entities is largely undocumented.[37]

Public and private finance, then, represent two distinct methods of financing campaigns, and they create different sorts of challenges to sustaining robust political discourse. Long before the advent of public financing, campaigns were funded by private resources of the candidates themselves, of their supporters, and of political parties. Private finance takes many forms. There are at least four distinct forms of private finance of campaigns evident in democracies. (1) Self-financing: An individual may use his or her own resources to finance a bid for office. One out of every five dollars raised by the typical challenger in U.S. congressional elections comes from personal resources.[38] (2) Charitable or nonprofit contributions: Individuals and organizations may contribute money, goods and services, or labor to a campaign, much as they contribute to other civic or social activities and charities. This is in fact the model for campaign finance adopted under FECA in the form of low contribution limits from individuals and the requirement that organizations set up separate and segregated funds in order to make contributions. (3) Profit-oriented contributions: A firm may give directly from its treasury with the funds mixed with or derived from other funds that are geared to making profits. The Corrupt Practices Act of 1911 banned such contributions in U.S. federal elections, though they are still permitted in some states.[39] (4) Party owned property: Political parties in many democracies own assets, ranging from newspapers to sports teams to factories to real estate, and the profits from those assets can be used to pay for election activities and to sustain party organizations.[40] Private property holdings of

(2010), find that over two-thirds of democracies provide public subsidies to parties and document the electoral advantage that incumbent parties maintain through these funds.

[37] See Farrell and Webb, *Political Parties* (cited in note 3).

[38] Federal Election Commission, "Congressional Candidates Raised $1.42 Billion in 2007–2008," news release, Dec 29, 2009. The FEC reports that in 2008 $51 million of the $231 million raised by U.S. House challengers took the form of contributions or loans by the candidate to his or her own campaign.

[39] For a fifty-state chart listing contribution limits from corporations, see National Conference of State Legislatures, *2011–2012 Limits on Contributions to Candidates* (Sept 30, 2011), online at http://www.ncsl.org/Portals/1/documents/legismgt/Limits_to_Candidates_2011-2012.pdf.

[40] See, for example, Ingrid van Biezen, *Financing Political Parties and Election Campaigns— Guidelines* 19 (Council of Europe, 2003).

the parties likely originated with newspapers, which served also as tools for campaigning and propaganda. The nonprofit tax status of the American political parties prevents the parties from receiving profits from any assets they may own, such as party headquarters, but such profit-making party enterprises are not uncommon in Europe. Finance of campaigns and elections in the United States relies extensively on the first two types of private fund-raising.

Paying for democracy through private financing presents two considerable problems: ensuring there is enough money to run an adequate campaign and preventing private interests from corrupting elected officials or political parties. First, raising money from voluntary donations or charitable contributions means that campaigns face collective-action problems when soliciting funds from individuals and groups. Electoral campaigns and political discourse, like many other aspects of democracy, have characteristics of public goods. Almost all Americans benefit from being informed about their options, as that enables them to make choices consistent with their true preferences, but no individual has a strong incentive to become informed if a large number of other persons are informed. Anthony Downs famously termed this problem "rational ignorance." This line of thinking extends further to political discourse generally. The general benefits of such activities are not divisible, as with private goods and services. As a result, the marketplace of democracy invariably suffers from market failures. Almost all Americans benefit individually from the information that political campaigns convey and from having an engaged and active electorate, but there is very little private incentive to pay anything for that information. Economic theory has long taught us that public goods are underproduced, and that is especially true of collective action in the electoral arena.[41]

Second, private finance creates the opportunity for corruption, or at least the impression of corruption. Those who can amass resources and overcome collective action will gain added leverage. Corporations, unions, even political parties may wield power in Washington, DC, not because their ideas are convincing, but because they have the resources to fund campaigns. Politicians, desperate for the funds required to mount a credible campaign, may change the way they behave in office or the issues they choose to

---

[41] Mancur Olson, *The Logic of Collective Action: Public Goods and the Theory of Groups* ch 1 (Harvard, 1961).

discuss in order to attract contributions from private donors. Even if there is no explicit quid pro quo, it is alleged by some observers that the near universal reliance of members of Congress on organized interests for campaign funds creates a culture of corruption.[42]

The possibility and appearance of corruption are especially acute when resources come directly from the treasuries of for-profit corporations. This problem is most forcefully expressed in the dissenting opinions, one by Justice White and one by Justice Rhenquist, in *First National Bank of Boston v Bellotti*.[43] The management of a firm invests and spends its capital precisely to make profits, not to engage in social or political ventures. A firm's owners and investors have made capital available to management precisely so that they can earn return on their investment. An inadequate return on investment may lead investors to seek other investment opportunities. Political contributions made directly from the corporate treasury are subject to the same pressures and scrutiny from owners as any other sort of expenditure or investment in labor or capital that management makes. Every contribution or expenditure directly from a for-profit corporation is thought to come with the expectation of something in return to that corporation. Political contributions coming directly from accounts of for-profit corporations are suspect as involving an explicit profit motivation or purchase of political favors, a quid pro quo. Precisely this problem, exposed in the New York Life Insurance scandal of 1905, led to the century-old prohibition on direct corporate contributions embodied in the Corrupt Practices Act.[44] Of course, participation by other types of organizations and individuals seeks to influence the outcomes of elections, public discourse, and ultimately public policy, but such activities are not seen as exacting a private benefit in return. Rather they seek to persuade others of their point of view and to sway elections through the marketplace of ideas, rather than to make that

---

[42] See, for example, Lawrence Lessig, *Democracy after Citizens United*, Boston Rev (Sept/Oct 2010), online at http://bostonreview.net/BR35.5/lessig.php; Richard L. Hasen, *Citizens United and the Illusion of Coherence*, 109 Mich L Rev 581, 584 (2011); John M. de Figueiredo and Elizabeth Garrett, *Paying for Politics*, 78 S Cal L Rev 591, 604 (2005); Thomas Stratmann, *What Do Campaign Contributions Buy? Deciphering Causal Effects of Money and Votes*, 57 S Econ J 606, 615 (1991).

[43] 435 US 765, 802–28 (1978) (dissenting opinions of Justices White and Rhenquist).

[44] Richard L. McCormick, *From Realignment to Reform: Political Change in New York State 1893–1910* at 197–205 (Cornell, 1981).

worried about the undue influence of the entire class of wealthy donors, rather than the power of a single wealthy individual. And, those in power—incumbents and the national party establishment— seemed only to grow in financial advantages under this private system of campaign finance.[47] Indeed, since the moment *Buckley v Valeo* was handed down, reformers have sought another way, one not reliant on private sources of funds at all. The objective seems to remain: to remove the threat of corruption by driving private money out of the electoral system. In that spirit, European systems of public financing have provided the model for those striving to change state and federal campaign finance laws in the United States over the past two decades.[48]

Public finance of elections is common in the world's democracies and takes many forms. (1) Subventions and grants for campaign expenses: The most common form of public financing consists of subventions or grants to political parties for the conduct of election activities during the general election. This model of public finance is tailored to parliamentary systems with short election periods, such as five weeks, and it is often tied to limits on candidates' expenditures. Additionally, many countries provide grants to candidates directly. (2) Matching funds: Public finance programs often tie subsidies to performance criteria, such as the amount of money raised. The U.S. presidential primary matching funds program provides public funds equal to private funds for all candidates who have qualified.[49] (3) Tax credits: Some public finance mechanisms subsidize donors, rather than candidates or parties, through tax credits or by allowing contributions to be counted as charitable donations. Before the 1979 amendments to FECA, U.S. tax law allowed donors to deduct campaign contributions as charitable gifts.[50] (4) Free media: Nearly all democratic systems provide free access to media to candidates in the form of free advertising time, public debates and forums on television or radio, or televised conventions. (5) Public grants or subventions to parties for day-to-day operations: Parties in most parliamentary systems, which tend to have very short elec-

---

[47] Sorauf, *Inside Campaign Finance* (cited in note 30).

[48] David Donnelly, Janice Fine, and Ellen Miller, *Going Public: New Directions in Campaign Reform*, Boston Rev (Apr/May 1997), online at http://bostonreview.net/BR22.2/donnelly.php.

[49] 26 USCA § 9033.

[50] Revenue Act of 1971, §§ 701, 702, and 703.

tion seasons of one to two months, are rarely in campaign mode. They must still maintain their political infrastructure, and many governments provide grants for these day-to-day operations of party headquarters and local offices.[51]

Candidates and parties in the United States rely on some public funds to conduct campaign activities. The Federal Election Campaign Act provides public grants, worth approximately $84 million in 2008, to nominees for president who have won the endorsement of one of the two major parties or who qualify by winning at least 7 percent of the vote in the general election. Presidential primary candidates can also qualify for matching funds from the national government. And, federal grants provided $16.3 million to each of the parties for their national conventions in 2008.[52] Over the past four decades, the states have turned increasingly to public financing for legislative and executive offices as well. The challenge for these systems is to provide for adequate funding, especially when politicians as a class are unpopular.[53]

Public financing schemes, however, suffer from three significant drawbacks. First, and most important, public funds are provided to qualified candidates and parties, and the criteria to qualify are usually not politically neutral. In most systems, the major parties automatically receive grants, but minor parties are either locked out or have to demonstrate their worthiness for grants. This has been a long-standing objection to the presidential public finance system in the United States.[54] The Democratic and Republican nominees automatically qualify for public funds, but a third party or independent candidate, such as John Anderson in 1980 or Ross Perot in 1992, must receive at least 5 percent of the vote in the general election to qualify for matching funds. That of course means that third parties do not know if they qualify for public support until after the election is over. In European countries, public funds often have discriminatory effects against minor parties.[55]

Second, it is exceedingly difficult to get the level of public subsidy

---

[51] For an overview of countries that subsidize parties, see Kevin Casas-Zamora, *Paying for Democracy: Political Finance and State Funding for Parties* 30–31 (ECPR, 2005).

[52] Federal Election Commission, *Quick Answers: Public Funding*, online at http://www.fec.gov/ans/answers_public_funding.shtml.

[53] Nathaniel Persily and Kelli Lammie, *Perceptions of Corruption and Campaign Finance: When Public Opinion Determines Constitutional Law*, 153 U Pa L Rev 119 (2004).

[54] *Buckley v Valeo*, 424 US 1, 251 (1976).

[55] Booth and Robbins, 16 Party Politics at 640 (cited in note 36).

right. The typical public grant is a lump sum provided to any qualified candidate or party. Some states, such as Hawaii, have long had
public funding systems, but the amount of the grant was too small
to be attractive to serious candidates. Facing budget shortfalls or
political deadlock, some states have chosen not to appropriate funds
to public finance programs.[56]

A fixed, lump-sum grant is also extremely inefficient. It's a one-
size-fits-all solution that is not attuned to the variation in electoral
competition across legislative districts. A fixed amount provides either too much money or, worse, too little.

Third, public finance does not necessarily eliminate independent
expenditures. Public financing schemes subsidize candidates and
parties. Such funds do not replace or eliminate expenditures by
organizations and individuals separate from the candidates' and parties' campaigns. If public money levels the playing field between
competing candidates or parties, any independent expenditures become more significant in determining the outcome of the election.
For instance, labor unions spend approximately $50 million per
campaign advocating for the election of the Labor Party in a country
without the party having to pay for advertising, get-out-the-vote
activities, and the like. A system with public funds and low expenditure limits may even create an opening for independent expenditures.

Even with these flaws, public financing has proved increasingly
attractive as an alternative to privately financed campaigns in the
United States. By 2010, twenty-five states had some form of public
finance in their legislative or executive elections.[57] Arizona's Clean
Elections law was one of the most comprehensive and sophisticated.
It sought to create a sustainable and workable public financing program in the American states. The law was conceived and enacted
as part of a political effort in states across the nation to pass "clean
elections" legislation.[58] Connecticut, Florida, Maine, Minnesota,
New Jersey, New Mexico, North Carolina, and Vermont passed
similar laws in the late 1990s and early 2000s.[59] Using a variety of

---

[56] Rick Klein, *Supreme Judicial Court Ruling: Fund or Repeal Clean Elections*, Boston Globe
A1 (Jan 26, 2002).

[57] National Council of State Legislatures, *Public Financing of Campaigns: An Overview*
(2010), online at http://www.ncsl.org/Default.aspx?TabId=16591.

[58] Donnelly, Fine, and Miller, *Going Public* (cited in note 48).

[59] National Council of State Legislatures, *Public Financing of Campaigns* (cited in note
57).

mechanisms tied to public funds, such as low contribution limits and triggers for additional public funds in response to independent spending or privately financed opponents, these new state campaign finance laws sought to minimize the role of private money in state elections, or eliminate it entirely.

II. Arizona Free Enterprise v Bennett

At issue in *Bennett* was a peculiar feature of Arizona's public financing scheme. Arizona's law, passed through the initiative process in 1998, provided public funds to candidates who agreed to spend no more than $500 of their personal money, to participate in at least one debate, and to return any unspent money. Candidates qualify for public funding by raising a certain amount of money in very small donations, as little as $5 each. The law also provided matching public funds. The match, however, was not of the amount of money raised by the qualified candidate, but of the amount spent by opposing candidates, party committees, or groups. Any candidate who participated in the public financing program would receive additional funds if privately financed opponents or independent groups spent above a certain level. The additional funds amounted to 96 cents for every dollar spent by the privately financed candidate or group, and candidates outspent by a privately financed candidate or group were provided up to three times the original public grant. Those matching funds troubled the Supreme Court in *Bennett* because private spending by or in support of a candidate would make possible an almost equally large amount of spending by a publicly financed opponent. Moreover, independent spending by a group—not coordinated with the privately financed candidate—would also qualify the publicly financed candidate for additional public funds.

The trigger mechanism that lay at the heart of the Arizona public financing scheme was thus both the innovation that promised to make this a workable and sustainable program and the feature that troubled the Court. The trigger mechanism was designed to encourage candidates to stick with this public financing system. It attempts to mimic a competitive private campaign system by increasing spending where it is needed. It also tries to counter what was at the time seen as the greatest threat to the private system: outside money in the form of independent expenditures. Large expenditures by either a privately financed candidate or independent group would raise the level of public funding, and thus keep can-

speech and more robust discourse by providing public funds and leveling the playing field from the bottom up, rather than the top down?

Curiously, the answer to both questions appears to be yes. The Arizona law furthered the ultimate aim of the First Amendment: it created more speech and more robust electoral competition. This was plainly evident in the social science research mounted in support of the case. Over the decade that the Arizona law operated, total campaign expenditures in midterm elections increased from approximately $1 million to $12 million.[69] The number of candidates who ran for state legislative elections rose, the number of incumbents in contested general election races increased only approximately 10 percent, and the average vote margin of incumbents dropped slightly.[70] In addition, amicus curiae briefs filed in support of the law found no evidence that the trigger mechanism altered campaign spending behavior.[71] Privately financed candidates rarely exceeded the threshold at which matching funds were triggered, and candidates showed no tendency to spend up to the threshold and stop. Privately financed candidates appeared to spend what they were able to raise.[72] There appeared to be no effect of the imposition of the law in 2000 or of the injunction staying the law in 2010 on the total amount of private money spent in elections.[73] The law mainly served as a mechanism for efficiently allocating public money to competitive races and of increasing the amount of electoral competition in the state, especially in state legislative contests.

The problem for the advocates of the law lay not in the facts on the ground, but in a decision issued by the Court two years earlier, *Davis v Federal Election Commission*.[74] In *Davis*, the Supreme Court overturned a provision of the Bipartisan Campaign Reform Act (BCRA) called the Millionaire's Amendment. The Millionaire's

---

[69] Calculated by author from data downloaded from the website of the Arizona Secretary of State. *Campaign Finance Search—Candidates*, online at http://www.azsos.gov/cfs/CandidateSummarySearch.aspx.

[70] Mayer, Werner, and Williams, *Do Public Funding Programs Enhance Electoral Competition?* at 255–57 (cited in note 63).

[71] Brief for Amici Curiae Costas Panagopoulos, PhD, Ryan D. Enos, PhD, Conor M. Dowling, PhD, and Anthony Fowler in Support of Respondents, *Arizona Free Enterprise Club's Freedom PAC v Bennett*, Nos 10-238, 10-239, *13 (US filed Feb 22, 2011).

[72] Id at *9, *10.

[73] Id at *15.

[74] 554 US 724.

Amendment was also a trigger mechanism, but for contributions rather than expenditures. Under this provision, any candidate whose opponent spent a very large amount of personal money (in excess of $350,000) on his campaign was allowed to raise campaign contributions at three times the normal contribution limit under federal law and could receive coordinated party expenditures without any limitation.

The Court held that the Millionaire's Amendment imposed an impermissible burden on the self-financing candidate's "First Amendment right to spend his own money for campaign speech."[75] The scheme, Justice Alito wrote in the majority opinion, is "not constitutional simply because it attaches as a consequence of a statutorily imposed choice . . . [A] candidate who wishes to exercise [the right to unlimited speech] has two choices: abide by a limit on personal expenditures or endure the burden that is placed on that right by the activation of a scheme of discriminatory contribution limits."[76] Further, raising contribution limits could not be justified as a compelling governmental interest. If anything, that approach would only increase "the threat of corruption."[77]

The mechanism struck down in *Davis* bore a striking resemblance to the mechanism in question in *Bennett*. If a candidate's spending—personal funds in *Davis* and privately raised funds in *Bennett*—exceeded a threshold, the law rewarded his or her opponent. Under BCRA, the Millionaire's Amendment raised the contribution limit of the opponent of the self-financed candidate. Under Arizona's Clean Elections Act, privately financed expenditures above the threshold qualified the opposing candidate for public funds. Was the difference between these cases substantial? Did higher contribution limits of BCRA make the issue meaningfully different from the public subsidies of the Arizona Clean Elections Act?

A majority of the Court answered no. Chief Justice Roberts wrote the opinion of the Court, and was joined by Justices Alito, Kennedy, Scalia, and Thomas—the same five Justices who had made up the majority in *Davis*. The logic of the decision in *Davis*, Roberts wrote, "largely controls our approach to this case."[78] Quoting the majority opinion in *Davis*, Roberts put the matter simply: "the matching

---

[75] Id at 736.

[76] Id at 737.

[77] Id at 738.

[78] *Arizona Free Enterprise*, 131 S Ct at 2818.

funds provision 'imposes an unprecedented penalty on any candidate who robustly exercises [his] First Amendment right[s.]'"[79] The nature of the burden, of course, is that expenditures by privately financed candidates or groups above the threshold automatically translated into new resources for the opposing candidates. Hence, the law created an implicit constraint on the speech of privately funded candidates. Moreover, there was no equivalent grant of public funds to privately funded candidates; all of the public funds would go to publicly funded candidates in opposition to the expenditures by privately funded candidates. Roberts concluded that ". . . If the law at issue in *Davis* imposed a burden on candidate speech, the Arizona law unquestionably does so as well."[80]

Indeed, the majority saw the BCRA's Millionaire Amendment as less problematic than Arizona's public funds trigger. Chief Justice Roberts identified three particular problems with granting public funds in response to excessive spending by a privately funded candidate. First, under the BCRA the candidate who benefited from the higher contribution limit still had to go out and raise the money. Under the Arizona law the money is automatically released. That was seen as a "far heavier burden" because each dollar spent by the privately funded candidate automatically became 96 cents in the opponent's war chest.[81] Second, in a multicandidate election, the expenditure of the privately funded candidate could have a multiplier effect, as many opponents could receive the almost dollar-for-dollar subsidy.[82] Third, privately financed candidates are penalized by the expenditures of independent groups, even if their expenditures are unwelcome or unhelpful.[83]

More troubling still were the restrictions on independent expenditures. The Arizona law treated independent expenditures by groups exactly the same way it treated expenditures by privately funded candidates. If the trigger mechanism unfairly burdened candidate speech, then it also unfairly burdened those engaged in independent spending, and independent expenditures have consistently received constitutional protection from *Buckley* on. Roberts discerned an added burden on independent expenditures:

---

[79] Id.

[80] Id.

[81] Id at 2819.

[82] Id.

[83] Id.

Once the spending cap is reached, an independent expenditure group
. . . can either opt to change its message from one addressing the merits
of the candidates to one addressing the merits of an issue, or refrain from
speaking at all. . . . And forcing that choice—trigger matching funds,
change your message, or do not speak—certainly contravenes "the fundamental rule of protection under the First Amendment, that a speaker
has the autonomy to choose the content of his own message."[84]

As persuasive as Chief Justice Roberts's argument is, four of his
colleagues lined up squarely in opposition and joined a spirited
dissent written by Justice Elena Kagan. She put the matter in equally
simple terms. The Arizona law did not prevent anyone from speaking and served only to increase the amount and variety of speech
in the electoral setting. In this regard, the public financing grants
and the matching funds furthered the core purpose of the First
Amendment "to foster a healthy, vibrant political system full of
robust discussion and debate."[85] The statute does not constrain
anyone's speech ex ante, and allows any candidate to join the public
financing program. "What the law does—and all that the law does—
is fund more speech."[86]

Nor did the dissent see any significant harm or burden from the
program's trigger mechanism or public grants. In this regard, Justice
Kagan's opinion draws the parallel not to contribution limits in
Davis but to public funding in *Buckley*. Like FECA, the Arizona law
provides a preset amount of financial support to candidates, with
the added stipulation to privately financed candidates that subsidy
to publicly financed candidates will increase with overall spending.[87]
Providing the opportunity of public funds to candidates does not
violate the First Amendment; rather it facilitates and enlarges public
discourse; it "subsidizes and so produces more political speech."[88]
Any candidate who wishes to spend private resources does so voluntarily, just as with the public grants under FECA. "Except in a
world gone topsy-turvy, additional campaign speech and electoral
competition is not a First Amendment injury."[89]

Ultimately, though, Justice Kagan saw the Arizona law as justified

---

[84] Id at 2819–20, quoting *Hurley v Irish-American Gay, Lesbian, and Bisexual Group of Boston, Inc.*, 515 US 557, 573 (1995).

[85] Id at 2830 (Kagan, J, dissenting).

[86] Id at 2834.

[87] Id.

[88] Id at 2833.

[89] Id.

among many distinct interests in society, rather than simple majority rule by the largest faction. The presence of diverse and competing interests in the political arena produces an equilibrium among the different interests in society that allows individuals to achieve their goals. The more, and the more diverse, the interests involved in the political arena the more fully politics and policy will reflect the public will. Individual rights, such as free speech, are essential to allowing plural politics to emerge and run their course. Let anyone speak, the truth will emerge, and the proof of the power of the idea lay in its acceptance. Ideas and claims must be tested in the court of public opinion; there they either fail or succeed.[94]

The ultimate end of free speech in the pluralist theory is to ensure a robust democratic process that can hold government accountable. Free speech is not the end in itself, though it too is valued. If government can no longer be held accountable, then free speech becomes hollow. This is why corruption is a grave concern, serious enough to serve as a counterweight to First Amendment rights when contribution limits are at issue.

The flaw, from Justice Kagan's perspective, is that the pluralist's open and universal political marketplace does not emerge naturally. Pluralist political theory has long been understood by political scientists and political theorists to have many weaknesses.[95] Two arise most clearly in Justice Kagan's critique of the majority, and in earlier opinions by Justice White in *Buckley*, Justice Marshall in *Austin*, and Justice Stevens in *Randall*. First, not all legitimate interests and concerns will be expressed. Those who can overcome the collective-action problem will make their voices heard. Corporations and unions, for example, find ample representation in the political arena. Many segments of society may be unable to solve collective-action problems, especially those groups with very broad interests, such as "all consumers" or "poor people," and their perspectives and ideas may find no voice at all.[96] Second, considerable resources are needed to engage in public debate on a large scale in our democracy.

---

[94] The classic expression of pluralism is Robert Dahl, *Who Governs?* (Yale, 1961). See also David Truman, *The Governmental Process: Political Interests and Public Opinion* (Knopf, 1951); Nelson Polsby, *How to Study Community Power: The Pluralist Alternative*, 22 J Politics 474–84 (1960).

[95] For a survey, see William Kelso, *American Democratic Theory: Pluralism and Its Critics* (Greenwood, 1978).

[96] This was the thrust of the critique of pluralism contained in Mancur Olson's *Logic of Collective Action* (Harvard, 1965).

Assembling the resources required pulls candidates, parties, and other organizations inexorably toward the interests of those who have and are willing to provide the resources. "The flaw in the Pluralist heaven," E. E. Schattschneider wrote, "is that the heavenly chorus sings with a strong upper-class accent."[97]

The marketplace of ideas, then, from Justice Kagan's perspective, can function effectively, but it needs tending. Laws, such as the Arizona statute, might ensure greater access to the public sphere and the expression of many more ideas and perspectives than in a completely unstructured political marketplace. Indeed, the political marketplace is not completely free, open, and unstructured. Other election laws determine the number of seats, the nomination of general election candidates, the size of the constituency, and so on. They determine the confines of the political contest to take place. Campaign finance law is invariably viewed in that context, because those rules determine the nature of the election and the campaign itself.

Most elections in the United States take the form of contests for single-member districts in which two major parties, Democrat and Republican, nominate candidates for the general election in primary elections, and individuals and other parties may qualify for the general election ballot as well. Proportional representation, by comparison, is very rare in the United States. Political scientists have long noted that such a system of single-member districts creates strong pressures to narrow the electoral choices down to two principal contestants.[98] American election law, especially campaign finance law, is necessarily structured around the nation's long-standing two-party system, as well as other features of our electoral institutions.

It is at this point that Justice Kagan's view of electoral politics most clearly departs from that of the majority. The majority opinion says little about the electoral context within which campaign finance laws function. Chief Justice Roberts adheres to a particular theory of politics that melds seamlessly with the free speech philosophy set forth in *Buckley*. Justice Kagan's dissenting opinion in *Bennett* takes a more pragmatic approach. Legislatures and courts cannot address or solve the failings of pluralist theory in the political arena;

---

[97] E. E. Schattschneider, *The Semi-Sovereign People* 35 (Holt-Reinhart, 1960).

[98] William H. Riker, *The Two-Party System and Duverger's Law: An Essay on the History of Political Science*, 76 Am Pol Sci Rev 753–66 (1982).

they cannot avoid the logic of collective action or rational ignorance. However, the legislatures and the courts can try to make laws that compensate for the failings of that theory in ways that improve the functioning of the democratic process. They can do so by encouraging political competition within the existing electoral framework. Perhaps the most striking difference between the opinions of Justices Roberts and Kagan is the emphasis on the importance of electoral competition. The means to achieving democratic governance for Justice Roberts is free speech; Justice Kagan insists additionally on competitive elections. Justice Kagan uses the words competition or competitive fourteen times; Justice Roberts just twice.[99]

Like Justices White, Stevens, and Marshall before her, Justice Kagan sets forth an adversarial model of electoral politics and public discourse. What is important from this perspective is that the Court's decisions weigh the robustness of speech and political competition. Invoking Justice Holmes's dissenting opinion in *Abrams v United States* that "The best test of the truth is the power of the thought to get accepted in the competition of the market,"[100] Kagan observes that allowing unrestricted speech may be insufficient to achieve this goal if it is entirely one-sided. For Kagan, the strength of the Arizona Clean Elections Act is that it levels the playing field, and it does so from the bottom up. It offers subsidies to all candidates in all races, but it provides additional campaign resources for publicly funded candidates who face privately funded candidates with even greater resources.[101]

In the context of the electoral system in the United States, the First Amendment takes on a particular meaning. The electoral setting in Justice Kagan's view is much more constrained than in Chief Justice Roberts's view. The adversarial setting in a given election campaign or legislative district is such that voters focus their choices on competing candidates, one of whom will serve as the constituents' representative. Robust political discourse in this context must focus on the abilities of the competing candidates within a given district to express themselves fully. Expenditures need not be equal, but there must be sufficient campaigning by both sides that the

---

[99] Computed by the author from the opinions of Justice Roberts and of Justice Kagan in *Arizona Free Enterprise*, 131 S Ct 2806.

[100] 250 US 616, 630 (1919).

[101] *Arizona Free Enterprise*, 131 S Ct at 2832–33 (Kagan, J, dissenting).

voters can reach an informed decision about which candidate best reflects their views and would serve their interests better. Electoral discourse becomes dysfunctional when a well-funded Democrat faces a poorly funded Republican in Phoenix, and a well-funded Republican faces a poorly funded Democrat in Scottsdale. There may be a great deal of speech in the state, and from both sides; however, in this example, the voters in Phoenix would never hear the Republican side of the argument, and the voters in Scottsdale would never hear the Democratic side. The marketplace of ideas envisioned by Holmes would fail in such an example, because there would be no meaningful competition within each of the districts. The Arizona law increases competition within each district by providing public grants and matching grants, and it does so without increasing reliance on contributions from private sources. The Arizona law, Justice Kagan concludes, furthers the twin objectives of the First Amendment of ample political discourse and robust political competition.

That model fits poorly with the pluralist theory. From the pluralist perspective, it is not entirely clear what increased political competition means, aside from simply more people involved in the political process and more speech. It is not enough to have speech from many different voices. If one or both of the major party's candidates do not or cannot get their message out, then there may be a failure of political competition. Specifically, groups may advocate for one candidate or another, but not correctly reflect what that candidate would do or promises to do in office. If that candidate lacks the resources to get his or her message across, then voters do not have the correct information on which to base their decisions. Independent spending by groups simply is not a substitute for candidates' own representations of what they stand for or have accomplished. Suppose, for example, that a group purchases most of the prime-time advertising on the major networks in a local market, leaving no time available for candidates to air their commercials to the largest segment of the electorate. Likewise, if one candidate has the resources to conduct an extensive advertising effort, but the opponent does not, then there is similarly a failure of robust political competition.

It is the particular weakness of the pluralist view that it fails to take into account other features of the election process and laws, even though the campaign finance laws do try to take them into account. The election laws in the United States put at the center of the electoral arena two competing candidates, each from one of the major parties. That is the choice that voters face. People do not vote for one group or another or for one idea or another; they vote for one of the two competing candidates. U.S. campaign finance laws treat candidates as the center of the electoral system. Other advanced democracies, especially those with proportional representation, place parties at the center of the electoral arena, and their campaign finance laws reflect this fact. It is in the context of the broader election laws of the United States that the First Amendment objective of ensuring robust political discourse and fostering informed electoral decision making takes on concrete meaning. Against the backdrop of a single-member district electoral system with two major parties, the First Amendment objective of ensuring robust political debate and creating an informed electorate becomes an imperative to ensure the fullest possible electoral competition between the candidates and parties. That vision of the First Amendment is most clearly embraced in the lineage of decisions from Justice White's dissenting opinion in *Buckley v Valeo* to Justice Stevens's majority opinion in *McConnell v FEC* to Justice Kagan's dissenting opinion in *Arizona Free Enterprise v Bennett*.

The Court's opinion in *Arizona Free Enterprise v Bennett* leaves us with little more than the pluralist view of the First Amendment. Competition between candidates or parties is of no particular importance, in this view. Rather, the objective is to encourage anyone who wishes to stand up and speak. Political competition in this view goes well beyond competition between two candidates; it extends to individuals, political parties, and organized interests in our society. Often when a candidate at the national level, such as one running for U.S. House, has a shot of winning a race but lacks the resources, political parties and interest groups will direct enormous amounts of money to that race, and these organizations often can mobilize funds much faster than the candidate. Campaign contributions and spending are often exceedingly difficult to regulate precisely because of the readiness of organizations to channel money, sometimes through very creative means, to support their preferred candidates and philosophy.[102] And the possibility of such "independent speech" makes it unclear how to design and imple-

---

[102] Samuel Issacharoff and Pamela S. Karlan, *The Hydraulics of Campaign Finance Reform*, 77 Tex L Rev 1673 (1999).

ment a workable public financing scheme, short of full public funding, that will simultaneously satisfy the First Amendment aims of free and unfettered speech and of robust political discourse. The reformers who backed the Arizona law thought they had found such a solution. That law would have satisfied the more narrow view of the First Amendment, with the objective of ensuring greater competition among the major party candidates. It failed to satisfy the broader notion of the First Amendment, expressed in the per curiam decision in *Buckley* and reinforced by Justice Roberts in the majority opinion in *Arizona Free Enterprise v Bennett*, precisely because the trigger mechanism created a burden on the speech of independent groups and privately financed candidates.

IV. The Unsolved Campaign Finance Problems

Over the past five years, the Roberts Court's decisions in *Bennett, Davis,* and other cases have clarified what had become an increasingly unsettled area of law. Reform efforts of the 1990s and early 2000s introduced a wide range of new methods of regulating campaign spending and contributions, and the courts allowed many to stand for the better part of a decade. The *Buckley* architecture seemed to suffer its biggest blow in *McConnell v FEC*, in which the Court accepted some regulation of expenditures, not just contributions, and embraced the idea of fair competition and leveling the playing field. The Court, however, never established a clear theory for allowing expenditure limits, as had been done for contributions, and never broached the tricky question of what a "competitiveness" standard might be. Thereafter, from 2006 to 2011, the Court reversed course and once again embraced the First Amendment approach to campaign finance law developed in *Buckley*.

The practicalities of campaign finance will continue to press against constitutional standards. Three persistent problems will force this issue back into the legislatures, and ultimately back to the Court. These problems have not vanished.

A. TOO LITTLE SPENDING

In the area of campaign finance, the logic of collective action immediately raises the prospect that there will be insufficient money to run adequate political campaigns. How robust is the electoral marketplace of ideas? The short answer is not very, and it probably never has been.

According to public records of the Federal Election Commission, the 2008 House elections cost approximately $1.2 billion. That sounds like a lot of money. It was, after all, another record year in campaign spending. But how much actual communication with voters did that amount of money buy? Campaign communications, such as television advertising and direct mail, are priced on the basis of per person reached. A good baseline is direct mail, because the prices are fairly constant throughout the country. A single mailing, including design, printing, and postage, costs approximately $1 per unit.[103] Using that as the basis for calculating the amount of communication, the per-person expenditure is actually quite paltry. The U.S. Bureau of the Census estimates that the eligible electorate in the United States in 2008 consisted of approximately 231 million adults. Thus, campaigns for election to the House of Representatives spent a total of about $5.25 per eligible voter. This is hardly the picture of robust political discourse—two and a half mailings on average per U.S. House candidate.

The picture of political discourse becomes weaker still when we consider the distribution of funds across races. Campaign spending is not equal across districts or states. Some contests are hard-fought affairs, and the heat they generate attracts national attention and considerable amounts of campaign donations. Candidates in such races spend far above the average amount, but even more candidates spend little or nothing. In forty or so uncontested House elections each election cycle, there is no discourse at all, as all of the spending comes from one side of the political aisle.

Whether you embrace the pluralist theory or the adversarial model, there is likely too little spending in U.S. elections to consider our system to be one of robust discourse. The image of robust political discourse is one of exchange of ideas and facts and understanding of the world, and the audience is taken to be the entire electorate. The amounts of money spent reveal that most campaigns involve no back and forth, no alternative ideas shared. Rather, there is a thin amount of campaign advertising, the equivalent of two to three pieces of mail to each household. That fact,

---

[103] Alan Gerber and Donald Green, *Get Out the Vote* (Brookings, 2007).

of course, has provided little check on the amount of legal rhetoric
about free and robust discourse. Those words are meaningful in
legal opinions, but in the electoral arena they have much less
substance.

B. ONE-SIDED SPENDING, OR THE PROBLEM OF CHALLENGERS

Since the 1970s, political scientists have documented severe in-
equities in the amount of money raised and spent by candidates.
One of the most salient and persistent facts has been the difference
between incumbent and challenger spending. In a typical year,
total incumbent spending is roughly three to four times challenger
spending.[104] But the discrepancy in a typical election is even
greater.

Consider spending patterns in the 2008 election. According to
expenditure reports from the Federal Election Commission, the
average House incumbent expenditure was $1,255,000, and the
average House challenger expenditure was $403,000. The voting-
age population in a typical congressional district was in the neigh-
borhood of 500,000 persons. At a cost of $1 per mailing per eligible
voter, the typical House challenger could send only one mailing
to only 80 percent of the district's voters, while the incumbent
could reach each voter two and a half times.

The distribution of expenditures, especially challenger expenditures, is highly skewed and concentrated in just a few competitive
districts. Here's the kicker. The *median* incumbent expenditure
was $954,000, whereas the *median* challenger expenditure was only
$70,000. That is barely enough money to send one piece of mail
to one-seventh of the voters in a congressional district. And, half
of the challengers spent less than $70,000. Even the least well-
funded incumbents have enough money to send mail to every
household in the district.

Almost all of the challenger spending is concentrated in the
forty most hotly contested races. In these races the challengers
spent at least $1.5 million, and the opposing incumbents spent on
average $2 million. Figure 1 displays the amounts spent by in-
cumbents and challengers in U.S. House elections from 1978 to
2008 in real dollars in each congressional race. The horizontal
axis is the incumbents' share of the two-party vote in the given

---

[104] Sorauf, *Inside Campaign Finance* (cited in note 30).

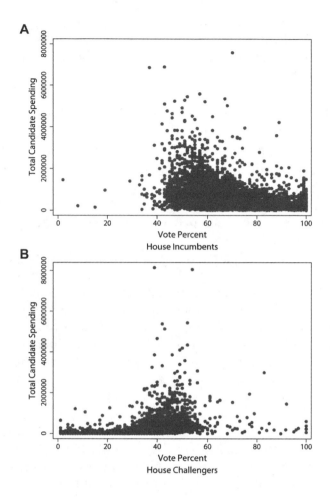

Figure 1. Distribution of party spending across U.S. House districts, by incumbent percentage of the two-party vote in the district. Source: compiled by author using data from the Federal Elections Commission.

election. Nearly all incumbents spend at least $750,000 today regardless of the level of competition, and the amounts are much larger in the very competitive seats. Challengers, as displayed in the lower panel, spend very little except in the very close elections. What all this means is that outside a fairly narrow band of races, there is insufficient challenger spending to qualify as true discourse or dialogue. Incumbents have the money in our privately funded campaign finance system; challengers do not. The electorate in

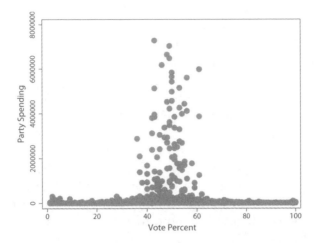

Figure 2. Distribution of party spending across U.S. House districts, by Democrat percentage of the two-party vote in the district. Source: compiled by author using data from the Federal Elections Commission.

75 percent of U.S. House races hears from only one side of the political equation.

C. PARTY AND GROUP CAMPAIGNS

Why do incumbents spend so much money? One explanation is that they spend it because they can, and it's not really that much money. Another explanation is that they are afraid. But of whom? The answer is, among others, parties and groups. Independent spending by parties and groups represents a growing segment of campaign money, though still only a small share of the total. In 2008, independent expenditures for and against candidates by political action committees totaled a little over $100 million, or 2.5 percent of the total amount spent on all election activities that year.

Although a modest amount of the total funds spent in the campaign finance system, party and group expenditures are highly targeted, which elevates their importance and their sensationalism. Figure 2 displays the total amount of money in party spending in House elections from 2000 through 2008. Almost all of the spending falls in races where the Democrat's share of the two-party vote was between 40 and 60 percent, and outside that range the amounts are so small as to be effectively zero.

Independent spending follows competition. Candidates in a close race can expect considerable sums of party and group money to flow into their races. The prospect of slipping into a close election strikes fear in incumbents. Senator John McCain, one of the principal co-sponsors of BCRA, defended the Millionaire's Amendment as a protection against a well-financed challenger. "Everyone is scared to death of waking up one morning and reading in the newspaper that some Fortune 500 CEO or heir or heiress is going to run against them and spend $15 million of their own money."[105] Whatever the forces that bear on a close election, the challenger will often be able to raise nearly as much as the incumbent from private donors, and the amounts often exceed $2 million. The prospect that the race might turn on a few thousand votes one way or the other will, in turn, attract parties and groups, and these organizations collectively are capable of pouring millions of dollars into a hotly competitive race.

Upon considering the amounts of money in and the dynamics of the campaigns, a distinction between the Millionaire's Amendment and the Clean Elections Law becomes clearer. The Millionaire's Amendment was intended to keep races from becoming competitive by keeping out one class of well-financed challengers. The Clean Elections Laws sought to keep the elections competitive by providing funds to credible candidates who face well-financed opponents. The line for Kagan in this case is quite clear. It is the difference between (1) the anemic sort of competition in which incumbents, who have little trouble raising money, face off against an occasional well-financed challenge, and (2) dynamic competition with considerable campaign spending on both sides in almost every legislative district. Such high-spending races arise in only about one in four U.S. House elections, and typically only in the competitive seats (those shown in the mid-range of figures 1 and 2). Wealthy challengers, targeted by the Millionaire's Amendment, are relatively rare. Poorly funded challengers facing incumbents willing to raise and spend many times more than their opponents, on the other hand, are the norm.

Ultimately, it is unclear how these facts should weigh on the

---

[105] Jill Zuckerman, *Senate Votes to Level Election Playing Fields*, Chicago Tribune 10 (March 21, 2001).

strictly construed First Amendment view of campaign finance. On the one hand, Chief Justice Roberts argues that the data are not relevant. The First Amendment principle of unrestricted free expression is indifferent to the data. The problem is that although the First Amendment principle is designed to produce intense political discourse and engagement, it rarely does so in practice. It is possible, of course, that the infrequency of robust political debate in actual election contests simply reflects the efficiency of private markets in allocating resources where they are best spent. But the only place where there is real competition, in the sense that Justice Kagan describes it, there is also competition in the way that Justice Roberts describes it. In congressional districts and states where we observe robust campaigning between competing candidates, we also observe independent spending by parties and groups. Unfortunately, that is a very small number of districts. In recent elections (2006, 2008, and 2010), only about 50 to 100 of the 435 U.S. House seats saw such intense, robust political discourse. In the other three-quarters of U.S. House districts, voters heard a one-sided campaign of incumbents, with little or no spending by the challenger, the parties, or outside groups.

I see these data as a shot across the bow for campaign finance law generally. Judges all too easily slide into debate over the meaning of the marketplace of ideas. As these data make clear, the marketplace of ideas envisioned in various Court opinions is not the norm in legislative elections in the United States today. The marketplace of ideas involves intense and robust exchange of ideas, and it facilitates the ability of the public to choose among competing views of government and candidates. Typically, only 20 percent of all congressional elections approximate this ideal. In the remaining 80 percent of congressional contests, there is a lack of both competition and discourse. Campaigns are one-sided, favoring incumbents, and parties and groups stay out. This seems to me a failure of the notion of the First Amendment under the *Buckley* framework to achieve the objective of robust political discourse.

V. What Is the Role of the First Amendment in Campaign Finance Law?

Supreme Court opinions commonly frame the issue of campaign finance as a trade-off between free speech and political corruption. The forty-year-long debate among the Justices over campaign finance, from *Buckley* to *Bennett*, cleaves along quite a different dimension. The great campaign finance debate within the Court is not over speech versus corruption, but over how we weigh the twin objectives of free speech and political competition. These two goals, it would seem, go hand in hand. Yet, from the very start of this debate in *Buckley*, the per curiam decision of the Court and the dissent of Justice White divided over exactly this matter. The Court adhered to strict First Amendment scrutiny of regulation of spending under the theory that money is essential to speech in the electoral arena and that limitations on spending fail that strict scrutiny. Justice White, however, saw political competition and robust debate as the objective of the First Amendment, and in his view that objective justified leveling the playing field. Nearly every major decision in the field of campaign finance in the years since *Buckley* divides along similar lines. Usually, one side follows the logic of *Buckley*, whereas the other cites the need for robust political *competition*. That distinction is as sharp as ever in *Bennett*.

The difference in how the Justices read the First Amendment is rooted in how they treat politics. Here again there is a basic duality. One view holds that electoral politics ought to be pluralistic, with ample discourse and debate among many different perspectives. Pluralism is in full bloom in highly competitive elections, as groups and party committees spend large sums advocating for their favored candidates and issues. Even when there is no debate, voters can still reach judgments based on what they know about the choices, and even the decision of some not to campaign vigorously. The other view takes as its starting point the adversarial structure of U.S. elections in which two candidates, each representing one of the two major parties, square off in the general election. Almost all elections, however, boil down to the head-to-head competition between the nominees of the two parties because our election law structures elections as plurality rule in single-member districts, and the winner takes all. The two competing major party candidates are the essential alternatives in an election, and campaign finance laws must, at a minimum, facilitate political discourse that produces informed public choice among those alternatives.

The pluralist model of politics fits neatly with the view of the

First Amendment set forth in *Buckley*. Let a thousand flowers bloom, and the best way to cultivate such a garden is for the government to get out of the way. The adversarial model, however, conflicts with *Buckley*'s assumption that unfettered speech is the ideal. Unfettered speech does not necessarily lead to robust political discourse. Campaign finance law, from the adversarial perspective, must somehow encourage more speech, and also more competitive speech.

The realities of campaign spending in the United States reveal the unfortunate failings of the pluralist model and the principle of unfettered campaign spending. It is true that many voices are raised in competitive elections, but plural politics occur only in those relatively unusual elections. If the ultimate objective is to create a robust marketplace of ideas where the public can learn about the choices and reach a reasoned judgment, then the approach in *Buckley* has failed. Campaign finance law in the United States has not served the ultimate purpose of the First Amendment. Rather, it has generally produced elections with one-sided political competition—a lecture, not a debate.

It is against this empirical backdrop that the adversarial model gains traction. And for a time, from *Austin* to *McConnell*, the Court seemed to warm up to this idea as the foundation for a new approach to campaign finance law. The challenge, though, rested with the legislators and reformers. Was it possible to forge a new campaign financing system that would produce *both* more speech and more competition? The advocates of the Clean Elections Law hoped that they had found an answer: public financing with matching funds triggered by private spending. Such a solution seemed more likely to pass constitutional muster than yet another charge into the breech with spending limits.

The Supreme Court's decision in *Bennett* has now closed off that approach. It may be possible to tinker further with clean election laws like the Arizona law, and I suspect many states will try. More important than the specific legislation, though, the Court's decision reasserts the primacy of the approach set out in *Buckley*. That approach is flawed, not necessarily as legal doctrine, but certainly as good policy. The history of campaign finance laws since *Buckley* demonstrates that this is the case. In other areas of election law, such as one-person-one-vote, the core issues are settled quickly and the state legislatures set about implementing the rule within the strictures of judicial rulings. In campaign finance, we have seen repeated attempts to alter state and federal laws in ways that challenge *Buckley* directly or that set out entirely new approaches to campaign finance. The reason for this is not that *Buckley* is wrong given the view of politics that it embraces. Rather, the reason is that the view of politics embraced by *Buckley* is out of alignment with the realities of contemporary political competition, and the Courts' subsequent rulings are therefore frequently at odds with the policy need.

What, then, is the real policy failure in campaign finance? Put simply, Americans get their democracy on the cheap. The public treasuries of the state and federal governments pay almost nothing for the purpose of ensuring an educated and engaged electorate. Public funding of presidential campaigns and conventions came to just $242 million in 2008.[106] The average American donates no money to candidates for office, parties, or political organizations. Most money comes from a wealthy few or through organizations such as corporations and unions. In one sense, then, campaign finance in the United States amounts to a wealth transfer from the small number of mostly higher-income Americans who pay for election-related activities to those who pay nothing.[107] But, in another, more fundamental sense, wealthy individuals and organizations now wield tremendous influence on politics because they are the font of the money needed to run political campaigns. This is inevitable in a campaign finance system that relies primarily on private sources of funds.

How do we get more speech and more competition into the political system? That seems to me the essential question for the future. Incumbents are unlikely to want to address this question because answering it would mean accepting more competition that endangers their own jobs. Perhaps that is too much to ask of human nature. *Davis* certainly exposed that very human instinct of self-preservation in the Bipartisan Campaign Reform Act. Incumbents used the Millionaire's Provision to keep challengers out. Similar objections can likely be said of restrictions on party soft money and issue advertising, which are designed to limit the power

---

[106] Federal Election Commission, *Presidential Campaign Finance Summaries*, online at http://www.fec.gov/press/bkgnd/pres_cf/pres_cf.shtml.

[107] Ansolabehere, de Figueiredo, and Snyder, *So Little Money* (cited in note 33).

of parties, groups, and wealthy opponents—all potential threats to incumbents.

In this regard, the First Amendment has served as an important corrective. The Roberts Court has dismantled parts of the BCRA and state laws that imposed such restrictions on campaign activities. Decisions following the principle of *Buckley* have refused to let legislators cap what candidates and groups can spend. In this respect, the application of the First Amendment has served as a policy corrective by preventing incumbents from writing election laws in ways that cynically further their own interests.

The First Amendment, however, is not a solution. Even if the Court struck down all campaign finance regulations under the First Amendment, this would not solve the critical problems of ensuring that campaigns are adequately funded, of ensuring greater competition and discourse among competing candidates, or of lessening concerns about corruption. Merely eliminating spending restrictions leaves most private citizens without any strong incentive to make voluntary contributions to candidates, and leaves most campaigns woefully underfunded. It also leaves unaddressed the problems of weak competition at the congressional district level and the problems of corruption and bribery.

The challenge today is that the space for available solutions just got smaller. *Bennett* makes clear that mechanisms that level the playing field remain unacceptable to the majority, even when such mechanisms increase the total amount of speech and the degree of electoral competition. This leaves policy makers with really two choices: full public financing or full private financing. The past forty years of full private financing of elections have exposed serious deficiencies with this approach—especially the inadequacy of resources, the threat of corruption and bias, and the public distrust that such an approach engenders. As the Court continues to push the United States away from more modest attempts at campaign finance regulation, then, it is increasingly pushing public policy toward the one alternative that many conservatives most abhor: full public financing of all federal elections along the lines of the presidential general election fund created by FECA. This, of course, does not eliminate private sources of money, but it would convert private money entirely into issue advocacy and independent spending.

FREDERICK SCHAUER

HARM(S) AND THE FIRST AMENDMENT

The First Amendment has always had a delicate relationship with harm. Although any robust free speech principle must protect at least some harmful speech despite the harm it may cause,[1] much public rhetoric, academic commentary, and even legal doctrine seems often to deny this now well understood dimension of freedom of speech. Typically, the denial takes the form of pointing out examples—and they are admittedly legion—in which officials have targeted as dangerous or harmful instances of speech that were in reality clearly benign.[2] On other occasions, the arguments for freedom of speech are lumped together with arguments for protecting a wide range of self-regarding conduct from governmental sanction.[3] Or sometimes it is simply claimed that speech is generally

Frederick Schauer is David and Mary Harrison Distinguished Professor of Law at the University of Virginia.

[1] This claim is developed at length in Frederick Schauer, *Free Speech: A Philosophical Enquiry* (Cambridge, 1982). For a more recent version, see Frederick Schauer, *On the Relation Between Chapters One and Two of John Stuart Mill's On Liberty*, 39 Cap U L Rev 571 (2011).

[2] A valuable survey of wartime examples of the phenomenon is Geoffrey R. Stone, *Perilous Times: Free Speech in Wartime: From the Sedition Act of 1798 to the War on Terrorism* (Norton, 2004).

[3] A prominent example of this approach is Ronald Dworkin, *Taking Rights Seriously* 275–76 (Harvard, 1977), although Ronald Dworkin, *A Matter of Principle* 336–38 (Harvard, 1985), is more forthcoming about the harm-producing capacities of communication. In more or less the same vein is C. Edwin Baker, *Human Liberty and Freedom of Speech* (Oxford, 1989), but C. Edwin Baker, *Autonomy and Free Speech*, 27 Const Comm 251 (2011), presents a more nuanced approach.

less harmful than conduct.[4] And often the harms occasioned by speech are attributed to the listener, whose thin skin is allegedly the source and cause of the problem, rather than what some speaker has spoken.[5]

The Supreme Court has often been complicit in denying or downplaying the harm-producing capacity of speech, framing even its most strongly speech-protective First Amendment decisions in a way that emphasizes the importance of the speech and de-emphasizes the possibility that even the speech we rightfully protect has substantial harm-producing capacities. Thus, if all we need do is avert our eyes, as in Justice Harlan's opinion in *Cohen v California*,[6] or recognize the responsibilities of living in an open democracy, as in Justice Brennan's now obsolete plurality opinion in *Rosenbloom v Metromedia, Inc.*,[7] or trust in counterspeech to remedy the harms of false speech, as in the claim in *Gertz v Robert Welch, Inc.*[8] that under the First Amendment "there is no such thing as a false idea,"[9] or rely on the marketplace of ideas to sort truth from falsity, as is explicit in *Gertz*[10] and implicit in *Lorillard Tobacco Co. v Reilly*,[11] then we need not concern ourselves very much with harmful speech.

---

[4] See Martin H. Redish, *Freedom of Expression: A Critical Analysis* 19 n 48 (Michie, 1984) ("It is almost certainly true in the overwhelming majority of cases that speech is less immediately dangerous than conduct.").

[5] *Harper v Poway Unified School Dist.*, 445 F3d 1166, 1207 (9th Cir 2006) (Kozinski dissenting), vacated as moot, 549 US 1262 (2007); Rodney A. Smolla, *The Libel Game: Suing the Press* 169 (Oxford, 1986); James F. Fitzpatrick, *The Sensitive Society*, 47 Fed Comm L J 237, 237 (1994). See also Judith Jarvis Thomson, *The Realm of Rights* 249–59 (Harvard, 1990) (suggesting that belief-mediated distress is different from other harms because one can "steel oneself" against such distress).

[6] 403 US 15, 21 (1971). See also *Erznoznik v City of Jacksonville*, 422 US 205, 212 (1975).

[7] 403 US 29, 48 (1971) (Brennan, J, for a plurality) ("Voluntarily or not, we are all 'public' men to some degree."). Although the plurality opinion in *Rosenbloom* would have extended the stringent protections of *New York Times Co. v Sullivan*, 376 US 254 (1964), to libel actions brought by all persons—public or private—who were involved in matters of public importance, *Gertz v Robert Welch, Inc.*, 418 US 323 (1974), superseded *Rosenbloom* by holding that nonpublic figures need only prove negligence in order to prevail. *Time, Inc. v Hill*, 385 US 374, 388 (1967), is somewhat consistent with *Rosenbloom* in limiting the remedies available to private individuals who become involved in public matters.

[8] 418 US 323 (1974).

[9] Id at 339. Even more to the point is the succeeding sentence: "However pernicious an opinion may seem, we depend for its correction . . . on the competition of other ideas." Id at 339–40.

[10] Id. And so too, of course, in Holmes's famous claim that the "best test of truth is the power of the thought to get itself accepted in the competition of the market." *Abrams v United States*, 250 US 616, 630 (1919) (Holmes, J, dissenting).

[11] 533 US 525 (2001).

There are, of course, some cases in which the Court has recognized the harms of speech, several of which have allowed restrictions,[12] and a few of which have even acknowledged the existence
of harms while refusing to allow the government to attempt to
restrict them.[13] But by and large, not very much of the Court's
rhetoric and doctrine has directly faced the issue of speech-created
harm.

Three cases in the last two Terms, however, have put harm more
squarely on the free speech agenda than we have typically seen in
the past. In *United States v Stevens*,[14] the Court dealt with a federal
restriction on films depicting (and typically produced in conjunction
with) the worst sort of cruelty to animals; in *Snyder v Phelps*,[15] the
question was whether the First Amendment would permit an action
by the family of a dead soldier for intentional infliction of emotional
distress against a group that decided that the funeral of the soldier
was the appropriate forum for advancing their campaign against
homosexuality; and in *Brown v Entertainment Merchants Association*,[16]
the Court was asked to allow the states to restrict minors' access
to interactive video games in which the minors could experience
the thrill of killing, maiming, and flouting the law. In none of these
cases would a claim of harmlessness have been taken seriously, and
thus the three cases together, all coming down in favor of the
speaker and against the restriction, represent the Court's most recent and sustained confrontation with speech-created harm. That
the Court did so in a somewhat evasive and unfocused way may be
attributable to its desire to avoid the central question, but it may
also have much to do with the fact that the three cases, while all
presenting clear harms, involved harms of very different types. In
sorting out this trilogy of harms, we may better understand this
delicate relationship between harm and free speech, and perhaps

---

[12] See, for example, *Hill v Colorado*, 530 US 703 (2000) (recognizing harms of targeted
picketing); *Frisby v Schultz*, 487 US 474 (1988) (same); *Dun & Bradstreet, Inc. v Greenmoss
Builders, Inc.*, 472 US 749 (1985) (recognizing harms of commercial defamation).

[13] For example, the protection of "reprehensible" hate speech in *R.A.V. v St. Paul*, 505
US 377 (1992), and the explicit recognition of the harm of protected defamation of public
officials in Justice White's concurring opinion in *Ocala Star-Banner Co. v Damron*, 401
US 295, 301 (1971) (White, J, concurring), and *Monitor Patriot Co. v Roy*, 401 US 265,
301 (1971) (White, J, concurring).

[14] 130 US 1577 (2010).

[15] 131 S Ct 1207 (2011).

[16] 131 S Ct 2729 (2011).

begin to understand how the doctrine might accommodate it.

I. THE CASES

A. UNITED STATES V STEVENS

In 1999 Congress enacted 18 USC § 48,[17] which made it a federal crime to create, sell, or possess in interstate commerce any "depiction of animal cruelty," defining that term to encompass the visual or auditory depiction of "conduct in which a living animal is intentionally maimed, mutilated, tortured, wounded, or killed. . . ."[18] The statute was passed in response to the apparent proliferation of "crush videos," videos in which live animals are slowly crushed or otherwise tortured or mutilated, typically in a sexualized context, and typically catering to people with a very specific sexual fetish.[19]

Although the impetus for 18 USC § 48 was the proliferation of such crush videos, the Supreme Court decision arose in a different context. The case began when the statute provided the basis for the indictment in the Western District of Pennsylvania of Robert Stevens, who ran an illegal dogfighting business and sold videos of the illegal dogfights and of dogs attacking other animals.[20] In moving to dismiss the indictment, Stevens challenged the constitutionality of 18 USC § 48, arguing that the videos he was charged with selling as well as the other depictions prohibited by the statute were protected by the First Amendment. Stevens was unsuccessful in the district court, and was thereafter convicted and sentenced to 37 months' imprisonment. On appeal, however, the Third Circuit held § 48 to be unconstitutional on its face and

---

[17] Pub L No 106-152, 113 Stat 1732 (codified at 18 USC § 48 (2006)).

[18] 18 USC § 48(c) (2006).

[19] HR Rep No 106-397, p 2 (1999), as described and quoted in *United States v Stevens*, 130 S Ct 1577, 1583 (2010).

[20] It is not clear from the record whether the deeper impetus for the prosecution was the videos, or instead the desire to prosecute Stevens because of a suspected more pervasive involvement with the dogfighting business itself. The question is of some interest because of the fact that many child pornography prosecutions appear to be indirect ways of reaching people suspected of actual "hands-on" pedophiliac behavior. See *United States v Garthus*, 652 F3d 715 (7th Cir 2011); Angela W. Eke, Michael C. Seto, and Jennette Williams, *Examining the Criminal History and Future Offending of Child Pornography Offenders: An Extended Prospective Follow-Up Study*, 35 L & Human Behav 466 (2011). See also Frederick Schauer, *Bentham on Presumed Offences*, 23 Utilitas 363 (2011).

vacated the conviction.[21] The Supreme Court granted the United States's petition for certiorari, but, with Chief Justice Roberts writing for an 8–1 majority (Justice Alito dissenting[22]), upheld the Third Circuit's conclusion that the statute was substantially overbroad and consequently unconstitutional on its face.

In upholding the Third Circuit, the Court rejected multiple arguments by the government for the statute's constitutionality. Most significantly, Chief Justice Roberts's majority opinion dismissed as "startling and dangerous" the government's contention, seemingly derived from the well-known language in *Chaplinsky v New Hampshire*,[23] that the coverage of the First Amendment was to be determined by weighing the relative social costs and benefits of a particular category of speech. Although such so-called definitional balancing[24] has often been thought to undergird the exclusion of obscenity and fighting words, inter alia, from even the coverage[25] of the First Amendment, the Court made clear that such a characterization should be understood as an after-the-fact description of certain historical exclusions, and decidedly not as

---

[21] *United States v Stevens*, 533 F3d 218 (3d Cir 2008).

[22] 130 S Ct at 1592. Justice Alito dissented from the majority's overbreadth ruling, but also wrote at length to emphasize the extent and severity of the genuine harms to animals that he believed the statute would be effective in addressing.

[23] "There are certain well-defined and narrowly limited classes of speech, the prevention and punishment of which have never been thought to raise any Constitutional problem. . . . [Such categories are] of such slight social value as a step to truth that any benefit that may be derived from them is clearly outweighed by the social interest in order and morality." *Chaplinsky v New Hampshire*, 315 US 568, 572 (1942). For a recent overview of *Chaplinsky*'s history and implications, see Rodney A. Smolla, *Words "Which By Their Very Utterance Inflict Injury": The Evolving Treatment of Inherently Dangerous Speech in Free Speech Law and Theory*, 36 Pepperdine L Rev 317 (2009).

[24] The label and the analysis come from Melville Nimmer, *The Right to Speak from "Times" to "Time": First Amendment Theory Applied to Libel and Misapplied to Privacy*, 56 Calif L Rev 935, 942–43 (1968), who emphasized that it was important to recognize that balancing could occur at the level of defining the scope of the First Amendment or of a particular First Amendment rule or principle or doctrine, and not necessarily in the context of any particular case. See also Joseph Blocher, *Categoricalism and Balancing in First and Second Amendment Analysis*, 84 NYU L Rev 375, 393–96 (2009); Joseph Blocher, *School Naming Rights and the First Amendment's Perfect Storm*, 96 Georgetown L J 1, 2 n 2 (2007); Norman T. Deutsch, *Professor Nimmer Meets Professor Schauer (and Others): An Analysis of "Definitional Balancing" as a Methodology for Determining the "Visible Boundaries of the First Amendment,"* 39 Akron L Rev 483 (2006).

[25] The Court explicitly (although not consistently) talks about "coverage," for the question of what the First Amendment covers—what activities occasion the use of First Amendment-generated tests, doctrines, and scrutiny—is different from the question of whether the application of those tests, doctrines, and scrutiny actually produces protection in the particular case. See Frederick Schauer, *The Boundaries of the First Amendment: A Preliminary Exploration of Constitutional Salience*, 117 Harv L Rev 1765, 1769–74 (2004).

a test. "Maybe there are some categories of speech that have been historically unprotected," the Chief Justice wrote, "but have not yet been specifically identified or discussed as such in our case law. But if so, there is no evidence that 'depictions of animal cruelty' is among them. We need not foreclose the future recognition of such categories to reject the Government's highly manipulable balancing test as a means of identifying them."[26]

Having emphatically declined the government's offer to create new categories of noncoverage by the use of even a categorial balancing test, and having apparently rejected as well the entire notion of definitional balancing,[27] the Court proceeded to invalidate the statute on overbreadth grounds. The Court seems to have been persuaded by many of the amicus briefs that the statute as written would extend far beyond crush videos, and far beyond glorifying depictions of illegal acts such as those shown in Stevens's products, and could well encompass a wide range of legitimate and valuable hunting and adventure depictions, and cover in addition some depictions whose political goal was to call attention to the evils of animal cruelty. And because the overbreadth, in the Court's view, was so substantial,[28] there became no need to address the question whether the First Amendment would permit a statute narrowly tailored to reach crush videos, or precisely aimed at portrayals of illegal acts where the portrayal was an integral part of the same illegal enterprise (as arguably it was in the case of Stevens himself).

Although the Court thus declined to address the constitutionality of a (much) more narrowly tailored statute, and although

---

[26] 130 S Ct at 1586.

[27] Although it should be obvious that the First Amendment cannot possibly even cover all instances of "speech," it does not follow that the speech that is covered and the speech that is not need be determined by a balancing test, even a balancing test deployed at the level of category definition. It is quite possible, for example, to focus the coverage question entirely on the purposes of the First Amendment (the evaluation of which need not be based on the intent of the drafters or the ratifiers) or on the scope of the broader idea of freedom of speech. Speech that is within those purposes would be covered regardless of the desirability of regulation, a matter which could then be addressed at the level of protection. And speech that is outside those purposes would not be covered, no matter how weak were the arguments for regulation. See Frederick Schauer, *Categories and the First Amendment: A Play in Three Acts*, 34 Vand L Rev 265 (1981).

[28] The most recent articulation of the Court's overbreadth test is *United States v Williams*, 553 US 285 (2008), and the most comprehensive analysis of overbreadth and of the standards for determining its existence is Richard H. Fallon Jr., *Making Sense of Overbreadth*, 100 Yale L J 853 (1991).

Congress has since passed a significantly narrower one,[29] the tenor of the opinion should not give much hope to proponents of anything other than almost a pointlessly narrow law.[30] The Court (but not Justice Alito in dissent) dismissed the obvious analogy with *New York v Ferber*,[31] flicking it aside as based on the "special case" of a conjunction among speech that was an "integral part" of a nonspeech crime, a market for the speech that was "intrinsically related" to the underlying illegality (of child abuse), and the "compelling interest" in protecting children from abuse.[32] And the Court made abundantly clear as well that it would not look kindly on efforts to expand the categories of speech uncovered by the First Amendment—that is, speech that can be regulated without satisfying First Amendment standards of justification. At the end of the day, the Court left the impression that the harms to animals coming from such videos were ones that a society with a strong commitment to freedom of speech would simply have to endure.

B. SNYDER V PHELPS

Relatively early in the Term following *Stevens*, the Court again confronted a case involving moderately clear speech-caused harm in, again, a situation that was largely novel. *Snyder v Phelps*[33] arose

---

[29] The replacement statute is the Animal Crush Video Prohibition Act of 2010, Pub L No 111-294, 124 Stat 3179, codified as (and replacing the previous version of) 18 USC § 48 (2012). The new statute is more narrowly restricted to depictions of extreme cruelty, and even more narrowly restricted to depictions of extreme cruelty that are also "obscene." The limitation to the obscene, however, presents a number of issues. First, might the limitation be understood as a viewpoint-based limitation of even uncovered "nonspeech," and thus still be unconstitutional under *R.A.V. v St. Paul*, 505 US 377 (1992)? Insofar as the new statute treats legally obscene cruelty to animals differently from legally obscene noncruel depictions of animals, there might well be just the kind of viewpoint discrimination in the domain of uncovered speech that we can think of as an *R.A.V.* problem. Second, does the fact that the new statute could not reach Stevens himself or any others whose animal cruelty videos were not sexual indicate that the statute is more political symbol than anything else? And, finally, and relatedly, does the statute serve any purpose that could not be served by existing obscenity law? A charitable interpretation would suggest that the statute is designed to satisfy the "specifically defined" component of the "patent offensiveness" prong of the test in *Miller v California*, 413 US 15, 24 (1973), but as long as there is a requirement in the statute that the material be legally obscene as well as depicting animal cruelty, it is hardly clear that the new statute is necessary to cover sexualized animal crush videos, and thus it is hardly clear that it is very much more than a political stunt.

[30] See note 29.

[31] 458 US 747 (1982).

[32] 130 S Ct at 1586.

[33] 131 S Ct 1207 (2011).

not in the context of a criminal prosecution, as in *Stevens*, but out of a civil lawsuit for intentional infliction of emotional distress and related torts. The suit was brought by the family of Marine Lance Corporal Matthew Snyder, who had been killed while on duty in Iraq. Lance Corporal Snyder's family planned a funeral at the Catholic church in their hometown, Westminster, Maryland. On the day of the funeral, Fred Phelps and other demonstrators from the Westboro Baptist Church, located in Topeka, Kansas, and founded by Phelps in 1955, arrived at the funeral and engaged in a demonstration and picketing on public land and public streets in view of the attendees at the funeral, just as they had done at nearly 600 previous military funerals. The motive behind the demonstration was entirely unrelated to Matthew Snyder or his family personally, other than the fact that he had died while in military service. Rather, the demonstration was inspired by the belief by Phelps and other members of Westboro Baptist that the death of American soldiers as well as other American calamities were the product of God's vengeance against the United States for its tolerance of homosexuality generally and in the military in particular. The picket signs carried by Phelps and others reflected this belief, and among the signs were ones announcing that "God Hates Fags," "God Hates the USA/Thank God for 9/11," "Priests Rape Boys," and "Thank God for Dead Soldiers."[34]

Although Albert Snyder, Matthew Snyder's father, was unaware of the specific wording on the signs until he saw them on a news broadcast later in the day, he was aware of their general import at the time of the funeral, and aware as well that the funeral was the target of a demonstration. He brought a diversity action based on Maryland law against Phelps in the United States District Court for the District of Maryland, and although the court dismissed some of the causes of action, it upheld the principal one for intentional infliction of emotional distress. A trial was held, and the jury found for Snyder, awarding him $2.9 million in compensatory damages and $8 million in punitive damages, the latter then remitted by the trial judge to $2.1 million. The verdict was reversed in its entirety on First Amendment grounds in the Fourth Circuit, however, and the Supreme Court granted certiorari.

As in *Stevens*, Chief Justice Roberts wrote for an 8–1 majority

---

[34] Id at 1210.

upholding the First Amendment claim, with Justice Breyer writing
a concurring opinion and Justice Alito again as the only dissenter.
In affirming the Fourth Circuit, the Chief Justice acknowledged
that a content-neutral prohibition on picketing in the vicinity of
a funeral might well be consistent with the First Amendment.[35]
But this restriction was not content-neutral, he concluded, precisely because the essence of the claim of (and verdict for) intentional infliction of emotional distress was that the content of the
demonstration had caused the distress to the Snyder family. Moreover, the Court concluded, the content of the speech that had
produced the damages award was content relating to a matter of
public concern, thus entitling Phelps's speech to a degree of "special protection" under the First Amendment.[36]

---

[35] Id at 1218.

[36] Although not the principal theme of this article, the Court's emphasis on the distinction between speech that is a matter of public concern and speech that is of only
private concern is potentially highly significant. If the Court's use of the distinction in
Snyder was intended to be limited to private tort actions for defamation, invasion of privacy,
and intentional infliction of emotional distress, then perhaps *Snyder* does little more than
restate a distinction explicit in the difference between *New York Times Co. v Sullivan*, 376
US 254 (1964), and *Curtis Publishing Co. v Butts*, 388 US 130 (1967), on the one hand,
and *Dun & Bradstreet, Inc. v Greenmoss Builders, Inc.*, 472 US 749 (1985), on the other.
Even in the context of defamation and related torts, however, the stress on public concern
raises an issue regarding the understanding and interpretation of *Gertz v Robert Welch,
Inc.*, 418 US 323 (1974). The plaintiff in *Gertz* was a private figure under the Court's
approach to defamation, and the defamatory publication was in what might broadly be
considered the "media." In that context, and with the presence there of what now might
be labeled a matter of public concern, the Court held that a plaintiff need not show
Sullivan actual malice, but would have to show at least negligence. The question now,
given the focus on the speech being a matter of public concern in *Snyder*, is whether a
non-public-figure plaintiff bringing an action for defamation against the media on a matter
not of public concern would still have to meet *Gertz*'s negligence standard, or whether,
as in the nonmedia and non-public-concern case of *Dun & Bradstreet*, nonconstitutionalized
application of common law principles would satisfy the First Amendment. Even more
significantly, there is now a question whether the emphasis on the presence of a matter
of public concern in *Snyder* signals the Court's willingness to apply the distinction between
public concern and so-called private concern across all or most of the First Amendment.
If that is so, the effect on existing doctrine could be substantial. To offer just one example,
is it now the case that Paul Cohen (*Cohen v California*, 403 US 15 (1971)) would not have
prevailed had he omitted the words, "the Draft," from his jacket? These are important
and now-open questions, but it is not clear that a more widespread emphasis on the public-
concerning nature of the speech at issue would command a majority of the Court, given
that Justice Scalia's majority opinion in *Brown v Entertainment Merchants Association*, 131
S Ct 2729 (2011), commented that "we have long recognized that it is difficult to distinguish politics from entertainment, and dangerous to try." 131 S Ct at 2733. Indeed, the
difficulties to which Justice Scalia alluded are apparent in the cases involving the speech
of public employees. Compare *Borough of Duryea v Guarnieri*, 131 S Ct 2488 (2011), with
Garcetti v Ceballos, 547 US 410 (2006), with *Connick v Myers*, 461 US 138 (1983), with
Pickering v Bd. of Educ., 391 US 563 (1968). And for a broad-based skepticism expressed
some years ago, see Cynthia L. Estlund, *Speech on Matters of Public Concern: The Perils of
an Emerging First Amendment Category*, 59 Geo Wash L Rev 1 (1990).

There can be little doubt that the Westboro picketers selected the location of their picketing because of the presence of Matthew Snyder's funeral, and thus the question arises as to how this case differs from those allowing restrictions on targeted residential picketing, as in *Frisby v Schultz*,[37] or upholding buffer zones and other restrictions on picketing at abortion clinics, as in *Hill v Colorado*[38] and *Madsen v Women's Health Center, Inc*.[39] The Court announced that such cases presented "obviously quite different" facts, and the majority noted that the Westboro protesters had a right to be where they were, had complied with all of the relevant regulations and police directions, and were neither unruly, nor profane, nor violent. But does this suggest that nonviolent targeted picketing of a private residence but on public streets is now protected, some of the language in *Frisby* notwithstanding? Or that targeted but peaceful picketing in the vicinity of abortion clinics might now receive greater solicitude than it did in *Hill* and *Madsen*? We do not know, but given that the constitutional validity of a content-based locational restriction on picketing is precisely the matter at issue, the fact that the Westboro protesters had obeyed the existing law seems rather question-begging.

Be that as it may, the Court's ultimate conclusion in *Snyder* itself was emphatic and unqualified: However much pain the protests had caused the Snyders, and the Court used that very word, the First Amendment would not permit a restriction on the speakers who caused it, especially where the pain was caused in the process of engaging in "public discourse" on matters of "public import." As a case about the First Amendment and harm, *Snyder* represents a clear statement, among the clearest the Court has ever issued, about the extent to which the First Amendment protects even personally harmful speech, and thus the extent to which requiring victims to endure such harm is a component of the Court's current approach to the First Amendment.[40]

---

[37] 487 US 474 (1988).

[38] 530 US 703 (2000).

[39] 512 US 753 (1994).

[40] Justice Breyer's concurrence stressed the particular facts of this case, especially the extent to which the protesters were at some distance from the funeral and in an area where picketing was lawful. 131 S Ct at 1221–22. Justice Alito's dissent, however, made much of the fact that none of the Snyders were public figures, and that many of the verbal attacks by the picketers were on and about Matthew Snyder and the Snyder family directly and personally. Justice Alito stressed the "great injury" suffered by the Snyder family as

C. BROWN V ENTERTAINMENT MERCHANTS ASSOCIATION

On the last day of the 2010 Term, the Supreme Court handed down the final of the three cases under discussion here. In *Brown v Entertainment Merchants Association*,[41] the Court considered and invalidated a California law prohibiting the sale or rental to minors of "violent video games."

The phenomenon that concerned California has received wide-spread publicity. Perhaps starting with the public attention to a video game called "Grand Theft Auto," there has been growing acknowledgment that a significant number of minors, and a not insignificant number of adults, spend a considerable amount of time playing interactive video games, many of which provide the participants with an opportunity to participate and exist in a virtual world in which they commit murder, assault, and various other unlawful and antisocial acts.

In response to this phenomenon, California in 2005 enacted a prohibition on minors' access to such material. The statute in some respects tracked the formulas of existing obscenity doctrine, especially with respect to patent offensiveness and lack of serious literary, artistic, political, or scientific value.[42] But the omission of the "appeal to prurient interest" component of the *Miller* test[43] was no accident, for California's concern was not sex but violence. And although *Ginsberg v New York*[44] allows the application of the test for obscenity to be adjusted to take into account the age of a portion of the target audience where that audience includes minors, California's attempt to shift some of the features of obscenity doctrine to depictions of violence, most of which are not sexualized except perhaps in some deeper and inaccessible way, represents not just the minor modification that was at the heart of *Ginsberg*, but an entirely distinct focus, and a focus not previously acknowledged in the case law under the First Amendment.[45]

Relying heavily on its recent decision in *Stevens*, the Supreme

a result of the picketing, concluding that to him it was "not necessary to allow the brutalization of innocent victims like the petitioner" in order to have open and vigorous public debate on matters of public concern. Id at 1228–30.

[41] 131 S Ct 2729 (2011).

[42] 131 S Ct at 2732–33.

[43] *Miller v California*, 403 US 15 (1973).

[44] 390 US 629 (1968).

[45] Among the academic ancestors of this approach is Kevin W. Saunders, *Violence as Obscenity: Limiting the Media's First Amendment Protection* (Duke, 1996).

Court upheld the District Court and the Ninth Circuit in invalidating California's law.[46] The division on the Court, however, was sharper than in either *Stevens* or *Snyder*, with Justice Scalia writing for himself and Justices Kennedy, Ginsburg, Sotomayor, and Kagan. Justice Alito, joined by the Chief Justice, concurred in the result only,[47] and Justices Thomas and Breyer dissented. For the majority, this was a case, like *Stevens*, in which the fundamental issue was whether new categories of noncoverage or nonprotection could be added to the existing array, and, if so, what the standard was to be for such additions. Rejecting as largely irrelevant California's attempt to mimic obscenity law but apply it to an entirely different domain and an entirely different problem,[48] the question for Justice Scalia was whether, for the first time,[49] the Court should recognize extreme violence as a justification for controlling a depiction.

Justice Scalia's rejection of the arguments for creating a new category, even in the context of a restriction only on minors and thus not on the adult population, relied rather more heavily on historical tradition—both the absence of a legal or cultural tradition of restricting minors' access to violence and also the presence of violence in literature for millennia—than would likely have been the case had another member of the majority written the opinion.[50] But the message was still clear: The creation of new categories of nonprotection faced a very heavy burden of justification. Indeed, at one point the majority insisted that there would in this case have to be a showing of a "direct causal link between video games and harm to minors."[51] And later in the opinion the Court announced that creating such a new category would require a showing of that "high degree of necessity" that had traditionally

---

[46] *Brown v Entertainments Association*, 131 S Ct 2729 (2011).

[47] The Chief Justice, joined by Justice Alito, was troubled by the vagueness and consequent lack of notice in the California law, but indicated that he might well be inclined to approve a law that eliminated this flaw.

[48] "The California Act is something else entirely. . . . [California] wishes to create a wholly new category of content-based regulation that is permissible only for speech directed at children." 131 S Ct at 2735.

[49] The Court noted that an earlier attempt to regulate violent depictions had been invalidated in *Winters v New York*, 333 US 507 (1948).

[50] And Justice Thomas's dissent, consistent with his concurrence in *Morse v Frederick*, 551 US 393 (2007), relied heavily on history to support his claim that the First Amendment essentially gave minors no free speech rights at all.

[51] 131 S Ct at 2738.

been "described as a compelling state interest."[52] Furthermore, the Court made it clear that California could not even come close to meeting such a high standard of justification. California had attempted to argue that video games, because of their interactive nature, presented a special case and special problems, but the argument was unavailing. The Court was dismissive of the empirical evidence,[53] but having established such a heightened standard of justification it seems clear that even substantially better empirical evidence than California, in the majority's view, was able to offer would still have been insufficient.

II. A Trilogy of Harms

Issues of campaign finance[54] aside, *Stevens*, *Snyder*, and *En-*

---

[52] Id at 2741.

[53] The Court quoted from the Ninth Circuit decision below (*Video Software Dealers Assn. v Schwarzenegger*, 556 F3d 950 (9th Cir 2009)) to the effect that "'[n]early all of the research is based on correlation, not evidence of causation, and most of the studies suffer from significant, admitted flaws in methodology." 556 F3d at 964, quoted at 131 S Ct 2729. Yet although everyone who is paying attention in Statistics 101 can parrot the flaw of necessarily inferring causation from correlation, few of the studies at issue suffered from that problem. Many had problems of construct and external validity, but a controlled laboratory experiment, as with many of the ones relied upon by California and located by Justice Breyer, is designed precisely to focus on causation. That does not, of course, mean that the causation located is necessarily relevant to the ultimate question. Identifying the causes of aggression in the laboratory does not necessarily translate to identifying the causes of aggression outside of the laboratory, and even identifying the extent of aggression outside of the laboratory is not the same as identifying a necessary or sufficient cause of actual violence. But this is not the error of confusing correlation with causation, and the ease with which the Ninth Circuit and the *Entertainment Merchants* majority accepted this questionable claim should give pause to those who would too easily trust the Court to make proper use of sophisticated empirical research.

Another intriguing issue about the empirical research may have even broader implications. Justice Breyer's dissenting opinion relied heavily on a substantial quantity of research on the effect of violent video games, much of which was not in the record. This practice has become standard operating procedure for Justice Breyer; see, for example, *Parents Involved in Community Schools v Seattle School Dist. No. 1*, 551 US 701, 803 (2007) (Breyer, J, dissenting); *Kumho Tire, Ltd. v Carmichael*, 526 US 137 (1999); *United States v Lopez*, 514 US 549 (1995) (Breyer, J, dissenting)—and it is noteworthy that in *Entertainment Merchants* Justice Scalia's majority opinion seemed to go out of its way to note that the "vast preponderance" of the research located by Justice Breyer "is outside the record." 131 S Ct at 2739. On the issue of Supreme Court independent factual research generally, see Frederick Schauer, *The Dilemma of Ignorance: PGA Tour v Casey Martin*, 2001 Supreme Court Review 267; Frederick Schauer and Virginia J. Wise, *Non-Legal Information and the Delegalization of Law*, 29 J Legal Stud 495 (2000); Elizabeth G. Thornburg, *The Curious Appellate Judge: Ethical Limits on Independent Research*, 28 Rev Litig 131 (2008). See also David L. Faigman, *Constitutional Fictions: A Unified Theory of Constitutional Facts* (Oxford, 2008).

[54] *Arizona Free Enterprise Clubs Freedom Club PAC v Bennett*, 131 S Ct 2806 (2011); *Citizens United v FEC*, 130 S Ct 876 (2010).

tertainment Merchants represent a good window into the current Court's current thinking about the First Amendment. But in some respects the cases look very different from each other. One (*Entertainment Merchants*) concerns a state law, another (*Stevens*) is about a federal law, and the third (*Snyder*) arises in the context of a common law cause of action. *Entertainment Merchants* is about violence, *Snyder* about harassment, and *Stevens* about animal cruelty. And in *Stevens* the objects of concern are animals, in *Entertainment Merchants* children, and in *Snyder* grieving adults. There are numerous other dissimilarities as well, some of which are suggested by the very different alignment of Justices in *Stevens* and *Snyder*, on the one hand, and *Entertainment Merchants* on the other.

Yet for all the dissimilarities, there is an important similarity— the presence in all three cases of reasonably patent harm. This itself is noteworthy. If one looks at the modern and not-so-modern history of Supreme Court free speech adjudication, one sees numerous examples of cases in which the alleged harmfulness of the speech at issue was, to put it mildly, hardly clear. Holmes may have noted in *Gitlow* that "every idea is an incitement,"[55] but six years earlier he had gone out of his way in his *Abrams* dissent to belittle the "silly" leaflet distributed by the "unknown" Jacob Abrams as a "puny anonymit[y],"[56] thereby suggesting that Abrams's leaflets were hardly likely to produce a revolution. Subsequently, Charlotte Whitney's membership in the Communist Labor Party of California[57] or even Clarence Brandenburg's speech to a few Klansmen and the cattle on an open field in Hamilton County, Ohio,[58] seem unlikely to have spurred many people to much action. The possibility that Commissioner of Public Safety L. B. Sullivan's reputation was injured in Alabama in 1963 by virtue of his being charged with hostility to the civil rights movement[59] is laughable, and even as far back as 1969 it seems far-fetched to imagine that very many people suffered very much anguish over their involuntary exposure to the words on Paul

---

[55] *Gitlow v New York*, 268 US 652, 673 (1925) (Holmes, J, dissenting).

[56] *Abrams v United States*, 250 US 616, 628–29 (1919) (Holmes, J, dissenting).

[57] *Whitney v California*, 274 US 357 (1927).

[58] *Brandenburg v Ohio*, 395 US 444 (1969) (per curiam). The "cattle" image, perhaps a bit hyperbolic but accurately suggestive of the setting, comes from L. A. Powe Jr., *Mass Speech and the Newer First Amendment*, 1982 Supreme Court Rev 243, 283.

[59] *New York Times Co. v Sullivan*, 376 US 254 (1964).

Cohen's jacket.[60] Similarly, the administrative functioning of the New Hampshire Highway Department seems to have survived George and Maxine Maynard's desire not to display a "Live Free or Die" license plate,[61] and the decorum and education mission of the Des Moines public schools were not much in danger from Mary Beth Tinker's protest armband.[62] Indeed, in one of the cases in which the claims of harm were the greatest—*New York Times Co. v United States*,[63] the case of the *Pentagon Papers*—Solicitor General Griswold, while insisting that his and government's ex ante assessment of possible danger was right when made on the basis of the information then available, also acknowledged that the ex post assessment showed that publication had in fact produced no damage.[64]

These examples are not intended to be either systematic or representative, but they do indicate a theme in First Amendment adjudication and commentary—the conclusion that the dangers alleged to come from speech are frequently exaggerated. And it is against this background that *Stevens*, *Snyder*, and *Entertainment Merchants* stand out. Even acknowledging some of the empirical disagreements in *Entertainment Merchants*, none of these cases represents the kind of largely baseless overreaction to trivial or imagined harms that is a significant strand in the history of the First Amendment, an enduring theme of much of the First Amendment literature, and the prevailing tone of civil libertarian public advocacy. Animals were really mutilated to make the videos that prompted the enactment of the statute in *Stevens*, the effects on victims of the persistent glorification of violence to impressionable minors is at least plausible, and no one who has lost a close relative, especially a young one, can fail to understand the genuine pain that the Snyders must have endured when an already tragic event was hijacked by someone else's nutty cause.

I do not claim that the Court's reactions to the harms in the three cases were the same. Indeed, there is substantially more acknowledgment of the harm in *Snyder* than in either *Stevens* or

---

[60] *Cohen v California*, 403 US 15 (1971).

[61] *Wooley v Maynard*, 430 US 705 (1977).

[62] *Tinker v Des Moines Independent Community School Dist.*, 393 US 503 (1969).

[63] 403 US 713 (1971) (per curiam).

[64] Erwin N. Griswold, *Secrets Not Worth Keeping: The Courts and Classified Information*, Washington Post A25 (Feb 15, 1989).

Entertainment Merchants. Perhaps this is because the harm to the Snyders was more patent and immediate than the harm to the animals in *Stevens* and the potential harm to unknown third-party victims of juvenile violence in *Entertainment Merchants.* Perhaps it is because, as parents of a soldier killed while on duty abroad, the Snyders presented a special reason for the Court's sympathy. And perhaps it is because the harm to the Snyders was connected with actual identifiable human beings, presenting once again the tendency of people, including Justices, to see harm in individual cases with faces and names more than in aggregates and statistics.[65]

Thus, there are differences in the way the Court discusses the harms in the three cases, and there are numerous possible explanations for why the harms in *Stevens* and *Entertainment Merchants* seem to have been, especially comparatively, de-emphasized. Maybe it is because of the majority's discomfort in *Entertainment Merchants* with empirical evidence that it did not locate and could not really understand. Maybe it is because the Court was uncomfortable even hinting at a similarity between the harm to children in *Ferber* and the harm to animals in *Stevens*, however obvious the latter harm was. And maybe there are other explanations, some of which I noted in the foregoing paragraph and the outset of this article. But perhaps it is simply because neither the case law nor the First Amendment tradition of harm denial has given the Court the conceptual and doctrinal arsenal necessary for grappling with speech-associated harm. *Stevens, Snyder,* and *Entertainment Merchants* thus provide an occasion not only to examine the current Court's approach to First Amendment issues, but also to reflect more broadly on the role that genuine harm can and might play in understanding free speech theory and fashioning First Amendment doctrine. Although it is (or should be) by now well settled that any robust free speech principle will protect speech not (only) because it is harmless, but despite the harm it may cause,[66] the pervasive and at times pernicious effect of the harmlessness model

---

[65] Thus the well-known fact that people are willing to have far more money spent to save six people trapped in a mine than they are to prevent a much larger number of miners from being trapped in mines in the first place. The example is analyzed extensively, and the common intuitions challenged on normative grounds, in Charles Fried, *An Anatomy of Values* 207–27 (Harvard, 1970).

[66] See Schauer, *Free Speech* (cited in note 1); Frederick Schauer, *The Phenomenology of Speech and Harm,* 103 Ethics 635 (1993).

of free speech—the "sticks and stones" model, to oversimplify[67]—
has stunted the development of theoretical and doctrinal tools
adapted to the phenomenon of harmful speech. The three cases
of the last two Terms can assist this process, partly because they
present the problem of genuine harm in such stark relief, but also
because the harms they present are of three different types. By
understanding the differences among these three kinds of speech-
induced harm, we can recognize the immature state of a doctrine
that treats them all the same to the extent that it even recognizes
them at all.

A. BROWN V ENTERTAINMENT MERCHANTS ASSOCIATION AND THE
   HARMS OF ADVOCACY

Going back at least as far as *Schenck v United States*,[68] the classic
speech-related harm is the harm of *advocacy*. Or we might call it
a harm of *persuasion*. Or a harm of *influence*. Or a harm of *facilitation*. Advocacy may differ from persuasion, which may differ
from influence, which may differ from encouragement, which may
differ from facilitation, but what all of these concepts share is the
idea that the words may be intended to have or may actually have
(whether intended to or not) an effect on subsequent actions taken
by the listener. An advocacy or persuasion or influence or encouragement or facilitation harm exists when a speaker is heard
(or read) by a sympathetic listener, who then proceeds to commit
some nonspeech act as a result of the intentional or unintentional
urging or inspiration or assistance by the speaker. But let us unpack
this a bit. Initially, the ultimate harm is ordinarily not one that is
itself defined by or necessarily even connected to speech. The
harm in *Schenck* was the failure of draft-eligible men to report for
the draft or serve in the military, and similarly in the other cases
of the *Schenck* era,[69] in which the feared harm was the harm of

---

[67] For a nonoversimplified examination of the issue, see Larry Alexander, *Banning Hate
Speech and the Sticks and Stones Defense*, 13 Const Comm 71 (1996).

[68] 249 US 47 (1919).

[69] For example, *Gitlow v New York*, 268 US 652 (1925) (urging Communist revolution
in the United States); *Abrams v United States*, 250 US 616 (1919) (encouraging interference
with war production); *Debs v United States*, 249 US 211 (1919) (encouraging draft evasion
and disobedience within the military); *Frohwerk v United States*, 249 US 204 (encouraging
draft evasion); *Masses Pub. Co. v Patten*, 244 Fed 535 (SDNY 1917) (same). On the background of these and other related cases of the period, see Richard Polenberg, *Fighting
Faiths: The Abrams Case, the Supreme Court, and Free Speech* (Viking, 1987). See also Stone,
Perilous Times (cited in note 2).

disobedience to the draft laws, or disobedience within the military, or armed revolution, or some other activity falling within that general category. The harm in *Brandenburg* was the potential assault on African-Americans and Jews. The harms alleged to come from some pornographic materials are the harms to victims of sexual assaults committed by readers or users of the material at issue.[70] The harms of inflammatory pretrial publicity are the harms produced by listeners or readers who find themselves on a jury and proceed to deliver biased verdicts.[71] And we could add numerous other examples of an argument that has the same basic structure. Although in all of these instances there are serious questions that could and should be asked about the causal relationship, if any, between the speech and the ultimate action, the ultimate actions are ones whose proscription is not itself typically controversial. And thus the alleged harm in scenarios of this general type is the harm that arises out of the possibility that some act of writing or speaking will increase the probability of something else that is uncontroversially and intrinsically harmful actually occurring.

The essence of this type of harm thus emanates from the reader or viewer or listener who then proceeds to *do* something as a result of what she has read, seen, or heard. Such an outcome may have been desired by the speaker, as in *Schenck* and *Abrams* and some number of other seditious advocacy cases, where we might safely assume that Charles Schenck and Jacob Frohwerk[72] really did want draft-eligible young men to resist conscription and that Eugene Dennis really did want a socialist revolution[73] and that Clarence Brandenburg (probably) really did want violence against African-Americans and Jews. Or the persuasion may have been unintended and perhaps inadvertent, as in *Herceg v Hustler Magazine*,[74] *Olivia*

---

[70] See Frederick Schauer, *Causation Theory and the Causes of Sexual Violence*, 1987 Am Bar Found Res J 737.

[71] *Sheppard v Maxwell*, 384 US 333 (1966).

[72] *Frohwerk v United States*, 249 US 204 (1919).

[73] *Dennis v United States*, 341 US 494 (1951).

[74] 814 F2d 1017 (5th Cir 1987) (holding that the First Amendment bars liability in a case in which a teenage boy had died while imitating a magazine article about autoerotic asphyxiation). The *Herceg* scenario has arisen in a number of subsequent cases involving video games, and with the same legal outcome. See *Watters v TSR, Inc.*, 901 F2d 378 (6th Cir 1990); *Waller v Osborne*, 763 F Supp 1144 (M D Ga 1991). *Wilson v Midway Games, Inc.*, 198 F Supp 2d 167 (D Conn 2002), is similar, but not exactly a suicide.

N. v National Broadcasting Co.,[75] *Rice v Paladin Enterprises, Inc.,*[76] and some number of other cases in which crime victims or their families brought suit—typically tort actions for wrongful death— against the speaker or publisher who allegedly caused the perpetrator (or suicide victim) to commit the crime, or at least facilitated his commission of it. And thus the basic idea behind the harms of "persuasion" might include pure advocacy or pure encouragement as well as the provision of facts, information, and instructions that someone might then proceed to use to commit some further act.[77] But although there are important differences among the ways in which the speech of one person might (probabilistically) cause someone else to commit a regulable antisocial act, the basic similarity is still there, and throughout the variations we have a speaker whose speech is then used by a listener to commit what is usually noncontroversially a wrong against some victim.

In important respects, *Entertainment Merchants* fits this mold. Although an obsession with playing violent interactive video games may not be the best path toward responsibility, maturity, and mental health for the person who is actually playing the games, many of the arguments for the restriction, and many of the studies noted (and disparaged) in the majority opinion and cited by Justice Breyer in his dissent, are arguments or research purporting to show that those who play interactive video games are as a result

---

[75] 126 Cal App 3d 488, 178 Cal Rptr 888 (Cal App 1st Dist 1981) (holding that *Brandenburg* precluded tort liability based on a claim by a victim of a sexual assault that the assault had imitated the assault on the television movie "Born Innocent"). The results were the same in some number of other cases involving claims by a victim that a video game had inspired the perpetrator. *James v Meow Media, Inc.,* 300 F3d 683 (6th Cir 2002); *Sanders v Acclaim Entertainment, Inc.,* 188 F Supp 2d 1264 (D Colo 2002).

[76] 128 F3d 233 (4th Cir 1997) (refusing to dismiss a suit by a victim of a contract killer who had relied on a book—*Hit Man*—containing instructions on how to perform contract killings). See also *Eimann v Soldier of Fortune Magazine, Inc.,* 680 F Supp 863 (S D Tex 1988) (allowing cause of action against publisher of advertisement for contract killer).

[77] See also *United States v Progressive, Inc.,* 467 F Supp 990 (W D Wis 1979), mandamus denied sub nom *Morland v Sprecher,* 443 US 709 (1979), case dismissed, 610 F2d 819 (7th Cir 1979) (information that might have assisted someone in constructing and detonating a hydrogen bomb). The problem of plans and instructions, as opposed to pure advocacy and argument, was presciently anticipated in Thomas Scanlon, *A Theory of Freedom of Expression,* 1 Phil & Pub Aff 204 (1972), posing the problem of someone who published instructions for making nerve gas out of gasoline, urine, and table salt. 1 Phil & Pub Aff at 211. On the issue generally, see David A. Anderson, *Incitement and Tort Law,* 37 Wake Forest L Rev 957 (2002); Rodney A. Smolla, *Information as Contraband: The First Amendment and Liability for Trafficking in Speech,* 96 Nw U L Rev 1099 (2002); Leslie Kendrick, Note, *A Test for Criminally Instructional Speech,* 91 Va L Rev 1973 (2005).

more likely to be aggressive toward *others* than they would have
been absent the violent video game experience. Apart from the
question of the validity of these studies, what inferences might
appropriately be drawn from them, and what standards of scientific
reliability and causal efficacy are required in this or that legal and
constitutional context, it is clear that the principal argument in
Entertainment Merchants was a victim-focused one. More specifically, the putative victims were not the viewers (or listeners, or
players), but rather those who would be harmed by the viewers
as a consequence of what the viewers had viewed. In this respect
Entertainment Merchants is of a piece with *Schenck*, *Abrams*, *Brandenburg*, and a host of other cases at all levels expressing a primary
concern for the harms that might be caused to third parties from
acts committed by listeners (the second parties) as a result of
speeches made by speakers (the first parties). Indeed, thinking of
these as third-party harms may be a useful way of distinguishing
them from other harms commonly associated with speech.

B. SNYDER V PHELPS AND THE HARMS OF VERBAL ASSAULT

It may be a bit cumbersome to distinguish among first, second,
and third parties in the *Entertainment Merchants* advocacy scenario,
but the distinction does assist us in appreciating the important
difference between the third-party harms at issue in such situations
and harms that arise, or are claimed to arise, in the situations in
which the speech causes harm directly to the second party, the
listener. To take a paradigmatic example, the claims of harm in
the Skokie litigation[78] were hardly claims that the Nazis were going
to Skokie in order to persuade its residents of the value of the
Nazi cause. Instead, Skokie's claim was that the very speech of
the Nazis would be harmful to the viewers and the listeners, who
would be harmed simply by what they saw and heard.

Harms such as these were suggested in *Chaplinsky* by its reference to words "which by their very utterance inflict injury,"[79]
but that way of characterizing the situation is somewhere between
misleading and wrong. The words cause an injury not because of
something they necessarily do in all contexts, and not because of

---

[78] *Collin v Smith*, 578 F2d 1197 (7th Cir), cert denied, 439 US 916 (1978); *Village of
Skokie v National Socialist Party of America*, 373 N E 2d 21 (1978).

[79] 315 US at 572.

some intrinsic property of words as words, but because of the effect that the words are expected to have on the mental state of those who hear (or see) them under certain circumstances. The important point is not that the very utterance is necessarily always dangerous, but that it is the uttering of the utterance rather than what the hearer might do to someone else as a result of hearing it that represents the essence of the harm. So although it would be useful to have more systematic psychological research on just how what we can call the "Skokie effects" might come about, the idea is that the words cause the injury *to* the listener, and not to someone whom the listener might then injure as a result of the words. More importantly, the category of injuries caused to those who hear or see words or images by virtue of that seeing or hearing is far wider than just the "fighting words" category spawned in *Chaplinsky*. The harms of threats, whether they be face-to-face or somewhat broader, as certainly in *Virginia v Black*[80] and probably in *R.A.V. v St. Paul*,[81] have nothing to do with third parties, and are harms that come to the receiver by virtue of the very reception of the threatening language.[82] And even apart from threats, and even apart from fighting words, it is often claimed—sometimes by use of the word "offense"[83]—that simply seeing or hearing certain words or images will itself cause the kind of distress that in some circumstances would be described as "pain," and in some circumstances would count as harm. This may be most obvious with respect to the Nazi images in Skokie and the cross burnings in *Virginia v Black*, but the claims are similar even when the harms are more debatable. California's claim in *Cohen* was thus structurally similar to the claim in Skokie, even if most of us are far more skeptical about the extent of the harm in *Cohen*, and the structural similarity exists as well in *Hustler Magazine v Falwell*,[84]

---

[80] 538 US 343 (2003). See Frederick Schauer, *Intentions, Conventions, and the First Amendment: The Case of Cross-Burning*, 2003 Supreme Court Review 197.

[81] 505 US 377 (1992).

[82] Of course the harm exists by virtue of some mental mediation, but so too when someone intentionally spits in my face, or slaps me on the cheek.

[83] The word "offense" is rarely used by the targets. The word is typically used by others to downplay the magnitude of what the targets are more likely to describe as "harm."

[84] 485 US 46 (1988). Given that Jerry Falwell was a public figure most likely well accustomed to harsh public criticism, there is a distinct possibility that his suit was more motivated by a desire to punish a publication he abhorred than by a degree of mental distress different in kind from the mental distress he would have typically suffered from some degree of persistent negative press coverage. And there is also a possibility that

Erznoznik v Jacksonville,[85] *FCC v Pacifica Foundation*,[86] and other cases involving claims of direct and harmful effects on viewers of involuntary exposure to allegedly indecent words and images and ideas. And even apart from indecency in its broadest sense, the claims about the effect of flag burning on viewers in *Texas v Johnson*[87] and *United States v Eichman*,[88] the effect of some of the anti-abortion protests on women in *Hill v Colorado*[89] and *Madsen v Women's Health Center, Inc.*,[90] and the effect of racist and other forms of hate speech on members of targeted minorities are claims about what speech will do to the listener, and not about what speech will prompt the listener to do to someone else.

Harms of this variety are precisely what were at issue in *Snyder v Phelps*. Indeed, the very name of the tort—intentional infliction of emotional distress—makes it clear that these are listener harms and not third-party harms. The Snyder family was hurt by the words themselves (although the extent to which they were also hurt by the commotion caused by the words complicates things somewhat, as does the fact that, based on what we know from the record, they learned about the words in a less direct way than was present in many of the hate-speech and flag-burning scenarios), and the harms they claimed had nothing to do with the reactions of sympathizers (had there been any), or even very much to the reactions of hostile audiences to Phelps's message. At the heart of the claim, intention aside, is that the distress caused to the Snyder family is of the same structural nature as the distress allegedly caused in *Cohen* and *Erznoznik* and *Falwell*, and almost certainly caused in *Texas v Johnson, United States v Eichman, R.A.V v St. Paul*, and *Virginia v Black*. And these are harms in which the victims are not the people who are hurt by what the listeners might do to others, but are the listeners themselves.

---

being an object of ridicule, which was the primary point of the *Hustler* parody, produced a harm different from even harsh and even false public criticism.

[85] 422 US 205 (1975).

[86] 438 US 726 (1978).

[87] 491 US 397 (1989).

[88] 496 US 310 (1990).

[89] 530 US 703 (2000).

[90] 512 US 753 (1994).

C. UNITED STATES V STEVENS AND PARTICIPANT HARMS

As should be obvious, the victims in *Stevens* were the animals. And especially the animals mutilated or killed in order to make the videos, which is the case in most of the videos at issue. Plainly the animals were not willing participants in making the videos, assuming we can ascribe intentionality to animals in this context, but they were participants nonetheless. And they would have been harmed as participants even had no one ever purchased or viewed the videos in which the animals' abuse appeared. While harms may flow to viewers from seeing such videos, and harms may flow to third parties (including other animals) from actions that watching the videos may inspire or promote,[91] the primary harms, in the eyes of Congress and in reality, are those that are part of the production process and not part of the viewing or listening process.

Such participant harms have not been nearly as prominent in the history of speech regulation and the First Amendment as have been the third-party and listener harms discussed above. But they have not been absent. Most prominently, participant harms are at the heart of the concern about child pornography, and of the Supreme Court's special approach to it. In *New York v Ferber*[92] and subsequent child pornography cases,[93] the essence of the Court's willingness to treat child pornography differently from obscenity or indecency was precisely the harm done to children in the process of production. It is true that some of the harm the Court noted in *Ferber* was the harm that comes to the participants from the images being permanently available for perpetual public consumption, and this harm looks like one mediated by a public— that is, a viewer—reaction to the material, but the primary harm the Court stressed was the harm that was done to the child participants in the process of production. And the subsequent litigation about the important difference between child pornography

---

[91] It is noteworthy that Jeremy Bentham endorsed criminalizing cruelty to animals not only because of his views about animal suffering (Jeremy Bentham, *Principles of Morals and Legislation*, ch XVII, § 4, at 311 (1789, London, 1988)), but also because he thought that cruelty to animals would inspire "cruelty towards men." Jeremy Bentham, *Principles of the Penal Code*, bk 4, ch 15, in *The Theory of Legislation*, trans. Richard Hildreth from Étienne Dumont, ed C. K. Ogden (London, 1931), at 425–27.

[92] 458 US 747 (1982).

[93] *United States v Williams*, 553 US 285 (2008); *Osborne v Ohio*, 495 US 103 (1990); *Massachusetts v Oakes*, 491 US 576 (1989).

said about him in the advertisement in the *New York Times*,[102] or that Benjamin Gitlow's "Left Wing Manifesto" was in any danger of creating the Communist revolution that he so earnestly desired.[103] But many more modern cases, including the ones under discussion here, present more substantial empirical issues. As Justice Breyer's citation-laden dissent in *Entertainment Merchants* shows, especially in contrast with the majority's discussion of much the same research, the empirics of the harm were a genuinely important question. Obviously, there are difficult questions to be asked about what kind of evidence would be necessary to establish a new category of nonprotection under the *Entertainment Merchants* majority's "high degree of necessity" and "compelling state interest" standard,[104] but it is not implausible to suppose that one or more members of the majority might have reached a different conclusion had they viewed the empirical data more favorably, or that Chief Justice Roberts or Justices Alito and Breyer might have reached a different conclusion had they assessed the empirical data less favorably. Or consider Justice Harlan's seeming reliance in *Cohen* and the Court's reliance in *Erznoznik* on people's ability to avert their eyes from a distasteful image or word. Assuming that even Justice Harlan would have agreed that one cannot avert one's eyes until one's eyes have seen what one would want to avert them from, the issue then turns on how much, if at all, the mind and the memory will retain that which one wishes he had not seen in the first place. This may or may not have been important for the outcome in *Cohen*, but in a significant number of genuinely difficult verbal assault or verbal harassment cases we should want to know just what the effect of those words is on the audience, how great that effect is, and how long it is likely to last. Justice Thomas's dissenting opinion in *Virginia v Black*,[105] for example, accuses the majority of underestimating the magnitude of the harm that comes

---

[102] *New York Times Co. v Sullivan*, 276 US 254 (1964).

[103] *Gitlow v New York*, 268 US 652 (1925). It is possible that the calls for draft resistance by Schenck and Debs would actually have had some causal effect on the rate of draft resistance during the First World War, especially among those already disposed to be sympathetic with Schenck's and Debs's broader political program, but by the time we get to the 1960s and the Vietnam War, the likelihood that Benjamin Spock's call for draft resistance (see *United States v Spock*, 416 F2d 165 (1st Cir 1969)) would have had a similar causal effect on draft-eligible men in the 1960s seems far less.

[104] 131 S Ct at 2741.

[105] 538 US at 388.

from witnessing a targeted cross burning, but whether the majority underestimated the harm, overestimated the harm, or got it just right is once again an empirical psychological question, as to which we might think serious research would be of some assistance. Similarly, the majority in *Snyder v Phelps* notes that the signs were 1,000 feet away from the church at which Matthew Snyder's funeral was held,[106] but would the result have been different had the signs been waved in the Snyder family's faces, and, if so, why? And in *Stevens*, would the result have differed had there been— seemingly counterfactually—evidence of a market in crush videos and dogfighting videos equivalent in size to the market for child pornography?

As the empirical dimension of Supreme Court decision making becomes more apparent and more extensive generally, and as genuine social science research is brought to bear on such questions with increased frequency,[107] it should come as no surprise that this phenomenon has not escaped First Amendment adjudication. And in large part the empirical dimension in First Amendment context is about the extent and causes of speech-associated consequences, primarily but not exclusively harms in a moderately direct sense. But it is impossible to evaluate these harms, or even to know which harms we are talking about, unless we have a better sense of exactly what kinds of harms are at issue, and thus what kind of evidence would bear, one way or another, upon their existence and extent. We take an important first step when we recognize that much First Amendment argument is about consequential and often harmful speech, but the necessary second step is to understand the nature of those harms, for without that we cannot hope to evaluate (or generate) the data that would enable courts to determine the extent of the harms involved, and whether the doctrine should allow any redress against them.

Disaggregating the various speech-associated harms is also important in properly focusing nonempirical normative argument about the contours of First Amendment doctrine. Consider, for example, the common claim that parents and not the government should protect juveniles from the effects of certain kinds of im-

---

[106] 131 S Ct at 1213.
[107] See note 53.

ages,[108] a claim that is in important ways at the heart of *Entertainment Merchants*. If we are concerned about the welfare of the juveniles themselves, then the claim seems to have a certain kind of resonance, at least on the assumption that parents are (or are assumed to be) more responsible for their children's welfare than the government. But if the claim is instead about the safety of those who become the victims of media-inspired juvenile violence, then arguments focused on and deflecting the concern to the importance of parental control are largely beside the point. Without sorting out carefully just what kind of harm is at issue, however, there is little hope of even considering the normative issue in the correct way.

IV. ASSIGNING THE COSTS OF HARM

Stevens, Snyder, and *Entertainment Merchants* all involved moderately clear harms—to animals, to grieving parents, and, perhaps more controversially, to potential victims of the aggressiveness of teenagers. And harms, of course, are costs, even if not always financial ones. Moreover, the speech-protective outcomes in each of the three cases represent an intriguing similarity in how those costs are to be assigned. Whenever the First Amendment prevails in a case of harmful speech, it means, in that case and presumably others, that some harm will go unredressed. But an unredressed harm is a cost, and the question then arises as to how that cost will or should be allocated.

Thus, in *Snyder*, the Snyders bore or were required to absorb the cost of the First Amendment, in the sense that they were required simply to "take" the harm to them, without the possibility of a constitutional permissible remedy. Indeed, because there is no reason to believe that the modified verdict was subject to anything other than a First Amendment challenge, and since that challenge was unsuccessful, we might say that the First Amendment cost the Snyders five million dollars. And although some of this amount might be offset insofar as the Snyders can be considered to be among the diffuse beneficiaries of the First Amendment itself, it is clear that the Snyders spent far more for everyone's

---

[108] This issue is central to *FCC v Fox TV Stations, Inc.*, No 10-1293, now pending before the Supreme Court and focusing on the continuing validity *vel non* of *FCC v Pacifica Foundation*, 438 US 726 (1978).

Amendment than they are, individually, likely to gain. Indeed, this might be even more obvious in *Stevens*. Except possibly in the most attenuated sense, dogs do not seem to benefit from the First Amendment at all, and there is no reason to believe, controlling for income level and the like, that dogs are better off in the United States than they are in any other country,[109] or that, if they are, the First Amendment has anything to do with it. Yet after *Stevens*, and especially if the replacement statute is, as suggested above, largely inconsequential except as a symbol, there is scant reason to believe that animal crush videos and dogfighting videos will not continue to proliferate, very much to the detriment of the animals that are abused and featured in such videos. The costs of the First Amendment are thus assigned to the animals. And in *Entertainment Merchants*, the costs of the First Amendment are borne by those who would be the victims of violent-video-inspired violence, at least if Justice Breyer and the research upon which he relies is even partially sound.

I have in the past suggested some rather unconventional ways of dealing with this problem,[110] and there is no need to repeat those suggestions here. But it is worth emphasizing that most free speech cases involve a claim by some individual (as in *Snyder*) or government (as in *Stevens* and *Entertainment Merchants*) that some item of communication has some antisocial effect of some sort, thus producing some cost to the individual or to society. In many of those cases the claim of antisocial effect is in error or greatly exaggerated, and thus in such cases the cost of the First Amendment is nonexistent or negligible. But in many others, including *Stevens*, *Snyder*, and *Entertainment Merchants*, the claims of antisocial effects are at least plausible, and thus in those cases there are social costs to upholding the First Amendment claim. And it is almost always the case that those social costs are not equally distributed among all 300 million of us who benefit from the First Amendment. Thus, while, in theory, all 300 million of us benefit from the First Amendment, our collective benefits are largely paid for by the Snyders, the animals, and the victims of video-inspired violence. It is quite possible that nothing can or should be done about this, but perhaps observing, as others have before, that

---

[109] Or at least any other country that does not consider dogs to be consumption items in the most literal sense.

[110] Frederick Schauer, *Uncoupling Free Speech*, 92 Colum L Rev 1321 (1992).

"there is no such thing as a free speech"[111] will be useful in at least alerting us to the costs of rights, and to the fact that those costs are rarely borne equally, or even fairly.

V. CONCLUSION: IS FIRST AMENDMENT DOCTRINE WORKING ITSELF PURE?

The First Amendment, as much if not more than the rest of the Constitution, is a mandate to the courts to engage in a common law process of developing the rules, principles, standards, maxims, canons, and precedents that together produce what we call legal doctrine.[112] But in considering the common law nature of the development of First Amendment doctrine, it is important to bear in mind Lord Mansfield's optimistic assessment that the common law "works itself pure."[113] In light of this assessment, or aspiration, it is often appropriate to ask of any common law domain of doctrine whether the progression of time, the increase in the stock of examples, and the continued testing of provisional rules and principles has produced improvement, and thus whether we are approaching, if not purity, at least manageability.

One of the surprising things about *Stevens*, *Snyder*, and *Entertainment Merchants*, taken as a group, is that they give little cause for optimism about the continuing refinement of First Amendment doctrine. Given the controversial nature of the issues and the change in Court personnel, we should not expect too much. But the cases together produce some cause for concern. Is the "public concern" of an act of communication relevant or not? What is the standard to be applied when novel issues raise the question of coverage or noncoverage? What is the relevance of empirical social science research, how should it be located, and by what standards should it be evaluated? And there are many other questions that are raised by just these three cases. And it does not seem too harsh to note that the cases may have raised more questions than they

---

[111] Eric Neisser, *Charging for Free Speech: User Fees and Insurance in the Marketplace of Ideas*, 74 Georgetown L J 257, 258 (1985).

[112] David A. Strauss, *The Living Constitution* (Oxford, 2010); David A. Strauss, *Freedom of Speech and the Common-Law Constitution*, in Lee C. Bollinger and Geoffrey R. Stone, eds, *Eternally Vigilant: Free Speech in the Modern Era* 32 (Chicago, 2002).

[113] *Omychund v Barker*, 26 Eng Rep 15, 23 (Chancery 1744). See also Lon L. Fuller, *The Law in Quest of Itself* 140 (Beacon, 1940).

have answered, hardly a good sign for a process seeking to work itself pure.

It would be the height of hubris to suggest that understanding and sorting out the various types of speech-associated harm will send the development of First Amendment doctrine in a new and better direction. Indeed, it would be hubris even to suggest that the failure to consider seriously the nature and varieties of speech-related harms is a major cause of an area seeming less systematic than even the balance of constitutional law. Still, the question of harm is one of huge First Amendment significance, and it has been one that has largely been avoided, perhaps in part because of the looming presence of a still pervasive but nonetheless implausible harmlessness model of speech and its protection. If we face the question of speech-associated harm directly, and if we recognize that we are talking about harms and not harm, then perhaps just a little bit of First Amendment doctrine can become slightly more pure.

JOHN F. MANNING

THE NEW PURPOSIVISM

In the past quarter-century, the Court has rethought its approach
to statutory interpretation. Throughout most of the twentieth century, the Court subscribed to the traditional purposivist framework
of *Holy Trinity Church v United States.*[1] That precedent, of course,
stood for the proposition that Congress enacts statutes to achieve
certain purposes, and that judges should construe statutory language
to fulfill those purposes. On the assumption that Congress legislates
against the constraints of limited time, imperfect foresight, and
imprecise human language, *Holy Trinity* suggested that when the
plain import of a statutory text did not correspond to available
evidence about the law's purposes, principles of legislative supremacy required judges to enforce the "spirit" rather than the "letter"
of the law.[2] The Court embraced this approach until the last decade
of the twentieth century.[3]

The Court, however, has not cited *Holy Trinity* positively for more
than two decades.[4] Rather than sacrificing letter for spirit, the Court

---

John F. Manning is Bruce Bromley Professor of Law, Harvard Law School.

AUTHOR'S NOTE: I am grateful to Amy Barrett, Michael Boudin, Joshua Chafetz, Bradford
Clark, Kevin Clermont, Michael Dorf, Abbe Gluck, William Kelley, Gillian Metzger,
Bernadette Meyler, Henry Monaghan, David Strauss, Matthew Stephenson, and Amanda
Tyler for valuable comments on an earlier draft. I am also grateful to participants in the
Cornell Law School Faculty Workshop for their thoughtful questions. I thank Matthew
Rowen for excellent research assistance.

[1] 143 US 457 (1892).

[2] Id at 459.

[3] See sources cited in note 57.

[4] See John F. Manning, *Second-Generation Textualism*, 98 Cal L Rev 1287, 1312–14
(2010).

has become increasingly inclined to do the opposite. While one can point to the rare exception,[5] the Court in the last two decades has mostly treated as uncontroversial its duty to adhere strictly to the terms of a clear statutory text, even when doing so produces results that fit poorly with the apparent purposes that inspired the enactment.[6]

As one might expect, the Court's textualists—Justices Scalia and Thomas—have been at the leading edge of this trend.[7] These Justices have advanced several now-familiar arguments: Texts enacted pursuant to the constitutionally prescribed processes of bicameralism and presentment trump unenacted purposes for which no legislator voted.[8] Because lawmaking entails compromise, and because no legislative majority pursues its purposes at all costs, interpreters must look carefully at the means prescribed by the enacted text.[9] Finally, the most common source of extratextual purpose—a statute's legislative history—supplies unreliable evidence of what the enacting Congress as a whole sought to accomplish by passing a law.[10]

The convictions of the two textualist Justices alone, however, cannot account for *Holy Trinity*'s demise. One prominent scholar has suggested that on a closely divided Court, it takes only one or

---

[5] See, for example, *Clinton v New York*, 524 US 417, 428–29 (1998); *Lewis v United States*, 523 US 155, 160 (1998). It is important to mention a more systemic, but idiosyncratic, exception. Despite the Court's movement away from atextual purposivism, it has continued to find that state law can be preempted when it presents an obstacle to the purposes of federal statutes. See Daniel J. Meltzer, *The Supreme Court's Judicial Passivity*, 2002 Supreme Court Review 343, 362–68. A recent concurring opinion by Justice Thomas has shown this purposive approach to preemption to be at odds with the Court's broader themes about legislative purpose. See *Wyeth v Levine*, 555 US 555, 601–02 (2009) (Thomas, J, concurring in the judgment). Analysis of the Court's idiosyncratic approach to implied preemption is the subject for another paper.

[6] See text accompanying notes 66–86.

[7] Most observers count Justices Scalia and Thomas as committed textualists. See, for example, Thomas W. Merrill, *Textualism and the Future of the Chevron Doctrine*, 72 Wash U L Q 351, 351 (1994); Michael P. Van Alstine, *Dynamic Treaty Interpretation*, 146 U Pa L Rev 687, 717 (1998). Conventional wisdom also treats Justice Kennedy as sympathetic to textualism, but not a full-on textualist. See, for example, Merrill, 72 Wash U L Q at 356.

[8] See text accompanying note 68.

[9] See text accompanying notes 61–62 and 68–72; see also text accompanying notes 66–67 (discussing opinions that laid groundwork for the textualist critique).

[10] See, for example, *Wisconsin Public Intervenor v Mortier*, 501 US 597, 620 (1991) (Scalia, J, concurring in the judgment) (contending that the understanding of a statute expressed in committee reports "does not necessarily say anything about what Congress as a whole thought").

two unyielding textualists to change the way the Court frames its decisions; to build coalitions, nontextualist Justices will write like textualists in order to get the textualists' votes.[11] But while that hypothesis perhaps explains why nontextualists would strategically eschew reliance on legislative history to win textualists' votes in cases in which letter and purpose point in the same direction, it cannot explain why nontextualist Justices have increasingly embraced text over purpose when the two conflict. The latter approach does not simply involve the decisions' rationales; rather, it produces substantively different outcomes from those which would have prevailed had the Court credited the purposes gleaned from the legislative history—or, for that matter, from any other source.[12]

Why have nontextualist Justices gone along with the rejection of *Holy Trinity*? All of the nontextualist Justices are willing to consult legislative history as evidence of statutory meaning.[13] The entire Court, moreover, believes that laws are purposive and that statutory purpose is relevant to ascertaining meaning.[14] So why does the Court now treat the letter of the law as a trump when, until so recently, it was willing to give decisive weight to the law's background purpose, even when it contradicted the text? One possibility, explored here, is that this shift reflects factors that go well beyond the claims made by the Court's textualists. Rather, the Court's new approach may also reflect a new understanding of what purposive interpretation properly entails. In particular, this approach may just assimilate a growing sense that the law's "purpose," properly understood, embodies not merely a statute's substantive ends (its "ulterior purposes"),[15] but also Congress's specific choices about the means to carry those ends into effect (its "implemental purposes").

---

[11] See Merrill, 72 Wash U L Q at 365–66 (cited in note 7).

[12] The Court derives purpose from many sources. See, for example, *United States v Katz*, 271 US 354, 357 (1926) ("In ascertaining . . . purpose, we may examine the title of the act, the source in previous legislation of the particular provision in question, and the legislative scheme or plan by which the general purpose of the Act is to be carried out.") (citations omitted). For simplicity, I focus on purpose as derived from the legislative history because that source has been such a focal point in the statutory interpretation debate. The analysis here applies with equal force, however, to any form of purpose that shifts the level of generality of a discrete statutory provision.

[13] See note 93.

[14] See note 91.

[15] See Max Radin, *Statutory Interpretation*, 43 Harv L Rev 863, 876 (1930) (using the term "ulterior purpose" to describe the background aims that inspired a piece of legislation).

On this account, even if one believes that law is inescapably purposive and that interpreters should interpret a statute to fulfill its
purpose, an interpreter must take seriously the signals that Congress
sends through the level of generality reflected in its choice of words.
A precise and specific command signals an implemental purpose to
leave relatively little discretion to the law's implementer. An open-
ended and general one signals the opposite. That is, a "no dogs in
the park" statute has a very different implemental purpose from
one using the formulation "no dangerous animals."[16] Both may be
inspired by the same ulterior purpose of safeguarding parkgoers
from harm, but the former achieves this end through a precise rule
that assures predictability but leaves interpreters relatively little discretion, while the latter opts for a standard that favors flexibility
rather than certainty in implementation.[17] If interpreters treat the
statutory text as simply a proxy for the law's ulterior purpose, they
deny legislators the capacity, through their choice of words, to distinguish those statutes meant to embody specific policy choices from
those meant to leave policy discretion to the law's implementers.

The traditional purposivism represented by *Holy Trinity* made it
difficult, if not impossible, for legislators to send predictable signals
of that sort. Two recent opinions for the Court by Justice Kagan,
however, typify a new purposivism that relies on Congress's choice
of words to determine how and to what extent an interpreter may
account for the policy rationale or ulterior purpose of a statute.
First, in *Milner v Department of the Navy*,[18] Justice Kagan's opinion
for an 8–1 Court concluded that the Freedom of Information Act's
exemption for an agency's "personnel rules and practices"[19] was
determinate enough to preclude the Navy from invoking it to with-
hold internal maps pertaining to the storage of munitions. Finding
the statutory text to be clear, the Court treated as out of bounds
the government's (and dissent's) claims that the legislative history

---

[16] Variants of the "no dogs" hypothetical, which I invoke throughout, are common in
the literature of statutory interpretation. See, for example, Frederick M. Schauer, *Playing
by the Rules: A Philosophical Examination of Rule-Based Decision-Making in Law and in Life*
16–37 (1991); Frank H. Easterbrook, *Statutes' Domains*, 50 U Chi L Rev 533, 546 (1983);
Robert E. Keeton, *Statutory Analogy, Purpose, and Policy in Legal Reasoning: Live Lobsters
and a Tiger Cub in the Park*, 52 Md L Rev 1192, 1205 (1993).

[17] Easterbrook, 50 U Chi L Rev at 535 (cited in note 16) (discussing these distinct
legislative strategies and their implications for interpretation).

[18] 131 S Ct 1259 (2011).

[19] 5 USC § 552(b)(2).

and the imperative of workable government required a different result.[20] Second, in *Fox v Vice*,[21] Justice Kagan's opinion for a unanimous Court read the open-ended language of a fee-shifting statute, which entitles a prevailing party to "a reasonable attorney's fee,"[22] almost entirely in light of the Court's perception of the statute's ulterior purposes.[23] In that case, the Court read the text to invite such an inquiry. Under the new purposivism employed in these two opinions, ulterior purpose plays a decisive role if and only if Congress has framed the text at a high enough level of generality to accommodate it.[24] Given this textually-structured approach to purposivism, all that distinguishes new purposivists from textualists is the new purposivists' willingness to invoke legislative history in cases of genuine semantic ambiguity.[25]

Despite its overlap with important aspects of textualism, the new purposivists' approach may be, if anything, truer to the core premises of purposivist theory than was *Holy Trinity* itself. The most influential formulation of purposivist theory—the Legal Process materials created by Professors Hart and Sacks—derives purposivism from three central premises: legislation is purposive by nature;[26] our system of government makes the legislature the chief

---

[20] *Milner*, 131 S Ct at 1266.

[21] 131 S Ct 2205 (2011).

[22] 42 USC § 1988(b).

[23] *Vice*, 131 S Ct at 2213–15.

[24] Professor Abbe Gluck has identified a similar phenomenon in state court practice, in which a "new modified textualism" apparently allows for consideration of legislative history if and only if the interpreter first determines that the statutory text is ambiguous. See Abbe R. Gluck, *The States as Laboratories of Statutory Interpretation: Methodological Consensus and the New Modified Textualism*, 119 Yale L J 1750, 1758 (2010).

[25] See William N. Eskridge Jr., *Textualism: The Unknown Ideal?* 96 Mich L Rev 1509, 1512 (1998) ("Doctrinally, the new textualism's most distinctive feature is its insistence that judges should almost never consult, and never rely on, the legislative history of a statute. . . ."); Jonathan T. Molot, *The Rise and Fall of Textualism*, 106 Colum L Rev 1, 38 (2006) ("Textualists tend to exclude one particular piece of evidence: legislative history."). Textualists would exclude reliance on legislative history even in cases of ambiguity, arguing that such history is unenacted and does not reliably reflect legislative understandings of statutory meaning. See, for example, Antonin Scalia, *Common-Law Courts in a Civil-Law System: The Role of United States Federal Courts in Interpreting the Constitution and Laws*, in Amy Gutmann, ed, *A Matter of Interpretation: Federal Courts and the Law* 3, 29–37 (Princeton, 1997) ("*A Matter of Interpretation*"). New purposivists, in contrast, do not hesitate to use legislative history to resolve statutory ambiguity. See, for example, Part II.C and note 272.

[26] Henry M. Hart Jr. and Albert M. Sacks, *The Legal Process: Basic Problems in the Making and Application of Law* 1124 (Foundation, 1958) (William N. Eskridge Jr. and Philip P. Frickey, eds, 1994) ("*The Legal Process*").

posivism in a variety of ways,[36] of interest here is the predominant American version that welds purposivism to the constitutional premise that federal judges must act as faithful agents of Congress.[37] Rooted in requirements of legislative supremacy derived from the U.S. Constitution, the traditional version of purposivism holds that judges must implement, as accurately as possible, the directives that Congress embeds in statutes.[38]

From that starting point, it is not difficult to derive purposivism. As Felix Frankfurter wrote: "Legislation has an aim; it seeks to obviate some mischief, to supply an inadequacy, to effect a change of policy, to formulate a plan of government."[39] And if a legislature enacts a statute in order to accomplish something, then presumably a judge who wishes to respect the constitutional supremacy

---

[36] For example, one account of purposivism rests on the theory that judges have intrinsic power to make the law more coherent and just. See, for example, James McCauley Landis, *Statutes and the Sources of Law*, in Roscoe Pound, ed, *Harvard Legal Essays* 213, 214–18 (Ayer, 1934). As discussed below, I focus on the version of purposivism that is grounded in the ideal of legislative supremacy. See note 38.

[37] See Cass R. Sunstein, *Interpreting Statutes in the Regulatory State*, 103 Harv L Rev 405, 415 (1989) (describing the faithful agent theory as "the most prominent conception of the role of courts in statutory construction").

[38] See, for example, Richard A. Posner, *Legal Formalism, Legal Realism, and the Interpretation of Statutes and the Constitution*, 37 Case W Res L Rev 179, 189 (1986) ("In our system of government the framers of statutes . . . are the superiors of the judges. The framers communicate orders to the judges through legislative texts. . . ."). I focus on that version of purposivism here for two reasons: First, as I have argued at length in previous writing, specific constitutional traditions associated with, and structural inferences derived from, Articles I and III support a theory of legislative supremacy requiring judges to act as Congress's faithful agents. See John F. Manning, *Textualism and the Equity of the Statute*, 101 Colum L Rev 1, 58–105 (2001). But see William N. Eskridge Jr., *All About Words: Early Understandings of the "Judicial Power" in Statutory Interpretation, 1776–1806*, 101 Colum L Rev 990 (2001) (arguing that the judicial power includes power to read laws equitably and purposively). Second, from nearly the beginning of the republic, the Supreme Court has started from the dual presumptions of legislative supremacy and faithful agency. See, for example, *Philbrook v Glodgett*, 421 US 707, 713 (1975) ("Our objective . . . is to ascertain the congressional intent and give effect to the legislative will."); *United States v American Trucking Associations*, 310 US 534, 542 (1940) ("In the interpretation of statutes, the function of the courts is easily stated. It is to construe the language so as to give effect to the intent of Congress."); *ICC v Baird*, 194 US 25, 38 (1904) ("The object of construction, as has been often said by the courts and writers of authority, is to ascertain the legislative intent, and, if possible, to effectuate the purposes of the lawmakers."); *Pennock v Dialogue*, 27 US (2 Pet) 1, 21 (1829) ("[T]he will of the legislature must still be obeyed."); *United States v Fisher*, 6 US (2 Cranch) 358, 386 (1805) (Marshall) ("Where the intent is plain, nothing is left to construction."); *Pennington v Coxe*, 6 US (2 Cranch) 33, 52 (1804) (Marshall) (explaining that the object of interpretation is to "discover[ ] the mind of the legislature"). Because the aim of the present analysis is to account for the Supreme Court's interpretive strategy, I think it fair to proceed from the constitutional framework that has defined the Court's practice since the early days of the Republic.

[39] Felix Frankfurter, *Some Reflections on the Reading of Statutes*, 47 Colum L Rev 527, 538–39 (1947).

of the legislature should read the legislation to achieve that purpose.

To be sure, traditional purposivism acknowledged that there was "no more persuasive evidence of the purpose of a statute than the words [adopted] by . . . the legislature" and that "those words are [often] sufficient in and of themselves to determine the purpose of the legislation."[40] Still, lawmakers have limited foresight, legislative time and resources are scarce, and human language is imprecise. So all laws will, in some applications, seem overinclusive and underinclusive in relation to their ultimate purposes.[41] For traditional purposivists, therefore, fidelity to Congress meant examining all available clues to figure out what Congress was really driving at, even if it did not always correspond to what the statute said.[42] Accordingly, they thought it appropriate to adjust the clear semantic import of the text to capture accurately the purpose reflected in sources such as the tenor of the statute, patterns of policy reflected in similar legislation, or statements of purpose found in the legislative history.[43]

These starting assumptions explain *Holy Trinity Church v United States*.[44] The facts are too familiar to require extensive recitation. Congress enacted a statute forbidding anyone from contracting with an alien to come to this country and perform "labor or service of any kind."[45] The Holy Trinity Church contracted with Reverend E. Walpole Warren to come to New York to serve as minister to their congregation. After reviewing the text and structure of the statute, the Court thought it clear that the letter of the statute

---

[40] *United States v American Trucking Associations*, 310 US 534, 543 (1940).

[41] See Frederick Schauer, *Statutory Construction and the Coordinating Function of Plain Meaning*, 1990 Supreme Court Review 231, 236.

[42] See, for example, *Treat v White*, 181 US 264, 267–68 (1901) (explaining "that a fair consideration of [a statute's] surroundings may indicate that that which is within the letter is not within the spirit, and therefore must be excluded from its scope[,]" but that such a course "implies that there is something which makes clear an intent on the part of Congress against enforcement according to the letter") (citation omitted); *United States v Goldenberg*, 168 US 95, 102–03 (1897) ("[T]here are cases in which the letter of the statute is not deemed controlling, but [such] cases . . . only arise when there are cogent reasons for believing that the letter does not fully and accurately disclose the intent.").

[43] See, for example, *United Steelworkers of America v Weber*, 443 US 193, 201–07 (1979) (legislative history); *Keifer & Keifer v Reconstruction Finance Corp.*, 306 US 381, 389 (1939) (related statutes); *United States v Katz*, 271 US 354, 357 (1926) (various sources of purpose).

[44] 143 US 457 (1892).

[45] Alien Contract Labor Act of 1885, 23 Stat 332, repealed by the Immigration and Nationality Act, Pub L No 82-414, 66 Stat 163 (1952).

applied to the church's contract with Reverend Warren.[46]

Despite that view, the Court had no difficulty further concluding that the statute did not cover the church's contract with Warren. Invoking the "familiar rule" that "a thing may be within the letter of the statute and yet not within the statute, because not within its spirit nor within the intention of its makers,"[47] the Court emphasized that the title of the statute, the political context of the legislation, and the committee reports accompanying the bill all indicated that the purpose of the statute was to prevent the "the influx of . . . cheap unskilled labor."[48] In addition, because of the religious character of the nation, the Court refused to impute to Congress a purpose to disadvantage religion by passing a law that precluded the importation of a minister.[49] Reasoning that the letter of the act "unexpectedly . . . reach[ed] cases and acts which . . . could not have been intentionally legislated against," the Court found that clipping back even a clear statutory text to conform to its purpose was not "the substitution of the will of the judge for that of the legislator,"[50] but rather a more effective way of effectuating Congress's designs.[51]

Accordingly, *Holy Trinity* is predicated on the idea that, in order to be a truly faithful agent of the legislature, judges must read between the lines drawn by the statutory text—and sometimes even go outside them.[52] This idea reached its apogee after the New Deal. In *United States v American Trucking Associations*[53]—the

---

[46] See *Holy Trinity*, 143 US at 458 ("It must be conceded that the act of the corporation is within the letter of this section, for the relation of rector to his church is one of service, and implies labor on one side with compensation on the other."). For an opposing view of the statute's clarity, see note 266.

[47] *Holy Trinity*, 143 US at 459.

[48] Id at 465. See also id at 463–65 (discussing the evidence of purpose).

[49] Id at 465.

[50] Id at 472.

[51] Id at 459.

[52] See Richard A. Posner, *The Problems of Jurisprudence* 268 (Harvard, 1990) ("Suppose I ask my secretary to call Z [to cancel lunch]. The secretary notices that on my calendar I have marked lunch with Y, not Z. . . . Is it not plain that the secretary should call Y, even though there was no semantic or internal ambiguity in my instruction?"); Lon L. Fuller, *The Case of the Speluncean Explorers*, 62 Harv L Rev 616, 625–26 (1949) ("The correction of obvious legislative errors or oversights is not to supplant the legislative will, but to make that will effective.").

[53] 310 US 534 (1940).

case said to have sealed the doom of the plain-meaning approach to interpretation[54]—the Court wrote:

> When [plain] meaning has led to absurd or futile results . . . this Court has looked beyond the words to the purpose of the act. Frequently, however, even when the plain meaning did not produce absurd results but merely an unreasonable one "plainly at variance with the policy of the legislation as a whole" this Court has followed that purpose, rather than the literal words. When aid to construction of the meaning of words, as used in the statute, is available, there certainly can be no "rule of law" which forbids its use, however clear the words may appear on "superficial examination."[55]

By making clear that purpose was the touchstone of interpretation and that no "aid to construction" was off limits in ascertaining purpose, *American Trucking* helped usher in a period of increasing judicial reliance on legislative history[56] and the unapologetic use of such material to ascertain whether the statutory text adequately captured the legislative purpose.[57]

B. MODERN TEXTUALISM

Many have written about the challenge that "textualism" leveled at traditional purposivism starting a quarter-century ago.[58] Developed largely by Justice Scalia and Judge Easterbrook, the new textualism has two major components, which overlap incompletely both conceptually and in practice. The first—and, initially, the more prominent—element is evidentiary. New textualists object to the use of legislative history as a source of meaning on pragmatic

---

[54] See Hart and Sacks, *The Legal Process* at 1237 (cited in note 26).

[55] *American Trucking*, 310 US at 543–44 (citations omitted).

[56] See Jorge L. Carro and Andrew R. Braunn, *The U.S. Supreme Court and the Use of Legislative Histories: A Statistical Analysis*, 22 Jurimetrics J 294, 302–03 (1982) (chronicling the post–New Deal rise in legislative history citations).

[57] See, for example, *Public Citizen v U.S. Department of Justice*, 491 US 440, 452–54 (1989); *California Federal Savings & Loan Association v Guerra*, 479 US 272, 284 (1987); *Anderson Bros. Ford v Valencia*, 452 US 205, 222 n 20 (1981); *Train v Colorado Public Interest Research Group, Inc.*, 426 US 1, 10 (1976); *United Housing Foundation, Inc. v Forman*, 421 US 837, 849 (1975); *National Woodwork Manufacturers Association v NLRB*, 386 US 612, 620 (1967); *United States v Public Utility Commission of California*, 345 US 295, 315 (1953); *Johansen v United States*, 343 US 427, 431 (1952); *International Longshoremen's & Warehousemen's Union v Juneau Spruce Corp.*, 342 US 237, 243 (1952).

[58] See, for example, Manning, 98 Cal L Rev at 1312–14 (cited in note 4); Philip P. Frickey, *From the Big Sleep to the Big Heat: The Revival of Theory in Statutory Interpretation*, 77 Minn L Rev 241, 254–56 (1992); William N. Eskridge Jr., *The New Textualism*, 37 UCLA L Rev 621, 640–56 (1991).

and formalist grounds: At a pragmatic level, they argue that even if one thinks of legislative history as mere evidence of legislative intent or understanding, interpreters simply have no way to know whether the enacting majority subscribed to the understanding expressed in a floor statement or committee report.[59] At a formal level, they add that if judges treat (unenacted) legislative history as authoritative evidence of meaning, such practice enables Congress to make an end run around the constitutional requirements of bicameralism and presentment.[60]

More important for present purposes, the second strand of the new textualism challenges the legitimacy of using purpose, however derived, to deviate from the clear terms of the enacted text. This critique of the *Holy Trinity* approach builds on the idea that lawmaking represents the product of compromise, and that compromises often fall short of the ultimate purposes that inspired a piece of legislation.[61] Hence, if the text of the statute is clear, deviation from the clear import of the text cannot be justified on the ground that it better promotes fidelity to legislative purposes.[62]

Both strands of the new textualism have attracted criticism,[63]

---

[59] See, for example, Scalia, *A Matter of Interpretation* at 34 (cited in note 25) ("One of the routine tasks of the Washington lawyer-lobbyist is to draft language that sympathetic legislators can recite in a prewritten 'floor debate'—or, even better, insert into a committee report.").

[60] See, for example, *Begier v IRS*, 496 US 53, 68 (1990) (Scalia, J, concurring in the judgment) ("Congress conveys its directions in the Statutes at Large, not in excerpts from the Congressional Record. . . .").

[61] See, for example, *Wyeth v Levine*, 129 S Ct 1187, 1215–16 (2009) (Thomas, J, concurring in the judgment) ("[A] statute's text might reflect a compromise between parties who wanted to pursue a particular goal to different extents."); *Eastern Associated Coal Corp. v United Mine Workers of America, District 17*, 531 US 57, 68–69 (2000) (Scalia, J, concurring in the judgment) ("The final form of a statute . . . is often the result of compromise among various interest groups, resulting in a decision to go so far and no farther.").

[62] See, for example, *Babbitt v Sweet Home Chapter of Committees for a Great Oregon*, 515 US 687, 726 (1995) (Scalia, J, joined by Rehnquist, CJ, and Thomas, J, dissenting) ("Deduction from the 'broad purpose' of a statute begs the question if it is used to decide by what *means* (and hence to what *length*) Congress pursued that purpose; to get the right answer to that question there is no substitute for the hard job . . . of reading the whole text.").

[63] For example, some commentators have challenged the textualists' empirical premise that legislative history does not reliably reflect the understandings of the enacting majority. See Daniel A. Farber and Philip P. Frickey, *Law and Public Choice: A Critical Introduction* (Chicago, 1991); McNollgast, *Legislative Intent: The Use of Positive Political Theory in Statutory Interpretation*, 57 L & Contemp Probs 3, 24–25 (1994). Others have suggested that the proposed exclusion of legislative history from consideration is overbroad and that judges should develop techniques for identifying reliable legislative history. See, for example, Daniel B. Rodriguez and Barry R. Weingast, *The Positive Political Theory of Legislative History: The 1964 Civil Rights Act and Its Interpretation*, 151 U Pa L Rev 1417 (2003);

and it is not my aim to rehearse the entirety of this intricate debate here. For present purposes, what is significant is that the Court appears to have accepted the textualist critique of *Holy Trinity*. The Court has not cited *Holy Trinity* favorably in more than two decades.[64] Indeed, in that period, only a lone concurrence by Justice Stevens has cited the case for the proposition that interpreters properly enforce the spirit rather than the letter of the law.[65] Instead, broad majorities of both the Rehnquist and Roberts Courts have taken pains to emphasize the unyielding quality of a semantically clear statutory text.

This approach began to take shape the last year of the Burger Court, when Chief Justice Burger wrote for a unanimous Court:

> Congress may be unanimous in its intent to stamp out some vague social or economic evil; however, because its Members may differ sharply on the means for effectuating that intent, the final language of the legislation may reflect hard-fought compromises. Invocation of the "plain purpose" of legislation at the expense of the terms of the statute itself takes no account of the processes of compromise. . . .[66]

The very next year, a per curiam opinion joined by seven Members of the newly convened Rehnquist Court similarly opined:

Nicholas S. Zeppos, *Legislative History and the Interpretation of Statutes: Toward a Fact-Finding Model of Statutory Interpretation*, 76 Va L Rev 1295, 1307–08 (1990). Critics have also challenged the second strand of textualism on various grounds, including the concern that it strains too hard to identify semantic clarity and, in so doing, arbitrarily excludes from consideration other valuable contextual clues about statutory meaning. See, for example, Eskridge, 96 Mich L Rev at 1532–42 (cited in note 25); Molot, 106 Colum L Rev at 50–53 (cited in note 25).

[64] The last favorable citation came in Justice Brennan's opinion for the Court in *Public Citizen v U.S. Department of Justice*, 491 US 440, 452–54 (1989).

[65] See *Zuni Public School District No. 89 v Department of Education*, 550 US 81, 107 n 3 (2007) (Stevens, J, concurring). In the same period, two dissenting opinions have cited *Holy Trinity* for the proposition that the Court can construe a statute to avoid an absurd result. See *United States v Dodd*, 545 US 353, 369 (2005) (Stevens, J, joined by Souter, Ginsburg, and Breyer, JJ, dissenting); *Chapman v United States*, 500 US 453, 476 (1991) (Stevens, J, joined by Marshall, J, dissenting). All of the Justices, including the textualists, subscribe to some version of the absurdity doctrine. See John F. Manning, *The Absurdity Doctrine*, 116 Harv L Rev 2387, 2391–92 (2003). I have previously addressed the legitimacy of that distinctive doctrine and do not do so here. See id at 2431–54.

[66] *Board of Governors of the Federal Reserve System v Dimension Financial Corp.*, 474 US 361, 374 (1986). One might also trace the origins of this trend to the Burger Court's famously text-driven opinion in *Tennessee Valley Authority v Hill*, 437 US 153, 194 (1978) ("Our individual appraisal of the wisdom or unwisdom of a particular course consciously selected by the Congress is to be put aside in the process of interpreting a statute. Once the meaning of an enactment is discerned and its constitutionality determined, the judicial process comes to an end."). I think it more accurate, however, to say that a sustained reconsideration of the relative roles of text and purpose did not begin in earnest until *Dimension Financial*.

> [N]o legislation pursues its purposes at all costs. Deciding what com-
> peting values will or will not be sacrificed to the achievement of a
> particular objective is the very essence of legislative choice—and it
> frustrates rather than effectuates legislative intent simplistically to as-
> sume that *whatever* furthers the statute's primary objective must be the
> law.[67]

By the early 1990s, the Court's (recently appointed) textualists began to run with those themes. In numerous cases, they were able to attract majorities for the proposition that the Court must adhere to the clear import of the statutory text even when it conflicts with a statute's apparent background purpose. In this vein, compare *Holy Trinity*'s premises about letter and spirit with the way the Court described its interpretive practice in a pivotal 1991 opinion:

> [T]he purpose of a statute includes not only what it sets out to change,
> but also what it resolves to leave alone. The best evidence of that
> purpose is the statutory text adopted by both Houses of Congress and
> submitted to the President. Where that contains a phrase that is un-
> ambiguous[,] . . . we do not permit it to be expanded or contracted by
> the statements of individual legislators or committees during the course
> of the enactment process. Congress could easily have [enacted a statute
> that reflected the broader purposes expressed in the legislative history],
> as it did in contemporaneous statutes; it chose instead to enact more
> restrictive language, and we are bound by that restriction.[68]

Like statements of the Court's new approach were soon to follow: "[T]he reach of a statute often exceeds the precise evil to be eliminated," and "it is not, and cannot be, [the Court's] practice to restrict the unqualified language of a statute to the particular evil that Congress was trying to remedy—even assuming that it is possible to identify that evil from something other than the text of the statute itself."[69] "[S]tatutory prohibitions often go beyond the principal evil to cover reasonably comparable evils, and it is ultimately the provisions of our laws rather than the principal concerns of our legislators by which we are governed."[70] "[Judges

---

[67] *Rodriguez v United States*, 480 US 522, 525–26 (1987) (per curiam).

[68] *West Virginia University Hospitals, Inc. v Casey*, 499 US 83, 98–99 (1991) (Scalia, J, joined by Rehnquist, CJ, and White, O'Connor, Kennedy, and Souter, JJ) (citations omitted).

[69] *Brogan v United States*, 522 US 398, 403 (1998) (Scalia, J, joined by Rehnquist, CJ, and O'Connor, Kennedy, Souter, and Thomas, JJ).

[70] *Oncale v Sundowner Offshore Services, Inc.*, 523 US 75, 79 (1998) (Scalia, J, for a unanimous Court).

are] bound, not only by the ultimate purposes Congress has selected, but by the means it has deemed appropriate, and prescribed,
for the pursuit of those purposes."[71] One could easily go on.[72]

The resulting change in attitude is perhaps best captured by the
Court's oft-cited opinion in *Connecticut National Bank v Germain*,[73]
which emphasized that "courts must presume that a legislature
says in a statute what it means and means in a statute what it says
there. When the words of a statute are unambiguous, then, this
first canon is also the last: 'judicial inquiry is complete.'"[74] Indeed,
the Court's textualists have been able to articulate this basic position again and again in opinions of the Court, often supported
by broad majorities.[75] Most (but not all) legislation scholars have

[71] *MCI Telecommunications Corp. v AT&T Co.*, 512 US 218, 231 n 4 (1994) (Scalia, J,
joined by Rehnquist, Kennedy, Thomas, and Ginsburg, JJ).

[72] For other examples of this approach, see *Cooper Industries, Inc. v Aviall Services, Inc.*,
543 US 157, 167 (2004) (Thomas, J, joined by Rehnquist, CJ, and O'Connor, Scalia,
Kennedy, Souter, and Breyer, JJ) ("Given the clear meaning of the text, there is no need
to resolve this dispute or to consult the purpose of CERCLA at all."); *Barnhart v Sigmon
Coal Co., Inc.*, 534 US 438, 461 (2002) (Thomas, J, joined by Rehnquist, CJ, and Scalia,
Kennedy, Souter, and Ginsburg, JJ) ("Dissatisfied with the text of the statute, the Commissioner attempts to search for and apply an overarching legislative purpose to each
section of the statute. Dissatisfaction, however, is often the cost of legislative compromise.
. . . The deals brokered during a Committee markup, on the floor of the two Houses,
during a joint House and Senate Conference, or in negotiations with the President are
not for us to judge or second-guess."); *Pennsylvania Department of Corrections v Yeskey*, 524
US 206, 212 (1998) (Scalia, J, for a unanimous Court) ("[A]ssuming . . . that Congress
did not envisio[n] that the [Americans with Disabilities Act] would be applied to state
prisoners, in the context of an unambiguous statutory text that is irrelevant.") (second
alteration in original) (citation and quotation marks omitted); *City of Chicago v Environmental Defense Fund*, 511 US 328, 339 (1994) (Scalia, J, joined by Rehnquist, CJ, and
Blackmun, Kennedy, Souter, and Ginsburg, JJ) ("It is not unusual for legislation to contain
diverse purposes that must be reconciled, and the most reliable guide for that task is the
enacted text.").

[73] 503 US 249 (1992) (Thomas, J, joined by Rehnquist, CJ, and Scalia, Kennedy, and
Souter, JJ).

[74] Id at 253–54 (citations omitted), quoting *Rubin v United States*, 449 US 424, 430
(1981).

[75] See, for example, *Morrison v National Australia Bank Ltd.*, 130 S Ct 2869, 2886 (2010)
(Scalia, J, joined by Roberts, CJ, and Thomas, Kennedy, and Alito, JJ) ("It is our function
to give the statute the effect its language suggests, however modest that may be; not to
extend it to admirable purposes it might be used to achieve."); *Hardt v Reliance Standard
Life Insurance Co.*, 130 S Ct 2149, 2156 (2010) (Thomas, J, for a unanimous Court) ("As
in all . . . cases [of statutory construction], we begin by analyzing the statutory language,
'assum[ing]' that the ordinary meaning of that language accurately expresses the legislative
purpose.' We must enforce plain and unambiguous statutory language according to its
terms."), quoting *Gross v FBL Financial Services, Inc.*, 129 S Ct 2343, 2350 (2009) (quotation
marks omitted); *Hartford Underwriters Insurance Co. v Union Planters Bank, N.A.*, 530 US
1, 6 (2000) (Scalia, J, for a unanimous Court) ("[W]hen the statute's language is plain,
the sole function of the courts—at least where the disposition required by the text is not
absurd—is to enforce it according to its terms.") (quotation marks omitted); *Hughes Aircraft*

acknowledged this trend,[76] noting the Court's greatly increased reliance on semantic evidence (such as dictionaries),[77] as well as its significant reduction in citations of legislative history.[78] Indeed, even the Court's strongest purposivists—Justices Stevens and Breyer—have acknowledged (while resisting) this trend.[79]

Of course, I do not mean to suggest here that the Court unerringly adheres to the statutory text. Surely, one could identify a number of recent cases in which a fair reading of the text could

---

Co. v Jacobson, 525 US 432, 438 (1999) (Thomas, J, for a unanimous Court) ("As in any case of statutory construction, our analysis begins with 'the language of the statute.' And where the statutory language provides a clear answer, it ends there as well."), quoting *Estate of Cowart v Nicklos Drilling Co.*, 505 US 469, 475 (1992).

[76] See, for example, Philip P. Frickey, *Revisiting the Revival of Theory in Statutory Interpretation: A Lecture in Honor of Irving Younger*, 84 Minn L Rev 199, 205 (1999) ("The Court is less likely to cite legislative history today, and when it does, the citations seem less important to the outcome. The Court pays careful attention to statutory text and is much more likely than in earlier eras to use dictionaries to assist in constructing textual meaning."); Molot, 106 Colum L Rev at 32–34 (cited in note 25) (noting the Court's increased emphasis on textualist principles); Schauer, 1990 Supreme Court Review at 231 (cited in note 41) (same). For some contrasting views on this point, see note 78.

[77] See, for example, Jeffrey L. Kirchmeier and Samuel A. Thumma, *Scaling the Lexicon Fortress: The United States Supreme Court's Use of Dictionaries in the Twenty-First Century*, 94 Marq L Rev 77, 86 (2010) (charting the increase in the use of dictionaries since the beginning of the 1980s); Samuel A. Thumma and Jeffrey L. Kirchmeier, *The Lexicon Remains a Fortress: An Update*, 5 Greenbag 2d 51 (2001); Samuel A. Thumma and Jeffrey L. Kirchmeier, *The Lexicon Has Become a Fortress: The United States Supreme Court's Use of Dictionaries*, 47 Buff L Rev 227, 252–60 (1999). See also Merrill, 72 Wash U L Q at 372 (cited in note 7) (noting the rise of that textualism also produced increased reliance on other semantic cues).

[78] See, for example, James J. Brudney and Corey Ditslear, *The Decline and Fall of Legislative History? Patterns of Supreme Court Reliance in the Burger and Rehnquist Eras*, 89 Judicature 220 (2006) (describing a dramatic drop in the Court's reliance on legislative history in workplace cases during the Rehnquist Court); Michael H. Koby, *The Supreme Court's Declining Reliance on Legislative History: The Impact of Justice Scalia's Critique*, 36 Harv J Leg 369, 386–87 (1999) (calculating that in the half dozen years prior to Justice Scalia's appointment, the Court averaged 3.47 citations of legislative history per opinion and that the average dropped to 1.87 in the dozen years after his appointment).

Other scholars view the case as more complicated. See, for example, Frank B. Cross, Essay, *The Significance of Statutory Interpretive Methodologies*, 82 Notre Dame L Rev 1971, 1979–88 (2007) (arguing that textualism peaked in 1994); Jane S. Schacter, *The Confounding Common Law Originalism in Recent Supreme Court Statutory Interpretation: Implications for the Legislative History Debate and Beyond*, 51 Stan L Rev 1 (1998) (noting that the Court relied on multiple sources of meaning, including legislative history, during October Term 1996); Anita S. Krishnakumar, *Statutory Interpretation in the Roberts Court's First Era: An Empirical and Doctrinal Analysis*, 62 Hastings L J 221 (2010) (arguing that, in statutory cases, some Justices stress judicial administrability while others stress policy coherence).

[79] See *Koons Buick Pontiac GMC, Inc. v Nigh*, 543 US 50, 65 (2004) (Stevens, J, joined by Breyer, J, concurring) ("In recent years the Court has suggested that we should only look at legislative history for the purpose of resolving textual ambiguities or to avoid absurdities. It would be wiser to acknowledge that it is always appropriate to consider all available evidence of Congress' true intent when interpreting its work product.").

not justify the outcome.[80] What is striking, however, is that, except in cases of absurdity, the Court no longer claims the authority to deviate from the clear import of the text—to prefer spirit over letter. That represents a significant departure from the Court's practice prior to the Rehnquist Court.

II. THE NEW PURPOSIVISM DEFINED

Perhaps even more striking than the shift away from *Holy Trinity* is the fact that all but two of the Court's nontextualist Justices seem to have gone along with this change in approach without much hesitation.[81] I have previously noted that nontextualist Justices now frequently join text-bound opinions for the Court written by textualists.[82] It is also true that most of the nontextualist Justices have themselves written opinions that profess a strict duty of adherence to the text or question the legitimacy of using purpose as a trump. Accordingly, Justice Sotomayor has written for the Court that "[w]hen the statutory language is plain, the sole function of the courts—at least where the disposition required by the text is not absurd—is to enforce it according to its terms."[83] Justice Ginsburg has written for a unanimous Court that "we ordinarily resist reading words or elements into a statute that do not appear on its face."[84] Justice Alito has written that where "the

---

[80] Indeed, the Court's textualists continue to argue that their nontextualist colleagues, at times, disregard the plain import of the text in order to achieve some extratextual purpose or goal. See, for example, *Hamilton v Lanning*, 130 S Ct 2464, 2485 (2010) (Scalia, J, dissenting) ("[T]aking liberties with text in light of outcome makes sense only if we assume that we know better than Congress which outcomes are mistaken.") (citation omitted); *Small v United States*, 544 US 385, 395 (2005) (Thomas, J, joined by Scalia and Kennedy, JJ, dissenting) ("[T]he Court distorts the plain meaning of the statute and departs from established principles of statutory construction."). Textual missteps are not the exclusive preserve of nontextualist Justices. See, for example, *AT&T Mobility LLC v Concepcion*, 131 S Ct 1740, 1748–53 (2011) (Scalia, J) (reading a purposive limitation on class actions into the Federal Arbitration Act); *FDA v Brown & Williamson Tobacco Corp.*, 529 US 120, 143–61 (2000) (opinion joined by Justices Scalia and Thomas limiting otherwise broad regulatory language in light of postenactment legislative history).

[81] See Molot, 106 Colum L Rev at 32–33 (cited in note 25) ("Although one finds more textualist rhetoric in the opinions of Justices Scalia and Thomas than in those of other Justices, other Justices regularly join the opinions of these self-proclaimed textualists, and even embrace textualist values in some of their own opinions."). The two adherents to traditional purposivism are Justices Stevens and Breyer. See note 168.

[82] See note 75 and accompanying text.

[83] *Carr v United States*, 130 S Ct 2229, 2241–42 (2010) (Sotomayor, J, joined by Roberts, CJ, and Stevens, Kennedy, and Breyer, JJ), quoting *Arlington Central School District Board of Education v Murphy*, 548 US 291, 296 (2006) (quotation marks and citation omitted).

[84] *Bates v United States*, 522 US 23, 29 (1997) (Ginsburg, J, for a unanimous Court).

statutory language is clear, there is no need to reach . . . arguments based on statutory purpose, legislative history, or the rule of lenity."[85] Examples of this sort could easily be multiplied.[86]

This phenomenon raises the important question of why these nontextualist Justices have embraced this approach. Most commentators assume that the change simply reflects the response of the other Justices to Justice Scalia's assertive campaign against legislative history and in favor of the statutory text.[87] As Professor Jonathan Molot explains it, "the broad appeal of textualism's underlying premises has led judges who do not consider themselves adherents to heed textualism's warnings about the pitfalls of strong purposivism and to alter their approach to statutory interpretation."[88]

Even if accurate, however, explanations of this sort fail to explain *why* judges holding quite different priors from Justice Scalia would embrace some or all of the premises of textualism. With the exception of Justices Scalia and Thomas, almost none of the Justices self-identify as textualists.[89] Indeed, because purposivism defined

---

[85] *Boyle v United States*, 129 S Ct 2237, 2246 (2009) (Alito, J, joined by Roberts, CJ, and Scalia, Kennedy, Souter, Thomas, and Ginsburg, JJ). One commentator has argued that Justice Alito should be considered a textualist. See Elliott M. Davis, Note, *The Newer Textualism: Justice Alito's Statutory Interpretation*, 30 Harv J L & Pub Pol 983 (2007). Justice Alito, however, has no trouble relying on legislative history to identify legislative intent or purpose. See, for example, *Zedner v United States*, 547 US 489, 501 (2006) (noting that the Speedy Trial Act's legislative history shows that "the Act was designed not just to benefit defendants but also to serve the public interest").

[86] See, for example, *Milavetz, Gallop & Milavetz, P.A. v United States*, 130 S Ct 1324, 1332 n 3 (2010) (Sotomayor, J, joined by Roberts, CJ, and Stevens, Kennedy, Breyer, and Alito, JJ) (noting that "reliance on legislative history is unnecessary in light of the statute's unambiguous language"); *Lockhart v United States*, 546 US 142, 146 (2005) (O'Connor, J, for a unanimous Court) ("'The fact that Congress may not have foreseen all of the consequences of a statutory enactment is not a sufficient reason for refusing to give effect to its plain meaning.'"), quoting *Union Bank v Wolas*, 502 US 151, 158 (1991); *Till v SCS Credit Corp.*, 541 US 465, 483 (2004) (plurality opinion of Stevens, J, joined by Souter, Ginsburg, and Breyer, JJ) (noting that, if the text of the statute were in fact unambiguous, "that would be the end of the matter"); *United States v Gonzales*, 520 US 1, 6 (1997) (O'Connor, J, joined by Rehnquist, CJ, and Scalia, Kennedy, Souter, Thomas, and Ginsburg, JJ) ("Given the straightforward statutory command, there is no reason to resort to legislative history."), citing *Connecticut National Bank v Germain*, 503 US 249, 254 (1992).

[87] See, for example, Frickey, 84 Minn L Rev at 205 (cited in note 76) ("Justice Scalia's arguments have had some effect upon the Supreme Court."); Bradley C. Karkkainen, *"Plain Meaning": Justice Scalia's Jurisprudence of Strict Statutory Construction*, 17 Harv J L & Pub Pol 401, 402 (1994) (noting that while many Justices disagree with Justice Scalia's premises, he "undoubtedly is forcing the Court to re-examine its jurisprudence of statutory interpretation").

[88] Molot, 106 Colum L Rev at 32 (cited in note 25).

[89] Even if one were to count Justice Kennedy as a textualist, see note 7, adding him to the lineup would still only yield three votes.

the consensus approach to statutory interpretation when all of the Justices of the past quarter-century went to law school,[90] it is fair to assume that they all began their careers steeped in the premises of purposivism. In case after case, moreover, all of the Justices have reaffirmed that statutory purpose properly guides interpretation.[91] And while legislative history rarely, if ever, plays the decisive role that it once did in the Court's jurisprudence,[92] all of the Justices—except Justices Scalia and Thomas—have expressly reaffirmed that such materials may be a source of probative and legitimate evidence of statutory meaning.[93]

---

[90] The purposive approach set forth in the Legal Process materials reflected the canonical understanding of statutory interpretation in the post–New Deal period. See note 173. Indeed, at least five of the Justices in that period (Scalia, Kennedy, Souter, Ginsburg, and Breyer) actually took the Legal Process course while in law school. See William N. Eskridge Jr. and Philip P. Frickey, *The Supreme Court 1993 Term—Forward: Law as Equilibrium*, 108 Harv L Rev 26, 27 (1993).

[91] See, for example, *CSX Transportation, Inc. v McBride*, 131 S Ct 2630, 2642–43 (2011) (plurality opinion of Ginsburg, J, joined by Breyer, Sotomayor, and Kagan, JJ) ("[W]hen the legislative text uses less legalistic language . . . [such as] 'resulting in whole or in part from,' and the legislative purpose is to loosen constraints on recovery, there is little reason for courts to hark back to stock, judge-made proximate-cause formulations."); *Fowler v United States*, 131 S Ct 2045, 2049 (2011) (Breyer, J, joined by Roberts, CJ, and Kennedy, Thomas, Sotomayor, and Kagan, JJ) ("[A]ny such limitation would conflict with the statute's basic purpose."); *Abbott v United States*, 131 S Ct 18, 31 n 9 (2010) (Ginsburg, J, for a unanimous Court, excluding Justice Kagan, who took no part in the case) ("Although the clause might have been more meticulously drafted, the 'grammatical possibility' of a defendant's interpretation does not command a resort to the rule of lenity if the interpretation proffered by the defendant reflects 'an implausible reading of the congressional purpose.'"), quoting *Caron v United States*, 524 US 308, 316 (1998); *Milavetz, Gallop & Milavetz, P.A. v United States*, 130 S Ct 1324, 1339 (2010) (Sotomayor, J, joined by Roberts, CJ, and Stevens, Kennedy, Ginsburg, Breyer, and Alito, JJ) ("As the foregoing shows, the language of the statute, together with other evidence of its purpose, makes this narrow reading of § 526(a)(4) not merely a plausible interpretation but the more natural one."); *Harbison v Bell*, 129 S Ct 1481, 1487 n 6 (2009) (Stevens, J, joined by Kennedy, Souter, Breyer, and Ginsburg, JJ) ("Such a rigid limit on the authority of appointed federal counsel would be inconsistent with the basic purpose of the statute."); *Watson v Philip Morris Companies, Inc.*, 551 US 142, 147–52 (2007) (Breyer, J, for a unanimous Court) (relying on the history and purpose of the federal removal statute to construe its scope); *Koons Buick Pontiac GMC, Inc. v Nigh*, 543 US 50, 62–64 (2004) (Ginsburg, J, joined by Rehnquist, CJ, and Stevens, Kennedy, Souter, Ginsburg, and Breyer, JJ) (resolving an ambiguity in light of common sense and the legislative aims suggested by the statutory history). Even Justice Scalia acknowledges the sometimes decisive relevance of purpose. See, for example, *Asgrow Seed Co. v Winterboer*, 513 US 179, 192 (1995) (Scalia, J, joined by Rehnquist, CJ, and O'Connor, Kennedy, Souter, Thomas, Ginsburg, and Breyer, JJ) ("While the meaning of the text is by no means clear, this is in our view the only reading that comports with the statutory purpose. . . .").

[92] These days, the Court tends to consult legislative history largely by way of showing that it confirms the Court's reading of the text or that it is inconclusive. See notes 258–59.

[93] Just last Term, all of the Court's Members except Justices Scalia and Thomas joined

So why would the nontextualist members of the Court seemingly abandon traditional purposivism when they apparently accept so many of the key premises underlying it? One hypothesis is that many, if not most, of core assumptions of the contemporary Court's statutory jurisprudence fit not only with the tenets of modern textualism, but also with those of purposivism, properly understood. The key to understanding the potential overlap lies in the fact that neither approach eschews consideration of purpose. Rather, the Court now takes its cues directly from Congress about how and to what degree to take background purpose or policy into account. Those cues derive from a signal that traditional purposivism tended to overlook (if not override)—the level of generality at which Congress frames its statutory commands. The following three cases illustrate this development.

A. DISCRETION-CONSTRAINING COMMANDS

If a statute frames the relevant command in a crisp and precise

---

an opinion by Justice Stevens stating:

> Legislative history materials are not generally so misleading that jurists should never employ them in a good-faith effort to discern legislative intent. Our precedents demonstrate that the Court's practice of utilizing legislative history reaches well into its past. We suspect that the practice will likewise reach well into the future.

Samantar v Yousuf, 130 S Ct 2278, 2294 (2010), quoting *Wisconsin Public Intervenor v Mortier*, 501 US 597, 611–12, n 4 (1991) (alteration in original; citations omitted). Indeed, all of the Justices, at one time or another, have joined opinions relying on legislative history. See, for example, *Samantar*, 130 S Ct at 2289 n 12 (Stevens, J, joined by Roberts, CJ, and Kennedy, Ginsburg, Breyer, Alito, and Sotomayor, JJ) ("The legislative history makes clear that Congress did not intend the FSIA to address position-based individual immunities such as diplomatic and consular immunity."); *Corley v United States*, 129 S Ct 1558, 1568–69 (2009) (Souter, J, joined by Stevens, Kennedy, Breyer, and Ginsburg, JJ) ("Further legislative history not only drives that point home, but conclusively shows an intent that subsection (c) limit *McNabb-Mallory*, not replace it."); *Scheidler v National Organization for Women, Inc.*, 547 US 9, 20 (2006) (Breyer, J, for a unanimous Court, excluding Justice Alito, who took no part in the case) (holding that the 1948 revision to the U.S. Criminal Code did not intend to change the Hobbs Act because "the Reviser's Notes indicate that the linguistic changes to the Hobbs Act simply amount to 'changes in phraseology and arrangement necessary to effect consolidation'"), quoting HR Rep No 304, 80th Cong, 1st Sess A131 (1947); *Scarborough v Principi*, 541 US 401, 417 (2004) (Ginsburg, J, joined by Rehnquist, CJ, and Stevens, O'Connor, Kennedy, Souter, and Breyer, JJ) ("Permitting amendment [of an attorney's fee application] thus advances Congress' purpose, in enacting EAJA, to reduce the 'emphasi[s], virtually to the exclusion of all other issues, [on] the cost of potential litigation' in a party's decision whether to challenge unjust governmental action.") (alteration in original), quoting HR Rep No 1005, 96th Cong, 2d Sess 7 (1980). Still, both Justices Scalia and Thomas continue to object to the use of legislative history on principle, sometimes declining to join an opinion, in full, because it has relied on legislative history. See note 169.

way, the Court now takes Congress to have defined the relevant statutory purpose with specificity. Thus, in *Milner v Department of the Navy*,[94] Justice Kagan's opinion for eight Members of the Court straightforwardly applied Exemption 2 of the Freedom of Information Act (FOIA), which excludes from the Act's compelled disclosure any agency records that are "related solely to the internal personnel rules and practices of an agency."[95] At issue was whether Exemption 2 shielded from disclosure documents containing Explosive Safety Quantity Distance (ESQD) information—data used by the Navy to help design storage facilities to house munitions at safe distances from each other. Milner had made an FOIA request for the Navy's documents containing ESQD information for a particular naval base. The Navy invoked Exemption 2 as the basis for withholding the requested documents.[96]

The Ninth Circuit upheld the Navy's assertion of Exemption 2, reasoning that the documents related to "predominantly internal" matters whose "disclosure presents a risk of circumvention of agency regulation."[97] That two-part test, in turn, came from a nearly three-decade-old D.C. Circuit decision—*Crooker v Bureau of Alcohol, Tobacco & Firearms*[98]—which had used a traditionally purposive approach to bring a Bureau of Alcohol, Tobacco and Firearms field-training manual within the purview of Exemption 2. Although the court in *Crooker* held that the language of Exemption 2 limited its scope to documents predominantly for internal agency use,[99] the balance of its test derived from inferences about legislative purpose. The court began from the general proposition that while FOIA's "primary purpose" was disclosure, Congress also had "a secondary purpose . . . of preserving the effective operation of governmental agencies."[100] From that starting point, an extended consideration of FOIA's "overall design," its legis-

---

[94] 131 S Ct 1259 (2011).

[95] 5 USC § 552(b)(2); see also *Milner*, 131 S Ct at 1261.

[96] *Milner*, 131 S Ct at 1263–64.

[97] *Milner v United States Department of the Navy*, 575 F3d 959, 967–68 (9th Cir 2009).

[98] 670 F2d 1051 (DC Cir 1981) (en banc).

[99] The court reasoned that "predominantly internal" struck a balance between the apparent narrowness of the word "solely" and the apparent breadth of the word "related" in Exemption 2's requirement that any documents withheld be "related solely to the internal personnel rules and practices of an agency." See id at 1056–57.

[100] Id at 1074.

lative history, and "even common sense" convinced the court that Congress could not have purported to enact a statute whose provisions "undermined . . . the effectiveness of law enforcement agencies."[101] In particular, these sources led the court to conclude that a "predominantly internal" document should be exempt under Exemption 2 if its disclosure "significantly risk[ed] circumvention of agency regulations or statutes."[102]

In her opinion for the Court in *Milner*, Justice Kagan rejected the *Crooker* test as inconsistent with the language of Exemption 2. Noting that "comparatively little attention has been focused on [Exemption 2's] 12 simple words," Justice Kagan wrote:

> The key word in that dozen—the one that most clearly marks the provision's boundaries—is "personnel." When used as an adjective, as it is here to modify "rules and practices," that term refers to human resources matters. "Personnel," in this common parlance, means "the selection, placement, and training of employees and . . . the formulation of policies, procedures, and relations with [or involving] employees or their representatives." *Webster's Third New International Dictionary* 1687 (1966) (hereinafter Webster's). So, for example, a "personnel department" is "the department of a business firm that deals with problems affecting the employees of the firm and that usually interviews applicants for jobs." *Random House Dictionary* 1075 (1966) (hereinafter Random House). "Personnel management" is similarly "the phase of management concerned with the engagement and effective utilization of manpower to obtain optimum efficiency of human resources." Web-

---

[101] Id.

[102] *Crooker*, 670 F2d at 1074. The court drew its inference about the risk of circumvention primarily from legislative history in the House of Representatives. For example, the court cited a statement by the bill's House sponsor suggesting that Exemption 2 "'was intended to cover . . . instances such as the manuals of procedure that are handed to an examiner—a bank examiner, or a savings and loan examiner, or the guidelines given to an FBI agent.'" Id at 1059, quoting Federal Public Records Law (Part 1): Hearings before a Subcommittee of the Committee on Government Operations on HR 5012 et al, 89th Cong, 1st Sess 29 (1965) (statement of Rep. Moss). To similar effect, the court pointed to a passage of the House Report stating that "[o]perating rules, guidelines, and manuals of procedure for Government investigators or examiners would be exempt" under Exemption 2. *Crooker*, 670 F2d at 1060, quoting HR Rep No 1497, 86th Cong, 2d Sess 10 (1966).

The court found further support for its test in the language and history of related FOIA provisions. For example, the court noted that the language of a clause mandating disclosure of "administrative staff manuals," 5 USC § 552(a)(2)(C), had been narrowed in apparent response to concerns that the original language ("staff manuals") might require disclosure of investigative techniques. See *Crooker*, 670 F2d at 1062–63. Similarly, the court noted that a 1974 amendment to Exemption 7—which shielded records that might reveal "investigative techniques and procedures," 5 USC § 552(7)(E)—was accompanied by legislative history suggesting that the amendment merely clarified and reaffirmed what FOIA already required. *Crooker*, 670 F2d at1063–65.

ster's 1687. And a "personnel agency" is "an agency for placing employable persons in jobs; employment agency." Random House 1075.[103]

From this semantic evidence Justice Kagan inferred that "personnel rules and practices" "concern the conditions of employment in federal agencies—such matters as hiring and firing, work rules and discipline, compensation and benefits."[104] She added, moreover, that this reading gave effect to FOIA's background goal of broad disclosure "through the simple device of confining [the exemption's] meaning to its words."[105]

Justice Breyer—the current Court's most traditional purposivist[106]—was the sole dissenter and strongly endorsed the *Crooker* test. He emphasized that this test properly rested on "Congress' broader FOIA objectives and a 'common sense' view of what Congress did and did not want to make available."[107] Reflecting the classical rationale for traditional purposivism, he added that this "practical approach"[108] was imperative given the realities of a broad-gauged framework statute such as FOIA:

> [Such an approach] reflects this Court's longstanding recognition that it cannot interpret the FOIA (and the Administrative Procedure Act (APA) of which it is a part) with the linguistic literalism fit for interpretations of the tax code. . . . That in large part is because the FOIA (like the APA but unlike the tax code) must govern the affairs of a vast Executive Branch with numerous different agencies, bureaus, and departments, performing numerous tasks of many different kinds. Too narrow an interpretation, while working well in the case of one agency, may seriously interfere with congressional objectives when applied to another. The D.C. Circuit's answer to this legal problem here was to interpret Exemption 2 in light of Congress' basic effort to achieve a "workable balance between the interests of the public in greater access to information and the needs of the Government to protect certain kinds of information from disclosure."[109]

---

[103] *Milner*, 131 S Ct at 1264.

[104] Id at 1265.

[105] Id at 1266.

[106] See notes 162 and 168.

[107] *Milner*, 131 S Ct at 1275 (Breyer, J, dissenting), quoting *Crooker*, 670 F2d at 1074.

[108] *Milner*, 131 S Ct at 1275 (Breyer, J, dissenting), quoting *John Doe Agency v John Doe Corp.*, 493 US 146, 157 (1989).

[109] *Milner*, 131 S Ct at 1276 (Breyer, J, dissenting), quoting *John Doe Agency*, 493 US at 157. Justice Breyer also cited several committee reports asserting the objective of workable government. See *Milner*, 131 S Ct at 1276, citing S Rep No 1219, 88th Cong, 2d Sess 8, 11 (1964); S Rep No 813, 89th Cong, 1st Sess 3, 5 (1965); HR Rep No 1497, 86th Cong, 2d Sess 2, 6 (1966).

Justice Kagan replied that "the *Crooker* interpretation . . . suffers from a patent flaw: It is disconnected from Exemption 2's text."[110] Even assuming that Justice Breyer and the *Crooker* court, moreover, accurately read FOIA's legislative history,[111] the "more fundamental point" for Justice Kagan was that "[l]egislative history, for those who take it into account, is meant to clear up ambiguity, not create it."[112]

One might be tempted to read the opinions in *Milner* as a clash between traditional purposivism (Breyer) and textualism (Kagan). Certainly, Justice Breyer's endorsement of *Crooker* seems to assume that, at least in the context of a government-wide framework statute such as FOIA, Congress cannot plausibly enact a set of *rules* that will ensure workable government agency by agency. Given that the desire for workable government represents a reasonable starting assumption about the purpose of all such statutes, the courts have good cause to read them purposively to ensure the achievement of Congress's ultimate purpose.

Justice Kagan, by contrast, might be seen as a hard-edged textualist, insisting that the Court follow plain meaning at the expense of Congress's presumed goals. Upon analysis, however, that characterization is not the most plausible view of Justice Kagan's position. Consider her telling response to Justice Breyer's contention that the *Crooker* test served FOIA's ultimate purpose of ensuring disclosure without sacrificing a workable government:

> [N]othing in FOIA either explicitly or implicitly grants courts discretion to expand (or contract) an exemption on this basis. In enacting FOIA, Congress struck the balance it thought right—generally favoring disclosure, subject only to a handful of specified exemptions—and did

---

[110] *Milner*, 131 S Ct at 1267 (majority opinion). Justice Kagan elaborated as follows:

> The [*Crooker*] test (in addition to substituting the word "predominantly" for "solely") ignores the plain meaning of the adjective "personnel," and adopts a circumvention requirement with no basis or referent in Exemption 2's language. Indeed, the only way to arrive at [the *Crooker* approach] is by taking a red pen to the statute—"cutting out some" words and "pasting in others" until little of the actual provision remains.

Id, quoting *Elliott v United States Department of Agriculture*, 596 F3d 842, 845 (DC Cir 2010).

[111] The Court disputed that proposition, suggesting that there was an irreconcilable difference between the House and Senate Reports about whether Exemption 2 extended beyond the conventional meaning of "personnel rules and practices." See *Milner*, 131 S Ct at 1267.

[112] Id.

so across the length and breadth of the Federal Government. The judicial role is to enforce that congressionally determined balance rather than, as the dissent suggests, to assess case by case, department by department, and task by task whether disclosure interferes with good government.[113]

This passage shows that Justice Kagan's analysis does not reject legislative purpose, but rather embraces it at a deeper level. The derivation of purpose is not, as Justice Breyer suggests, merely the attempt to approximate the policy objectives that the evidence suggests a reasonable legislator would pursue in the circumstances. Instead, as Justice Kagan's reasoning suggests, the idea of purpose necessarily includes the congressional purpose to grant or with-hold discretion from those charged with implementing the statute. Because Congress "struck the balance" between disclosure and workability rather precisely in Exemption 2, it expressed a purpose to withhold from courts (and, for that matter, agencies) "discretion to expand (or contract) [that] exemption" in order to make gov-ernment more workable. The kind of purposivism practiced by Justice Kagan in *Milner* recognizes that, in a system of legislative supremacy, Congress must have the capacity, through the relative specificity or generality of its chosen language, to set meaningful boundaries on the purposes it wishes courts and agencies to pursue. In contrast with *Holy Trinity*, the *Milner* Court declined to deviate from those boundaries in order to pursue the goals that Congress apparently sought to achieve but that did not make their way into the final text.

B. DISCRETION-CONFERRING COMMANDS

This view of the new purposivism finds support in Justice Ka-gan's rather different calibration of the relative importance of text and purpose in *Fox v Vice*,[114] a case interpreting the broad, open-ended language of Section 1988. That statute provides that in specified classes of civil rights litigation, "the court, in its discre-tion, may allow the prevailing party, other than the United States, a reasonable attorney's fee. . . ."[115] At issue was how to handle the fees awarded to a prevailing defendant in a case in which the

---

[113] Id at 1265 n 5.

[114] 131 S Ct 2205 (2011).

[115] 42 USC § 1988(b).

plaintiff filed both frivolous and nonfrivolous claims. Justice Kagan's opinion for a unanimous Court paid almost no attention to the text of the statute. Instead, it rested entirely upon the purposes of Section 1988, as developed in common law fashion by prior opinions of the Court.

Under the Court's precedents, a prevailing plaintiff is presumptively entitled to attorney's fees.[116] In contrast, the Court had made clear that a prevailing defendant was entitled to fees only if the trial court found "that the plaintiff's action was frivolous, unreasonable, or without foundation."[117] In *Fox v Vice*, Fox—an ultimately successful candidate for municipal office—had brought a variety of claims against the previous incumbent, Vice, in connection with alleged "dirty tricks" committed during the election campaign.[118] Fox sued under 42 USC § 1983 alleging that Vice's and the municipality's conduct had interfered with his federally protected right to seek public office.[119] He also brought pendent state law claims alleging, inter alia, defamation. At the conclusion of discovery, the district court granted summary judgment for the defendant (Vice) on the federal claims and declined to exercise supplemental jurisdiction over Fox's state claims.[120] The court awarded attorney's fees to Vice on the ground that the federal claims were frivolous. Even though the district court had not found Fox's state law claims to be frivolous (indeed, they remained live claims), the court nonetheless awarded Vice fees for all of the litigation expenses he had incurred, noting that all of the claims, frivolous and nonfrivolous, had arisen from the same transaction and were factually interrelated.[121]

In an opinion by Justice Kagan, a unanimous Court reversed, holding that the "congressional policy" underlying Section 1988 "allows a defendant to recover reasonable attorney's fees incurred because of, but only because of, a frivolous claim."[122] In contrast with *Milner*, Justice Kagan expended no effort in *Vice* parsing or analyzing the operative language of the statute. Rather, building

---

[116] See *Newman v Piggie Park Enterprises, Inc.*, 390 US 400, 402 (1968) (per curiam).

[117] *Christiansburg Garment Co. v EEOC*, 434 US 412, 421 (1978).

[118] *Fox v Vice*, 131 S Ct 2205, 2211 (2011).

[119] *Fox v Vice*, 594 F3d 423, 425 (5th Cir 2010).

[120] Id at 425–26.

[121] Id at 429.

[122] *Vice*, 131 S Ct at 2215.

on legislative purposes identified in prior opinions, her opinion distinguished the situation of a prevailing plaintiff from a prevailing defendant such as Vice. With respect to a prevailing plaintiff, Justice Kagan explained that fee-shifting statutes such as Section 1988 seek to create "private attorney[s] general"[123] to remedy civil rights violations and that fee awards to plaintiffs make federal law violators accountable for their wrongs.[124] Accordingly, plaintiffs "may receive fees . . . even if they are not victorious on every claim" because "[a] civil rights plaintiff who obtains meaningful relief has corrected a violation of federal law and, in so doing, has vindicated Congress's statutory purposes."[125] Although plaintiffs are not entitled to fees for work "that bore no relation to the grant of relief," they can recover for work that reasonably went into the development of both the successful and unsuccessful claims.[126]

In contrast, Justice Kagan noted that because "'quite different equitable considerations'" apply to prevailing defendants, Section 1988's policy merely called for fee awards that would "'protect defendants from burdensome litigation having no legal or factual basis.'"[127] Defendants, therefore, are only entitled to fees when the plaintiff brings a frivolous or baseless claim.[128] When the plaintiff brings both frivolous and nonfrivolous claims, moreover, Section 1988 "serves to relieve a defendant of the expenses [only] for the frivolous charges" that the plaintiff "acted wrongly in leveling."[129]

In light of these background policies, Justice Kagan concluded that a prevailing defendant may "recover reasonable attorney's fees incurred because, but only because of, a frivolous claim"—that is, the frivolous claim must be a "but-for" cause of the particular fees awarded.[130] The "legislative purpose[ ]" of compensating plaintiffs "for the costs of redressing civil rights" required full compensation

---

[123] Id at 2213, quoting *Newman v Piggie Park Enterprises, Inc.*, 390 US 400, 402 (1968) (per curiam).

[124] See *Vice*, 131 S Ct at 2213, discussing *Riverside v Rivera*, 477 US 561, 577–78 (1986); *Christiansburg Garment Co. v EEOC*, 434 US 412, 416, 418 (1978); *Newman*, 390 US at 402.

[125] *Vice*, 131 S Ct at 2214.

[126] Id.

[127] Id at 2213, quoting *Christiansburg Garment Co.*, 434 US at 419, 420.

[128] See *Vice*, 131 S Ct at 2213.

[129] Id at 2214.

[130] Id at 2215.

of fees jointly expended on successful and unsuccessful claims.[131] The contrasting purpose of relieving defendants of "the burden associated with fending off frivolous claims" required the reimbursement only of the "fees that those claims caused him to incur."[132]

The Court emphasized that "[i]n each context, the standard for allocating fees in 'mixed' cases matches the relevant congressional purpose."[133] None of its analysis consulted or depended on the meaning of the text. Instead, the Court drew a rather exact standard of causation (but-for cause) from rather broadly framed attributions of legislative purpose developed in common law fashion by earlier opinions of the Court. Still, even the Court's most committed textualists—Justices Scalia and Thomas—joined without protest. One can perhaps explain this broad consensus, again, by thinking about the relationship between text and purpose. Though reasonable minds could differ on the best reading of Section 1988,[134] the Court understood the key provision's open-endedness ("reasonable attorney's fee") to invite development of a common law of fee shifting. Except in contexts in which it may constitute a term of art, "reasonable" is one of those words that "have so little color of their own that they can be made to take on almost any hue."[135] Accordingly, legislative language of that sort conveys to interpreters an implemental purpose to confer discretion, within broad boundaries, to develop the details of statutory policy in light of the objectives that lurk in the background. In contrast with *Holy Trinity*, therefore, the Court in *Fox v Vice*

---

[131] Id at 2215 n 3.

[132] Id at 2215 n 3.

[133] Id.

[134] For example, as noted, the statute provides that "the court, in its discretion, may allow *the prevailing party, other than the United States*, a reasonable attorney's fee as part of the costs." 42 USC § 1988(b) (emphasis added). Because the statute does not differentiate between prevailing plaintiffs and defendants (and, in fact, singles out only the United States for distinctive treatment), one might question whether the Court's adoption of separate rules for prevailing plaintiffs and defendants read too much into Congress's invitation to develop the meaning of a "reasonable attorney's fee." Still, the important point, for present purposes, is this: Whether or not one could quibble with the Court's particular reading of Section 1988, *Fox v Vice* illustrates the way new purposivism works when the Court understands Congress to have conferred discretion through the use of open-ended language. I am grateful to David Strauss for raising this point.

[135] Radin, 43 Harv L Rev at 883–84 (cited in note 15). For the textualist take on such provisions, see Easterbrook, 50 U Chi L Rev at 544 (cited in note 16) ("The statute books are full of laws, of which the Sherman Act is a good example, that effectively authorize courts to create new lines of common law.").

viewed itself as invoking background purposes at Congress's invitation.

C. TEXTUALLY STRUCTURED PURPOSIVISM

A final example—almost surely the most purposivist statutory opinion of the Roberts Court—drives home the extent to which new purposivists accept the constraints of the statutory text while also displaying a willingness to derive purpose from the legislative history in cases of statutory ambiguity. In *Zuni Public School District No. 89 v Department of Education*,[136] the Court purposively construed a complex statutory formula for awarding federal education grants to states under the Impact Aid Act (IAA).[137] Under the IAA, the federal government provides aid to local school districts whose finances are compromised by activities of the federal government (as, for example, when a military base increases the number of school age children).[138] The statute prohibits states from offsetting federal aid by cutting state aid, except when doing so would be necessary to implement a state program to equalize per-pupil expenditures across the state.[139]

Accordingly, the U.S. Secretary of Education must determine whether a given state has a program to "equalize expenditures" on school funding throughout the state.[140] This entails determining whether the per-pupil expenditures in the district with the highest such expenditures exceed those of the district with the lowest by more than 25 percent.[141] In making that calculation, the Secretary must "disregard local educational agencies [school districts] with per-pupil expenditures . . . above the ninety-fifth percentile or below the fifth percentile of such expenditures."[142] The question presented in *Zuni* was whether this "disregard instruction" required the Secretary to calculate the fifth and ninety-fifth percentiles based on the simple number of school districts (for example, pick the top and bottom five out of one hundred districts)

---

[136] 550 US 81 (2007).

[137] 20 USC § 7701 et seq.

[138] See *Zuni*, 550 US at 84–85.

[139] See id at 85.

[140] 20 USC § 7709(b)(1) (2006).

[141] § 7709(b)(2)(A).

[142] § 7709(b)(2)(B)(i).

or to do so based on their enrollment (for example, pick those districts that in aggregate contain the top and bottom 5,000 students out of 100,000).[143] The Secretary used the latter method.[144]

No one disputed the applicability of the *Chevron* framework,[145] which called upon the Court to ask whether the IAA spoke "directly . . . to the precise question at issue" and, if not, whether the Secretary's interpretation was "reasonable."[146] What made *Zuni* controversial was the Court's decision to reverse the usual order of inquiry by beginning with the statutory purpose rather than the text.[147] In an opinion for the Court joined by Justices Stevens, Kennedy, Ginsburg, and Alito, Justice Breyer explained that "because of the technical nature of the language in question, we shall first examine the provision's background and basic purposes."[148] He noted, in that regard, that the Secretary had for two decades used the present calculation method under a prior version of the IAA, that the amendment adding the disregard instruction came from an administration bill drafted by the Secretary, and that no one in the legislative process "expressed the view that [the] language [of the disregard instruction] was intended to . . . change the Department's [long-standing] system of calculation."[149] More importantly, the Court noted that the language of the statute evinced a "purpose to exclude statistical outliers" in determining whether the state equalized expenditures across districts.[150] Calculating the "percentiles" based on the number of districts rather than the aggregate number of students in the districts, the Court concluded, would contradict that purpose.[151] Accordingly, the

---

[143] *Zuni*, 550 US at 88–89.

[144] Id at 86–87.

[145] See *Chevron USA, Inc. v Natural Resources Defense Council, Inc.*, 467 US 837 (1984).

[146] Id at 842–44.

[147] See *Zuni*, 550 US at 89–90. The Court has frequently reiterated its duty to begin statutory interpretation inquiries with the text of the statute. See, for example, *CSX Transportation, Inc. v Alabama Department of Revenue*, 131 S Ct 1101, 1107 (2011) ("We begin, as in any case of statutory interpretation, with the language of the statute."); *Landreth Timber Co. v Landreth*, 471 US 681, 685 (1985) ("It is axiomatic that '[t]he starting point in every case involving construction of a statute is the language itself.'"), quoting *Blue Chip Stamps v Manor Drug Stores*, 421 US 723, 756 (1975) (Powell, J, concurring).

[148] *Zuni*, 550 US at 90.

[149] Id at 90–91.

[150] Id at 91.

[151] The Court illustrated the point as follows:

To understand the Secretary's first problem, consider an exaggerated example,

Court found that the Secretary's calculation method "carrie[d] out Congress' likely intent in enacting the statutory provision before us."[152]

Because the Court focused first and foremost on statutory purpose, it drew a strongly worded dissent from Justice Scalia. He argued that the disregard instruction explicitly directs the Secretary to focus on "local educational agencies" whose per-pupil expenditures lie above or below the specified percentiles.[153] Finding the text to be clear,[154] Justice Scalia described the Court's opinion as heralding "the return of that miraculous redeemer of lost causes, *Church of the Holy Trinity*."[155] He denounced the Court's reliance on legislative history, reasoning that such evidence could never tell us "what a law was 'intended' to mean, for the simple reason that it is never voted upon—or ordinarily even seen

---

say, a State with 80 school districts of unequal size. Suppose 8 of the districts include urban areas and together account for 70 percent of the State's students, while the remaining 72 districts include primarily rural areas and together account for 30 percent of the State's students. If the State's greatest funding disparities are among the 8 urban districts, [the challenger's] calculation method (which looks only at the number of districts and ignores their size) would require the Secretary to disregard the system's 8 largest districts (i.e., 10 percent of the number 80) even though those 8 districts (because they together contain 70 percent of the State's pupils) are typical of, indeed characterize, the State's public school system. It would require the Secretary instead to measure the system's expenditure equality by looking only to noncharacteristic districts that are not representative of the system as a whole, indeed districts accounting for only 30 percent of the State's pupils. Thus, according to Zuni's method, the Secretary would have to certify a state aid program as one that "equalizes expenditures" even if there were gross disparities in per-pupil expenditures among urban districts accounting for 70 percent of the State's students. By way of contrast, the Secretary's method, by taking into account a district's size as well as its expenditures, would avoid a calculation that would produce results so contrary to the statute's objective.

Zuni, 550 US at 92–93.

[152] Id at 93.

[153] Id at 111–12 (Scalia, J, joined by Roberts, CJ, and Thomas, J, dissenting).

[154] Justice Scalia reasoned as follows:

The word "per" *connotes* that the expenditure or revenue is a single average figure assigned to a unit the *composite members of which* are individual pupils. And the only such unit mentioned in the statute is the local educational agency. See 20 USC § 7709(b)(2)(B)(i). It is simply irrelevant that "[n]o dictionary definition . . . suggests that there is any single logical, mathematical, or statistical link between [per-pupil expenditures or revenues] and . . . the nature of the relevant population." Of course there is not. It is the text at issue which must identify the relevant population, and it does so here quite unambiguously: "local educational agencies with per-pupil expenditures or revenues."

Id at 113, quoting § 7709(b)(2)(B)(i).

[155] *Zuni*, 550 US at 116 (Scalia, J, joined by Roberts, CJ, and Thomas, J, dissenting).

or heard—by the 'intending' lawgiving entity, which consists of both Houses of Congress and the President (if he did not veto the bill)."[156] In fact, he added, "what judges believe Congress 'meant' (apart from the text) has a disturbing but entirely unsurprising tendency to be whatever judges think Congress must have meant, *i.e.*, *should* have meant."[157] Accordingly, contrary to *Holy Trinity*, "[w]e must interpret the law as Congress has written it, not as we would wish it to be."[158]

Justice Stevens wrote separately to respond to Justice Scalia. Defending traditional purposivism, Justice Stevens argued that "[t]here is no reason why we must confine ourselves to, or begin our analysis with, the statutory text if other tools of statutory construction provide better evidence of congressional intent with respect to the precise point at issue."[159] Because he found *Zuni* "to be a case in which the legislative history is pellucidly clear and the statutory text is difficult to fathom," he would have upheld the agency's position based on the legislative history as such.[160] Citing *Holy Trinity*, however, he further stressed that the clarity of the congressional intent would have led him to the same result even if he had thought that the challenger's "literal reading of the statutory text was correct."[161]

Significantly, the Court did not endorse Justice Stevens's views or profess to have the authority to enforce purpose irrespective of the meaning of the text. Rather, consistent with shared premises of textualism and the new purposivism, Justice Breyer's opinion articulated the following framework for dealing with legislative purpose and the statutory text:

> The [literal language] is important, for normally neither the legislative history nor the reasonableness of the Secretary's method would be determinative if the plain language of the statute unambiguously indicated that Congress sought to foreclose the Secretary's interpretation. . . . Under this Court's precedents, if the intent of Congress is clear and unambiguously expressed by the statutory language at issue, that would be the end of our analysis. A customs statute that imposes a tariff

---

[156] Id at 117.

[157] Id.

[158] Id at 122.

[159] Id at 106 (Stevens, J, concurring).

[160] Id.

[161] Id at 106–07 & 107 n 3.

on "clothing" does not impose a tariff on automobiles, no matter how
strong the policy arguments for treating the two kinds of goods alike.
But we . . . believe that the Secretary's method falls within the scope
of the statute's plain language.[162]

From that starting point, the Court carefully examined the
"technical" meaning of the term "percentile" in the statute's disregard instruction. After consulting conventional, mathematical,
and scientific dictionaries, the Court concluded that the statute's
"percentile" cut-off simply tells us that the Secretary must construct a "distribution of values" consisting of "a 'population'
ranked according to a characteristic."[163] It does not, however, specify precisely what population is to be ranked for that purpose—
that is, whether it is to be the districts themselves or the aggregate
numbers of students within those districts.[164] Accordingly, the
Court concluded that nothing in the statutory language precluded
the Secretary from using "the State's students as the relevant population for calculating the specified percentiles" of local school
districts.[165]

Whether the majority or the dissent had the better of this difficult statutory question is quite beside the point. Rather, the important point, for present purposes, is that the Court thought it
necessary to go to great lengths to establish that the language of
the statute could accommodate the Secretary's result. Contrary to
Justice Stevens's attempt to revive the *Holy Trinity* framework, the
Court evidently did not think it sufficient to establish that the
legislative purpose, as derived from the tenor of the act and its
legislative history, clearly supported the Secretary's position. Instead, the Court thought it necessary to show "that the language

---

[162] Id at 93–94 (majority opinion). It is worth noting that Justice Breyer himself seems
to subscribe to traditional purposivism. Stephen Breyer, *Active Liberty: Interpreting Our
Democratic Constitution* 85–101 (Knopf, 2005) ("*Active Liberty*") (defending strong purposivism).

[163] *Zuni*, 550 US at 95. See also id at 94–95 (examining the definitions found in John
Black, *A Dictionary of Economics* 348–49 (2d ed 2002); Christopher Clapham and James
Nicholson, *The Concise Oxford Dictionary of Mathematics* 378–79 (3d ed 2005); *The American
Heritage Science Dictionary* 468 (2005); *Merriam-Webster's Medical Desk Dictionary* 612
(2002); *Webster's Third New International Dictionary* 1675 (1961)).

[164] See *Zuni*, 550 US at 96 ("No dictionary definition we have found suggests that there
is any *single* logical, mathematical, or statistical link between, on the one hand, the characterizing data (used for ranking purposes) and, on the other hand, the nature of the
relevant population or how that population might be weighted for purposes of determining
a percentile cutoff.").

[165] Id.

of the statute is broad enough to permit the Secretary's reading."[166] That fact alone allowed the Court "to look beyond the language to determine whether the Secretary's interpretation is a reasonable, and hence permissible, implementation of the statute."[167]

Zuni is, therefore, of a piece with *Milner* and *Vice*. Although the Court in *Zuni* was more deeply divided over the indicia of meaning than it was in the other two cases, the basic framework in all three was identical: The statute's background purpose was relevant and might even have been dispositive. But the Court felt it necessary to take its cues from the statute itself about how and to what extent it had discretion to take such purpose into account. Accordingly, in contrast with the traditional purposivism of *Holy Trinity*, the Court's new purposivism makes clear that background statutory purpose cannot trump the clear import of the statutory text.

III. The New Purposivism and the Purposivist Tradition

Milner, *Vice*, and *Zuni* suggest a new synthesis in the Court. In recent years, only two Members of the Court—Justices Stevens and Breyer—have endorsed *Holy Trinity*'s premise that expressions of intent or purpose culled from the legislative history can trump the statutory text.[168] At the same time, however, at most two others—Justice Scalia and perhaps Justice Thomas—have subscribed fully to the implications of the new textualism, professing opposition to the use of legislative history even to resolve ambiguity or confirm statutory meaning.[169] The balance of the Court seems

---

[166] Id at 100.

[167] Id.

[168] Indeed, in the past two decades, only Justice Stevens's concurring opinion in *Zuni* has cited *Holy Trinity* for the proposition that the spirit can trump the letter of the law. Justice Breyer has explicitly endorsed atextual purposivism only in academic writing. See Breyer, *Active Liberty* 85–101 (cited in note 162) (defending traditional purposivism). Justice Stevens, joined by Justice Breyer, has also written separate opinions stating that judges should rely on legislative history regardless of whether a statute is ambiguous—a position closely allied with *Holy Trinity*-style purposivism. See, for example, *Exxon Mobil Corp. v Allapattah Services, Inc.*, 545 US 546, 573–77 (2005) (Stevens, J, joined by Breyer, J, dissenting); *Koons Buick Pontiac GMC, Inc. v Nigh*, 543 US 50, 65–66 (2004) (Stevens, J, joined by Breyer, J, concurring).

[169] Justice Scalia has expressed that view in a number of well-known separate opinions declining to join opinions of the Court that relied on legislative history. See, for example, *Wisconsin Public Intervenor v Mortier*, 501 US 597, 620 (1991) (Scalia, J, concurring in the judgment); *Blanchard v Bergeron*, 489 US 87, 99 (1989) (Scalia, J, concurring in part and concurring in the judgment). Justice Thomas has not taken the same categorical stance

to consist of textually constrained purposivists (or, what may be the same thing, purpose-sensitive textualists). Two decades ago, it was black letter law that the Court had legitimate authority to enforce statutory purpose in the teeth of the statutory text.[170] As *Milner*, *Vice*, and *Zuni* illustrate, however, the Court's propensity to rely on background purpose now depends upon the degree to which the text of the statute permits it.

Justices raised within the purposivist tradition have been essential to this trend—including the Court's rather decisive repudiation of *Holy Trinity*. This fact invites the question, Why have they gone along with this quite significant change in practice? Have they simply bought into the premises of the new textualism, or might some other factor explain their abandonment of the traditional idea that spirit trumps letter?

This part argues that if one takes seriously the core premises of purposivism—that Congress passes legislation for a purpose and that a faithful agent must interpret the statute to fulfill its purposes—then the textual constraint element of the new purposivism follows. Consider these key structural features of the U.S. Constitution. While Congress lacks constitutional authority to execute its own laws, the Necessary and Proper Clause gives Congress express authority to determine, within constitutional limits, how law executors are to carry statutes into effect—to prescribe an implemental purpose for its legislation. In particular, the Court's recent nondelegation doctrine decisions (including *Chevron*) have firmly established that Congress's power over law implementation includes very broad authority over the degree of discretion it wishes to assign to agencies or courts.[171] By paying attention to the divergent levels of generality at which Congress writes its laws,

---

against legislative history that Justice Scalia has. From time to time, however, Justice Thomas will decline to join an opinion of the Court simply because of its citation on legislative history. See, for example, *Samantar v Yousuf*, 130 S Ct 2278, 2293 (2010) (Thomas, J, concurring in part and concurring in the judgment) (joining "the Court's opinion except for those parts relying on the legislative history"); *Wyeth v Levine*, 555 US 555, 594 (2009) (Thomas, J, concurring in the judgment) ("The cases improperly rely on legislative history, broad atextual notions of congressional purpose, and even congressional inaction in order to pre-empt state law.").

[170] See, for example, *United States v Ron Pair Enterprises, Inc.*, 489 US 235, 242 (1989) ("The plain meaning of legislation should be conclusive, except in the 'rare cases [in which] the literal application of a statute will produce a result demonstrably at odds with the intentions of its drafters.'"), quoting *Griffin v Oceanic Contractors, Inc.*, 458 US 564, 571 (1982).

[171] See text accompanying notes 141–54.

interpreters enable Congress to express that crucial implemental purpose through its choice of words. Precise laws leave implementers little discretion; open-ended statutes leave a great deal. One cannot fully account for the purpose of a statute without acknowledging that crucial signal.

Traditional purposivism as reflected in *Holy Trinity* and its ilk erred in focusing exclusively on what Professor Max Radin called the "ulterior purposes" of a statute—the background public policy justification that inspired legislators to act.[172] Such cases did not recognize the importance of "implemental purpose"—the decision about how much discretion interpreters should have in carrying out a statute's ulterior purposes. By giving effect to both types of legislative purpose, the new purposivists' emphasis on textual constraints serves rather than disserves the fundamental premises of purposivist theory. In other words, the Court's new approach, though constrained by the statutory text, nonetheless remains a theory of purposivism.

Section A offers a purposivist justification for textually constrained purposivism, focusing on the idea of institutional settlement that lies at the core of the most prominent account of purposivism—Hart and Sacks's Legal Process materials. Section B preliminarily explores some of the implications of the new, textually constrained purposivism. In particular, it considers the new purposivists' appropriate posture toward the use of legislative history and the various forms of semantic evidence conventionally used to determine textual meaning.

A. THE NEW PURPOSIVISM AND INSTITUTIONAL SETTLEMENT

In examining whether the textual constraints of the new purposivism fit within the purposivist tradition, I rely primarily on the work of Professors Hart and Sacks, whose influential Legal Process materials supplied the most widely accepted justification of the practice in the postwar period.[173] First, at least as relevant here, purposivism rests on the premise of legislative supremacy.[174]

---

[172] Radin, 43 Harv L Rev at 876 (cited in note 15).

[173] For discussion of Hart and Sacks's influence, see, for example, T. Alexander Aleinikoff, *Updating Statutory Interpretation*, 87 Mich L Rev 20, 26–27 (1988); William N. Eskridge Jr. and Philip P. Frickey, *Legislation Scholarship and Pedagogy in the Post-Legal Process Era*, 48 U Pitt L Rev 691, 698–99 (1987).

[174] See note 38.

As Hart and Sacks emphasized, interpreters in our system of government must "[r]espect the position of the legislature as the chief policy-determining agency of the society, subject only to the limitations of the constitution."[175] Second, Congress passes laws to accomplish something; hence, "[t]he idea of a statute without an intelligible purpose is foreign to the idea of law and inadmissible."[176] Third, given those starting premises, interpreters should determine "what purpose ought to be attributed to the statute" and then "[i]nterpret the words of the statute immediately in question so as to carry out its purpose as best it can."[177]

These starting premises can of course support traditional, *Holy Trinity*-style purposivism, and Hart and Sacks at various points suggest that it does.[178] At the same time, however, one can also see the new purposivism in key elements of the Hart and Sacks materials. After considering both positions, I contend here that the new purposivism better reconciles the core premises of the Legal Process approach with those of our constitutional structure.

1. *The purposivist case for traditional purposivism.* One can easily derive *Holy Trinity*-style traditional purposivism from the previously described elements of the Hart and Sacks framework. No one has explained it more cogently than Max Radin, a prominent legal realist whose late-career embrace of purposivism helped lay some of the intellectual groundwork for the Legal Process approach.[179] Like Hart and Sacks, Radin believed that "[t]he legislature that put the statute on the books had the constitutional right and power to set [the statute's] purpose as a desirable one for the community, and the court or administrator has the undoubted duty to obey it."[180] In addition, he contended that because the words in a statute have been selected "primarily to let us know

---

[175] Hart and Sacks, *The Legal Process* at 1374 (cited in note 26).

[176] Id at 1124. See also Archibald Cox, *Judge Learned Hand and the Interpretation of Statutes*, 60 Harv L Rev 370, 370 (1947) (noting that some "purpose lies behind all intelligible legislation"); Frankfurter, 47 Colum L Rev at 538–39 (cited in note 39) ("Legislation has an aim; it seeks to obviate some mischief, to supply an inadequacy, to effect a change of policy, to formulate a plan of government.").

[177] Hart and Sacks, *The Legal Process* at 1374 (cited in note 26).

[178] See text accompanying notes 185–93.

[179] See Max Radin, *A Short Way with Statutes*, 56 Harv L Rev 388 (1942). For discussion of Radin's contribution to the intellectual movement culminating in the Legal Process approach, see William N. Eskridge Jr., and Philip P. Frickey, *Statutory Interpretation as Practical Reasoning*, 42 Stan L Rev 321, 332–33 (1990).

[180] Radin, 56 Harv L Rev at 398 (cited in note 179).

the statutory purpose,"[181] they must be read with that function in mind. These starting premises led him to question the impulse toward strict textual fidelity:

> To say that the legislature is "presumed" to have selected its phraseology with meticulous care as to every word is in direct contradiction of known facts and injects an improper element into the relation of courts to the statutes. The legislature has no constitutional warrant to demand reverence for the words in which it frames its directives. If the purposes of the statute cannot be learned except by examining the precise words and by troubling our ingenuity to discover why this word was used rather than another of approximately similar effect, then this process of anxious cogitation must be employed. But it is rarely necessary.[182]

In other words, if the courts in our constitutional system have an obligation to see a statute's apparent purpose fulfilled, they must not fasten on every semantic detail. Rather, "if the purpose is clear, the implemental part of the statute should be subordinated to it."[183]

Although Hart and Sacks, as discussed below, exhorted interpreters not to give statutes a meaning their language would not bear,[184] elements of their analysis seem more in sync with the Radin position. Implicitly endorsing the New York Court of Appeals's famously atextual opinion in *Riggs v Palmer*,[185] Hart and Sacks questioned both the institutional legitimacy and institutional desirability of the judiciary's "laying down a flat rule that general words in a statute which are expressed without qualification are to be read without qualification."[186] As to legitimacy, they asked whether "human experience shows that a policymaker's purposes are usually best served if those who have to carry out his policies always take his general expressions literally, without regard to the possibility of unexpressed or unanticipated situations."[187] Turning to institutional desirability, they asked whether a literal approach

---

[181] Id at 400.

[182] Id at 406.

[183] Id at 407.

[184] See text accompanying notes 209–11.

[185] 115 NY 506 (1889). *Riggs* held that a legatee who killed the testator in order to gain his inheritance forfeited his rights under the will, even though the will had been duly executed under the statute of wills and the statute contained no applicable exception. See id at 514. The court reasoned that the statute implicitly incorporated an unwritten common law principle that a wrongdoer shall not profit from his or her wrong. See id at 511–12.

[186] Hart and Sacks, *The Legal Process* at 90 (cited in note 26).

[187] Id at 91.

would, in fact, provoke clearer, better drafting or, instead, un-realistically ask legislatures to "go[ ] into great detail in dealing with all possible problems."[188]

Consistent with these concerns, the relevant sections of Hart and Sacks emphasized that "[t]he meaning of words can almost always be narrowed if the context seems to call for the narrow-ing"[189]—a qualifier that nicely describes *Holy Trinity* itself.[190] In addition, although somewhat less clear in their endorsement of purposive extensions of a statute, Hart and Sacks also seemed willing to reach situations "seemingly within [a statute's] purpose but not within any accepted meaning of its words."[191] Although rejecting the idea that such a move could be grounded on a reading of the particular legislative command, Hart and Sacks suggested that "it may nevertheless be proper for the court to rely upon the policy expressed in the statute in formulating, upon its own re-sponsibility, a parallel ground of decision in the case at bar."[192] This flexible approach had other important subscribers in the post-war heyday of traditional purposivism.[193]

2. The purposivist case for respecting textual constraints. While Ra-din's take on basic purposivism is more than plausible, it presents a serious conceptual difficulty that becomes apparent when one reads Radin's work from an earlier, realist phase. In a famous article entitled simply "Statutory Interpretation," Radin argued that reliance on legislative purpose created serious difficulties re-lating to the level of generality at which one describes the relevant purpose.[194] Even the early Radin acknowledged that statutes are

---

[188] Id at 92.

[189] Id at 1376.

[190] See text accompanying notes 44–51.

[191] Hart and Sacks, *The Legal Process* at 1194 (cited in note 26).

[192] Id.

[193] The most prominent example would be the defense of atextual purposivism attributed to the fictional Justice Foster in Lon L. Fuller's article, *The Case of the Speluncean Explorers*:

> There are those who raise the cry of judicial usurpation whenever a court, after analyzing the purpose of a statute, gives to its words a meaning that is not at once apparent to the casual reader who has not studied the statute closely or examined the objectives it seeks to attain. . . . The correction of obvious leg-islative errors or oversights is not to supplant the legislative will, but to make that will effective.

Fuller, 62 Harv L Rev at 625–26 (cited in note 52).

[194] See Radin, 43 Harv L Rev at 876–78 (cited in note 15).

enacted for a purpose; indeed, he thought it "rare indeed that we can not say positively what any particular statute is for, by reading it."[195] He quickly added, however, that "[t]here are purposes and purposes" and that "nearly every end is a means to another end."[196] In fact, if one carries the idea far enough, "the avowed and ultimate purposes of all statutes, because of all law, are justice and security."[197] Accordingly, he wrote, "to interpret a law by its purposes requires the court to select one of a concatenated sequence of purposes, and this choice is to be determined by motives which are usually suppressed."[198]

To make Radin's point more concrete, consider the previously discussed example, "No dogs in the park."[199] One way to describe its purpose is that it is "to ban dogs from the park." One could, with equal justification, say that it is "to keep disruptive animals out of the park," "to promote the hygiene and safety of the park," "to promote recreational enjoyment," or, indeed, "to promote human welfare." If so, how does an interpreter determine at what level of generality to describe the purpose of the statute? Read at the lowest level of generality ("no dogs"), the statutory purpose might not ban potentially disruptive noncanines such as ferrets, potbellied pigs, or even pet tiger cubs. At a higher level of generality ("promote recreational enjoyment"), one might say that the statutory purpose could justify excluding loud music or go-carts from the park.

In contrast with the Court's traditional purposivism as reflected in *Holy Trinity*, the new purposivism takes a crucial cue about purpose more directly from Congress's choice of words. Legislation ranges from the breathtakingly open-ended to the mind-numbingly precise.[200] And, as some leading purposivists have rec-

---

[195] Id at 876.

[196] Id.

[197] Id.

[198] Id at 878.

[199] See text accompanying note 16.

[200] Compare 47 USC § 307(a) (instructing the FCC to allocate radio station licenses in conformity with what will serve the "public convenience, interest, or necessity"), with 21 USC § 841(b)(1)(B)(vi) (imposing a mandatory minimum penalty for persons who possess with intent to distribute "40 grams or more of a mixture or substance containing a detectable amount of N-phenyl-N-[1-(2-phenylethyl)-4-piperidinyl] propanamide or 10 grams or more of a mixture or substance containing a detectable amount of any analogue of N-phenyl-N-[1-(2-phenylethyl)-4-piperidinyl] propanamide"). Of course, even a statute as precise as § 841(b)(1)(B)(vi) will present some interpretive challenges. Compare *Chap-*

ognized, Congress sends a very different signal to judges, executors, and the regulated public when it uses open-ended ("no disruptive animals") rather than precise ("no dogs") language.[201] This reality has implications for how one thinks about the core principles underlying purposivism.

It may seem senseless to limit a "no dogs" statute to *canis familiaris* when the evils at which it was directed surely reach a tiger cub. Indeed, legislative history may irrefutably demonstrate that such a statute was inspired by an ulterior purpose to free the parks of disruptive animals. But specifying "no dogs" also conveys the purpose to adopt a hard-edged rule, which is a choice to opt for definiteness at the cost of inevitable over- and underinclusiveness.[202] To borrow *Holy Trinity*'s conceit, lawmakers may have misspoken when they said dogs rather than disruptive animals. But using ulterior purpose to convert a "no dogs" statute into a "no disruptive animals" statute denies legislators the power to use precise language to limit the discretion of implementers and to define the space within which interpreters properly take ulterior purposes into account. If one accepts the constitutional tradition of legislative supremacy and the reality of purposive legislation, it is odd, to say the least, to assume that Congress conveys no binding purpose in the decision to opt for a rule versus a standard or a standard versus a rule.

Although, as noted, Hart and Sacks can be read to support

---

man v United States, 500 US 453, 457–64 (1991) (giving an inclusive reading to the "mixture or substance" language as used in a related provision), with id at 469–74 (Stevens, J, dissenting) (reading the same language more narrowly). That reality, however, does not alter the fact that Congress chooses to express itself at many different levels of statutory precision and generality.

[201] See, for example, Jerome Frank, *Words and Music: Some Remarks on Statutory Interpretation*, 47 Colum L Rev 1259, 1267 (1947) ("A legislature can make plain when it wants literalness, and when it wants to authorize judicial legislation."); Frankfurter, 47 Colum L Rev at 534 (cited in note 39) ("Even in matters legal some words and phrases, though very few, approach mathematical symbols and mean substantially the same to all who have occasion to use them. Other law terms like 'police power' are not symbols at all but labels for the results of the whole process of adjudication. There are differing shades of compulsion for judges behind different words. . . .").

[202] This argument is a staple of textualist theory. See Easterbrook, 50 U Chi L Rev at 546–47 (cited in note 16) (noting that the treatment of rules as standards or standards as rules "denies to legislatures the choice of creating or withholding gapfilling authority"). For the reasons discussed in this article's text, however, this approach also fits comfortably within the framework of purposivist theory. For discussion of the many factors that go into choice between rules and standards, see, for example, Louis Kaplow, *Rules Versus Standards: An Economic Analysis*, 42 Duke L J 557, 591 (1992); Colin S. Diver, *The Optimal Precision of Administrative Rules*, 93 Yale L J 65, 73 (1983).

traditional purposivism, one can also see the foundation for the new purposivism in the Legal Process materials. One of Hart and Sacks's central assumptions was that of "institutional settlement."[203] The idea is straightforward. To prevent social chaos, we have established "regular and peaceable methods of decision."[204] And "[t]he principle of institutional settlement expresses the judgment that decisions which are the duly arrived at result of duly established procedures . . . ought to be accepted as binding."[205] This principle justifies observing positive law, even when it produces awkward results that are hard to justify on the merits. As Hart and Sacks wrote:

> When the principle of institutional settlement is plainly applicable, we say that the law "is" thus and so, and brush aside further discussion of what it "ought" to be. Yet the "is" is not really an "is" but a special kind of "ought"—a statement that, for the reasons just reviewed, a decision which is the duly arrived at result of a duly established procedure for making decisions of this kind "ought" to be accepted as binding upon the whole society unless and until it has been duly changed.[206]

When a "particular settlement" is "the product of a particular kind of procedure," Hart and Sacks noted that considerations peculiar to that procedure will "aid in determining the effect to be given decisions arrived at in accordance with that procedure."[207]

Of course, it does not necessarily follow that the idea of institutional settlement leads to a textually constrained form of purposivism.[208] Still, if Congress has the authority to determine how much discretion to leave to its interpreters, the idea of institutional settlement suggests that interpreters should respect the level of generality through which lawmakers specified the means of statutory implementation. Hart and Sacks seem to have thought the same, even if they showed some inconstancy in application. They emphasized that while interpreters should read statutes purpo-

---

[203] Hart and Sacks, *The Legal Process* at 4 (cited in note 26).

[204] Id.

[205] Id.

[206] Id at 5.

[207] Id.

[208] Indeed, in their discussion of institutional settlement, Hart and Sacks noted that the concept left many questions to be answered, including: "'Ought' this statute to be read as reaching this situation which its words literally cover but its apparent purpose does not?" Id.

sively, they must not "give the words . . . a meaning they will not
bear."[209] Importantly, they elaborated as follows:

> The proposition that a court ought never to give the words of a statute
> a meaning they will not bear is a corollary of the propositions that
> courts are bound to respect the constitutional position of the legislature
> and the constitutional procedures for the enactment of legislation.
>
>   The words of the statute are what the legislature has enacted as law,
> and all that it has the power to enact. Unenacted intentions or wishes
> cannot be given effect as law.[210]

Indeed, sounding the theme that semantic meaning is the currency
used by a legislature to express its purposes, Hart and Sacks added
that interpreters "cannot permit the legislative process, and all the
other processes which depend upon the integrity of language, to
be subverted by the misuse of words."[211] This element of Hart
and Sacks sounds very much like the new purposivism.

Again, these passages of Hart and Sacks coexist awkwardly with
the simultaneous endorsement of practices that call for interpreters
to clip back statutes or to extend their reach to omitted cases falling
within a statute's purposes. Still, it may be possible to reconcile
at least some of Hart and Sacks's seemingly atextual impulses with
the respect for textual constraint that characterizes the new purposivism. For example, when Hart and Sacks endorsed the practice
of paring back the generality of language, they emphasized "the
recurrent possibilities of reading general language as subject to
assumed but unexpressed qualifications in terms of customary defenses or other limiting policies of the law."[212] As I have argued
elsewhere, because textual meaning depends on the practices of a
relevant linguistic community and because the legal community
shares a rich set of *established* background conventions that apply
in recognizable situations, this sort of contextual "narrowing" is

---

[209] Id at 1374.

[210] Id at 1375.

[211] Id.

[212] Id at 1192. This principle may better account for their famous endorsement of *Riggs
v Palmer*. See note 185. Far from treating that case as a precedent for atextual interpretation, Hart and Sacks defended it as an application of the convention that statutes are
to be read in light of the settled common law principle that a person should not profit
from his or her own wrongdoing. See Hart and Sacks, *The Legal Process* at 89 (cited in
note 26).

fully consistent with the premises of fidelity to textual meaning.[213] Similarly, when Hart and Sacks endorsed a court's using the policy of a statute as the basis for "formulating, upon [the court's] own responsibility, a parallel ground of decision in the case at bar," they seem to be referring to those contexts in which courts independently have common law powers.[214] Accordingly, that proposition may not support purposive expansion of a statute to cover omitted cases in the routine context in which federal courts lack independent common law powers.[215]

I am prepared, however, to assume that both the traditional and new versions of purposivism find some support in the great book. In the section that follows,[216] I argue that the new purposivism's emphasis on implemental purpose fits more tightly with the Court's contemporary structural constitutional doctrine. In par-

---

[213] See Manning, 116 Harv L Rev at 2465–76 (cited in note 65). Indeed, this intuition underlies the Court's practice of assuming that Congress enacts legislation against the backdrop of its established interpretive conventions. Textualist Justices, moreover, routinely read established doctrines of tolling into facially unqualified statutes of limitations and established defenses into facially unqualified criminal statutes. See, for example, *Young v United States*, 535 US 43, 49–50 (2002) (Scalia, J) (holding that "Congress must be presumed to draft limitations periods in light of th[e] background principle" that statutes of limitations are subject to equitable tolling); *Staples v United States*, 511 US 600, 605 (1994) (Thomas, J) ("[W]e must construe [a criminal] statute in light of the background rules of the common law, in which the requirement of some *mens rea* for a crime is firmly embedded.") (citations omitted).

Hart and Sacks also defended contextual narrowing in light of the principle that one should read language, where appropriate, in its specialized or colloquial sense rather than in its literal or dictionary sense. See Hart and Sacks, *The Legal Process* at 1192 (cited in note 26); see also text accompanying notes 287 and 291 (elaborating on those techniques). For example, Hart and Sacks relied on such a principle to argue that locomotives fell within a railroad safety statute requiring that "any car" have automatic couplers. See Hart and Sacks, *The Legal Process* at 1142–43 (cited in note 26) (critiquing *Johnson v Southern Pacific Co.*, 117 F 462 (8th Cir 1902), reversed by 196 US 1 (1904)). Hart and Sacks argued that even if a locomotive is literally distinct from a railroad car, common usage would include a locomotive within that descriptor. See id at 1142 (arguing that a child who asked for a "'train of cars'" for a gift would surely expect not only "a string of shiny . . . non-self-propelling cars," but also a locomotive). Whether or not their particular analysis is correct, Hart and Sacks made the effort, as new purposivists do, to show that an accepted understanding of the text would accommodate the statute's apparent purpose. See Part II.C and note 272.

[214] Hart and Sacks, *The Legal Process* at 1194 (cited in note 26). In support of a court's power to use statutory policy to derive its own rule of decision, Hart and Sacks relied on *The T.J. Hooper*, 60 F2d 737 (2d Cir 1932), an admiralty case.

[215] See, for example, *Texas Industries, Inc. v Radcliff Materials, Inc.*, 451 US 630, 641 (1981) (holding that federal courts possess common law powers only in limited enclaves involving "the rights and obligations of the United States, interstate and international disputes implicating the conflicting rights of States or our relations with foreign nations, and admiralty cases") (citations omitted).

[216] See Part III.A.3.

ticular, the Court's structural cases have emphasized that Congress cannot retain *direct* control over the implementation of its own laws but can determine, within very broad limits, how much discretion to confer upon those who do implement such laws. As discussed below, these related developments accentuate the need to take seriously the implemental purpose conveyed by the level of generality in Congress's choice of words.

3. *Congressional control over implemental discretion.* While the foregoing discussion suggests that both the traditional and new versions of purposivism can plausibly find support in the Legal Process tradition, let me suggest that the new purposivism and its emphasis on implemental purpose fit better with certain core assumptions of the American constitutional structure. Both versions of purposivism represent plausible accounts of how to give effect to the idea of legislative supremacy—of how best to serve as a faithful agent of the legislature. But legislative supremacy means little in the abstract; it carries distinctive meanings in different constitutional traditions.[217] Under the United States Constitution, the idea of legislative supremacy must be understood in light of the fact that the Constitution explicitly assigns *Congress* authority to determine the means by which federal power is to be effectuated. The Necessary and Proper Clause of course confers upon Congress the power "[t]o make all Laws which shall be necessary and proper for carrying into Execution the foregoing Powers, and all other Powers vested by this Constitution in the Government of the United States, or in any Department or Officer thereof."[218] As the Court explained in its pivotal decision in *McCulloch v Maryland*,[219] even "in the absence of this clause, congress would have some choice of means."[220] Under traditional rules of construction, a grant of power implies a further grant of incidental powers necessary to implement the underlying grant.[221] The Necessary and

---

[217] Cf Manning, 101 Colum L Rev at 36–78 (cited in note 38) (contrasting the American constitutional conception of legislative supremacy with the common law conception that had prevailed in England).

[218] US Const, Art I, § 8, cl 18.

[219] 17 US (4 Wheat) 316 (1819).

[220] Id at 419.

[221] See, for example, Thomas M. Cooley, *A Treatise on the Constitutional Limitations Which Rest Upon the Legislative Power of the United States of the American Union* 77 (1883) (Lawbook Exchange, ltd ed 1998) (noting the "general rule, that when a constitution gives a general power, or enjoins a duty, it also gives, by implication, every particular power necessary for the exercise of the one or the performance of the other").

new purposivism, the brute reality is that long-settled doctrine has by now placed the permissibility of broad delegations beyond reasonable doubt.[231] The Court has, of course, repeatedly affirmed that Article I vests nondelegable "legislative" power exclusively in Congress.[232] At the same time, however, the Court has, with equal force, stressed that as long as Congress provides an "intelligible principle" to guide the law's implementation, a delegatee can be thought of as merely carrying out or executing congressional policy rather than exercising legislative power as such.[233] In applying this weak nondelegation doctrine, the Court has only twice—both times in the same year—found that Congress had impermissibly delegated legislative power to an agency.[234] In countless other cases, the Court has sustained "intelligible principles" as vaporous as "fair and equitable,"[235] "just and reasonable,"[236] and "public interest, convenience, and necessity."[237]

tolerate such grants to the executive). Adjudication of this hard-fought historical dispute is beyond this paper's scope.

[231] See, for example, *Textile Workers Union of America v Lincoln Mills of Alabama*, 353 US 448, 455–56, 459 (1957) (sustaining a delegation of power to the courts to make federal common law for the enforcement of collective bargaining agreements); *Lichter v United States*, 334 US 742, 785–86 (1948) (upholding a statute authorizing agency to recoup "excessive profits" on war contracts); *American Power & Light Co. v SEC*, 329 US 90, 104 (1946) (sustaining a statute authorizing the SEC to reject public utility reorganizations that are "unduly or unnecessarily complicate[d]" and do not "unfairly or inequitably distribute voting power among security holders"); see also text accompanying notes 235–37.

[232] See, for example, *Loving v United States*, 517 US 748, 758 (1996) ("The fundamental precept of the delegation doctrine is that the lawmaking function belongs to Congress, U.S. Const., Art. I, § 1, and may not be conveyed to another branch or entity."); *Touby v United States*, 500 US 160, 164–65 (1991) ("The Constitution provides that: '[a]ll legislative Powers herein granted shall be vested in a Congress of the United States.' From this language the Court has derived the non-delegation doctrine: that Congress may not constitutionally delegate its legislative power to another branch of Government.") (citations omitted).

[233] See, for example, *ICC v Goodrich Transit Co.*, 224 US 194, 214 (1912) ("The Congress may not delegate its purely legislative power to a commission, but, having laid down the general rules of action under which a commission shall proceed, it may require of that commission the application of such rules to particular situations and the investigation of facts, with a view to making orders in a particular matter within the rules laid down by the Congress."); *Union Bridge Co. v United States*, 204 US 364, 386 (1907) (holding that in implementing a permissibly definite delegation, "the Secretary of War will only execute the clearly-expressed will of Congress, and will not, in any true sense, exert legislative or judicial power").

[234] See *ALA Schechter Poultry Corp. v United States*, 295 US 495 (1935); *Panama Refining Co. v Ryan*, 293 US 388 (1935).

[235] See *Yakus v United States*, 321 US 414, 420, 423–26 (1944) (wartime price control).

[236] See *Federal Power Commission v Hope Natural Gas Co.*, 320 US 591, 600 (1944) (natural gas ratemaking).

[237] See *National Broadcasting Co. v United States*, 319 US 190, 225–26 (1943) (broadcast licensing).

The resultant legislative authority—to decide whether to sweat the details or to ask the coordinate branches to do so—necessarily reflects a judgment about Congress's implemental powers under the Necessary and Proper Clause. (Indeed, it is difficult to see from what other constitutional source that authority could derive.) As the Court thus explained in a pivotal nondelegation precedent that invoked *McCulloch* by name:

> Congress is not confined to that method of executing its policy which involves the least possible delegation of discretion to administrative officers. It is free to avoid the rigidity of such a system, which might well result in serious hardship, and to choose instead the flexibility attainable by the use of less restrictive standards. Only if we could say that there is an absence of standards for the guidance of the [law executor's] action, so that it would be impossible in a proper proceeding to ascertain whether the will of Congress has been obeyed, would we be justified in overriding its choice of means for effecting its declared purpose. . . .[238]

Other cases are to similar effect.[239] Within broad boundaries, Congress may ask the coordinate branches to fill in policy details when detailed legislative policymaking "would be impracticable, in view of the vast and varied interests which require national legislation from time to time."[240]

Indeed, in the period in which both textualism and the new purposivism emerged, two doctrinal developments underscored this deeply rooted structural reality. First, in a prominent nondelegation decision, the Court signaled that it was all but getting out of the business of policing the nondelegation doctrine through judicial review. In *Whitman v American Trucking Associations*,[241] the Court sustained a statutory provision requiring the Environmental

---

[238] *Yakus*, 321 US at 425–26 (citations omitted).

[239] See, for example, *Currin v Wallace*, 306 US 1, 15 (1939) ("The Constitution has never been regarded as denying to the Congress the necessary resources of flexibility and practicality, which will enable it to perform its function in laying down policies and establishing standards, while leaving to selected instrumentalities the making of subordinate rules within prescribed limits and the determination of facts to which the policy as declared by the Legislature is to apply."), quoting *Panama Refining*, 293 US at 421; *J. W. Hampton, Jr., & Co. v United States*, 276 US 394, 406 (1928) ("The field of Congress involves all and many varieties of legislative action, and Congress has found it frequently necessary to use officers of the executive branch within defined limits, to secure the exact effect intended by its acts of legislation, by vesting discretion in such officers to make public regulations interpreting a statute and directing the details of its execution. . . .").

[240] *Union Bridge Co. v United States*, 204 US 364, 386 (1907).

[241] 531 US 457 (2001).

Protection Agency to set ambient air quality standards at a level "requisite to protect the public health" with "an adequate margin of safety."[242] Despite the open-endedness of the standard, the Court found "adequate margin of safety" no less intelligible than countless statutory standards that it had approved in the past.[243] More importantly, however, the Court emphasized that virtually all laws leave their implementers some degree of discretion.[244] But determining the precise limits of permissibly delegable discretion lay beyond the Court's competence. Accordingly, as Justice Scalia wrote in an opinion for the Court joined by seven of his colleagues, "we have 'almost never felt qualified to second-guess Congress regarding the permissible degree of policy judgment that can be left to those executing or applying the law.'"[245] In other words, by the Court's lights, *Congress* has responsibility for determining the appropriate degree of discretion to confer upon agencies and courts.[246]

Second, the Court's most important administrative law decision of this period points to a like conclusion. In *Chevron USA, Inc. v Natural Resources Defense Council, Inc.*,[247] the Court abandoned an elaborate multifactor framework for determining when a reviewing court should "defer" to an agency's interpretation of the organic act administered by the agency.[248] Instead, in those procedural contexts in which the Court thinks it likely that Congress would wish to delegate interstitial lawmaking power to agencies,[249] *Chev-*

---

[242] 42 USC § 7409(b)(1).

[243] See *Whitman*, 531 US at 473–76.

[244] Id at 475 ("[A] certain degree of discretion, and thus of lawmaking, inheres in most executive or judicial action."), quoting *Mistretta v United States*, 488 US 361, 417 (1989) (Scalia, J, dissenting) (emphasis omitted).

[245] *Whitman*, 531 US at 474–75, quoting *Mistretta*, 488 US at 416 (Scalia, J, dissenting).

[246] See *Whitman*, 531 US at 474–75.

[247] 467 US 837 (1984).

[248] Under the pre-*Chevron* regime, reviewing courts were more likely to defer if, for example, the matter involved a question of lesser importance, the interpretive question called for agency expertise, or the organic act expressly granted rulemaking authority. See John F. Manning, *Constitutional Structure and Judicial Deference to Agency Interpretations of Agency Rules*, 96 Colum L Rev 612, 624 (1996) (describing the multifactor test).

[249] Subsequent to *Chevron*, the Court made clear that *Chevron* applies only in circumstances in which Congress has assigned agencies the authority to adopt interpretations that bind with the force of law. See *United States v Mead Corp.*, 533 US 218, 229–31 (2001). The Court thought it "fair to assume generally that Congress contemplates administrative action with the effect of law when it provides for a relatively formal administrative procedure tending to foster the fairness and deliberation that should underlie a pronouncement of such force." Id at 230. In the Court's view, the paradigmatic contexts

ron treats indeterminacy as the trigger for inferring delegation. If a reviewing court applying traditional tools of statutory construction concludes that Congress "has directly spoken to the precise question at issue," then "that is the end of the matter; for the court, as well as the agency, must give effect to the unambiguously expressed intent of Congress."[250] If, however, "the statute is silent or ambiguous with respect to the specific issue," then the reviewing court must uphold the agency's position if it is "reasonable" or "permissible."[251] Under this framework, because the indeterminacy represents an "implicit" legislative delegation to the agency, the reviewing court "may not substitute its own construction [of the statute] for a reasonable interpretation made by the . . . agency."[252]

Interestingly, the *Chevron* framework does not require a reviewing court to conclude that the enacting coalition in Congress consciously meant a given instance of statutory indeterminacy to signify delegation. To the contrary, the Court emphasized that it did not know why Congress failed to strike the relevant policy balance at the level of specificity presented by the facts of the case before it:

> Perhaps . . . [Congress] consciously desired the [agency] to strike the balance at this level, thinking that those with great expertise and charged with responsibility for administering the provision would be in a better position to do so; perhaps it simply did not consider the question at this level; and perhaps Congress was unable to forge a coalition on either side of the question, and those on each side decided to take their chances with the scheme devised by the agency.[253]

For purposes of determining whether to treat the indeterminacy as a delegation, the Court found that "it matters not which of these things occurred."[254] By equating indeterminacy with delegation and precision with its absence, the Court in *Chevron* enabled Congress to use the level of generality of its statutes as a signal

---

for applying *Chevron* thus involve "the fruits of notice-and-comment rulemaking or formal adjudication." Id. The analysis here does not depend on whether *Mead* correctly assesses the conditions in which Congress would want *Chevron* to apply. Rather, what is important is that, within the pertinent domain, *Chevron* instructs reviewing courts to treat indeterminacy as a signal of legislative delegation.

[250] *Chevron*, 467 US at 842–43.

[251] Id at 843, 844.

[252] Id at 844.

[253] Id at 865.

[254] Id.

for when it wished to resolve a policy matter itself or when it wished a delegatee to resolve such a matter.

Obviously, the Court's generally forgiving approach to non-delegation and its decision to equate indeterminacy with delegation do not inexorably lead away from traditional purposivism and toward the new purposivism.[255] Still, these developments strongly suggest that as compared with traditional purposivism, the new version better respects the express allocation of constitutional authority effected by the Necessary and Proper Clause. Congress undeniably disagrees about, and compromises over, not only the law's ulterior purposes, but also the means by which the law is to be carried into effect.[256] As discussed, a statute banning "dogs" from public parks reflects a very different implemental purpose from one banning "dangerous animals," even though extrinsic evidence of various sorts might well demonstrate that the former was animated by an ulterior purpose to control dangerous animals while the latter was inspired by an ulterior purpose to control dogs.[257] If an interpretive approach makes all statutory texts mere proxies for their ulterior purposes, that regime denies Congress the capacity to use the semantic meaning of statutory texts to specify its implemental purposes—to signal when it wants the precision and fixity that typifies rules or the discretion and adaptability that typifies standards. Or, put another way, if a court transforms a rule into a standard or a standard into a rule in order to capture more faithfully a statute's perceived ultimate purpose—if it reads "no dogs" to mean "no dangerous animals" or vice versa—then it is the judiciary, and not Congress, that has taken responsibility

---

[255] Indeed, *Chevron* itself leaves open the possibility that a reviewing court might rely on legislative history to resolve indeterminacy that would otherwise give rise to an inference of delegation. See id at 851–53 (establishing that the legislative history of the Clean Air Act does not address the question before the Court). For further discussion of whether a reviewing court should consult legislative history under the *Chevron* framework, see note 283.

[256] Several prominent opinions by purposivist Justices have emphasized this divide between means and ends. See, for example, *Landgraf v USI Film Products*, 511 US 244, 286 (1994) (Stevens, J) ("Statutes are seldom crafted to pursue a single goal, and compromises necessary to their enactment may require adopting means other than those that would most effectively pursue the main goal."); *Pension Benefit Guaranty Corp. v LTV Corp.*, 496 US 633, 646–47 (1990) (Blackmun, J) ("'Deciding what competing values will or will not be sacrificed to the achievement of a particular objective is the very essence of legislative choice—and it frustrates rather than effectuates legislative intent simplistically to assume that *whatever* furthers the statute's primary objective must be the law.'"), quoting *Rodriguez v United States*, 480 US 522, 525–26 (1987) (per curiam).

[257] See text accompanying notes 199–202.

for prescribing the means of implementing federal policy.

The new purposivism seems to reflect just such concerns. By taking seriously the level of generality at which Congress frames its directives, the new purposivism better enables Congress to exercise its authority under the Necessary and Proper Clause to specify how much it wishes to decide for itself and how much it wishes others to decide. By giving Congress more effective control over implemental purpose, the new purposivism thus makes better sense of the particular form of legislative supremacy established by the text of Article I.

B. IMPLICATIONS OF THE NEW PURPOSIVISM

Although full exploration of the details of the new purposivism must await another day, two apparent implications merit brief mention. First, although new purposivists are more prone than new textualists to rely on legislative history, the premises of their approach should prevent its use to shift the level of generality at which Congress has expressed its policy. This implication means that the new purposivists should eschew legislative history not only when it contradicts a clear text, but also when it points to a more definite or more open-ended policy than that which is evident from the text. Second, because language has no intrinsic meaning, new purposivists should (and do) exhaust all semantic resources— including accepted linguistic canons of convention—to try to ascertain how a reasonable person conversant with applicable social and linguistic conventions would have understood the text in context.

1. *Legislative history and the new purposivism.* Although disagreement about the relevance of legislative history occupied a great deal of the statutory interpretation debate a quarter-century ago, the Court seems to have reached some equilibrium on the subject. These days, legislative history typically comes into play when the Court explains either that the legislative materials confirm the apparent import of the statutory text[258] or that they are too in-

---

[258] See, for example, *Jerman v Carlisle, McNellie, Rini, Kramer & Ulrich LPA*, 130 S Ct 1605, 1617 n 12 (2010) (Sotomayor, J, joined by Roberts, CJ, and Stevens, Thomas, Ginsburg, and Breyer, JJ) (deeming it unnecessary to rely on legislative history but citing to show that at least "some Members of Congress" shared the Court's understanding); *United States v Ressem*, 553 US 272, 275 (2008) (Stevens, J, joined by Roberts, CJ, and Kennedy, Souter, Ginsburg, Breyer, and Alito, JJ) ("The history of the statute we construe today further supports our conclusion that Congress did not intend to require the Gov-

conclusive or self-contradictory to alter the Court's conclusion about statutory meaning.[259] Perhaps because the textualist critique heightened awareness of the possibility of unrepresentative or even "cooked" legislative history, such materials only rarely play a dispositive role in the Court's opinions, even for purposes of resolving ambiguity.[260]

Still, one of the few things that divide the new purposivists from textualists is that the former will credit legislative history to resolve indeterminacy, even if they will not do so to vary the meaning of a clear text. Accordingly, it is worth saying a few words, first, about why clear legislative history should not trump clear text and, second, about when new purposivists should treat legislative history

---

ernment to establish a relationship between the explosive carried and the underlying felony."); *Begay v United States*, 553 US 137, 143 (2008) (Breyer, J, joined by Roberts, CJ, and Stevens, Kennedy, and Ginsburg, JJ) ("The statute's history offers further support for our conclusion that the examples in clause (ii) limit the scope of the clause to crimes that are similar to the examples themselves."). For discussion of the use of legislative history to confirm the apparent meaning of the text, see James J. Brudney, *Confirmatory Legislative History*, 76 Brooklyn L Rev 901 (2011).

[259] See, for example, *Graham County Soil and Water Conservation District v Wilson*, 130 S Ct 1396, 1407, 1409 (2010) (Stevens, J, joined by Roberts, CJ, and Kennedy, Thomas, Ginsburg, and Alito, JJ) (noting that "the drafting history" of the relevant provision "raises more questions than it answers"); *Richlin Security Service Co. v Chertoff*, 553 US 571, 584 n 8 (2008) (Alito, J, joined by Roberts, CJ, and Stevens, Kennedy, Ginsburg, Souter, and Breyer, JJ) ("Because the legislative history is a wash in this case, we need not decide precisely how much weight it deserves in our analysis."); *Long Island Care at Home, Ltd. v Coke*, 551 US 158, 168 (2007) (Breyer, J, for a unanimous Court) ("Nor can one find any clear answer in the statute's legislative history."); *Small v United States*, 544 US 385, 393 (2005) (Breyer, J, joined by Stevens, O'Connor, Souter, and Ginsburg, JJ) ("Thus, those who use legislative history to help discern congressional intent will see the history here as silent, hence a neutral factor, that simply confirms the obvious, namely, that Congress did not consider the issue.").

[260] Almost two decades ago, Professor Eskridge predicted precisely such a phenomenon. He argued that the textualist critique underscored that "the Court should devote more of its energy to analyzing statutory *texts*," "that legislative history is, at best, secondary and supporting evidence of statutory meaning," and that the Court must take greater care to ensure that the legislative history in question has sufficient indicia of reliability and relevance. Eskridge, 37 UCLA L Rev at 625 (cited in note 58). Indeed, legislative history is so often marginal to the outcome of the case that the Court has devised an innocuous way to introduce it so that even hard-core legislative history skeptics such as Justices Scalia and Thomas can join the discussion. See, for example, *Tapia v United States*, 131 S Ct 2382, 2391 (2011) (Kagan, J, for a unanimous Court) ("[F]or those who consider legislative history useful, the key Senate Report concerning the SRA provides one last piece of corroborating evidence."); *Microsoft Corp. v i4i Ltd. Partnership*, 131 S Ct 2238, 2249 n 8 (2011) (Sotomayor, J, joined by Scalia, Kennedy, Ginsburg, Breyer, Alito, and Kagan, JJ) ("For those of us for whom it is relevant, the legislative history of § 282 provides additional evidence that Congress meant to codify the judge-made presumption of validity, not to set forth a new presumption of its own making."); *Abbott v United States*, 131 S Ct 18, 29 n 7 (2010) (Ginsburg, J, for a unanimous Court, excluding Justice Kagan, who took no part in the case) ("For those who take legislative history into account, it is as silent as is the statute's text.").

as being in conflict with the text. These two points, as it turns out, are related.

a) *Favoring the text in cases of conflict.* Why should new purposivists allow the text to trump the legislative history? Even if one believes that an interpreter should closely follow the signals that Congress sends through the level of generality it picks, purposivists might well think it appropriate to assume (as they traditionally did) that the legislative history could, at times, supply more reliable clues than the text about what policy Congress actually meant to frame. Put another way, if one cares about implemental purpose but accepts the legitimacy of legislative history (as new purposivists do), one might look to the legislative history, as well as the text, for clues about how Congress intended to exercise its authority over means.[261] For example, to return to the "no dogs" statute, imagine a situation in which a committee report states that "no dogs" is merely a placeholder for a broader purpose of barring disruptive animals from the park. Imagine further that the bill's floor managers, as well as numerous rank-and-file members, rise to echo that sentiment, with no opposing view expressed in either house. For those who find probative value in legislative history, why shouldn't such materials supply determinative cues about the desired level of generality?

The answer lies in the premises of institutional settlement. The inescapable fact is that, in this example, the statutory text and the legislative history conflict because they address the problem of peaceful enjoyment of the park through policies framed at different levels of generality. The statutory text is narrow ("no dogs"); the legislative history is broad ("no disruptive animals"). In determining whether the statute applies to a pet tiger cub, a macaw, or a potbellied pig, a court or agency must inevitably decide which text to credit, the statute or the legislative history.

Why should new purposivists give the statute a superior claim to authoritativeness? The reason is not terribly different from Chief Justice Marshall's famous observation in *Marbury* that when a statute conflicts with the higher law of the Constitution, the former must yield.[262] Simply put, if the statute and the legislative

---

[261] I am grateful to Matthew Stephenson for suggesting this point.

[262] The relevant passage is as follows:

So if a law be in opposition to the constitution; if both the law and the constitution apply to a particular case, so that the court must either decide that

history genuinely conflict, Article I, Section 7 of the Constitution itself gives the text a greater claim to authoritativeness.

Of course, given that legislation suffers from limits on human foresight and inevitable glitches in expression, one might still think that legislative history could supply evidence of the true compromise, even in cases in which the statute is otherwise clear. But when a conflict is evident from the legislative history (the sponsor says that "no dogs" means "no disruptive animals"), then the legislative process itself has flagged the putative problem of expression that traditional purposivists would have used to justify reliance on legislative history.[263] If legislators, at that point, do not adjust the text to reflect their desired (but countertextual) understanding, one cannot help but suspect that the conflicting signal found in the legislative history could not, for whatever reason, have survived the legislative process.[264] Or, at least, the bill's managers may have acted on that belief. This possibility undercuts the plausibility of the traditional premise that crediting the legislative history furthers true legislative purpose by addressing unanticipated questions or slips of the pen.

---

case conformably to the law, disregarding the constitution; or conformably to the constitution, disregarding the law; the court must determine which of these conflicting rules governs the case. This is of the very essence of judicial duty.

If then the courts are to regard the constitution; and the constitution is superior to any ordinary act of the legislature; the constitution, and not such ordinary act, must govern the case to which they both apply.

Marbury v Madison, 5 US (1 Cranch) 137, 178 (1803).

[263] See John F. Manning, *Textualism as a Nondelegation Doctrine*, 97 Colum L Rev 673, 728 (1997) ("If something appears in the legislative history—clarification of how a term applies, a stated preference for a given interpretive approach, etc.—then someone in the enactment process necessarily anticipated the point. This makes it at least theoretically possible for Congress to address the question in the legislation itself.").

[264] The preeminent example of this phenomenon comes from *Holy Trinity* itself. The statute, as noted, prohibited contracting with aliens to come to the United States to perform "labor or service of any kind." See text accompanying note 45. In holding that the statute applied only to "manual laborers" rather than to a broader category that included professionals, the Court relied on a Senate Committee Report stating that the bill's intended sweep was the narrower one and that the committee would have proposed narrowing language had it not been so late in the legislative session. See *Holy Trinity Church v United States*, 143 US 457, 464–65 (1892). As Professor Adrian Vermeule has shown, however, the bill did not pass during the session in which the Senate Report issued; rather, it passed in a later session. See Adrian Vermeule, *Legislative History and the Limits of Judicial Competence: The Untold Story of Holy Trinity Church*, 50 Stan L Rev 1833, 1845–50 (1998). The failure of anyone to propose the narrowing language despite the protracted consideration of the bill has led Vermeule to the reasonable conclusion that the bill's managers feared that such an amendment would have jeopardized the bill's enactment. See id at 1849. In my view, whenever the legislative history contradicts the text, it raises a question about whether the bill would have passed had the legislative history's formulation been substituted for that of the text.

b) Identifying conflicts. If the new purposivism is correct to credit text over legislative history in cases of conflict, then it remains necessary to identify what counts as a conflict. The task should draw guidance from the distinctive premise of the new purposivism—namely, that the text gives insight into the implemental purpose through the level of generality at which Congress has framed its policy. If Congress's choice of rules versus standards sends a signal about how much discretion to leave to law implementers, then conflicts will arise when the legislative history alters the level of statutory generality, asserting either more or less discretion for the interpreter than a fair reading of the text allows.

The first and most obvious example is the one offered above. The legislative history suggests that a narrow, rule-like text ("dogs") is really just a marker for a broader, standard-like ulterior purpose ("no disruptive pets"). As the Court's decision in *Milner* suggests, new purposivists would properly credit Congress's choice to regulate the problem of disruptive animals through a semantically determinate rule that, like all rules, will inevitably be overinclusive and underinclusive in relation to some identifiable ulterior purpose.

The second example involves narrowing a broad and encompassing statute in light of its ulterior purpose. This situation is slightly less straightforward because there is some sentiment, even among fairly modern purposivists such as Hart and Sacks, that broad statutory language can almost always be narrowed by context.[265] If one believes that the level of generality conveys an implemental purpose, however, one cannot easily justify the Hart and Sacks position on this point. Rules can convey narrow precision but they can also convey encompassing breadth. Recall the facts of *Holy Trinity*. The Court started from the premise that the Alien Contract Labor Act's prohibition against importing "labor or service of any kind" comprehensively referred to all forms of employment.[266] Thinking in terms of implemental purpose, an interpreter cannot discount the choice of such encompassing lan-

---

[265] See text accompanying note 189.

[266] See *Holy Trinity*, 143 US at 458–59. To be sure, some have detected more ambiguity in the text of the Alien Contract Labor Act than the Brewer Court did. See Eskridge, 96 Mich L Rev at 1517–18 (cited in note 25) (arguing that contemporaries would have understood the words "labor" or "service" more narrowly to exclude "brain toilers"). For purposes of illustrating the point about breadth, however, I start from the reasonable semantic assumptions made by the Court.

guage—which Congress might have chosen to avoid the need for fine judgment calls in the law's administration, to placate labor constituencies, to accommodate future changes in the labor market, or to achieve any number of implemental purposes that breadth might serve.[267] To the extent that the Court narrowed the statute in order to implement the ulterior purpose expressed in the legislative history (namely, excluding low-wage manual labor), it substituted an extratextual standard (or, at least, a more narrow-gauged rule) for the broad rule embedded in the enacted text.

The third—and final—example of conflict between text and legislative history requires more explanation. It entails the use of legislative history to add detail to a term that one might call vague or open-ended—something in the nature of a standard rather than a rule. For example, if Congress passed a "no disruptive animals" statute, should a new purposivist read the statute narrowly in light of legislative history indicating that the bill's supporters sought only to address the problem of dogs? Certainly, since the term "no disruptive animals" is so indefinite, one could imagine the argument that resorting to legislative history, if reliable, merely clarifies, rather than conflicts with, the text. This view would also seem to fit comfortably with the ancient idea that statutes should be interpreted to suppress the mischief at which they were directed.[268]

If one thinks about the problem in terms of generality shifting, however, using legislative history to narrow or sharpen a vague statutory term would seem to conflict with Congress's apparent implemental purpose to confer discretion upon the law's interpreters. To see why this is so, it is helpful to consider the distinction that interpretation scholars have sometimes drawn between ambiguity and vagueness or open-endedness.[269] On the one hand, they say that ambiguity describes situations in which words have more than one sense—leaving it to interpreters to figure out

---

[267] Cf. Manning, 116 Harv L Rev at 2424–27 (cited in note 65) (discussing factors that might have accounted for the Alien Contract Labor Act's breadth).

[268] See text accompanying note 35.

[269] See, for example, Randy E. Barnett, *Interpretation and Construction*, 34 Harv J L & Pub Pol 65, 67 (2011); Lawrence B. Solum, *The Interpretation-Construction Distinction*, 27 Const Comm 95, 97–98 (2010); E. Allan Farnsworth, *"Meaning" in the Law of Contracts*, 76 Yale L J 939, 953 (1967).

which of the available senses the lawmaker meant to use.[270] For example, a statute regulating "banks" could refer to riverbanks or financial institutions, and context narrows the meaning by identifying which sense is appropriate.[271] In such cases, if one were otherwise inclined to credit legislative history (as new purposivists are), it does not shift the level of statutory generality to rely on legislative history to determine which way Congress used the term. The interpreter *must* choose among the available competing meanings, and, since Congress uses statutory language purposively, a statute's ulterior purpose may indicate the sense in which Congress used the relevant term or terms.[272]

In contrast, vagueness or open-endedness says something quite different about the statute's assignment of interpretive discretion. Although I am not fully convinced that the line between ambiguity and vagueness is as sharply drawn as some have suggested, vagueness is said to entail the presence of borderline cases whose inclusion or exclusion requires judgment calls that one cannot make

---

[270] See, for example, Barnett, 34 Harv J L & Pub Pol at 67 (cited in note 269); Solum, 27 Const Comm at 97–98 (cited in note 269); Farnsworth, 76 Yale L J at 953 (cited in note 269).

[271] See Lawrence Lessig, *Understanding Changed Readings: Fidelity and Theory*, 47 Stan L Rev 395, 407–08 (1995).

[272] *General Dynamics Land System, Inc. v Cline*, 540 US 581 (2004), illustrates this phenomenon. At issue was whether the Age Discrimination in Employment Act of 1967 (ADEA), 29 USC §§ 621–34, prohibits discrimination in favor of older workers as well as against them. The ADEA makes it unlawful to "discriminate against any individual with respect to his compensation, terms, conditions, or privileges of employment, because of such individual's age." 29 USC § 623(a)(1). The plaintiff, who satisfied the Act's standing requirements, see 29 USC § 623(a)(1), claimed that his company discriminated against him in favor of older workers and argued that his claim fell squarely within the terms of the statute.

Justice Souter's opinion for the Court reasoned that the term "age" conveyed two competing meanings:

> [T]he word "age" standing alone can be readily understood either as pointing to any number of years lived, or as common shorthand for the longer span and concurrent aches that make youth look good. Which alternative was probably intended is a matter of context; we understand the different choices of meaning that lie behind a sentence like "Age can be shown by a driver's license," and the statement, "Age has left him a shut-in."

Cline, 540 US at 596. Because the phrase "discriminate . . . because of . . . age" therefore left a residue of ambiguity, the Court felt it appropriate to rely, inter alia, on legislative history suggesting that the statute's ulterior purpose was to protect older workers against discrimination in favor of younger ones. See id at 587–92. In that setting, using purpose to make an inevitable choice between two conflicting meanings of a word or phrase does not shift the statute's level of generality.

by reference to semantic meaning.[273] In such cases, the relevant statutes convey an implemental purpose—within the boundaries set by the statute—to leave the specification of policy detail to agencies or courts.[274] That is to say, they convey a purpose to delegate. This impulse is most familiar in the context of the classically open-ended administrative commands instructing agencies to regulate radio waves in the "public interest, convenience, or necessity"[275] or to determine "just and reasonable" utility rates.[276] But Congress is also not shy about using open-ended standards in judicially-administered statutes.[277]

In such circumstances, using legislative history to narrow statutory meaning risks shifting the level of generality at which Congress expressed its command, thereby negating the delegation. Consider a statute that attaches certain conditions to the finding that "substantially all" of a multiemployer pension fund's assets come from the trucking industry.[278] Although there is no bright line between what counts as a standard rather than a rule, a term such as "substantially all" surely has the feel of a standard. One could doubtless find specifications of that term that would fall outside of any plausible semantic meaning of the term—50 or 60 or perhaps even 70 percent, for example.[279] On the other hand, assuming that the phrase is not a term of art,[280] it would be a judgment call whether to say that 85 or 90 percent satisfied the definition. Imagine now that the originating committees and the sponsors all explain that they understand "substantially all" to

---

[273] See Barnett, 34 Harv J L & Pub Pol at 67 (cited in note 269); Solum, 27 Const Comm at 98 (cited in note 269); Farnsworth, 76 Yale L J at 953 (cited in note 269).

[274] For further discussion of this point, see, for example, Edward L. Rubin, *Law and Legislation in the Administrative State*, 89 Colum L Rev 369, 380–85 (1989); Richard J. Pierce Jr., *The Role of the Judiciary in Implementing an Agency Theory of Government*, 64 NYU L Rev 1239, 1244–46 (1989).

[275] 47 USC §§ 307(c)(1), 309(a), 310(d).

[276] 16 USC § 824d(a).

[277] See, for example, 15 USC § 2 (making it a felony to "monopolize, or attempt to monopolize, or combine or conspire with any other person or persons, to monopolize any part of the trade or commerce among the several States"); 42 USC § 1988(b) (authorizing courts to award a "reasonable attorney's fee" to prevailing parties in certain cases).

[278] This hypothetical adapts the facts of *Continental Can Co., Inc. v Chicago Truck Drivers, Helpers & Warehouse Workers Union*, 916 F2d 1154 (7th Cir 1990).

[279] In the Seventh Circuit case, the legislation's Senate sponsor entered a statement into the legislative record stating that "substantially all" meant 51 percent. See id at 1157.

[280] The Seventh Circuit concluded that "substantially all" was a term of art derived from preexisting Internal Revenue regulations. See id at 1158. For discussion of terms of art, see note 287.

mean 90 percent. Even though the statute is indeterminate, crediting the number articulated in the legislative history changes the level of generality at which Congress spoke. A soft-edged standard conferring discretion has now become a sharp-edged rule devoid of discretion. That conversion does not clarify the statute; rather, it contradicts its evident textual choice to give the responsible agency or court a range of discretion within which to determine what counts as "substantially all" the assets of the fund.

Obviously, there is no formula for determining when reliance on legislative history shifts the level of generality of a statute. Certainly, as the unanimous opinion in *Fox v Vice*[281] suggests, when an interpreter makes sense of an open-ended statute, it is appropriate if not necessary to read such a statute in light of the broad purposes that inspired its enactment. One could not decide what a "reasonable attorney's fee" is without some benchmark for determining reasonableness; hence, an interpreter would necessarily refer to the evident statutory goal to create private attorneys general or to make prevailing civil rights plaintiffs whole for their litigation expenses. At the same time, however, if the legislative history of the same statute spelled out a detailed formula for determining what constitutes a "reasonable" fee, crediting that detail would shift the level of generality at which Congress spoke and reduce the level of discretion that the statutory text itself conferred upon the interpreter chosen by the legislature.[282] However difficult

---

[281] 131 S Ct 2205 (2011), discussed in Part II.B.

[282] This conclusion suggests a reason for questioning a famous decision of the Rehnquist Court. In *Blanchard v Bergeron*, 489 US 87 (1989), a lopsided majority of the Court (everyone except Justice Scalia) construed the open-ended term "reasonable attorney's fee," 42 USC § 1988, in light of a detailed formula found in the committee reports. In particular, the Court emphasized that both committee reports accompanying Section 1988 conveyed an intent or purpose to embrace a twelve-factor test articulated in *Johnson v Georgia Highway Express, Inc.*, 488 F2d 714 (5th Cir 1974)—a Fifth Circuit opinion that had construed similar language in Title VII of the Civil Rights Act of 1964, 42 USC § 2000e-5(k). See *Blanchard*, 489 US at 91. As the *Blanchard* Court described it, that test consisted of the following factors:

> (1) the time and labor required; (2) the novelty and difficulty of the questions; (3) the skill requisite to perform the legal service properly; (4) the preclusion of other employment by the attorney due to acceptance of the case; (5) the customary fee; (6) whether the fee is fixed or contingent; (7) time limitations imposed by the client or the circumstances; (8) the amount involved and the results obtained; (9) the experience, reputation, and ability of the attorneys; (10) the "undesirability" of the case; (11) the nature and length of the professional relationship with the client; and (12) awards in similar cases.

Id at 91 n 5. In a much-discussed concurrence early in his campaign to promote textualism, Justice Scalia challenged the Court's approach, expressing confidence "that only a small

it may be at the margins to distinguish generality-shifting from non-generality-shifting uses of legislative history, the new purposivists' emphasis on implemental purpose suggests that just such a question should set the course of their decision making.[283]

2. *Identifying semantic meaning.* One final question merits attention. New purposivists seem to recognize that they should consider available sources of semantic evidence when determining whether a statutory text is too clear to permit consultation of extrinsic evidence of purpose. In some ways, that proposition seems obvious; if one is supposed to determine semantic meaning, look for evidence of usage. But traditional purposivists were notoriously skeptical of conventional semantic resources. For example, they admonished judges not to put too much stock in dictionary definitions.[284] They also emphasized that semantic canons should be "subordinated to the doctrine that courts will construe the details

---

proportion of the Members of Congress read either one of the Committee Reports in question" and that no member affirmatively ascertained and assented to the contents of cases cited in such reports. Id at 98–99 (Scalia, J, concurring in part and concurring in the judgment).

Even if one disagreed with Justice Scalia's critique of legislative history, the thrust for the new purposivism would suggest that the *Blanchard* Court erred in its approach. By substituting a very open-ended standard ("reasonable attorney's fees") with a more detailed twelve-factor test, the Court shifted the level of generality at which courts were to examine the availability of a reasonable attorney's fee. Given that the twelve-factor *Johnson* test was available and known to the responsible committees, it would not have been difficult to draft the statute to reflect that more detailed approach—if the bill's managers had thought that they could get agreement on the details without jeopardizing the bill. For whatever reason, the drafters instead framed the statute in a way that gave courts more open-ended discretion. *Blanchard* disregarded that apparent choice.

[283] This conclusion has implications for an ongoing dispute about the *Chevron* doctrine. See text accompanying notes 247–54 (describing *Chevron*). The judiciary has sent mixed signals about whether reviewing courts should rely on legislative history, at step one of the *Chevron* framework, to determine whether Congress has clearly spoken to the precise question at issue. See John F. Manning and Matthew C. Stephenson, *Legislation and Regulation* 886–87 (Foundation, 2010). *Chevron* itself suggested that the reviewing court rely on "traditional tools of statutory construction," and then went on to examine the legislative history of the statute at issue. *Chevron*, 467 US at 843 n 9; see also id at 851–53 (analyzing the legislative history of the Clean Air Act Amendments). Nevertheless, if one follows the new purposivism to its logical conclusion, a reviewing court should not use legislative history at step one if it would shift the level of generality at which Congress framed its delegation. If a vague or open-ended statute signals an implemental purpose for the agency to exercise discretion, legislative history imposing a more specific policy framework on the agency would contradict the text of the statute.

[284] See, for example, *Chapman v United States*, 500 US 453, 476 (1991) (Stevens, J, dissenting) ("In construing a statute, Learned Hand wisely counseled us to look first to the words of the statute, but 'not to make a fortress out of the dictionary; but to remember that statutes always have some purpose or object to accomplish, whose sympathetic and imaginative discovery is the surest guide to their meaning.'"), quoting *Cabell v Markham*, 148 F2d 737, 739 (2d Cir), aff'd, 326 US 404 (1945).

of an act in conformity with its dominating general purpose."[285]

New purposivists are more prone to consult semantic resources than their more traditional forebears. They frequently cite dictionaries.[286] They consult technical materials—including common law legal sources—to determine whether a statutory word or phrase carries the idiosyncratic connotations of a term of art.[287] Perhaps most surprisingly, many of the new purposivists resort to the once-discredited semantic canons of construction to ascertain the meaning of statutory texts.[288]

---

[285] *SEC v C.M. Joiner Leasing Corp.*, 320 US 344, 350 (1943). See also, for example, *Watt v Western Nuclear, Inc.*, 462 US 36, 44 n 5 (1983) (holding that legislative history can overcome the force of *ejusdem generis*).

[286] See, for example, *Tapia v United States*, 131 S Ct 2382, 2388 (2011) (Kagan, J) (invoking the dictionary definition of "recognize"); *DePierre v United States*, 131 S Ct 2225, 2228 (2011) (Sotomayor, J) (using, inter alia, *Webster's Third New International Dictionary* 434 (2002) to ascertain the meaning of "cocaine"); *Milner v Department of the Navy*, 131 S Ct 1259, 1264 (2011) (Kagan, J) (consulting the dictionary definition of "personnel" for purposes of the Freedom of Information Act); *Ransom v FIA Card Services, N.A.*, 131 S Ct 716, 724 (2011) (Kagan, J) (relying on several dictionary definitions to conclude that "an expense amount is 'applicable' within the plain meaning of the statute when it is appropriate, relevant, suitable, or fit"). Even the Court's most traditional purposivists recognize the utility of dictionaries. See, for example, *Fowler v United States*, 131 S Ct 2045, 2051 (2011) (Breyer, J) ("We find possible answers to this question in the dictionary definition of the word 'prevent.'"); *Muscarello v United States*, 524 US 125, 127–32 (1998) (Breyer, J) (determining the "primary meaning" of "carry" based on its dictionary definition); *Dunn v Commodity Futures Trading Commission*, 519 US 465, 470 (1997) (Stevens, J) (relying on a dictionary to determine whether an agency's interpretation "violates the ordinary meaning of the key word 'in'"); *MCI Telecommunications Corp. v AT&T Co.*, 512 US 218, 240–42 (1994) (Stevens, J, dissenting) (noting that dictionaries can be "useful aids in statutory interpretation" if words are also considered in context).

[287] See, for example, *Microsoft Corp. v i4i Ltd. Partnership*, 131 S Ct 2238, 2245 (2011) (Sotomayor, J) ("[W]here Congress uses a common-law term in a statute, we assume the 'term . . . comes with a common law meaning, absent anything pointing another way.'"), quoting *Safeco Insurance Co. of America v Burr*, 551 US 47, 58 (2007); *Willkie v Robbins*, 551 US 537, 563–64 (2007) (Souter, J) (presuming that "Congress meant to incorporate" the common law understanding of extortion in the Hobbs Act); *Field v Mans*, 516 US 59, 69 (1995) (Souter, J) ("The operative terms, . . . 'false pretenses, a false representation, or actual fraud,' carry the acquired meaning of terms of art."). Even a traditional purposivist like Justice Stevens has acknowledged the importance of unearthing the technical meaning of terms of art. See *Evans v United States*, 504 US 255, 259 (1992) (Stevens, J) ("[W]here Congress borrows terms of art . . . it presumably knows and adopts the cluster of ideas that were attached to each borrowed word in the body of learning from which it was taken and the meaning its use will convey to the judicial mind unless otherwise instructed.") (alteration in original; quotation marks omitted), quoting *Morissette v United States*, 342 US 246, 263 (1952). This approach is also a staple of textualism. See Manning, 116 Harv L Rev at 2464 (cited in note 65) (discussing the textualist rationale for crediting the technical meaning of terms of art).

[288] See, for example, *CSX Transportation, Inc. v Alabama Department of Revenue*, 131 S Ct 1101, 1113 (2011) (Kagan, J) (acknowledging the force and function of the *ejusdem generis* canon while explaining that it does not apply to the statutory language at issue); *Graham County Soil & Water Conservation District v Wilson*, 130 S Ct 1396, 1412–14 (2010) (Sotomayor, J, joined by Breyer, J, dissenting) (applying the *noscitur a sociis* principle that

Rehearsing the complex debates over the appropriate use, if any, of these forms of semantic evidence must await another day. Suffice it to say that if new purposivists believe that Congress's choice of words structures and constrains the interpreter's use of purpose, then they appropriately consult semantic evidence of textual meaning *before* deciding what role background purpose can properly play in the analysis. If Congress cannot dependably use words to express the level of generality at which it wishes to set policy— to differentiate "no dogs" from "no canines" from "no disruptive animals"—then Congress cannot effectively discharge its authority under the Necessary and Proper Clause to determine how policy is to be carried out. Accordingly, unless interpreters give priority to the shared semantic conventions that make it possible for legislators to communicate their policies to the law's implementers, a legislature cannot predictably use language as a tool to define the scope and limits of the background legislative policies that the statutory text carries into effect.[289]

---

words draw meaning from the words with which they are associated); *Washington State Department of Social and Health Services v Guardianship of Keffeler*, 537 US 371, 384 (2003) (Souter, J) (using "the established interpretative canons of *noscitur a sociis* and *ejusdem generis*" to clarify the meaning of a statutory phrase); *Chevron USA Inc. v Echazabal*, 536 US 73, 81 (2002) (Souter, J) (explaining that proper application of the *expressio unius* canon "depends on identifying a series of two or more terms or things that should be understood to go hand in hand, which [is] abridged in circumstances supporting a sensible inference that the term left out must have been meant to be excluded"); *TRW Inc. v Andrews*, 534 US 19, 28 (2001) (Ginsburg, J) (citing the *expressio unius* canon to support the proposition that "[t]he most natural reading of [the relevant statutory provision] is that Congress implicitly excluded a general discovery rule by explicitly including a more limited one"). Even a staunch traditional purposivist like Justice Stevens sometimes relied on the canons— despite his acknowledged reluctance to cite them. See, for example, *Conroy v Aniskoff*, 507 US 511, 516 (1993) (Stevens, J) (omitting to cite the *expressio unius* canon but holding that consideration of "the entire statute indicates that Congress included a prejudice requirement whenever it considered it appropriate to do so, and that its omission of any such requirement in § 525 was deliberate"); *Third National Bank in Nashville v Impac Ltd., Inc.*, 432 US 312, 322 & n 16 (1977) (Stevens, J) (applying the "familiar principle of statutory construction that words grouped in a list should be given related meaning" but adding that "'[o]ne hardly need rely on such Latin phrases as *ejusdem generis* and *noscitur a sociis* to reach this obvious conclusion'"), quoting *United States v Feola*, 420 US 671, 708 (1975) (Stewart, J, dissenting).

[289] See Gerald C. MacCallum Jr., *Legislative Intent*, 75 Yale L J 754, 758 (1966) ("The words [a legislator] uses are the instruments by means of which he expects or hopes to effect . . . changes in . . . society. What gives him this expectation or this hope is his belief that he can anticipate how others (*e.g.*, judges and administrators) will understand these words."); Jeremy Waldron, *Legislators' Intention and Unintentional Legislation*, in Andrei Marmor, ed, *Law and Interpretation: Essays in Legal Philosophy* 329, 339 (Clarendon, 1995) ("A legislator who votes for (or against) a provision like 'No vehicle shall be permitted to enter any state or municipal park' does so on the assumption that—to put it crudely— what the words mean to him is identical to what they will mean to those to whom they are addressed. . . . That such assumptions pervade the legislative process shows how much

This conclusion is not all that dramatic. It does not purport to tell interpreters *how* to take semantic evidence into account, merely *when* to do so. Even the casual student of interpretation, for example, knows that dictionaries have their limits. To be sure, because the editors identify the most common usages after broadly studying the way speakers and writers use a word in different contexts, dictionaries may offer at least a potential starting point for corroborating or disquieting the interpreter's general sense of the range of meanings attached to the word by its users.[290] Because of the vastness of linguistic experience and the limited time and resources of editors, no dictionary can capture every shred of nuance or each idiosyncratic meaning a word may acquire when combined with others.[291] Nor can a dictionary tell the interpreter

---

law depends on language, on the shared conventions that constitute a language, and on the reciprocity of intentions that conventions comprise.").

[290] See Ellen P. Aprill, *The Law of the Word: Dictionary Shopping in the Supreme Court*, 30 Ariz St L J 275, 283–92 (1998) (summarizing the standard practice of dictionary compilation); see also Lawrence A. Solan, *When Judges Use the Dictionary*, 68 Am Speech 50, 55 (1993) (arguing that dictionaries are appropriately used "to give the reader a general sense of the word"); Note, *Looking It Up: Dictionaries and Statutory Interpretation*, 107 Harv L Rev 1437, 1452 (1994) (arguing that interpreters act properly when "employing dictionaries to identify the general outlines of word meanings and then relying on contextual arguments from text, structure, history, or policy to determine which meaning is appropriate"). Hart and Sacks described that function in the following way: "A dictionary . . . never says what meaning a word *must* bear in a particular context. . . . A good dictionary always gives examples of the use of the word *in context* in each of the meanings ascribed to it." Hart and Sacks, *The Legal Process* at 1190 (cited in note 26).

[291] See Clark D. Cunningham et al, *Plain Meaning and Hard Cases*, 103 Yale L J 1561, 1615 (1994) ("Dictionary-making is an inexact art, and it often happens that usages are common for some time before lexicographers happen to collect enough of them and realize that they represent a distinct usage, and decide to revise an entry to include that usage."); Solan, 68 Am Speech at 53 (cited in note 290) ("To the lexicographer, the limitation of space is a very important issue. Inevitably, the lexicographer's success will only be partial, even in the best dictionaries.").

Smith v United States, 508 US 223 (1993), illustrates this limitation. At issue was a provision of the criminal code providing for sentence enhancement when a person "during and in relation to any crime of violence or drug trafficking crime . . . uses . . . a firearm." 18 USC § 924(c)(1)(A). The precise question was whether the defendant had triggered the penalty enhancement provision by trading a gun for illegal drugs. *Smith*, 508 US at 225. Relying on a broad dictionary definition that included "'[t]o convert to one's service'" or "'to employ,'" the Court concluded that by attempting to trade a gun for drugs, the defendant "'used' or 'employed' it as an item of barter to obtain cocaine." Id at 229, quoting *Webster's New International Dictionary* 2806 (2d ed 1939). In a dissent joined by Justices Stevens and Souter, Justice Scalia wrote that the Court had erred by relying on an acontextual dictionary definition of the term. See *Smith*, 508 US at 241–42. The dissent elaborated:

> When someone asks, "Do you use a cane?," he is not inquiring whether you have your grandfather's silver-handled walking stick on display in the hall; he wants to know whether you walk with a cane. Similarly, to speak of "using a firearm" is to speak of using it for its distinctive purpose, *i.e.*, as a weapon. To

which among multiple competing senses of a word Congress intended to use.[292] No one—not even the staunchest textualist— believes that the role of the dictionary in interpretation is straightforward, formulaic, or without complication.[293]

Similarly, legal analysts debate the proper use of semantic canons. Relatively few now accept Llewellyn's view that each canon has an equal and opposite countercanon, and that the whole enterprise masks judicial decision making on other grounds.[294] Modern defenders of the canons argue that, like any linguistic convention, the canons have resolving significance only when applied by a skilled user of language in context.[295] They are neither pre-

---

be sure, "one can use a firearm in a number of ways," including as an article of exchange, just as one can "use" a cane as a hall decoration—but that is not the ordinary meaning of "using" the one or the other. The Court does not appear to grasp the distinction between how a word can be used and how it ordinarily is used. . . . It is unquestionably not reasonable and normal, I think, to say simply "do not use firearms" when one means to prohibit selling or scratching with them.

Id at 243–43. In my view, this exchange illustrates the limited utility of dictionaries in interpretation. They can help identify a range of meanings but cannot capture the full contextual nuance of a complex language.

[292] See, for example, Sunstein, 103 Harv L Rev at 418–19 (cited in note 37) (arguing that the ordinary-meaning approach "is unhelpful when statutory words have more than one dictionary definition, or when the context produces interpretive doubt").

[293] As prominent textualist Judge Easterbrook has written, "the choice among meanings must have a footing more solid than a dictionary—which is a museum of words, an historical catalog rather than a means to decode the work of legislatures." Frank H. Easterbrook, *Text, History, and Structure in Statutory Interpretation*, 17 Harv J L & Pub Pol 61, 67 (1994). As noted, Justice Scalia, too, has rejected ordinary or dictionary meaning in favor of the colloquial or technical meaning of words. See note 291; see also, for example, *Moskal v United States*, 498 US 103, 122–25 (1990) (Scalia, J, dissenting) (arguing that the phrase "falsely made" has a technical meaning and should be read in its technical rather than ordinary sense).

[294] See Karl N. Llewellyn, *Remarks on the Theory of Appellate Decision and the Rules or Canons About How Statutes Are to Be Construed*, 3 Vand L Rev 395 (1950). In the past two decades, the canons have enjoyed a resurgence that cuts broadly across ideological lines. See, for example, Easterbrook, 50 U Chi L Rev at 540 (cited in note 16); Eskridge and Frickey, 108 Harv L Rev at 66 (cited in note 90); Scalia, *A Matter of Interpretation* at 26 (cited in note 25); David L. Shapiro, *Continuity and Change in Statutory Interpretation*, 67 NYU L Rev 921, 923 (1992); Sunstein, 103 Harv L Rev at 452–54 (cited in note 37).

[295] Professors Macey and Miller thus write:

[I]n a wide array of situations, common sense or practical wisdom will inform judges' decisions about which canon to employ in a given context. For example, one may tell a person standing on the edge of a deep gorge "he who hesitates is lost." One also might say "look before you leap." But, of course, common sense dictates that the latter maxim is more appropriate than the former in this context. Common sense similarly will inform the decision in other situations. Thus, while it is true that no meta-rule or formal model is available to instruct judges in picking and choosing among canons, in the same way that people who do not know the rules of grammar can employ grammatically correct language

scriptive nor mechanical, but rather serve as "axiom[s] of experience."[296] Consider the once-dreaded maxim of negative implication, *expressio unius est exclusio alterius*.[297] The specification of one thing surely does not always mean the exclusion of others.[298] If a parent tells a child who has asked for a drink, "you may have juice," that specification almost surely excludes soda.[299] Conversely, were one to ask a roommate to "'get milk, bread, peanut butter and eggs at the grocery,'" that request "probably does not mean 'do not get ice cream.'"[300] Still, while there is no master rule that can tell us when the maxim applies,[301] that does not mean that skilled users of language are utterly unable to identify when a speaker has used language in a way that creates a negative implication. We do so all the time. Sometimes the maxim's applicability is obvious;[302] other times, it is subject to reasonable disagreement.[303] Again, it is clear that at least some of the semantic

when speaking English, it seems plausible that judges can select among canons in a sensible and coherent fashion even in the absence of known rules to guide them.

Jonathan R. Macey and Geoffrey P. Miller, *The Canons of Statutory Construction and Judicial Preferences*, 45 Vand L Rev 647, 650–51 (1992).

[296] *Boston Sand & Gravel Co. v United States*, 278 US 41, 48 (1928) (Holmes, J).

[297] See Shapiro, 67 NYU L Rev at 927 (cited in note 294) ("The usefulness of this much-cited maxim has been frequently challenged.").

[298] See, for example, Sunstein, 103 Harv L Rev at 455 (cited in note 37) (noting that the omission of an item from a statutory list "may reflect inadvertence, inability to reach consensus, or a decision to delegate the decision to the courts, rather than an implicit negative legislative decision on the subject").

[299] For a similar example, see Harold Hongju Koh, *The President versus the Senate in Treaty Interpretation: What's All the Fuss About?* 15 Yale J Intl L 331, 335 (1990).

[300] *Longview Fibre Co. v Rasmussen*, 980 F2d 1307, 1313 (9th Cir 1992).

[301] The Court has said that *expressio unius* properly applies only when the "circumstances" surrounding a specification "support[ ] a sensible inference that the term left out must have been meant to be excluded." *Chevron USA Inc. v Echazabal*, 536 US 73, 81 (2002). Obviously, this meta-rule for applying the canon is too general to do real work.

[302] See Geoffrey P. Miller, *Pragmatics and the Maxims of Interpretation*, 1990 Wisc L Rev 1179, 1196:

If a statute says, "All cats born on or after January 1, 1989, shall be vaccinated for feline leukemia," this is not inconsistent logically with the proposition that cats born before January 1, 1989, shall be vaccinated; yet any reader would understand intuitively that construing the statute to cover this second class of cats would flout a standard convention of interpretation.

[303] Compare, for example, *Silvers v Sony Pictures Entertainment, Inc.*, 402 F3d 881, 885 (9th Cir 2005) (en banc) (applying the maxim to conclude that the enumeration of "exclusive rights" in the Copyright Act carries a negative implication excluding unenumerated rights), with id at 899–903 (Bea, J, dissenting) (arguing that the history of the statute's enactment shows that the enumeration was not meant to be exclusive of the right claimed by the plaintiff in the case).

canons nicely describe (rather than prescribe) linguistic habits of mind,[304] but equally clear that no magic formula can guide the interpreter in applying them. The best one can say is that when a judge encounters a situation in which a linguistic practice applies, the citation of a canon provides a shorthand way for the judge to describe the mental calculation that explains his or her conclusion.

The short of it is that virtually all of the most common semantic evidence will be context-dependent and often complicated to use. Sometimes these forms of evidence will help produce clear outcomes; sometimes they will not. This will be true whether these resources are deployed by textualists or purposivists. My point is that to the extent that these resources can help to yield clear answers to statutory questions (or to reveal that no clear answer exists), new purposivists—like textualists—should deploy them *before* examining evidence of ulterior purpose.[305] Given their commitment to ensuring that language can provide the currency in which Congress expresses its implemental purposes, the first order of business for the new purposivist is to ascertain how a reasonable member of the relevant linguistic community would have *used* the language that Congress chose. That places them in sharp contrast with traditional purposivists, who believed that semantic cues (such as the canons) should yield to persuasive extratextual evidence of purpose.

IV. Conclusion

For much of this nation's history, the Court unflinchingly practiced the traditional purposivism of *Holy Trinity Church v*

---

[304] Consider this example, borrowed from Justice Scalia: "If you tell me, 'I took the boat out on the bay,' I understand 'bay' to mean one thing; if you tell me, 'I put the saddle on the bay,' I understand it to mean something else." Scalia, *A Matter of Interpretation* at 26 (cited in note 25). That outcome can be described by the canon *noscitur a sociis*—which means that a word is "'known by its companions.'" Id.

[305] In prior writing, I drew the distinction between "semantic context" (or "evidence about the way a reasonable person conversant with relevant social and linguistic practices would have used the words") and "policy context" (or "evidence that goes to the way a reasonable person conversant with the circumstances underlying enactment would suppress the mischief and advance the remedy"). See John F. Manning, *What Divides Textualists from Purposivists?* 106 Colum L Rev 70, 91 (2006). I noted that whereas traditional purposivists thought it truer to legislative supremacy to give priority to policy context over semantic context, textualists believe the opposite. See id at 92–96. The textualist position is rooted in the idea that semantic meaning is "the currency of legislative compromise"— the medium through which legislators express the scope and limits of the policy to which they were able to agree. See id at 99. The same analysis accounts for the position of the new purposivists.

United States.[306] Congress enacted statutes to achieve some ulterior purpose or policy objective. If the details of the statutory text did not achieve, or even contradicted, the goals articulated in the legislative history, the judge's job in a system of legislative supremacy was to implement the spirit or purpose rather than the letter of the law. In the past quarter-century, the Court has rejected this approach. Nowadays, if the text of the statute is clear, that is the end of the matter (unless the statute produces an absurd result). The conventional wisdom is that this change is the product of the growing influence of textualism, which emphasizes that the text of the statute alone is law and that legislative history—the primary source of evidence about ulterior purpose—cannot be credited because it lacks both legitimacy and reliability.

The difficulty with this account is that the Court has, at most, two committed textualists. Although the remaining Justices are more cautious than in earlier times about the use of legislative history, they all believe that legislative history has the potential to shed light on legislative purpose and that purpose is an important touchstone of statutory meaning. So why do these non-textualist judges reject the idea that the purpose embodied in the legislative history can trump the statutory text?

The answer may lie in the development of a new purposivism. If one looks at the behavior of all but two of the nontextualist Justices, it becomes clear that they take their cues from Congress about how and when to rely on ulterior purpose to resolve statutory meaning. When the statute is clear and precise, ulterior purpose counts for little. When a statute is vague and open-ended, ulterior purpose can be dispositive. This approach fits nicely within the purposivist intellectual tradition and has origins in the Legal Process School developed by Hart and Sacks. Since Congress cannot implement the law itself, one of the most important purposes reflected in any legislation is its implemental purpose—the decisions whether to use rules or standards and, relatedly, how much discretion to leave to the coordinate branches. If interpreters do not respect the clear meaning of a statute—if they read the word "dog" to mean "disruptive animal," or vice versa—they deny Congress the capacity to set an implemental purpose through the level of generality at which it articulates its policies. In contrast

---

[306] 143 US 457 (1892).

with traditional purposivists, new purposivists respect the level of generality at which Congress speaks. They rely on evidence of ulterior purpose only when and to whatever extent Congress has deemed appropriate through the language it adopted in the statute.

ERWIN CHEMERINSKY

FORMALISM WITHOUT A
FOUNDATION: STERN v MARSHALL

The Supreme Court's recent decision in *Stern v Marshall*[1] has a
narrow holding, but potentially enormous implications for bankruptcy courts and litigation in the federal courts. The case received
media attention because it involved Anna Nicole Smith, known in
this litigation as Vickie Lynn Marshall, a young woman who married
a much older, very wealthy man. After the death of her husband,
J. Howard Marshall II, a fierce battle for his estate ensued between
her and his son, E. Pierce Marshall. Anna Nicole Smith became a
familiar figure in the tabloids, but the issue before the Supreme
Court was hardly one to make the cover of supermarket newspapers:
Can a bankruptcy court issue a final judgment on a state law counterclaim for tortious interference with property?

The Court held, in a 5–4 decision split along familiar ideological
lines,[2] that the bankruptcy court could not issue a final judgment
over the state law counterclaim even though Congress clearly had
given it the authority to do so. Chief Justice Roberts concluded the
majority opinion by painting it as a narrow holding and declaring:

Erwin Chemerinsky is Dean and Distinguished Professor of Law, University of California, Irvine School of Law.

AUTHOR'S NOTE: I am grateful to Diana Palacios for her research assistance and to
Catherine Fisk and Kenneth Klee for very helpful conversations.

[1] 131 S Ct 2594 (2011).

[2] Chief Justice Roberts wrote for the Court, joined by Justices Scalia (who wrote a short
concurrence), Kennedy, Thomas, and Alito. Justice Breyer wrote a dissent, which was
joined by Justices Ginsburg, Sotomayor, and Kagan.

"We conclude today that Congress, in one isolated respect, exceeded [the limitation of Article III] in the Bankruptcy Act of 1984."[3]

But if this provision of the Bankruptcy Act is unconstitutional, then what other provisions are similarly impermissible in giving bankruptcy courts authority to issue final judgments? Bankruptcy courts constantly decide state law questions; after *Stern v Marshall* when can they issue final judgments on these matters? This is potentially enormously important on a practical level because of the sheer volume of matters handled by bankruptcy courts. As Justice Breyer noted in his dissent, "the volume of bankruptcy cases is staggering, involving almost 1.6 million filings last year, compared to a federal district court docket of around 260,000 civil cases and 78,000 criminal cases."[4] *Stern v Marshall* may well mean that a significant number of bankruptcy court decisions must be reviewed by the federal district courts. Moreover, if bankruptcy courts cannot issue final judgments because their judges lack the life tenure required by Article III of the Constitution, what about other non-Article III judges, such as federal magistrate judges, and their ability to issue final judgments?[5]

Beyond trying to assess the impact of the decision, there is the basic normative question as to why it is objectionable for a bankruptcy judge to issue a final judgment on a state law counterclaim. Chief Justice Roberts's majority opinion emphasized the essential role of life tenure under Article III of the Constitution in ensuring judicial independence.[6] He wrote that "Article III could neither serve its purpose in the system of checks and balances nor preserve the integrity of judicial decisionmaking if the other branches of the Federal Government could confer the Government's judicial power on entities outside Article III."[7]

Stern v Marshall, though, does not involve Congress trying to undermine judicial independence by placing a matter of federal law or of great constitutional significance in a court where the judges lack life tenure. This case involves a *state* law counterclaim and state

---

[3] 131 S Ct at 2620.

[4] Id at 2630 (Breyer, J, dissenting).

[5] Magistrate judges are appointed by the federal district courts and serve eight-year terms. 28 USC § 636(c). Bankruptcy judges are appointed by the federal court of appeals and serve fourteen-year terms. 28 USC § 152(a). This is discussed below at text accompanying notes 113–14.

[6] *Stern*, 131 S Ct at 2608–09.

[7] Id at 2609.

law matters are usually adjudicated in state courts whose judges generally do not have life tenure. There is a significant disconnect between the lofty goal of protecting judicial independence and the holding that the bankruptcy court cannot issue a final judgment on a state law counterclaim for tortious interference with recovery from a large estate. Never does the Court explain why allowing a bankruptcy court to issue a final judgment on a state law counterclaim risks undermining judicial independence in any way.

The only way to understand *Stern v Marshall* is to see it as a very formalistic application of legal rules that have developed over more than a century and a half concerning when Congress can vest judicial matters in non-Article III judges. On examination, these rules make little sense, and so application of them in a formalistic way likewise is inherently unsatisfying.

Seeing *Stern v Marshall* in this way also helps to explain why the case divided 5–4 along ideological lines. After all, the scope of bankruptcy court authority would not be thought of as the type of issue, like gun control or affirmative action or abortion, that would divide the Court ideologically. But if the case is seen through the lens of a formalistic as opposed to a more functional approach to constitutional adjudication, a key difference between the conservative and liberal Justices on the current Court, then the basis for the 5–4 split in *Stern v Marshall* becomes much clearer.

In Part I, I briefly review the facts of *Stern v Marshall* and the Court's holding that it was unconstitutional for the bankruptcy court to issue a final judgment in favor of Vickie Lynn Marshall. Part II then focuses on the normative premise of *Stern v Marshall*— that it offends separation of powers to allow a non-Article III court to issue a final judgment as to a state law matter—and argues that this makes little sense and can be understood only as the Court following in a formalistic way a series of decisions that themselves make little sense. In fact, the case is a marked departure from other, more recent Supreme Court decisions that took a far more functional approach to deciding when Congress could assign judicial matters to non-Article III judges.[8] Part III then explores the implications of *Stern v Marshall* and especially the key question that is likely to determine its impact: Can consent solve the problem

---

[8] *Commodities Futures Trading Commission v Schor*, 478 US 833 (1986); *Thomas v Union Carbide Agricultural Products Co.*, 473 US 568 (1985).

and allow a non-Article III court to issue a final judgment in a matter otherwise beyond its power?

I. What Happened?

Chief Justice Roberts began his majority opinion by quoting from Charles Dickens's *Bleak House*, and the analogy certainly seems apt.[9] The litigation began even before J. Howard Marshall's death in 1995.[10] Only a relatively brief recitation of the facts is needed to understand the constitutional issue presented.

Vickie Lynn Marshall and J. Howard Marshall met in October 1991 and were married on June 27, 1994. Although he lavished gifts and significant sums of money on Vickie during their courtship and marriage, J. Howard did not include anything for Vickie in his will.[11] Before J. Howard passed away in August 1995, Vickie filed suit in Texas probate court, claiming that Pierce Marshall—J. Howard's younger son—fraudulently induced his father to sign a living trust that did not include her. She maintained that J. Howard meant to leave her half of his estate. Pierce denied any fraudulent activity and defended the trust and, after his father's death, the will.

Soon after J. Howard died, in January 1996, Vickie filed a petition for bankruptcy in the U.S. District Court for the Central District of California. In June 1996, Pierce filed a proof of claim in the federal bankruptcy proceeding, alleging that Vickie had defamed him when attorneys representing Vickie told members of the press that Pierce had engaged in forgery, fraud, and overreaching to gain control of his father's assets. Vickie answered, asserting truth as a defense. She also filed counterclaims, among them a claim that Pierce had tortiously interfered with a gift she expected. She contended that Pierce essentially imprisoned J. Howard against his wishes, surrounded him with hired guards for the purpose of preventing contact with Vickie, made misrepresentations to J. Howard,

---

[9] *Stern*, 131 S Ct at 2600 (citation omitted).

[10] The facts are recounted in more detail in *Marshall v Marshall*, 547 US 293 (2006), the first time the matter came to the Supreme Court on the issue of whether the probate exception precluded federal court jurisdiction (and the Court held that it did not). The Court also presents the key facts at the beginning of its opinion in *Stern*, 131 S Ct at 2601–03.

[11] Because there are three different individuals named Marshall involved—J. Howard Marshall, Pierce Marshall, and Vickie Lynn Marshall—it is easiest to refer to them by first names.

and transferred property against J. Howard's expressed wishes.[12]

The bankruptcy court granted summary judgment in favor of Vickie on Pierce's claim and, after a trial on the merits, entered judgment for Vickie on her tortious interference counterclaim.[13] The bankruptcy court also held that both Vickie's objection to Pierce's claim and Vickie's counterclaim qualified as "core proceedings" under the Bankruptcy Act, which meant that the court had authority to enter a final judgment disposing of those claims.[14] The court awarded Vickie compensatory damages of more than $449 million—less whatever she recovered in the ongoing probate action in Texas—as well as $25 million in punitive damages.[15]

The District Court concluded that the bankruptcy court lacked the authority to issue a final judgment on Vickie's counterclaim and thus said that it would treat the bankruptcy court's judgment as "proposed rather than final" and engaged in an "independent review of the record."[16] However, subsequent to the bankruptcy court decision, but prior to the decision of the District Court, the Texas probate court had conducted a jury trial and ruled in favor of Pierce Marshall. The District Court, however, did not give preclusive effect to this decision and agreed with the bankruptcy court that Pierce had tortiously interfered with Vickie's inheritance. The District Court reduced the damages to approximately $88 million, divided equally between compensatory and punitive damages.

The Ninth Circuit reversed the District Court based on the matter falling within the probate exception to federal jurisdiction, but the Supreme Court unanimously reversed and remanded the case back to the Ninth Circuit.[17] The Ninth Circuit then ruled in favor of Pierce, holding that the counterclaim was not properly within the core jurisdiction of the bankruptcy court and thus that it lacked

---

[12] *Marshall*, 547 US at 301.

[13] *In re Marshall*, 253 BR 550, 558–59 (Bankr CD Cal 2000).

[14] *In re Marshall*, 257 BR 35, 39–40 (CD Cal 2000).

[15] Id at 40.

[16] *In re Marshall*, 264 BR 609, 633 (CD Cal 2001) ("[A] counterclaim should not be characterized as core [if it] is only somewhat related to the claim against which it is asserted, and when the unique characteristics and context of the counterclaim place it outside the normal type of set-off or other counterclaims that customarily arise.").

[17] *Marshall v Marshall*, 547 US 293 (2006) (holding that the "probate exception" to federal court jurisdiction did not bar a federal court, including a bankruptcy court, from deciding a claim of tortious interference with recovery from an estate).

the authority to issue a final judgment.[18] Because the bankruptcy court could not issue a final judgment, its ruling lacked preclusive effect; thus, the Texas probate court decision was binding.

That was the issue before the Supreme Court. If the bankruptcy court had the authority to issue a final judgment, then its ruling was preclusive of the Texas probate court's decision and Vickie's estate wins. But if the bankruptcy court lacked the authority to issue a final judgment, then there was no preclusion of the Texas probate court and Pierce's estate wins. The Court, 5–4, took the latter approach.

Chief Justice Roberts wrote for the Court. The Court said that the Bankruptcy Act in § 157(b)(2)(c) expressly makes counterclaims "core" proceedings over which the bankruptcy court could issue a final judgment.[19] But the Court found that this violated the Constitution because bankruptcy judges do not have life tenure. Chief Justice Roberts's majority opinion began by stressing the essential nature of Article III protections for separation of powers and the protection of individual liberties. He wrote:

> Article III protects liberty not only through its role in implementing the
> separation of powers, but also by specifying the defining characteristics
> of Article III judges. . . . Article III could neither serve its purpose in
> the system of checks and balances nor preserve the integrity of judicial
> decisionmaking if the other branches of the Federal Government could
> confer the Government's "judicial Power" on entities outside Article III.
> That is why we have long recognized that, in general, Congress may not
> "withdraw from judicial cognizance any matter which, from its nature,
> is the subject of a suit at the common law, or in equity, or in admiralty."[20]

The Court concluded that it violated Article III for Congress to authorize the bankruptcy court to issue a final judgment over the state law counterclaim. The Court explained that this did not fit into any of the traditional exceptions where non-Article III courts are allowed, such as for "public rights" matters where it is a claim against the United States and Congress has waived its sovereign immunity but with the condition that the matter be heard in a non-

---

[18] *In re Marshall*, 600 F3d 1037, 1058–59 (9th Cir 2010).

[19] *Stern*, 131 S Ct at 2604–05. The Bankruptcy Act designates some matters as core, over which the bankruptcy court can issue a final judgment, and some matters as noncore, over which the bankruptcy court can issue a final judgment with consent of the parties or otherwise make a report and recommendation to the federal district court.

[20] Id at 2609 (citations omitted).

Article III court.[21] Nor, the Court said, could the bankruptcy court be seen as an "adjunct" of the district court. Chief Justice Roberts explained that given its expansive authority, "a bankruptcy court can no more be deemed a mere 'adjunct' of the district court than a district court can be deemed such an 'adjunct' of the court of appeals."[22]

In what is likely the most important language of the opinion in terms of when bankruptcy courts can issue final judgments, the Court said that "the question is whether the action at issue stems from the bankruptcy itself or would necessarily be resolved in the claims allowance process."[23] Vickie's counterclaim for tortious interference did not fit within this definition, and thus the bankruptcy court decision was not a final judgment and had no preclusive effect over the Texas probate court decision.

II. WHY?

The basis for the Court's decision was that it was unconstitutional for Congress to give non-Article III judges the authority to issue a final judgment over the state law counterclaim. But it is questionable as to why this is unconstitutional. Chief Justice Roberts focused, at some length, on the importance of Article III in ensuring the independence of the federal judiciary.[24]

The Court's emphasis on the importance of an independent judiciary would make sense if this were an issue of federal constitutional law, especially one where life tenure might make judges more inclined to withstand popular pressure and uphold the Constitution. But the issue in *Stern v Marshall* was a state law claim that by itself would not even fit within the scope of the matters that federal courts are allowed to hear under Article III, Section 2 of the Constitution. State law claims are generally adjudicated by state law judges who rarely have life tenure. What then was so objectionable about Con-

---

[21] Id at 2611 ("Vickie's counterclaim cannot be deemed a matter of 'public right' that can be decided outside the Judicial Branch."). The public rights exception is based on the notion that since sovereign immunity bars claims against the United States, Congress can waive sovereign immunity on the condition that the matter be brought in a non-Article III court. The public rights exception is derived from *Murray's Lessee v Hoboken Land and Improvement Co.*, 59 US 272 (1856).

[22] *Stern*, 131 S Ct at 2619.

[23] Id at 2618.

[24] Id at 2608–09.

gress authorizing bankruptcy judges without life tenure to hear the matters?

Chief Justice Roberts's only answer to this question comes at the end of the majority opinion. He writes: "Is there really a threat to the separation of powers where Congress has conferred the judicial power outside Article III only over certain counterclaims in bankruptcy? The short but emphatic answer is yes. A statute may no more lawfully chip away at the authority of the Judicial Branch than it may eliminate it entirely."[25]

But Congress has "chipped away" at the "authority of the Judicial Branch" by assigning judicial matters to non-Article III courts in many different situations since the earliest days of American history. The question, which the Court does not answer, is what is objectionable about this matter being assigned to a non-Article III court in light of all that proceeded it in terms of situations in which non-Article III judges are allowed. This question, of course, can be assessed only in the context of what the Court previously has said about when non-Article III courts are permitted. Section A reviews this history and shows that the Court never has developed a coherent explanation for why non-Article III courts are permissible under the Constitution. Section B then looks at the Supreme Court's decision in *Northern Pipeline Construction Co. v Marathon Pipeline Co.*,[26] which limited the ability of bankruptcy courts to decide state law claims.[27] *Northern Pipeline* is the foundation for *Stern v Marshall*, and yet it, too, lacks a persuasive justification for why bankruptcy courts cannot decide state law matters. Section C then concludes by arguing that the Court's decision in *Stern v Marshall* is deeply flawed because it is an exercise in formalism that is based on a foundation that cannot be justified.

A. ARTICLE III AND NON-ARTICLE III COURTS

The text of Article III seemingly requires that all federal judges have life tenure and salaries that cannot be decreased during their terms of office. Article III, Section 1 says that "[t]he judicial power of the United States shall be vested in one Supreme Court, and in such inferior courts as the Congress may from time to time

---

[25] Id at 2620.

[26] 458 US 50 (1982).

[27] Id at 87.

ordain and establish. The judges, both of the supreme and inferior courts, shall hold their offices during good behavior, and shall, at stated times, receive compensation, which shall not be diminished during their continuance in office."[28] This flatly declares that all inferior courts that Congress creates must have judges with these protections. No exceptions are mentioned.

But it never has been that way.[29] The first Congress authorized executive officers in the Treasury Department to decide matters, such as claims to veterans' benefits, that fell within Article III.[30] The Supreme Court has upheld the constitutionality of non-Article III courts, sometimes called "legislative courts," since 1828.[31] Over time, the Supreme Court has recognized three situations where it will allow Congress to create inferior courts whose judges do not have life tenure and salary protection.

First, the Court allowed non-Article III courts for the territories. In *American Insurance Co. v Canter*,[32] in 1828, the Court considered the constitutionality of a court created for the territory of Florida, which was not yet a state.[33] Judges on this territorial court were appointed for four-year terms. Chief Justice Marshall, writing for the Court, upheld the constitutionality of the territorial courts. The Court contrasted "constitutional courts" established by Congress pursuant to Article III, with "legislative courts," which were created pursuant to Congress's legislative powers under Articles I and IV of the Constitution. Chief Justice Marshall declared: "These Courts, then, are not constitutional Courts. . . . They are legislative Courts, created in virtue of that general right of sovereignty which exists in the government, or in virtue of the clause which enables Congress to make all needful rules and regulations, respecting the territory belonging to the United States."[34]

Congress created territorial courts with judges lacking life tenure primarily to avoid a surplus of federal judges after the terri-

---

[28] US Const, Art III, § 1.

[29] For a thorough history of the use of non-Article III courts, see James Pfander, *Article I Tribunals, Article III Courts, and the Judicial Power of the United States*, 118 Harv L Rev 643 (2004).

[30] Richard H. Fallon, *Of Legislative Courts, Administrative Agencies and Article III*, 101 Harv L Rev 915, 919 (1988).

[31] *American Insurance Co. v Canter*, 26 US (1 Pet) 511 (1828).

[32] Id.

[33] Id at 511.

[34] Id at 546.

tories were admitted into statehood.[35] The territorial courts decided all judicial matters—both federal and state law questions—
arising in the territories. Thus, there was a need for more territorial judges than there would be for federal judges once the territory became a state. In Florida, for example, there were five
territorial judges, but after it became a state, there was only one
federal court judge.[36] The Supreme Court later explained that "[i]t
would have been doctrinaire in the extreme to deny the right of
Congress to invest judges of its creation with authority to dispose
of the judicial business of the territories. It would have been at
least as dogmatic . . . to fashion on those judges a guarantee of
tenure that Congress could not put to use and that the exigencies
of the territories did not require."[37]

Yet it is questionable whether this policy rationale justifies the
Court's permitting a departure from the literal language of Article
III. Article III says that all inferior federal courts—that is, all
federal courts subordinate to the United States Supreme Court—
shall have judges with life tenure who are protected against re-
ductions in salary. By definition, the territorial courts are inferior
courts of the United States.

Second, the Supreme Court has allowed non-Article III courts
for the military. In *Dynes v Hoover*,[38] in 1858, the Supreme Court
upheld Congress's power to create legislative courts for the military.[39] The Court explained that Congress's authority under Article I permitted it "to provide for the trial and punishment of
military and naval offences . . . without any connection between
it and the 3rd article of the Constitution defining the judicial
power of the United States."[40]

The argument for separate courts for the military is that specialized tribunals and procedures are justified by the need for discipline and order in the armed services. But this only explains the
need for a distinct military court system and some differences in

---

[35] See *Glidden Co. v Zdanok*, 370 US 530, 544–47 (1962) (explaining the rationale behind
territorial courts).

[36] Id.

[37] Id.

[38] 61 US (20 How) 65 (1858).

[39] Id at 79. In *Weiss v United States*, 510 US 163, 181 (1994), the Supreme Court held
that the Due Process Clause does not require that military judges have fixed terms of
office.

[40] Id at 79.

procedures; it does not explain why judges in military courts should not be accorded life tenure and salary protections.

Third, the Supreme Court has allowed for non-Article III courts for deciding disputes between the U.S. government and private parties. These are often referred to as "public rights" cases, and this exception was expressly discussed in *Stern v Marshall*.[41] The use of legislative courts for civil disputes between the government and private citizens was first approved by the Supreme Court in *Murray's Lessee v Hoboken Land & Improvement Co.*,[42] which also was discussed in *Stern v Marshall*. In *Murray's Lessee*, the Court stated that Congress could not withdraw from federal "judicial cognizance any matter which, from its nature, is the subject of a suit at the common law, or in equity, or admiralty."[43] But the Court said, "there are matters, involving public rights, which may be presented in such form that the judicial power is capable of acting on them, and which are susceptible of judicial determination, but which Congress may or may not bring within the cognizance of the Courts of the United States."[44]

Under the public rights doctrine, many disputes between the government and private citizens are decided, at least initially, in administrative agencies or Article I courts. The Tax Court, for example, has judges who sit for fifteen-year terms.[45] Because the Tax Court resolves disputes between the government and citizens, Article I judges are permitted.[46]

Similarly, administrative agencies often perform adjudicatory tasks. Federal agencies, employing administrative law judges, decide a large volume of cases involving benefits under government entitlement programs, such as the Social Security Act. Immigration cases are yet another category of civil cases arising under

---

[41] 130 S Ct at 2611–15.

[42] 59 US (18 How) 272 (1856).

[43] Id at 284.

[44] Id. It should be noted that *Murray's Lessee* did not actually involve a legislative court. The holding was that Congress could authorize summary distraint of property to satisfy debts owed to the United States.

[45] See *Freytag v Commissioner of Internal Revenue*, 501 US 868, 890–92 (1991) (upholding the constitutionality of the Tax Courts and their ability to appoint judges for specific matters).

[46] For example, a constitutional challenge to the Tax Court was rejected on the ground that the Tax Court fit into the traditional public rights exception because it adjudicated disputes between the government and private citizens. *Simanonok v Commissioner of Internal Revenue*, 731 F2d 743 (11th Cir 1984).

federal law, albeit ones where the consequences of decisions are usually great, that are handled in administrative proceedings. These are just a few of countless instances in which civil disputes between the government and private citizens are decided by legislative courts.[47]

The Supreme Court has offered several explanations for why public law matters can be decided in non-Article III tribunals. One rationale is based on sovereign immunity. Because the U.S. government has sovereign immunity, it may be sued only if Congress authorizes such suit. Also, the federal government has the power to sue only if Congress grants it such authority. The argument is that because Congress has discretion whether to permit such litigation, it can choose to authorize the suits on the condition that they be brought in a particular tribunal, such as a legislative court. In fact, the Supreme Court has explained that "[t]he doctrine may be explained in part by reference to the traditional principle of sovereign immunity, which recognizes that the Government may attach conditions to its consent to be sued."[48]

Another justification for the public rights doctrine is that the framers intended that Congress should be able to create legislative courts for such matters. Justice Brennan explained that "the framers expected that Congress would be free to commit such matters completely to nonjudicial executive determination, and that as a result there can be no constitutional objection to Congress' employing the less drastic expedient of committing their determination to a legislative court or administrative agency."[49]

The Supreme Court also has invoked history to justify permitting Congress to assign public rights matters to legislative courts. The Court said that there is "a historically recognized distinction" between inherently judicial matters, which must be decided by an Article III court, and those that can be decided in other tribunals.[50] The Court stated that "[p]rivate rights disputes . . . lie at the core

---

[47] Similarly, a federal court of appeals upheld the authority of the Benefits Review Board, which reviews the award of benefits for conditions, such as black lung disease. The court emphasized the ability of Congress to assign the adjudication of statutorily created rights to administrative agencies. *Gibas v Saginaw Mining Co.*, 748 F2d 1112, 1119 (6th Cir 1984), cert denied, 471 US 1116 (1984).

[48] *Northern Pipeline*, 458 US at 67.

[49] Id at 68.

[50] Id.

of the historically recognized judicial power."[51] But according to the Court, public law matters—civil disputes between the government and private citizens—are not inherently judicial and may be assigned to legislative courts.

However, these rationales are open to question. A strong argument can be made that an independent judiciary is especially important in a dispute between the government and a private citizen. A primary purpose of the U.S. Constitution is to protect people from the arbitrary exercise of power by the federal government. Judges with life tenure and salary protection are more likely to perform this checking function than are those answerable to the legislature and executive branches.[52] Moreover, it can be argued that although Congress has discretion to allow the United States to be sued, once such suits are authorized it would be an "unconstitutional condition" to require the litigation be brought in courts that are otherwise unconstitutional.[53] Under this view, Congress can choose only whether the suit will be permitted; once litigation is allowed, it must be in an Article III court.

B. ARTICLE III MEETS BANKRUPTCY COURTS: NORTHERN PIPELINE

It was against this legal backdrop that the Supreme Court in 1982 decided *Northern Pipeline* and articulated the basis for the limits on the powers of the bankruptcy courts that was invoked in *Stern v Marshall*. In *Northern Pipeline*, the Court—without a majority opinion—declared unconstitutional the bankruptcy courts created by the Bankruptcy Act of 1978. Under that act, bankruptcy judges appointed to fourteen-year terms had broad jurisdiction to decide private civil disputes. The Court held that this authority violated Article III.

The facts of the case were simple. The Northern Pipeline Construction Company sued the Marathon Pipe Line Company in the U.S. District Court for the Western District of Kentucky. Subsequently, Northern Pipeline filed for bankruptcy in the U.S.

---

[51] Id at 70.

[52] See, for example, Kenneth S. Klein, *The Public Rights Doctrine in Light of the Historical Rationale of the Seventh Amendment*, 21 Hastings Const L Q 1013 (1994); Mary Ellen Fullerton, *No Light at the End of the Pipeline: Confusion Surrounds Legislative Courts*, 49 Brooklyn L Rev 207, 230–31 (1983).

[53] See, for example, Martin H. Redish, *Legislative Courts, Administrative Agencies, and the Northern Pipeline Decision*, 1983 Duke L J 197, 214 (1983).

Bankruptcy Court for the District of Minnesota. Northern Pipeline also filed a claim in the bankruptcy court against Marathon
Pipe Line for breach of contract. This was identical to the suit it
had filed in federal court in Kentucky. Marathon Pipe Line argued
that it was unconstitutional for the breach-of-contract claim to be
tried in the bankruptcy court because the judges lacked life tenure
and the salary protections required under Article III.

The Supreme Court agreed and ruled that the bankruptcy courts
were unconstitutional. There were three major opinions, none of
which was joined by a majority of the Court. Justice Brennan wrote
for a plurality including Justices Marshall, Blackmun, and Stevens.
Justice Brennan's plurality opinion stressed that legislative courts
were permitted only in a few instances—for territories, the military, and public rights disputes—and that bankruptcy did not fit
into these exceptions.[54] Moreover, the plurality opinion said that
legislative courts could be used as an adjunct to Article III courts
only under limited circumstances. The existence of review by an
Article III court was deemed insufficient to permit the use of a
legislative court. Justice Brennan wrote: "Appellants suggest . . .
that Art. III is satisfied so long as some degree of appellate review
is provided. But that suggestion is directly contrary to the text of
our Constitution. . . . Our precedents make it clear that the constitutional requirements for the exercise of the judicial power must
be met at all stages of adjudication."[55]

Justices Rehnquist and O'Connor concurred in the judgment.
Their position was that it was unconstitutional for Congress to
vest in the bankruptcy courts broad authority to adjudicate state
law matters that were only tangentially related to the adjudication
of bankruptcy under federal law.[56] They agreed with the plurality
that appellate review in an Article III court was insufficient to cure
this constitutional defect.[57] Unlike the plurality, the concurrence
said that it was unnecessary to express an opinion on anything
other than this aspect of the bankruptcy courts' jurisdiction. How-

---

[54] *Northern Pipeline*, 458 US at 86 n 39.

[55] Id at 81–86.

[56] Id at 91 (bankruptcy courts are not an adjunct to Article III courts).

[57] Chief Justice Burger also wrote a short, separate dissenting opinion to emphasize the
narrowness of the concurring opinion authored by Justices Rehnquist and O'Connor and
hence the narrowness of the ultimate holding in *Northern Pipeline*. Id at 92 (Burger, CJ,
dissenting).

ever, because Justices Rehnquist and O'Connor agreed that it was uncertain what Congress would have enacted had it been unable to vest plenary jurisdiction in the bankruptcy courts, they concurred in declaring the courts unconstitutional.

Justice White wrote a lengthy dissent joined by Chief Justice Burger and Justice Powell.[58] The dissent emphasized a functional approach to analyzing the constitutionality of legislative courts focusing on whether the particular court undermines separation of powers and checks and balances. Justice White explained: "The inquiry should, rather, focus equally on those Art. III values and ask whether and to what extent the legislative scheme accommodates them or, conversely, substantially undermines them. The burden on Art. III values should then be measured against the values Congress hopes to serve through the use of Art. I courts."[59] Justice White's approach openly balances the benefits of a legislative court against its effects on separation of powers and judicial independence.

In this instance, the dissent found little reason to object to the use of a legislative court. Justice White emphasized that when a legislative court is "designed to deal with issues likely to be of little interest to the political branches," there is no fear that Congress is creating such tribunals to aggrandize its own power.[60] Moreover, Justice White explained that, for the sake of flexibility, Congress understandably did not want to create several hundred bankruptcy judges with life tenure. In light of the existence of appellate review by Article III courts, the dissent would have upheld the constitutionality of the bankruptcy courts.

Thus, in *Northern Pipeline* six of the Justices found it objectionable to assign state law matters to a non-Article III judge. But why? Why did the plurality draw the line at legislative courts being permissible for the territories, the military, and public rights disputes but for nothing else? In *Palmore v United States*,[61] the Court spoke of the constitutionality of legislative courts for "specialized areas having particularized needs and warranting distinctive treatment."[62] Bankruptcy certainly is a "specialized area" with "partic-

---

[58] *Northern Pipeline*, 458 US at 115 (White, J, dissenting).

[59] Id.

[60] Id.

[61] 411 US 389 (1973).

[62] Id at 408.

ularized needs," especially the desire to make sure that all of the claims by or against the bankruptcy estate are resolved in a single proceeding. The plurality in *Northern Pipeline* found legislative courts for the territories, the military, and public rights matters to fit within this exception, but not bankruptcy courts. Yet, the Justices gave little explanation for why they were drawing the line at this point.[63]

Justice Brennan, writing for the plurality, said that if Congress creates a right, Congress can decide the forum where it will be adjudicated. But this is not so for state law claims since, by definition, they were not created by Congress. Justice Brennan wrote: "Indeed, the cases before us, which center upon appellant Northern's claim for damages for breach of contract and misrepresentation, involve a right created by *state* law, a right independent of and antecedent to the reorganization petition that conferred jurisdiction upon the Bankruptcy Court. Accordingly, Congress's authority to control the manner in which that right is adjudicated, through assignment of historically judicial functions to a non-Art. III 'adjunct,' plainly must be deemed at a minimum."[64]

But still there is no explanation for why it is objectionable for *state* law matters to be decided by a non-Article III court, or an answer to Justice White's arguments in dissent that this is not a situation in which the structural protections of Article III are needed. There is a highly formalistic approach by the plurality that seems uncharacteristic of Justice Brennan's approach to constitutional law.

I would suggest that the decision in *Northern Pipeline*—and especially the plurality comprised of the Court's most liberal Justices (Brennan, Marshall, Blackmun, and Stevens)—was a reflection of the context of the times. In 1980, Ronald Reagan won the presidency and Republicans gained control of the Senate. In 1981, a number of bills were introduced into the new Congress to strip the Supreme Court and the lower federal courts of the ability to decide particular issues, such as challenges to state laws restricting abortion or allowing prayer in public schools.[65] Tremendous at-

---

[63] *Northern Pipeline*, 458 US at 86 n 39.

[64] Id at 84 (emphasis in original).

[65] See, for example, S 158, 97th Cong, 1st Sess, in 127 Cong Rec S 496 (Jan 19, 1981); HR 3225, 97th Cong, 1st Sess, in 127 Cong Rec H 7324 (Apr 10, 1981) (bills restricting federal court jurisdiction in abortion cases); S 481, 97th Cong, 1st Sess, in 127 Cong Rec

tention was paid in law reviews in 1981 to whether such bills would be constitutional, including Professor Lawrence Sager's foreword to the November 1981 issue of the *Harvard Law Review*.[66]

It was in this context that the Court decided *Northern Pipeline* in June 1982. I always have believed that the liberal plurality in *Northern Pipeline* was attempting to send a message to Congress about limits on congressional power to take matters away from the Article III courts.[67] The jurisdiction of the bankruptcy courts to hear state law matters just happened to be the vehicle that was before the Court at exactly that time. The plurality could not articulate a persuasive reason why having bankruptcy courts decide state law matters was particularly objectionable, especially in light of other instances in which non-Article III courts were allowed, but it could and did make clear that the Court would prevent Congress from removing other matters from the Article III judiciary.

C. STERN V MARSHALL

After *Northern Pipeline*, Congress passed the Bankruptcy Amendments and Federal Judgeship Act of 1984, which provides that bankruptcy judges are appointed for fourteen-year terms by the U.S. Courts of Appeals.[68] Bankruptcy judges are said to be officers of the district courts. The 1984 act changed the jurisdiction of the bankruptcy courts. The new law drew a distinction between "core" and "noncore" bankruptcy proceedings. Core matters are those involving the bankrupt's property or assets within the jurisdiction of the bankruptcy court. Bankruptcy courts may "hear and decide" these core proceedings.

Noncore matters are those that earlier would have been within the bankruptcy courts' plenary jurisdiction. Here, the 1984 act draws a further distinction between noncore matters that would

---

S 2184 (Feb 16, 1981); HR 4756, 97th Cong, 1st Sess, in 127 Cong Rec H 24228 (Oct 15,1981) (bills restricting federal court jurisdiction over cases that involve voluntary school prayer).

[66] Lawrence Sager, *Foreword: Constitutional Limits on Congress' Authority to Regulate the Jurisdiction of the Federal Courts*, 95 Harv L Rev 17 (1981); see also Laurence Tribe, *Jurisdictional Gerrymandering: Zoning Disfavored Rights Out of the Federal Courts*, 16 Harv CR-CL L Rev 129 (1981).

[67] Professor Judith Resnik made this point not long after *Northern Pipeline* was decided. Judith Resnik, *The Mythic Meaning of Article III Courts*, 56 U Colo L Rev 581, 599 (1985).

[68] *Granfinanciera, S.A.*, 492 US 33 (1989).

have fit within federal court jurisdiction absent the Bankruptcy Act (e.g., because of diversity or federal question jurisdiction) and those that a federal court could not otherwise have heard. As to noncore matters for which there is an independent basis for federal jurisdiction, the bankruptcy courts make proposed findings of fact and conclusions of law to the federal district court. A final order is not entered until after the district court engages in de novo review of any matters to which an objection was made. But noncore matters, for which there is not a separate basis for federal jurisdiction, should be dismissed upon a motion if state proceedings exist that can provide a timely resolution of the issue. Also, the bankruptcy courts specifically are prevented from exercising jurisdiction over personal injury tort and wrongful death claims.

The statute delineates what are "core" proceedings and specifically includes within this "counterclaims by the estate against persons filing claims against the estate."[69] Thus, Vickie Lynn Marshall's state law counterclaim against Pierce Marshall was a "core" proceeding and the bankruptcy court was authorized by statute to issue a final judgment. But the Supreme Court held that Congress could not constitutionally authorize non-Article III courts to issue a final judgment over such state law matters.

The Court, though, never explains why it threatens the independence of the judiciary and individual liberty for the non-Article III bankruptcy courts to decide the state law counterclaim. There is a highly formalistic quality to Chief Justice Roberts's majority opinion. Indeed, he reasons in a syllogism:

Major premise: Congress may create non-Article III courts with power to issue final judgments only for territories, the military, and public rights matters.

Minor premise: The state law counterclaim of Vickie Lynn Marshall does not involve the territories, the military, or public rights matters.

Conclusion: It is unconstitutional for the bankruptcy court to issue a final judgment over Vickie Lynn Marshall's counterclaim.

But as with any syllogism, the conclusion follows only if the premises are true. The Court never explains why the line is to be drawn in that way, other than that is what *Northern Pipeline* said. Chief Justice Roberts emphasizes at length the importance of ju-

---

[69] 28 USC § 157(b)(2)(C).

dicial independence to protect individual liberties. He fails, however, to explain why that is implicated in a case involving a state
law counterclaim.

The Court's formalism is even more questionable because subsequent to *Northern Pipeline* the Court took a far more functional
approach to deciding when non-Article III courts are permissible.
In fact, in these later decisions the Court used exactly the functional approach urged by Justice White in his dissent in *Northern
Pipeline*.

The first post-*Northern Pipeline* decision was *Thomas v Union
Carbide Agricultural Products Co.*[70] In *Thomas*, the Supreme Court
upheld the constitutionality of an arbitration system designed to
resolve valuation disputes among participants in a pesticide reg-
istration program. Federal law required manufacturers to submit
research data regarding the health, safety, and environmental effects of all pesticides. The law permitted the data submitted by
one company to be used by another that sought to register the
same or a similar product, but a company using another company's
data had to pay for the costs of the data generation. The Environmental Protection Agency (EPA) was entrusted with determining the appropriate amount of compensation owed and resolving disputes. To relieve the EPA of this burden, Congress
shifted the task of valuation for compensation purposes to a system
of negotiations and binding arbitrations. Judicial review was limited to instances of "fraud, misrepresentation, or other miscon-
duct."[71]

The issue in *Thomas* was whether Congress could assign this
private law dispute to a non-Article III court. In upholding the
constitutionality of the arbitration system, the Court narrowly
stated what it understood to be the holding of *Northern Pipeline*.
Justice O'Connor, writing for the majority, said that the earlier
decision established only "that Congress may not vest in a non-
Article III court the power to adjudicate, render final judgment,
and issue binding orders in a traditional contract action arising
under state law, without consent of the litigants, and subject only
to ordinary appellate review."[72]

---

[70] 473 US at 584.

[71] 7 USC § 136a(c)(1)(D)(ii).

[72] *Thomas*, 473 US at 593–94.

The Court said that legislative courts were permissible for private disputes that were closely related to government regulatory activities. In perhaps the most important language of the majority opinion, Justice O'Connor stated: "Congress, acting for a valid legislative purpose pursuant to its constitutional powers under article I, may create a seemingly 'private' right that is so closely integrated into a public regulatory scheme as to be a matter appropriate for agency resolution."[73]

The Court adopted a functional approach, considering the desirability of a non-Article III tribunal and the degree of encroachment on the federal judiciary. In this way, the Court's approach seems similar to the balancing test endorsed by Justice White in *Northern Pipeline*.[74]

The Court again adopted a functional approach to the constitutionality of non-Article III courts in *Commodity Futures Trading Commission v Schor*.[75] The Commodity Futures Trading Commission has the statutory authority to provide reparations to individuals who are injured by fraudulent or illegally manipulative conduct by brokers.[76] The commission also promulgated regulations that enabled it to hear all counterclaims arising out of the same allegedly impermissible transactions.

The Court separately considered these two aspects of the commission's jurisdiction: the authority to provide reparations and the power to adjudicate counterclaims. As to the former, the Court found that the commission's jurisdiction to order reparations to injured consumers was "of unquestioned constitutional validity."[77] Because the commission could not enforce its own orders, which instead required federal court action, the Court concluded that the commission served as an adjunct to the federal court.

The more difficult question was whether the commission could hear state law counterclaims. In *Northern Pipeline*, both the plurality and the concurrence found objectionable the bankruptcy courts' authority to decide state law matters. However, in *Schor*, the Court approved the commission's authority to rule on the state law counterclaims. The Court expressly endorsed a balancing

---

[73] Id at 593.

[74] Id at 589–90, 593–94.

[75] *Schor*, 478 US 833 (1986).

[76] 7 USC § 18.

[77] *Schor*, 478 US at 856.

test in appraising the constitutionality of legislative courts.[78]

The Court identified the benefits of an administrative alternative to federal court litigation in terms of efficiency and expertise.[79] At the same time, the Court said that these interests had to be balanced against "the purposes underlying the requirements of Article III."[80] The Court considered two goals of Article III: ensuring fairness to litigants by providing an independent judiciary, and maintaining the "structural" role of the judiciary in the scheme of separation of powers. As to fairness, the Court said that the defendant had consented to the administrative proceedings as an alternative to federal court litigation and hence could not claim that the commission adjudication was inherently unfair.[81]

As to separation of powers, the Court declared: "In determining the extent to which a given congressional decision to authorize the adjudication of article III business in a non-article III tribunal impermissibly threatens the institutional integrity of the Judicial Branch, the Court has declined to adopt formalistic and unbending rules."[82] Justice O'Connor, writing for the majority, said that instead the Court focuses on several factors, including "the extent to which the 'essential attributes of judicial power' are reserved to article III courts, and conversely, the extent to which the non-article III forum exercises the range of jurisdiction and powers normally vested only in article III courts, the origins and importance of the right to be adjudicated, and the concerns that drove Congress to depart from the requirements of article III."[83]

It is not possible to reconcile the functional approach in *Thomas* and *Schor* with the formalistic approach in *Stern v Marshall*. The Court in *Stern v Marshall* returned to the earlier formalism of *Northern Pipeline*, but without ever acknowledging that the cases subsequent to it had taken a dramatically different method of analyzing when Congress can give authority to non-Article III courts. The Court in *Stern v Marshall* could have recognized and disavowed the functional approach of *Thomas* and *Schor* and reaffirmed the formalism of *Northern Pipeline*. Or it could have em-

---

[78] Id.

[79] Id at 847.

[80] Id at 849–50.

[81] Id at 851.

[82] Id.

[83] Id at 856.

braced the functional approach of *Thomas* and *Schor* and acknowledged that they had replaced the formalism of *Northern Pipeline*.
This would have required a very different majority opinion, and
likely a different result, in *Stern v Marshall*. But the Court did
neither and ignored the underlying differences in approaches in
these cases.

Chief Justice Roberts's majority opinion in *Stern v Marshall*
distinguished *Thomas* and *Schor*, but without acknowledging or
addressing their expressly functional approach to determining
when non-Article III courts are permissible.[84] The Court said that
Thomas was different because "any right to compensation result[ed]
from the statute" and did not "depend on or replace a right to
compensation under state law."[85] As for *Schor*, the Court said that
Vickie's claim to relief "is not completely dependent upon adjudication of a claim created by federal law, as in *Schor*. Pierce did
not truly consent to resolution of Vickie's claim in the bankruptcy
court proceedings. He had nowhere else to go if we wished to
recover from Vickie's estate."[86]

Although these are distinctions between *Stern v Marshall* and
Thomas and *Schor*, they miss the point that the Court was departing
from the functional and pragmatic approach of the latter decisions.
This was the central point of the dissent. Justice Breyer, writing
for the dissenting Justices, declared:

> Rather than leaning so heavily on the approach taken by the plurality
> in *Northern Pipeline*, I would look to this Court's more recent Article
> III cases *Thomas* and *Schor*—cases that commanded a clear majority. In
> both cases the Court took a more pragmatic approach to the consti-
> tutional question. It sought to determine whether, in the particular
> instance, the challenged delegation of adjudicatory authority posed a
> genuine and serious threat that one branch of Government sought to
> aggrandize its own constitutionally delegated authority by encroaching
> upon a field of authority that the Constitution assigns exclusively to
> another branch.[87]

---

[84] The Court in *Stern v Marshall* could have recognized and disavowed the functional
approach of *Thomas* and *Schor* and reaffirmed the formalism of *Northern Pipeline*. Or it
could have embraced the functional approach of *Thomas* and *Schor* and acknowledged that
they had replaced the formalism of *Northern Pipeline*. This would have required a very
different majority opinion, and likely a different result, in *Stern v Marshall*. But the Court
did neither and ignored the underlying differences in approaches in these cases.

[85] *Stern*, 131 S Ct at 2613, quoting *Thomas*, 473 US at 584.

[86] *Stern*, 131 S Ct at 2614.

[87] Id at 2624 (Breyer, J, dissenting).

The formalistic approach of *Stern* is very different from the functional approach of *Thomas* and *Schor*.[88] Chief Justice Roberts's opinion in *Stern* doesn't even try to reconcile these approaches. The difference between the majority and the dissent in *Stern v Marshall*, then, seems less about views over state law counterclaims in bankruptcy or even the proper role of non-Article III courts and much more a disagreement about how the Constitution should be interpreted. Formalism is inherent to the originalism of conservative Justices like Scalia and Thomas who believe that the meaning of a constitutional provision is fixed when it is adopted and changeable only by constitutional amendment. By contrast, more liberal Justices, who believe that the Constitution is a living document, which must be interpreted in light of modern circumstances, take a more pragmatic approach to constitutional law.[89] In this context, it is not surprising that *Stern v Marshall* was a 5–4 decision, split along traditional ideological grounds.

For all of the familiar reasons, formalism is inherently unsatisfying in constitutional law where the premises are almost always likely to be disputed and where there is a need to interpret constitutional provisions in light of modern circumstances.[90] In *Stern v Marshall*, the formalism is particularly unpersuasive because Chief Justice Roberts begins by emphasizing the need for judges with life tenure to ensure independence of the judiciary and to protect individual liberty, but he never explains why allowing bankruptcy judges to issue final judgments as to state law counterclaims compromises these goals. Furthermore, the Court through American history has used a functional approach in allowing other non-Article III courts. The use of formalism in deciding the powers of a legislative court thus seems particularly inappropriate and out of place.

Nor can the Court's decision in *Stern v Marshall* be reduced to

---

[88] Justice Breyer makes this point: "Insofar as the majority would apply more formal standards, it simply disregards recent, controlling precedent. *Thomas*, 473 US at 587 ("[P]ractical attention to substance rather than doctrinaire reliance on formal categories should inform application of Article III"); ("[T]he Court has declined to adopt formalistic and unbending rules" for deciding Article III cases).

[89] In fact, Justice Breyer, the author of the dissent, has written two recent books defending what he describes as a pragmatic approach to constitutional interpretation. Stephen G. Breyer, *Making Our Democracy Work: A Judge's View* (Knopf, 2010); Stephen G. Breyer, *Active Liberty: Interpreting Our Democratic Constitution* (Knopf, 2005).

[90] A critique of formalism and a defense of the view that it should be a "living Constitution" are obviously beyond the scope of this paper.

against the estate.[97] The Court's reasoning was that bankruptcy courts could issue final judgments over matters that would fit within the scope of supplemental jurisdiction. The Court in *Schor* explained that in *Katchen* "this Court upheld a bankruptcy referee's power to hear and decide state law counterclaims against a creditor who filed a claim in bankruptcy when those counterclaims arose out of the same transaction."[98]

But in *Stern v Marshall*, the Court does not accept that supplemental jurisdiction can bring matters within the scope of the bankruptcy court's authority to issue a final judgment. Justice Breyer's dissent urged this,[99] but the majority implicitly rejected it. As one commentator noted: "The *Stern v. Marshall* majority, however, very abruptly (and with no explanation) refuses to even acknowledge the possibility that supplemental jurisdiction is a valid concept in the context of non-Article III adjudications. The Court very conspicuously (to anyone who has read *Katchen* even casually) simply ignores *Katchen*'s primary reliance upon more general supplemental jurisdiction reasoning."[100]

The majority opinion in *Stern v Marshall* does give a clear indication as to its scope, and it is far broader than Chief Justice Roberts's conclusion acknowledged. The Court stated: "[T]he question is whether the action at issue stems from the bankruptcy itself or would necessarily be allowed in the claims allowance process."[101] This rule is quite restrictive and would place most state law counterclaims, and many other matters, outside the scope of bankruptcy courts to issue final judgments.

What difference would this make? It would seem that bankruptcy courts would have to make "reports and recommendations" to the district courts so that they could issue final judgments.[102] As Justice Breyer points out in dissent, there are 1.6 million bank-

---

[97] Id at 325–26.

[98] *Schor*, 478 US at 852.

[99] *Stern*, 131 S Ct at 2626, 2629 (Breyer, J, dissenting).

[100] Ralph Brubaker, *Article III's Bleak House (Part II): The Constitutional Limits of Bankruptcy Judges' Core Jurisdiction*, 31 Bankr L Let 1, 12 (Sept 2011).

[101] *Stern*, 131 S Ct at 2618.

[102] There actually is a statutory problem with this: The Bankruptcy Act recognizes two kinds of cases: core and noncore proceedings. It provides for bankruptcy courts to issue reports and recommendations as to the latter. But *Stern v Marshall* creates a third category: core proceedings where bankruptcy courts cannot issue final judgments. Are these to be treated as noncore proceedings under the statute?

ruptcy filings a year (as compared to 280,000 civil cases and 78,000 criminal cases), and to require that a significant portion of these now be reviewed by the federal district courts would have a staggering impact.[103] As Justice Breyer explains in his conclusion, "under these circumstances, a constitutionally required game of jurisdictional ping-pong between courts would lead to inefficiency, increased cost, delay, and needless additional suffering among those faced with bankruptcy."[104]

The crucial practical question will be whether consent can cure this and whether bankruptcy courts can issue final judgments with consent of the parties. If so, the effect of *Stern v Marshall* will be greatly reduced; if not, the implications of *Stern v Marshall* are enormous and transcend the bankruptcy context.

It is impossible to find an answer to this question in the majority's opinion. Chief Justice Roberts points out that Pierce Marshall consented to the bankruptcy court's jurisdiction for his claim of defamation against Vickie Lynn Marshall. The Court says: "Pierce repeatedly stated to the Bankruptcy Court that he was happy to litigate there. We will not consider his claim to the contrary, now that he is sad."[105] But this is in the context of Pierce's consent to have his claim heard in the bankruptcy court; it is not about whether he agreed to have Vickie's counterclaim heard there. As to that, the Court says: "Pierce did not truly consent to resolution of Vickie's claim in the bankruptcy court proceedings."[106]

No principle of federal jurisdiction is more clearly established than that a limit on the power of a federal court cannot be overcome by consent.[107] Article III defines the authority of a federal court, and because it is about the Constitution's structure, the consent of the parties cannot place a matter within the power of an Article III court that otherwise would not be there. *Stern v Marshall* held that Article III of the Constitution did not permit the bankruptcy court to issue a final judgment on Vickie Lynn

---

[103] *Stern*, 131 S Ct at 2630 (Breyer, J, dissenting).

[104] Id.

[105] Id at 2608.

[106] Id at 2614.

[107] See, for example, *Sosna v Iowa*, 419 US 393, 398 (1975); *Mitchell v Mauer*, 293 US 237, 244 (1934).

Marshall's counterclaim for tortious interference. Consent cannot increase the power of a federal court.

Some courts have argued that this is wrong because there is a distinction between the subject matter jurisdiction of a bankruptcy court and its power to issue final judgments; consent cannot cure a defect in the former, but it can allow for the latter.[108] The Court in *Stern* recognized that the bankruptcy court had subject matter jurisdiction pursuant to 28 USC § 1334 and that the division between core and noncore proceedings in the Bankruptcy Act did not implicate subject matter jurisdiction. Chief Justice Roberts wrote: "Section 157 allocates the authority to enter final judgment between the bankruptcy court and the district court. That allocation does not implicate questions of subject matter jurisdiction."[109] The Court cited to Section 157(c)(2), which provides that parties may consent to entry of final judgment by bankruptcy judges in noncore areas.[110] The assertion is that bankruptcy courts cannot gain subject matter jurisdiction by consent, but they can gain the power to issue final judgments via consent of the parties.

In fact, in the first months after *Stern v Marshall*, bankruptcy courts have consistently invoked this distinction and ruled that consent can cure the problem. Courts have relied on the language in *Stern* stating that Section 157 allocates authority to enter final judgments between bankruptcy and district courts—an allocation that does not implicate questions of subject matter jurisdiction.[111] Because subject matter jurisdiction is not implicated, consent permits a bankruptcy court's final judgment. Some courts have analogized to binding arbitration proceedings where parties can agree to final determinations made by arbitrators.[112] For courts that have followed this logic, if parties may consent to binding arbitration, then they should be permitted to consent to bankruptcy courts entering final judgments if they desire, especially because, as one court stated, arbitrators do not enjoy the same attributes as Article III judges or bankruptcy judges.[113]

---

[108] See *In re Olde Prairie Block Owner, LLC*, 457 BR 692, 700 (Bankr ND Ill 2011).

[109] *Stern*, 131 S Ct at 2607.

[110] Id.

[111] *In re Pro-Pac, Inc.*, 456 BR 894, 902–03 (Bankr ED Wis 2011); *In re Oxford Expositions, LLC*, 2011 WL 4074028, *8 (Bankr ND Miss).

[112] *In re Teleservices Group, Inc.*, 456 BR at 338.

[113] Id.; *In re Oxford Expositions, LLC*, 2011 WL 4074028 at *8 ("Indeed, many arbitrators

But this reasoning seems highly problematic. It assumes that a limit on the Article III power of a court can be overcome via consent. The argument is that there are two kinds of restrictions on the authority imposed by Article III: lack of subject matter jurisdiction and lack of power to issue a final judgment; consent cannot cure the former, but can solve the latter. But there is no apparent basis for this distinction. Article III is a constitutional, structural limit on the powers of the federal judiciary. There is no reason why any Article III deficiency can be overcome by consent.[114] It is one thing for parties by consent to submit a matter to an arbiter for a decision; that does not implicate the Article III powers of a federal court. But if Congress mandates binding arbitration over state law claims and gives the arbiters the authority to issue a binding judgment, then under the reasoning of *Stern v Marshall* and *Northern Pipeline*, there is every reason to believe that would be unconstitutional as well.[115]

In fact, that is why the implications of *Stern v Marshall* are so great. In addition to the constitutional problems with congressionally mandated binding arbitration for state law claims, any final decision by a non-Article III judge over state law claims would be unconstitutional. Federal magistrate judges are non-Article III judges who are appointed for eight-year terms. In *United States v Raddatz*,[116] the Supreme Court held that magistrate judges are constitutional as adjuncts of the federal district courts.[117] The Court concluded that because "the entire process takes place under the district court's total control and jurisdiction . . . [the act] strikes the proper balance between the demands of due process and the constraints of Art. III."[118]

---

are not licensed attorneys, and unlike United States Bankruptcy Judges, they are not appointed to fourteen year terms by an Article III Court of Appeals, nor do they have their compensation statutorily linked to the compensation of Article III district judges.").

[114] See Richard Lieb, *The Supreme Court, in Stern v. Marshall, by Applying Article III of the Constitution Further Limited the Statutory Authority of Bankruptcy Courts to Issue Final Orders*, 20 J Bankr L & Prac 4 Art 1 (2011).

[115] Professor Judith Resnik has made the point that the cases decided by non-Article III judges far outnumber those decided by Article III courts and that this will only increase. Judith Resnik, *Of Courts, Agencies, and the Court of Federal Claims: Fortunately Outliving One's Anomalous Character*, 71 Geo Wash L Rev 798, 808 (2003) ("My assumption is that one hundred years from now, life-tenured judges will at best comprise about one quarter of the federal judicial work force and will mostly do appellate work, reviewing decisions of non-Article III judges.").

[116] 447 US 667 (1980)

[117] Id at 687.

[118] Id at 681, 683–84.

But magistrate judges also can hold trials in civil proceedings, including jury trials, with consent of the parties. Consent need not even be explicit; in *Roell v Withrow*,[119] the Court held that consent to trial by a magistrate judge can be implied from a party's conduct during litigation.[120] In such matters, magistrate judges are not in any meaningful sense adjuncts of the district court, any more than the bankruptcy court in *Stern v Marshall* was functioning as an adjunct of the district court. Yet, ten circuits have upheld the Federal Magistrate Statute, which permits parties to consent to magistrate judges entering final judgments.[121] If consent is not sufficient to permit a non-Article III judge to issue a final judgment over state law matters, then these decisions are wrong at least as to state law claims, such as through supplemental state law claims or state law counterclaims, that would be presented for final judgments to magistrate judges.

IV. Conclusion

The easiest thing to say about *Stern v Marshall* is that it is causing enormous confusion and litigation concerning its scope. There is a desperate need for the Supreme Court to clarify the scope of its holding and whether consent is sufficient to cure the defect. In reading Chief Justice Roberts's majority opinion, it is apparent that the Court had not thought through the problems its ruling would create in countless cases in bankruptcy courts across the country. Chief Justice Roberts's attempt to dismiss the dissent's concern by saying that the ruling "does not change all that much"[122] indicates that the Court did not consider what it would mean to hold that bankruptcy courts, and likely other non-Article III courts, cannot issue binding judgments on some state law claims.

The Court's reasoning in *Stern v Marshall* is inherently unpersuasive because it is built on a framework that makes little sense. The language of Article III of the Constitution seemingly requires that all who exercise the federal judicial power have life tenure

---

[119] 538 US 580 (2003).

[120] Id at 590.

[121] *In re Safety Harbor Resort & Spa*, 456 BR 703, 718 (Bankr MD Fla 2011), citing *Sinclair v Wainwright*, 814 F2d 1516, 1519 (11th Cir 1987).

[122] *Stern*, 131 S Ct at 2620 ("If our decision today does not change all that much, then why the fuss?").

and salary protections, but for practical reasons that has not been the law since the early nineteenth century when the Court began to allow non-Article III courts. The Court has allowed them in three instances—for territories, for the military, and for public law matters—but never has explained why just these three and not others. *Northern Pipeline*, the predicate for *Stern v Marshall*, held that it was constitutionally impermissible for bankruptcy judges to decide state law claims, but never justified what is objectionable about this in terms of the need to assure judicial independence. The Court in *Stern v Marshall* likewise stresses the need for life tenure to ensure judicial independence, but does not explain why this means that a state law counterclaim must be decided by an Article III judge. Decisions after *Northern Pipeline*, *Thomas*, and *Schor* emphasized the need for a functional and not a formalistic approach to determining when non-Article III courts are permissible, but the Court in *Stern v Marshall* ignores this shift toward the pragmatic.

Ultimately, it is the highly formalistic approach of *Stern v Marshall* that makes it most unsatisfying and unpersuasive. The Court has rejected formalism in this area of the law in allowing other non-Article III courts for almost 200 years. The distinctions that need to be drawn to come to the Court's conclusion in *Stern v Marshall* are impossible to justify. More generally, formalism is inherently unsuitable for interpreting a Constitution written over 200 years ago for a vastly different society and that has to be applied to an infinite variety of problems that could not have been anticipated at the time.

The dispute between Vickie Lynn Marshall and Pierce Marshall made the tabloids because of interest in a beautiful woman in her twenties marrying a very rich man in his eighties and because of the nasty fight over a large inheritance. But the constitutional questions go to the very core of the meaning of Article III and how the Constitution should be interpreted.

WILLIAM P. MARSHALL
AND GENE R. NICHOL

NOT A *WINN*-WIN: MISCONSTRUING
STANDING AND THE ESTABLISHMENT
CLAUSE

In no line of cases over the past half-century has the Supreme Court
so directly faced the tension between constitutional accountability
and jurisdictional traditions of personal harm as in the taxpayer
standing decisions under the Establishment Clause. Sometimes,
most notably in *Flast v Cohen*,[1] the Justices have explicitly embraced
a broad understanding of standing to sue.[2] Other times, the Court
has sidestepped the standing question and proceeded directly to the
merits of the Establishment Clause claim, apparently assuming,
without explanation, the existence of standing.[3] More recently, the

William P. Marshall is Kenan Professor of Law, University of North Carolina. Gene
R. Nichol is Boyd Tinsley Professor of Law, University of North Carolina.

AUTHORS' NOTE: The authors would like to thank Fred Gedicks for his comments on
an earlier draft of this article and Laura Stephens Chipman and Katherine Slager for their
exceptional research assistance.

[1] 392 US 83 (1968) (granting taxpayer standing to challenge a federal spending program
used in part to assist private religious schools).

[2] Id at 94–101. Further examples include *Tilton v Richardson*, 403 US 672, 676 (1971)
(upholding taxpayer standing under the Establishment Clause to challenge a federal program providing funding to religiously affiliated colleges and universities); *Bowen v Kendrick*,
487 US 589, 618 (1988) (taxpayer standing allowed to challenge the federal Adolescent
Family Life Act).

[3] See, for example, *Mueller v Allen*, 463 US 388 (1983); *Committee for Public Ed. &
Religious Liberty v Nyquist*, 413 US 756, 762 (1973); *Hunt v McNair*, 413 US 734, 735
(1973); *Walz v Tax Comm'n of City of New York*, 397 US 664, 666 (1970). Also consider
Hibbs v Winn, 542 US 88, 92 (2004) (reaching only threshold jurisdictional issues).

Court has drawn back from its broad conception of standing and interpreted its prior standards and pronouncements in a remarkably wooden and rigid manner in order to deny standing and therefore restrict judicial review.[4] It seems safe to say that the Court's record in taxpayer standing cases has satisfied no one.

Last term, in *Arizona Christian School Tuition Organization v Winn*,[5] the Roberts Court turned for the second time in four years to this much-disputed arena of Article III authority. As in its earlier decision in *Hein v Freedom of Religion Foundation*,[6] the Court, sharply divided, rejected claims of taxpayer standing that would have seemed to follow easily from the language of *Flast* and similar precedents.[7] The Court held in *Winn* that though taxpayers might have standing to contest legislative *appropriations* designed to aid religious enterprises as in *Flast*, they have no standing to challenge legislative *tax credit* programs intended for the same purpose.[8] *Winn* thus constitutes a further, pointed step in the Court's narrowing of taxpayer standing under the Establishment Clause. Although not formally overruling *Flast*, *Winn* moves significantly in that direction by resting on a distinction between credits and appropriations that cannot be justified under either standing or Establishment Clause principles. Further, by purporting to distinguish tax credit programs that benefit religion from direct appropriations that do the same, *Winn*, as a practical matter, offers willing legislatures a ready and obvious path to shield religious assistance from constitutional review.

---

[4] See, for example, *Valley Forge Christian College v Americans United for Separation of Church and State*, 454 US 464, 486 (1982) (taxpayers do not have standing to challenge the transfer of federal surplus property to a religious organization); *Hein v Freedom from Religion Foundation*, 551 US 587, 605 (2007) (taxpayers do not have standing to challenge expenditures by the federal executive, although taxpayers would have standing to challenge the same types of expenditures if appropriated by Congress). Also consider *United States v Richardson*, 418 US 166, 167–68 (1974) (analogous constrained reading of standing requirements in taxpayer/citizen suit under the Accounts Clause). The Court also exhibited a restrictive approach to Establishment Clause standing in a pre-*Flast* case, *Doremus v Board of Education*, 342 US 429, 431–32 (1952) (denying taxpayer standing to challenge Bible reading in the public schools on grounds that the practice did not involve any government expenditures).

[5] 131 S Ct 1436 (2011).

[6] 551 US 587 (2007). The Roberts Court also addressed taxpayer standing outside the Establishment Clause context in *DaimlerChrysler Corp. v Cuno*, 547 US 332, 346 (2006) (denying taxpayer standing to challenge a state tax subsidy under the Commerce Clause). For a general assessment of standing and the Roberts Court, see Michael E. Solimine, *Congress, Separation of Powers, and Standing*, 59 Case W Reserve L Rev 1023, 1031–35 (2009).

[7] See *Flast v Cohen*, 392 US 83, 88 (1968); *Bowen v Kendrick*, 487 US 589, 618 (1988).

[8] *Winn*, 131 S Ct at 1447.

In this article, we will explore *Winn* and its implications for the judicial enforcement of the Establishment Clause. In Part I, we critique the *Winn* decision in some detail. We first set forth Justice Kennedy's claims that the action brought by the Arizona taxpayers (*a*) runs afoul of Article III's prohibition against judicial resolution of generalized grievances and (*b*) falls outside the taxpayer "exception" recognized in *Flast*. We then contest both conclusions. We argue that the majority opinion embraces formal distinctions that undermine constitutional accountability. In our view, the majority's reliance on a distinction between concrete, individual harms and shared, intangible claims is inescapably illusory, and its attempts to distinguish *Flast* as a specialized injury case based on the "extraction and spending" of tax dollars is incoherent. Although the Court posits that widely shared, intangible harms are insufficient to confer standing, it affirms *Flast*, which was grounded on precisely such injuries.

In Part II, we look more broadly at the purposes underlying the Establishment Clause and at the types of harms it was designed to address. We argue that the intangible, "psychic" harms that *Winn* implicitly rejects as a basis for standing are central to the core purposes of the Establishment Clause. By suggesting that such interests are noncognizable claims, *Winn* undercuts not only taxpayer standing but much that has been thought to underlie Establishment Clause jurisprudence itself.

I. Arizona Christian School Tuition Organization v Winn

Kathleen Winn and a group of Arizona taxpayers sought to challenge a state tax program[9] that provides dollar-to-dollar tax credit up to $1,000 per married couple and $500 per individual for

---

[9] Ariz Rev Stat Ann § 43-1089 (West, 2010). The relevant portion of the statute is as follows:

> A. A credit is allowed against the taxes imposed by this title for the amount of voluntary cash contributions by the taxpayer or on the taxpayer's behalf pursuant to section 43-401, subsection I during the taxable year to a school tuition organization that is certified pursuant to chapter 16 of this title at the time of donation. Except as provided by subsection C of this section, the amount of the credit shall not exceed:
> 1. Five hundred dollars in any taxable year for a single individual or a head of household.
> 2. One thousand dollars in any taxable year for a married couple filing a joint return.

contributions to "school tuition organizations" (STOs).[10] STOs are private, nonprofit organizations that were set up specifically to accept these contributions and then use the donated funds for "scholarships to students attending private schools, including religious schools."[11] The statute establishing the program prohibits STOs from providing scholarship aid to students attending schools that "discriminate on the basis of race, color, handicap, familial status or national origin"[12] but does not prevent STOs "from funding scholarships to schools that provide religious instruction or that give admissions preferences on the basis of religious affiliation."[13]

Since the program was adopted in 1997, its primary beneficiaries have been students attending religious schools. In 1998, for example, 94 percent of taxpayer donations went to STOs that granted scholarships exclusively to students at religious schools.[14] And in 2009, the state's four largest religiously affiliated STOs accounted collectively for "more than half of the more than $50 million in tax payments received by all Arizona STOs."[15] The total cost of the program between 1998 and 2008, according to the State's calculations, was "nearly $350 million in redirected tax revenue."[16]

The plaintiffs alleged that the program violated the Establishment Clause.[17] They argued that the tax break effectively constituted public financial support for religious teaching and provided government sustenance for schools that discriminate on the basis of religious affiliation in admissions.[18] They sought standing pursuant

---

[10] *Winn*, 131 S Ct at 1440.

[11] Id.

[12] Ariz Rev Stat Ann § 43-1089(H)(2)(a).

[13] *Winn v Arizona Christian School Tuition Organization*, 563 F3d 1002, 1005 (9th Cir 2009).

[14] *Winn v Hibbs*, 361 F Supp 2d 1117, 1119 (D Ariz 2005).

[15] Brief for Respondents, *Arizona Christian School Tuition Organization v Winn*, Nos. 09-987, 09-991, *12 (filed Sept 15, 2010) (available on Westlaw at 2010 WL 3624706). The four religious STOs were the Arizona Christian School Tuition Organization, the Catholic Tuition Organization of the Diocese of Phoenix, the Catholic Tuition Organization of the Diocese of Tucson, and the Jewish Tuition Organization. See id.

[16] *Winn*, 131 S Ct at 1458 (Kagan, J, dissenting). In 2008 alone, the state reported a total of $54.1 million in scholarships paid out by the student tuition organizations. See Arizona Department of Revenue, Individual Income Tax Credit for Donations to Private School Tuition Organizations: Reporting for 2009 (Apr 21, 2010), available at http://www.azdor.gov/Portals/0/Reports/private-school-tax-credit-report-2008.pdf.

[17] Id at 1440.

[18] Id at 1450 (Kagan, J, dissenting).

to the Warren Court's landmark ruling in *Flast v Cohen*,[19] which held that taxpayers have standing to challenge legislative expenditures supporting various costs of instruction in religious or sectarian schools.[20]

The federal district court in *Winn* ruled against the plaintiffs on the merits, holding that the plaintiffs' complaint failed to state a claim.[21] The Court of Appeals for the Ninth Circuit reversed and remanded for further proceedings and, citing *Flast*, also ruled that the plaintiffs had sufficient standing to maintain the action.[22] The Supreme Court reversed again. Justice Anthony Kennedy's opinion, joined by Chief Justice Roberts and Justices Scalia, Thomas, and Alito, held that Winn's suit was barred, for lack of standing, under Article III of the Constitution.[23]

Justice Kennedy's opinion did not contest the proposition that if the state had directly appropriated the credited funds for religious schools the expenditures could have been challenged under *Flast*.[24] But for the *Winn* majority, the use of a tax credit rather than an appropriation was sufficient to defeat federal jurisdiction.[25] Justice Elena Kagan, in her first dissenting opinion, observed on behalf of herself and Justices Ginsburg, Breyer, and Sotomayor that the Court's "decision devastates taxpayer standing in Establishment Clause cases."[26] The majority did not disagree.

A. WINN'S STANDING MOVE

Justice Kennedy opened the standing inquiry on familiar terrain. The federal courts have long refused, he reminded, to entertain cases asserting a mere "generalized interest in constitutional gov-

---

[19] 392 US 83 (1968).

[20] The federal statute at issue in *Flast* authorized the federal government to provide grants to assist in the education of children from low-income families. The beneficiaries of the statute apparently included students attending private religious and nonreligious schools. See id at 85–87.

[21] *Winn v Hibbs*, 361 F Supp 2d 1117, 1123 (D Ariz 2005).

[22] *Winn v Arizona Christian School Tuition Organization*, 562 F3d 1002, 1008 (9th Cir 2009).

[23] *Winn*, 131 S Ct at 1442–49.

[24] See *Flast v Cohen*, 392 US 83, 101 (1968) (allowing analogous challenge as within the scope of Article III).

[25] See *Winn*, 131 S Ct at 1442–49.

[26] Id at 1463 (Kagan, J, dissenting).

ernance."[27] To embrace such actions, he explained, would press beyond "the role assigned to the judiciary within the Constitution's tripartite allocation of power."[28] Instead, Article III demands allegations of "concrete and particularized injury" demonstrated to be "fairly traceable to the challenged action of the defendant," and "likely to be redressed by a favorable" decree.[29] In order to sustain federal judicial authority, a lawsuit must "affect the plaintiff in a personal and individual way."[30] Winn and her fellow taxpayers, Kennedy observed, could make no such claims.[31]

Justice Kennedy's conclusion is, of course, not surprising. A mere interest in assuring that one's tax dollars are used appropriately is widely shared and "general."[32] Because any actual financial stake is apt to be "remote, fluctuating and uncertain,"[33] such a claim sounds more in political disputation than in the enforcement of a legal right. Moreover, because tax credits and deductions sometimes secure "cost savings for the state,"[34] it is not always clear whether an objecting taxpayer's financial bottom line will be improved or diminished.[35] In such circumstances, Justice Kennedy determined that the plaintiffs in *Winn* had "not shown that any interest they have [in the Arizona] Treasury would be advanced."[36]

Justice Kennedy next turned to the harder question: is standing nonetheless appropriate under the "narrow exception" of *Flast v Cohen*?[37] Chief Justice Warren's opinion in *Flast* had announced a two-pronged standard for taxpayer standing. First, plaintiffs must demonstrate a "logical link" between their taxpayer status and the "type of legislative enactment" challenged. In *Flast*, that meant an attack upon an exercise of Congress's "authority both to collect

---

[27] Id at 1441–42, citing *Schlesinger v Reservists Committee to Stop the War*, 418 US 208, 214 (1974).

[28] Id at 1442 (quotation marks omitted).

[29] Id at 1442, citing *Lujan v Defenders of Wildlife*, 504 US 555, 560–61 (1992).

[30] Id at 1442.

[31] Id at 1442–43.

[32] Id at 1442–43, citing *Hein v Freedom from Religion Foundation*, 551 US 587, 599 (2007).

[33] Id at 1443, citing *Frothingham v Mellon*, 262 US 447, 487 (1923).

[34] Id.

[35] Id at 1443–44, citing *DaimlerChrysler v Cuno*, 547 US 332, 433 (2006).

[36] Id at 1444.

[37] 392 US 83 (1968).

and spend tax dollars."[38] Second, the taxpayer must demonstrate "a nexus" between her status and "the precise nature of the constitutional infringement allowed."[39] In *Flast*, this meant showing that the expenditure exceeded "specific constitutional limitations" imposed upon the taxing and spending power.[40]

The proffered test seemed suitably tailored for *Flast*'s occasion. There the litigants challenged a congressional spending program that paid for various instructional undertakings in private, sectarian schools, allegedly in violation of the Establishment Clause. The Court in *Flast* held that its newly crafted standard was satisfied, even though both the scope and underlying rationale of the standard were unclear.[41]

Justice Kennedy did not question the continuing vitality of *Flast*.[42] Rather, the key to *Flast*, he explained, was a claim by the plaintiffs that their "tax money [was] being extracted and spent in violation of specific constitutional protections against [such uses] of legislative power."[43] This "extraction and spending" was, in Kennedy's view, unlike the "generalized grievances" the Court had previously ruled "inappropriate for judicial redress."[44] Turning to James Madison's Memorial and Remonstrance Against Religious Assessments,[45] Kennedy named "the specific evil . . . identified by those who drafted" the Religion Clauses: "government should not force a citizen to contribute three pence of his property for the support of any one establishment."[46] Even such a modest gesture

---

[38] Id at 103; *Winn*, 131 S Ct at 1445.

[39] *Flast*, 392 US at 102.

[40] Id at 102–03.

[41] As Justice Scalia put it, concurring in *Hein v Freedom from Religion Foundation*, 551 US 587 (2007), "Enter the magical two-pronged nexus test. It has often been pointed out, and never refuted, that the criteria in *Flast*'s two-part test are entirely unrelated to the purported goal of ensuring that the plaintiff has a sufficient 'stake in the outcome of the controversy.'" Id at 623 (Scalia, J, concurring), citing *Flast*, 392 US at 121, 124 (Harlan, J, dissenting).

[42] Here, *Winn* followed the same path as *Hein* four years earlier—which may have derided *Flast* and applied it with a stilted rigidity, but refused to overrule it.

[43] *Winn*, 131 S Ct at 1446. *Flast* itself had characterized its holding quite differently: "[W]e hold that a taxpayer will have standing consistent with Article III to invoke federal judicial power when he alleges that congressional action under the taxing and spending clause is in derogation of" the Establishment Clause. *Flast*, 392 US at 105–06.

[44] *Winn*, 131 S Ct at 1446.

[45] Id. See, for example, *Everson v Board of Ed. of Ewing*, 330 US 1, 74 (1947) (supplemental appendix to dissent of Rutledge).

[46] Id (quotation marks omitted).

could "require the payment of taxes to support religious institutions with whose beliefs they disagreed."[47]

The "extract and spend" trigger, according to the *Winn* majority, distinguished the Arizona tax credit challenge from expenditure cases like *Flast*. In direct appropriation actions, the taxpayer "knows he has, in some small measure, been made to contribute to an establishment in violation of conscience"—even if his overall tax liability might not actually be affected.[48] The *Winn* tax credit, on the other hand, represented a mere determination by the state to "decline to impose" liability.[49] "When Arizona taxpayers choose to contribute [to the scholarship fund] they spend their own money, not money the state has collected from [them] or other taxpayers."[50] They remain free to pay their own tax bills without offering support for church-based education. The credit is not, therefore, "tantamount to a religious tithe" and "does not visit the injury identified in *Flast*."[51]

Further, the Court contended, although tax credits and government expenditures may have similar economic consequences, they do not "implicate individual taxpayers in sectarian activities" in the same fashion.[52] A dissenting taxpayer remains removed from the controversial act of religious support. The Arizona credit scheme "allowed citizens to retain control over their own funds in accordance with their own conscience[s]."[53] The program was "implemented by private action without state intervention,"[54] and any objecting Arizonan knew full well that her "fellow citizens," not the state, "opted to contribute."[55] The *Winn* plaintiffs' standing theory, therefore, strayed fatally beyond "the limits of *Flast*'s logic."[56]

Justice Kennedy still faced one hurdle in achieving dismissal.

---

[47] Id.

[48] *Winn*, 131 S Ct at 1447.

[49] Id.

[50] Id.

[51] Id.

[52] Id at 1447.

[53] Id.

[54] Id. This, of course, is an odd description of a tax program developed, monitored, certified, and enforced by the state—which is created by statute and outlined and triggered on the Arizona income tax form itself.

[55] Id.

[56] Id at 1447.

Over the past four decades, the Court had reached the merits of at least four significant Establishment Clause challenges in suits filed by taxpayers claiming that tax policies violated the First Amendment in contexts at least analogous to *Winn*.[57] Shortly after *Flast*, in 1970, the Court heard a challenge to local religion-based property tax exemptions in the much-cited *Walz v Tax Commission of City of New York*.[58] Three years later, in *Hunt v McNair*,[59] the Justices examined, and rejected, a taxpayer's action seeking to invalidate a state agency's decision to issue tax exempt bonds to sectarian institutions.[60] That same day, in *Committee for Public Education & Religious Liberty v Nyquist*,[61] the Court struck down a state tax credit for parents who paid tuition to religious schools.[62] A decade later, in *Mueller v Allen*,[63] the Court reached the merits and upheld a tax deduction program directed to various expenses associated with private religious education.[64] Thus, a not-insignificant chunk of Establishment Clause jurisprudence is premised on the seemingly conventional notion that taxpayers have standing to present Establishment Clause challenges against state and local governments *even when no direct spending program is implicated*.[65]

---

[57] See *Mueller v Allen*, 463 US 388, 392 (1983); *Committee for Public Ed. & Religious Liberty v Nyquist*, 413 US 756, 762 (1973); *Hunt v McNair*, 413 US 734, 735 (1973); *Walz v Tax Comm'n of City of New York*, 397 US 664, 666 (1970). Consider also *Hibbs v Winn*, 542 US 88, 92 (2004) (reaching only threshold jurisdictional issues).

[58] 397 US 664, 666 (1970).

[59] 413 US 734 (1973).

[60] Id at 735.

[61] 413 US 756 (1973).

[62] Id at 798.

[63] 463 US 388 (1983).

[64] Id at 391.

[65] Justice Kagan also pointed out in her spirited and effective dissent that: "[w]e have also several times summarily affirmed lower court decisions adjudicating taxpayer challenges to tax expenditures alleged to violate the Establishment Clause." *Winn*, 131 S Ct at 1454 n 3. See *Byrne v Pub. Funds for Pub. Sch. of N.J.*, 442 US 907 (1979), summarily affirming 590 F2d 514, 516 n 3 (3d Cir 1979) (holding that "plaintiffs, as taxpayers, have standing under *Flast*" to challenge a tax deduction for dependents attending religious and other private schools); *Grit v Wolman*, 413 US 901 (1973), summarily affirming *Kosydar v Wolman*, 353 F Supp 744, 749 (SD Ohio 1972) (three-judge court) (noting that no party had questioned the standing of taxpayers to contest tax credits for private-school tuition payments); *Franchise Tax Bd. of Cal. v United Americans for Pub. Sch.*, 419 US 890 (1974), summarily affirming No. C-73-0090 (ND Cal, Feb 1, 1974) (three-judge court) (invalidating a tax credit for children attending private schools). See also William P. Marshall and Maripat Flood, *Establishment Clause Standing: The Not Very Revolutionary Decision at Valley Forge*, 11 Hofstra L Rev 63, 89–90 (1982) (noting that the Court had long applied less stringent standing limitations to plaintiffs bringing establishment challenges to state

Even the *Winn* case itself had enjoyed an earlier trip to the Supreme Court, during which the Court once again assumed Article III standing.[66]

Justice Kennedy was not deterred. He declared that "those cases do not mention standing and so are not contrary to the conclusion reached here."[67] Since the jurisdictional "defect"—in this extensive array of decisions—was "neither noted nor discussed," those rulings could not be read to sustain jurisdiction in *Winn*.[68] That scholars, advocates, judges, and the Justices themselves had uniformly assumed, for over four decades, the existence of a broad embrace of taxpayer standing in these cases was of no significance. As Justice Kennedy argued, "the Court would risk error if it relied on assumptions that have gone unstated and unexamined."[69]

Justices Scalia and Thomas concurred in the majority opinion. They made clear, though, that a "principled reading of Article III" required *Flast*'s "repudiation" rather than its mere limitation.[70] Speaking for the four dissenters, Justice Kagan accused the majority of making an "end run" around principle, deploying "form over substance," to assure the "effective demise of taxpayer standing."[71] The majority opinion, she charged, offered an "instruction to any government that wishes to insulate its financing of religion

government actions purportedly supporting religion than to actions brought against the federal government).

[66] See *Hibbs v Winn*, 542 US 88, 112 (2004) (holding that a taxpayer action challenging the Arizona tax credit program was not barred by the Tax Injunction Act, 28 USC § 1341).

[67] *Winn*, 131 S Ct at 1448.

[68] Id, citing *Hagans v Lavine*, 415 US 528, 535 n 5 (1974) ("[W]hen questions of jurisdiction have been passed on in prior decisions sub silentio, this Court has never considered itself bound when a subsequent case finally brings the jurisdictional issue before us.").

[69] *Winn*, 131 S Ct at 1449.

[70] Id at 1449–50 (Scalia, J, concurring). There is, as is often the case, a good deal of rhetorical power in Justice Scalia's brief concurring opinion. The distinctions the Court continues to draw between *Flast* and other taxpayer cases are, indeed, fanciful. See, for example, *Hein v Freedom from Religion Foundation*, 551 US 587 (2007) (no standing to contest executive branch expenditures); *Valley Forge Christian College v Americans United for Separation of Church and State*, 454 US 464 (1982) (no standing to challenge federal gift of property to church). But whatever Justice Scalia seeks in his standing jurisprudence, it can hardly be described as "principled." See, for example, *Bennett v Spear*, 520 US 154 (1997) (opinion by Justice Scalia offering an extraordinarily generous vision of standing in case alleging that environmental enforcement against third party was too strict); *Adarand Constructors v Pena*, 515 US 200 (1995) (generous standing for complainant in affirmative action cases); *Shaw v Reno*, 509 US 630 (1993) (broad standing for white plaintiffs to challenge the use of race in redistricting process).

[71] *Winn*, 131 S Ct at 1450–58 (Kagan, J, dissenting).

from legal challenge"—to merely "structure the funding as a tax expenditure."[72] In the process, vital enforcement of the Establishment Clause would be foreclosed.[73]

B. WINN'S UNSUSTAINABLE PREMISES

There is much that can be said about the Supreme Court's ruling in *Winn*. One could start with the most obvious. As outlined in Justice Kagan's dissent, the case presents a virtual blueprint for how legislative bodies can support religious activities without the risk of judicial review.[74] Under *Winn*'s auspices, a legislature, city council, or Congress itself may now, in straightforward fashion, say:

> We mean to provide money to support religious undertakings, but we seek to avoid the annoyances of constitutional accountability and judicial review. Therefore, we will provide tax credits to compensate for various church activities. No one will miss the significance. They will be assured that we have thrown the power of the state behind religious endeavor. (Or, at least behind those religious endeavors that meet our approval). But no one will be allowed to use the courts to challenge our efforts.

Winn also offers no explanation of how far the credit/appropriation "distinction" will be extended. There is no reason, though, to think that the statutory benefits made subject to review in *Flast* itself couldn't simply be recast as tax credits. In effect, Congress can now reverse the holding of *Flast*—the case from which *Winn* claims to draw its central sustenance. And it could surely go farther. There is no limit to the number of programs designed to support religion through legislative appropriation that are capable of being recast as now-unreviewable tax credits. *Flast* remains in place, of course. It is, with the requisite nod and wink, simply drained of all content.[75]

Nor, one guesses, need the Congress stop at the tax credits. As

---

[72] Id at 1462 (Kagan, J, dissenting).

[73] Id at 1450, 1458 (Kagan, J, dissenting).

[74] Id.

[75] Professors Lupu and Tuttle have argued, convincingly, that *Hein v Freedom from Religion Foundation* was "an early step down a perilous path" in removing even greater expanses from First Amendment review. See Ira C. Lupu and Robert Tuttle, *Ball on a Needle: Hein v. Freedom from Religion Foundation, Inc. and the Future of Establishment Clause Adjudication*, 2008 BYU L Rev 115, 168 (2008). If true, *Winn* is a bold, mature stride.

Justice Kagan noted,[76] if a federal (or state) check-off tool were to be developed, allowing taxpayers to "consent" to the appropriation of their tax payments to support churches, the logic of Justice Kennedy's opinion suggests that there would be no judicial review. So long as the religion-sustaining funds were technically segregated, no "objecting" taxpayer would be harmed. An important element of the Establishment Clause could be thus interred.[77]

With this in mind, it is more than a little ironic that Justice Kennedy relied on James Madison and his famed Memorial and Remonstrance to justify the *Winn* calculus. The Virginia Statute for Religious Liberty, and the political contest that spawned it, demonstrated, for Kennedy, the central premise of nonestablishment: a foundational aversion to citizens being "required to pay taxes to support religious institutions with whose beliefs they disagree."[78] But the proposed religious tax levy to which Madison objected would have allowed Virginians, should they have chosen, to opt out of compulsory support for churches by giving instead to a fund for common schools.[79] It thus would not have compelled any objecting religious contribution whatsoever. The implication of *Winn* then is that, despite Justice Kennedy's invocation of the Memorial and Remonstrance as setting forth the substantive rationale underlying the Establishment Clause's protection of taxpayers, no taxpayer would have standing to challenge any modern-day resurrection of the Virginia establishment tax, the provision to which Madison's words were directed.[80]

---

[76] *Winn*, 131 S Ct at 1461 (Kagan, J, dissenting).

[77] *Winn*'s sidestep of *Flast* parallels Justice Kennedy's opinion in *Citizens United v Federal Election Commission*, 130 S Ct 876 (2010). There, he exercised great caution to avoid the invalidation of campaign contribution limits and to leave standing the landmark, if troubled, ruling in *Buckley v Valeo*, 424 US 1 (1976). Rather than overruling *Buckley*, Kennedy minted a new constitutionally protected right for corporations to spend unlimited amounts of their treasury funds to engage independently in electioneering. Id at 913. While that result may leave the contribution-restricting rule intact, it simply renders it pointless. What sense can it make to limit an individual to gifts of two or three or four thousand dollars, if the union or corporation down the road can spend millions to elect or defeat a candidate?

[78] *Winn*, 131 S Ct at 1447, quoting Noah Feldman, *The Intellectual Origins of the Establishment Clause*, 77 NYU L Rev 346, 351 (2002).

[79] See Vincent Blasi, *School Vouchers and Religious Liberty*, 87 Cornell L Rev 783, 784 (2002); *Winn*, 131 S Ct at 1461 (Kagan, J, dissenting).

[80] *Winn* is surely based, in at least significant measure, on the substantive belief that there is nothing wrong with providing public funding for church-based schools and, additionally, that it is unproblematic for such schools to discriminate, in their now publicly funded operations, on the basis of religious affiliation. To make the point by indirection,

1. *Direct harms and general grievances.* *Winn* also fails as comprehensible Article III standing analysis. Justice Kennedy structured his jurisdictional determination, initially, upon the Court's traditional injury framework. Litigants must demonstrate "more than the mere generalized interests of all citizens."[81] Rather, in order to invoke the federal judicial power, complainants must allege that they "have suffered 'injury in fact'" which is "concrete and particularized" and "affects the plaintiff in a personal and individual way."[82] The plaintiffs in *Winn* failed to meet this Article III requirement for the same reason that those seeking to enforce broad, public constitutional claims frequently do:

> The party who invokes the power [of the federal courts] must be able to show not only that the statute is invalid, but that he has sustained or is immediately in danger of sustaining some direct injury as a result of its enforcement, and not merely that he suffers in some indefinite way in common with people generally.[83]

Because the interests proffered by the plaintiffs in seeking to invalidate the Arizona tax credit program were "of a general character, not particular to certain persons,"[84] the constitutional standard rejecting "speculative" claims and demanding "particularized injury" barred judicial review.[85]

To this point, Justice Kennedy is correct, at least in his description of stated standing doctrine. Current doctrine does distinguish between specific, particularized, concrete harms suffered by individual litigants and broad, widely shared, intangible harms that are only the abstract objections of the citizenry at large.[86] The

---

imagine if the tax credit program challenged had allowed religious school recipients of state support to discriminate in admissions on the basis of race. See *Bob Jones v United States*, 461 US 574, 577 (1983). Would standing to challenge the operation of the tax credit program still be denied, even if no rejected student applicant sued? For our money, we don't think so.

[81] *Winn*, 131 S Ct at 1441–42, citing *Schlesinger v Committee to Stop the War*, 418 US 208, 217 (1974).

[82] *Winn*, 131 S Ct at 1442, citing *Allen v Wright*, 468 US 737, 751, and *Lujan v Defenders of Wildlife*, 504 US 555, 560 (1992).

[83] *Winn*, 131 S Ct at 1443, citing *Doremus v Bd of Education of Hawthorne*, 342 US 429, 434 (1952).

[84] Id at 1444.

[85] Id.

[86] See *United States v Richardson*, 418 US 166, 167–68 (1974) (holding that there is no standing for an individual to seek an accounting of the CIA budget under US Const, Art I, § 9, cl 7); *Schlesinger v Reservists Committee to Stop the War*, 418 US 208, 210–11 (1974) (no taxpayer standing to challenge to members of Congress serving in the armed forces under Incompatibility Clause, Art I, § 6).

former comprise the harms necessary to trigger federal lawsuits. The latter constitute mere ideological disputation—best resolved through the electoral and political processes.

But Kennedy fails to acknowledge that the proffered line between "direct, personal injuries" and objections held in "common with the people generally" has never been the rigid bar to a litigant's standing that his *Winn* opinion suggests. The Court has held, for example, that the "widely shared . . . climate-change risks" constitute distinct and palpable harms,[87] that the denial of access to Federal Election Commission information constitutes actionable injury though "shared in substantially equal measure by all or a large class of citizens,"[88] and that a disgruntled citizen is "distinctly" harmed by living in an (otherwise invisible) electoral district that has been purportedly gerrymandered on the basis of race—even though he can make no claim to either individual or group-based vote dilution.[89] The Court has also held that one is "personally" and "concretely" injured if her senator's district has 3 percent more inhabitants than the one next door.[90] A purported victim of racial affirmative action in higher education admissions suffers distinct and tangible harm even if he would never have been admitted to the university.[91] An unsuccessful federal contracting applicant is free to challenge the allocation process even though he would not have obtained the contract.[92] And an environmentalist's concern for the plight of a snail darter in the nation's rivers is neither intangible, subjective, nor sufficiently communal to thwart judicial review.[93]

This is a slalom that no one can successfully navigate. Yet Justice Kennedy deployed this analysis in *Winn* to conclude that a seeming violation of the Establishment Clause is incapable of judicial re-

---

[87] See *Massachusetts v EPA*, 549 US 497, 522 (2007).

[88] See *Federal Election Commission v Akins*, 524 US 11, 24 (1998) ("Where a harm is concrete, though widely shared, the Court has found 'injury in fact.'").

[89] See *Shaw v Reno*, 509 US 630, 633 (1993) (racial electoral gerrymandering case); *United States v Hays*, 515 US 737, 739 (1995) (though the challenger must live in the electoral district challenged).

[90] See *Baker v Carr*, 369 US 186, 206–08 (1962); *Reynolds v Sims*, 377 US 533, 560–61 (1964).

[91] See *Bakke v Regents of California*, 438 US 265, 280 (1978).

[92] See *Adarand Constructors v Pena*, 515 US 200, 212 (1995) (allowing generous standing to challenge affirmative action in federal contracting).

[93] See *Tennessee Valley Authority v Hill*, 437 US 153, 165 (1978) (allowing challenge lodged by "any person" under the Endangered Species Act).

dress. As Justice Scalia observed in his concurring opinion in *Hein*,[94] the Court has never explained why it has found particular allegations of injury to be "cognizable" in some cases and "insufficient" in others."[95] *Winn* continues this tradition.

2. *"Extraction and spending" in taxpayer cases.* The *Winn* majority opinion's most significant contribution to standing jurisprudence, however, was its conclusion that the Arizona tax credit challenge was distinguishable from *Flast*.[96] Building on the language of *DaimlerChrysler v Cuno*,[97] Justice Kennedy explained that *Flast* "understood the 'injury' alleged in Establishment Clause challenges to . . . spending to be the very 'extract[ion] and spend[ing]' of 'tax money' in aid of religion."[98] This, Kennedy concluded, is not a "general grievance about the conduct of government"—like those typically rejected in public constitutional actions.[99] Rather, the "dissenter" whose tax dollars are "extracted and spent" knows that he has "in some measure been made to contribute to an establishment in violation of conscience."[100] The wounding "connection would exist even if the [objectors'] tax liability were unaffected. . . ."[101]

Flast's concept of taxpayer standing is thus based on "the specific evils identified in the public arguments of those who drafted the Establishment Clause and fought for its adoption."[102] Because the "credit" challenged in *Winn* entailed no such worrying "extraction,"[103] the plaintiffs could not demonstrate that "they were required to pay taxes to support religious institutions with whose beliefs they disagreed." It "follows," Justice Kennedy ruled, that the challengers had "neither alleged an injury for standing purposes under general rules nor met the *Flast* exception."[104]

---

[94] *Hein v Freedom from Religion Foundation*, 551 US 587, 599 (2007).

[95] *Hein*, 551 US 620 (Scalia, J, concurring) (referring to "psychic" injury).

[96] *Winn*, 131 S Ct at 1445–49.

[97] *DaimlerChrysler v Cuno*, 547 US 348 (2006).

[98] *Winn*, 131 S Ct at 1446, citing *Flast*, 392 US at 103 (quotation marks omitted).

[99] See, for example, *Ex parte Levitt*, 302 US 633, 634 (1937) (challenge to Justice Black's seating on United States Supreme Court as violation of Emoluments Clause); *Frothingham v Mellon*, 262 US 447, 479, 486 (1923) (challenge to federal spending program by taxpayer under the Tenth Amendment and Due Process Clause).

[100] *Winn*, 131 S Ct at 1447.

[101] Id.

[102] Id at 1446 (quotation marks omitted).

[103] Id at 1447.

[104] Id.

The "extract and spend" recasting of taxpayer standing is intriguing. It is true, as shall be discussed,[105] that there is something different about having one's tax payments spent for religious purposes—something perhaps distinct from the simple argument that the government is failing to comply with the Constitution or is using one's payments to support disapproved ventures.[106] But if this harm is unanchored to a defensible claim of economic stake, it cannot, as Kennedy suggests, be characterized as a "particularized," consequential "injury" rather than as a "general grievance"—at least not if those terms are to have anything like the meaning the Court has traditionally asserted for them. Justice Kennedy's opinion, in short, denies standing based upon widely shared intangible harms while at the same time purporting to affirm *Flast*, which predicated standing on precisely this type of injury.

Justice Kennedy's opinion in *Winn* thus falls of its own analytical weight. It draws no sustenance from credible understanding of Article III. And, as we will argue in the following section, it ignores the fact that the Establishment Clause is directly aimed at protecting against an array of widely shared, intangible harms. By overlooking these injuries, *Winn*, without justification, renders underenforceable[107] broad categories of Establishment Clause interests that are central to the very purposes of the First Amendment.

II. Establishment Clause Harms

Winn, perhaps, can be understood as an attempt to bring Establishment Clause standing doctrine in line with nonestablishment standing doctrine by demanding that plaintiffs demonstrate

---

[105] See notes 120–29 and accompanying text.

[106] *Schlesinger v Reservists Committee to Stop the War*, 418 US 208, 214 (1974).

[107] We use the term "underenforceable" rather than "unenforceable" because we allow for the possibility that, in some circumstances, other types of plaintiffs could emerge that might be able to allege particularized harm resulting from the purportedly unconstitutional state action. In challenging the type of program at issue in *Winn*, for example, a laid-off public school teacher, if the facts allowed, might be able to allege that the injury of losing her job resulted from too many students abandoning the public school system to attend the religious schools supported by the state tax credit program. But see *Smith v Jefferson County Bd. of Sch. Comm'rs*, 641 F3d 197, 208–09 (6th Cir 2011) (denying standing to laid-off public school teachers to raise an Establishment Clause challenge to an agreement between a public school and a religious school for the religious school to provide services to public school students that the laid-off public school teachers had been previously providing).

concrete and particularized injury.[108] Article III standards should not be relaxed in Establishment Clause cases to accommodate broad, intangible injuries, including, as Justice Scalia suggested in *Hein*, the "psychic" harm that would not be sufficient to confer standing in non-Establishment Clause cases.[109] To be sure, Justice Kennedy's opinion in *Winn* fails, on its own terms, to accomplish this purpose.[110] By affirming *Flast* and allowing taxpayer standing when the government "extracts and spends," Kennedy effectively concedes that the injury necessary to confer standing need not be either concrete or individual.[111] But *Winn* and *Hein* clearly signal that a majority of the Court is moving in an ever more restrictive direction.

Winn's suggestion that intangible, widely shared Establishment Clause injuries are nonjusticiable has implications for the substantive scope of the Establishment Clause as well as for the standing doctrine. Establishment Clause violations can impose tangible and individualized injuries. A law that allows a church governing body to object to the issuance of a liquor license to a nearby restaurant can impose economic harm on a restaurant that is denied a license.[112] A regulation that requires employers to afford every employee the right not to work on the Sabbath burdens both the employer and other employees.[113] A statute that prohibits the teaching of evolution may lead to a teacher's criminal prosecution.[114]

But while such harms may be sufficient to confer standing, they are only the collateral consequence of the Establishment Clause violations. They are not the harms that directly implicate the core purposes of the Establishment Clause. More importantly, such particularized and concrete Establishment Clause harms are often the exception, not the rule. The reason is straightforward. The Establishment Clause is in large measure aimed at curbing injuries that are, by their very nature, intangible and widely shared.[115] That is,

---

[108] See notes 27–29 and accompanying text.

[109] See notes 122–25 and accompanying text.

[110] See notes 105–06 and accompanying text.

[111] Justice Scalia, of course, would go further. Inherent in Justice Scalia's assertion that *Flast* should be overruled is that concrete and individualized injury should always be demanded in establishment cases.

[112] *Larkin v Grendel's Den*, 459 US 116, 127 (1982).

[113] *Estate of Thornton v Caldor, Inc.*, 472 US 703, 709–10 (1985).

[114] *Epperson v Arkansas*, 393 US 97, 107 (1968).

[115] Consider Carl H. Esbeck, *The Establishment Clause as a Structural Restraint on Governmental Power*, 84 Iowa L Rev 1, 2–3 (1998) (contending that unlike the Free Speech

many of the purposes underlying the anti-establishment mandate are directed specifically at preventing precisely the broad, nonconcrete "psychic" harms that Justice Scalia derided in his opinion in *Hein* as nonjusticiable.[116] Concluding that this harm does not present cognizable injury for standing purposes suggests that the harm is also not cognizable as a substantive Establishment Clause concern—a contention that, as we shall see, is at odds with both history and constitutional doctrine.

The remainder of this section expands on these points. We begin by revisiting taxpayer injury in more detail—demonstrating that protecting taxpayers from the "psychic" harm of being compelled to support religion to which they do not adhere is a central substantive Establishment Clause concern. Denying standing to taxpayers bringing such claims, therefore, undermines the anti-establishment mandate, even if the injury is thought of as intangible. We then indicate that an array of commonly recognized Establishment Clause aims are directed at such intangible, "psychic" harms as well. Barring standing to litigants attempting to base jurisdiction upon these interests is flatly at odds with vital substantive Establishment Clause norms. We end by responding to an anticipated criticism that recognizing psychic harm as a basis for standing in Establishment Clause cases will open the federal courthouse doors too widely to First Amendment challenges. As we explain, the psychic harm addressed by the Establishment Clause is not open-ended but is specifically tied to the particular purposes the provision was designed to serve. Granting standing to litigants alleging such injuries, then, appropriately enforces the Establishment Clause mandate. Allowing litigants the standing to raise such claims accordingly fits fully within the appropriate role of judicial review.

A. PROTECTING TAXPAYERS FROM INTANGIBLE, WIDELY SHARED "PSYCHIC" HARM

Protecting taxpayers from being forced to involuntarily support religious beliefs or institutions has long been recognized as a principal substantive purpose of the Establishment Clause. Sometimes characterized as an anti-coercion principle (taxpayers should not

---

Clause or the Free Exercise Clause, for example, the Establishment Clause does not create individual rights).

[116] *Hein v Freedom from Religion Foundation*, 551 US 587, 619–20 (2007) (Scalia, J, concurring).

be compelled to support a religion to which they do not adhere)[117] and sometimes framed as a conscience-protecting principle (taxpayer support of religion may conflict with taxpayers' religious conscience),[118] an overarching concern for taxpayer religious compulsion has deep historical support.[119] As the Court explained in *Flast v Cohen*:[120]

> Our history vividly illustrates that one of the specific evils feared by those who drafted the Establishment Clause and fought for its adoption was that the taxing and spending power would be used to favor one religion over another or to support religion in general. James Madison, who is generally recognized as the leading architect of the Religion Clauses of the First Amendment, observed in his famous Memorial and Remonstrance Against Religious Assessments that "the same authority which can force a citizen to contribute three pence only of his property for the support of any one establishment, may force him to conform to any other establishment in all cases whatsoever." The concern of Madison and his supporters was quite clearly that religious liberty ultimately would be the victim if government could employ its taxing and spending powers to aid one religion over another or to aid religion in general. The Establishment Clause was designed as a specific bulwark against such potential abuses of governmental power, and that clause of the First Amendment operates as a specific constitutional limitation upon the exercise by Congress of the taxing and spending power conferred by Art. I, § 8.[121]

Despite its historical pedigree, though, taxpayer injury runs into serious obstacles as a basis for standing if a demonstration of concrete, particularized harm is required. As Justice Scalia stated in his *Hein* opinion, taxpayer harm has two components—wallet injury and psychic injury. Wallet injury means that "the plaintiff's

---

[117] Lupu and Tuttle, 2008 BYU L Rev at 122 (cited in note 75).

[118] Micah Schwartzman, *Conscience, Speech, and Money*, 97 Va L Rev 317, 338 (2011); Richard W. Garnett, *Standing, Spending, and Separation: How the No-Establishment Rule Does (and Does Not) Protect Conscience*, 54 Vill L Rev 655, 661 (2009).

[119] See, for example, *Hein*, 551 US at 638–39 (Souter, J, dissenting); Noah Feldman, *Divided by God: America's Church-State Problem—and What We Should Do About It* 37 (2005). But see Garnett, 54 Vill L Rev at 664 (cited in note 118).

[120] *Flast*, 392 US 83 (1968).

[121] Id at 103–04, citing Gaillard Hunt, ed, 2 *Writings of James Madison* 183, 186 (Putnam's Sons, 1901). Thomas Jefferson also expressed similar concerns to that of Madison. See Thomas Jefferson, *A Bill for Establishing Religious Freedom*, in Julian P. Boyd, ed, 2 *The Papers of Thomas Jefferson* 545 (Princeton, 1950) ("To compel a man to furnish contributions of money for the propagation of opinions which he disbelieves and abhors, is sinful and tyrannical.").

tax liability is higher than it would be, but for the allegedly unlawful government action."[122] Psychic injury:

> consists of the taxpayer's *mental displeasure* that money extracted from
> him is being spent in an unlawful manner . . . his conceptualizing of
> injury in fact in purely mental terms conflicts squarely with the familiar
> proposition that a plaintiff lacks a concrete and particularized injury
> when his only complaint is the generalized grievance that the law is
> being violated.[123]

As noted earlier, Justice Scalia's assessment that recognizing
psychic injury conflicts with settled justiciability principles may be
overstated, as standing limitations have proved to be far more
malleable than his *Hein* analysis admits.[124] But more importantly,
Justice Scalia's rejection of psychic injury in the Establishment
Clause context is particularly notable because the psychic injury
he describes appears to be exactly the type of harm that was of
concern to the Framers—the violation of an individual's conscience caused by supporting a religion to which she does not
adhere.[125] Thus, even if Justice Scalia is technically correct that
psychic harm should not be sufficient to establish standing generally, there is significant question as to whether it should also
not be sufficient to establish standing when the particular constitutional provision in question is directed at redressing precisely
this kind of harm. That is, if one of the core purposes underlying
the Establishment Clause is to prevent a taxpayer's psychic injury
harm, then taxpayers suffering that harm should have standing[126]
even if the asserted injury is thought to be intangible. Taxpayers
alleging Establishment Clause violations, therefore, are on different footing than citizens asserting that members of Congress
should not hold commissions in the armed forces reserves under
the Incompatibility Clause as in *Schlesinger v Reservists Committee
to Stop the War*,[127] or that the appointment of Hugo Black to the

---

[122] *Hein*, 551 US at 619–20 (Scalia, J, concurring).

[123] Id.

[124] See notes 87–93 and accompanying text.

[125] See notes 119–21 and accompanying text.

[126] As Mark Rahdert states, if preventing the compelled exaction of taxes to advance
religion is a core concern of the Establishment Clause, "then the most logical method for
enforcement is through taxpayer actions in federal court." Mark C. Rahdert, *Forks Taken
and Roads Not Taken: Standing to Challenge Faith-Based Spending*, 32 Cardozo L Rev 1009,
1033 (2011).

[127] 418 US 208, 210–11 (1974).

Supreme Court violated the Emoluments Clause as in *Ex parte Levitt*.[128] The taxpayers' claim in the Establishment Clause context is not merely that the government has acted unconstitutionally; it is, rather, that the taxpayers have suffered an injury at the very core of the Establishment Clause concern.[129]

This does not mean that any Establishment Clause challenge raised in the name of a taxpayer is automatically justiciable. The Court may have had it right, for example, when it held in *Doremus v Board of Education*[130] that a taxpayer did not have standing to challenge Bible reading in the public schools because he did not allege that the practice required the expenditure of state funds.[131] But when a taxpayer demonstrates actual taxpayer injury, she comes within the class of "direct and intended" beneficiaries of the First Amendment's prohibition of financial aid to religion and is therefore a "singularly proper and appropriate party" to raise the Establishment Clause claim.[132]

One might argue, of course, that taxpayer injury should not be recognized as a substantive Establishment Clause harm. After all, given the current scope of federal government expenditures, the notion that a taxpayer will suffer injury *as a taxpayer* because of the way government funds are appropriated may seem too attenuated in the modern context. As Noah Feldman has written, "[i]n the eighteenth century, no one seemed to have suggested that taxes for religious purposes could not be attributed to the taxpayer. In that environment, it might be said, the citizen knew where his taxes were going, especially at the local level. A tax for religious purposes felt like exactly that. By contrast, this is often not so today."[133]

It is also possible, we think, to see Establishment Clause taxpayer standing as underinclusive because it confines cognizable taxpayer

---

[128] 302 US 633, 633 (1937).

[129] We do not revisit here the question of whether a citizen's or taxpayer's interest in having the government act constitutionally is sufficient to confer standing. See *Valley Forge Christian College v Americans United for Separation of Church and State*, 454 US 464, 483 (1982) (holding that such interest is not sufficient to base standing). The point that we are making is that taxpayer standing to raise an Establishment Clause claim based on taxpayer injury is qualitatively distinguishable from the claim that the government has acted unconstitutionally even if the plaintiff's harm may be intangible and widely shared.

[130] 342 US 429 (1952).

[131] Id at 435.

[132] See *Valley Forge*, 454 US at 509 (Brennan, J, dissenting) (quotation marks omitted).

[133] Feldman, 77 NYU L Rev at 346, 420 (cited in note 78).

conscience injury to government expenditures for religious purposes.[134] The religious consciences of taxpayers can also be triggered by government expenditures for a host of other activities
that includes, for example, military actions, the death penalty, gov-
ernment-funded reproductive services, and environmental exploration.[135] And the claim that there is something unique that distinguishes religious conscience from all other deeply held
convictions can be blurred by the diversity of beliefs in present-
day American life.[136] As Micah Schwartzman has asserted, although
such a notion may have had resonance in the Founding era, "the
idea that there is something distinctive about *religious* conscience,
or that claims of conscience can only be religious in nature, has
become normatively untenable."[137]

Still, the textual and historical case for recognizing taxpayer
harm continues to be compelling. Imagine, for example, that a
local government issued a special assessment to fund the construction of a church. Few would disagree that this would constitute
an archetypical establishment violation.[138] Even Justice Scalia
would appear to recognize taxpayer standing in this circumstance
because this is the exact type of "wallet injury" in which the taxpayer's payment can be directly traced to the challenged govern-

---

[134] It may also be overinclusive in that it apparently grants standing to nonreligious
taxpayers who therefore cannot complain that their religious conscience has been infringed.
But see notes 136–37 (questioning whether there is a meaningful distinction between
nonreligious and religious conscience).

[135] Feldman, 77 NYU L Rev at 421 (cited in note 78). Also consider Steven D. Smith,
What Does Religion Have to Do with Freedom of Conscience? 76 U Colo L Rev 911, 930
(2005).

[136] As one of us has argued elsewhere, the lack of a basis for such a distinction supports
the Court's holding in *Employment Div., Dep't of Human Resources of Oregon v Smith*, 494
US 872, 877–80 (1990) (holding that religious beliefs are not uniquely entitled to exemptions from neutral laws under the Free Exercise Clause). See William P. Marshall,
*What Is the Matter with Equality? An Assessment of the Equal Treatment of Religion and Non-
religion in First Amendment Jurisprudence*, 75 Ind L J 193, 196–200 (2000); William P.
Marshall, *In Defense of Smith and Free Exercise Revisionism*, 58 U Chi L Rev 308, 319–23
(1991). See also Frederick Mark Gedicks, *An Unfirm Foundation: The Regrettable Indefen-
sibility of Religious Exemptions*, 20 U Ark Little Rock L J 555, 569–72 (1998); Christopher
L. Eisgruber and Lawrence G. Sager, *The Vulnerability of Conscience: The Constitutional
Basis for Protecting Religious Conduct*, 61 U Chi L Rev 1245, 1291–97 (1994).

[137] Schwartzman, 97 Va L Rev at 324 (cited in note 118). See also Garnett, 54 Vill L
Rev at 664 (cited in note 118).

[138] See *Everson v Board of Education*, 330 US 1, 15–16 (1947) ("The 'establishment of
religion' clause of the First Amendment means at least this: . . . No tax in any amount,
large or small, can be levied to support any religious activities or institutions, whatever
they may be called, or whatever form they may adopt to teach or practice religion.").

ment expenditure.[139] But while the taxpayer may have suffered the concrete harm of paying higher taxes, her increased financial burden is not what is of direct anti-establishment concern. Rather, her establishment injury is the affront to conscience caused by the government's use of her funds for religious purposes. Negating the constitutional significance of her injury contradicts the substantive regime that the Establishment Clause means to assure.[140]

Perhaps for this reason even the *Winn* Court does not deny that taxpayer injury should continue to be recognized as a substantive Establishment Clause concern. But Justice Kennedy broadly discounts shared injuries as insufficient to confer standing. In rhetorical thrust, he thus joins Justice Scalia, even while retaining *Flast*.

The problem in Kennedy's opinion, then, is that it makes little sense to purport to recognize taxpayer harm as a legitimate Establishment Clause concern while denying standing to those who bring such claims. Yet *Winn* does exactly that through a hypertechnical account of injury that is so convoluted it strains credibility. If taxpayer injury is a nonparticularized, intangible harm that stems from the government's use of taxpayer funds to support religion, the wound is the same regardless of whether taxes are directly levied to support a religious institution or credits are used to accomplish an identical result. Either way, tax obligations are being deployed to facilitate religious subsidy. In both cases, a contesting plaintiff presents only a nonparticularized psychic grievance.

It is also possible that Justice Kennedy was attempting to provide substantive definition to taxpayer injury by asserting that the taxpayer harm recognized by the Establishment Clause occurs only when the taxpayer's funds flow directly into religious coffers. That result, though, contradicts not only common sense but historical record. As noted earlier, the proposed religious tax levy to which Madison objected in the Memorial and Remonstrance allowed Virginians to opt out of compulsory support for churches by giving instead to a fund for common schools.[141] For Madison, the fact

---

[139] See note 122 and accompanying text. See also Lupu and Tuttle, 2008 BYU L Rev at 139–40 (cited in note 75) (presenting examples of cases in which taxpayer standing against federal government expenditures could be recognized based upon wallet injury).

[140] See notes 125–29 and accompanying text.

[141] See Blasi, 87 Cornell L Rev 783, 784 (cited in note 79). See also *Winn*, 131 S Ct at 1462 (Kagan, J, dissenting).

that the taxpayer's funds did not go directly to the religious institution was of no moment. The establishment injury accrued to the taxpayer because the government to which she was compelled to pay taxes devoted funds to religious purposes. This was true whether or not her dollars could be directly traced to religious aid. Madison, unlike Kennedy, did not believe establishment problems could be cured through inventive accounting.

B. COMMONLY RECOGNIZED INTANGIBLE AND WIDELY SHARED ANTI-ESTABLISHMENT INJURIES

Taxpayer injury is not the only generalized, intangible harm addressed by the Establishment Clause.[142] Rather, other core purposes of the clause are also directed toward preventing the same sort of "psychic injury" at issue in the taxpayer cases. The following subsections identify these Establishment Clause harms and explain how requiring litigants to demonstrate concrete, particularized injuries undercuts essential Establishment Clause concerns.

1. *The harms stemming from denominational preferences.* One of the central aims of the Establishment Clause is preventing the government from preferring one religious sect over another.[143] As the Court stated in *Larson v Valente*,[144] "[t]he clearest command of the Establishment Clause is that one religious denomination cannot be officially preferred over another."[145] *Larson*'s assertion is well founded in the historical record. Guarding against denominational preference was repeatedly raised as a driving purpose during the Founding period—in the statements of prominent political and religious leaders and in the constitutional provisions that were then enacted.[146]

Determining whether sect preferences inflict tangible harm,

---

[142] As numerous commentators have pointed out, the Establishment Clause has "multiple purposes." See Andrew Koppelman, *Corruption of Religion and the Establishment Clause*, 50 Wm & Mary L Rev 1831, 1831 (2009); see also Kent Greenawalt, 2 *Religion and the Constitution: Establishment and Fairness* 6–13 (2008); Steven H. Shiffrin, *The Pluralistic Foundations of the Religion Clauses*, 90 Cornell L Rev 9, 37–54 (2004).

[143] In *Wallace v Jaffree*, for example, then Justice Rehnquist appeared to assert that preventing sect discrimination may be the only cognizable purpose of the Establishment Clause (other than prohibiting the actual establishment of a church). *Wallace v Jaffree*, 472 US 38, 98 (1985).

[144] 456 US 228 (1982).

[145] Id at 244.

[146] Michael W. McConnell, John H. Garvey, and Thomas C. Berg, *Religion and the Constitution* 292–93 (Aspen, 3d ed 2011).

however, is often less straightforward. Sometimes a denominational preference can lead to concrete and particularized harm. A
law allowing only Christians to attend public schools, for example,
would no doubt impose specific, concrete harm on non-Christians
who were denied access. But a Christian-only admissions policy
would also likely violate the Free Exercise Clause[147] and the Equal
Protection Clause.[148] The inclusion of a separate Establishment
Clause inquiry adds little to the existing constitutional calculus.[149]
Allowing standing for this type of harm then does not do much
to assure that central Establishment Clause values are judicially
enforced.

Even cases that clearly appear to set forth denominational preferences (as opposed to discrimination against a particular sect) do
not always lead to easy standing determinations. Assume, for example, that a local government administering a drug treatment
program awards a competitive grant to a Baptist-related organization over a Lutheran agency, basing its decision at least in part
on the organization's Baptist religious affiliation. Although the
decision would clearly constitute denominational preference, the
only party specifically aggrieved by the preference is the Lutheran
agency. Other parties, such as concerned citizens, taxpayers, or
nonreligious agencies, might object on the grounds that the state

---

[147] See *Church of Lukumi Babalu Aye v City of Hialeah*, 508 US 520, 524–25, 542 (1993)
(striking down ordinances prohibiting a religious animal sacrifice ritual on the grounds
that those prohibitions targeted a particular religious group). See also *Employment Div.,
Dep't of Human Resources of Oregon v Smith*, 494 US 872, 888–89 (1990) (holding that
nonneutral laws that infringe upon religious exercise violate the Free Exercise Clause).

[148] *City of New Orleans v Dukes*, 427 US 297, 303 (1976) (Equal Protection Clause
prohibits discrimination on the basis of religion); Lupu and Tuttle, 2008 BYU L Rev at
135 (cited in note 75) (sectarian preference in the government's distribution of benefits
would be an Equal Protection violation).

[149] The relationship between the Free Exercise and Establishment Clauses in guarding
against denominational preferences was explicitly noted by the Court in *Larson*:

> This constitutional prohibition of denominational preferences is inextricably
> connected with the continuing vitality of the Free Exercise Clause. Madison
> once noted: "Security for civil rights must be the same as that for religious
> rights. It consists in the one case in the multiplicity of interests and in the other
> in the multiplicity of sects." Madison's vision—freedom for all religion being
> guaranteed by free competition between religions—naturally assumed that every
> denomination would be equally at liberty to exercise and propagate its beliefs.
> But such equality would be impossible in an atmosphere of official denomi-
> national preference.

Larson, 456 US at 245 (1982).

is improperly funding a religious organization.[150] That claim, though, would not sound in denominational preference.

The Lutheran organization, in turn, though directly presenting the sect-preference injury, may nevertheless be denied standing unless it can show that the favoritism resulted in a separate, tangible harm.[151] Accordingly, it would be required to demonstrate not only that it had applied for the grant but also that "but for" the denominational preference the Lutheran organization would likely have received the grant. Whether an organization can make such a showing, however, is typically both fact-specific and speculative.[152] And if it cannot make that showing, then the only remaining harm is the psychic injury of being on the disfavored end of an unconstitutional denominational preference.

In fact, the concrete and particularized injury requirement potentially immunizes even the most blatant examples of sect preferences from constitutional attack. Assume, for example, that a city, without expending any funds or providing other forms of tangible support, declares that Presbyterianism is its official religion. Who, if anyone, would suffer a particularized injury as a result of the city's action? If there is no tangible effect, then presumably no individual would suffer concrete harm. Rather, the "injury" would simply be the shared sense that the government has acted unconstitutionally, an injury the Court has, on numerous occasions, including *Winn*, characterized as insufficient for standing requirements.[153] To be sure, a member of another religious sect might go a step further and claim that she was particularly offended by the city's endorsement of a different denomination. But experiencing offense is no more than the psychic harm that the Court has otherwise indicated, except in limited circumstances

---

[150] See, for example, *Bowen v Kendrick*, 487 US 589, 620 (1988) (taxpayer standing allowed to challenge the federal Adolescent Family Life Act).

[151] See *Lewis v Casey*, 518 US 343, 351 (1996); *Warth v Seldin*, 422 US 490, 499 (1975). But see *Adarand Constructors v Pena*, 515 US 200, 212 (1995).

[152] Compare *Warth v Seldin*, 422 US 490, 493 (1975) (standing denied to an equal protection challenge to restricting zoning requirements), with *Arlington Heights v Metropolitan Housing Development Corp.*, 429 US 252, 261–62 (1977) (equal protection standing to challenge restrictive zoning requirements upheld). The distinction between *Warth* and *Arlington Heights* appeared to rest on whether the plaintiffs would be able to show that but for the zoning requirements they would be able to move in to the restricted community.

[153] *Winn*, 131 S Ct at 1441–42, citing *Schlesinger v Reservists Committee to Stop the War*, 418 US 208, 214 (1974). See also *Valley Forge*, 454 US at 476, 481.

that will be discussed below, is insufficient to sustain standing.[154]

Or consider *Larson* itself. At issue in *Larson* was the constitutionality of a Minnesota provision that exempted some, but not all, religious organizations from certain reporting and disclosure requirements that were otherwise applicable to all charitable organizations.[155] The eligibility for the exemption depended on whether the religious organization raised more of its funding from its membership than from outside sources. If the group raised more than half of its revenues from its members, it was exempt. If it drew more than 50 percent from outside sources, it was subject to the reporting and disclosure requirements. The Court granted standing to an organization that did not qualify for the exemption (the Unification Church) to challenge the provision as an impermissible sect preference. But, as the dissent pointed out, the Establishment Clause injury suffered by the Unification Church was not related to the purported denominational preference at issue in the statute.[156] The church did not allege any tangible harm to itself resulting from the exemption's operation. It did not, for example, claim that the disparate treatment placed it at some sort of competitive disadvantage. Rather, its injury was the regulatory burden imposed because the church was not exempt, a harm having nothing to do with the purported denominational preference set forth in the statute.[157]

The Court in *Larson* ultimately circumvented the standing issue by engaging in creative remedial tailoring. Rather than striking down the exemption as a sect preference (although it was the exemption that was challenged), the Court *expanded* the exemption to include *all* religious organizations, thereby lifting the Unification Church's regulatory burden and redressing its alleged injury.[158] But this left the central point open. When would a non-exempt religious institution have standing to challenge another organization's exemption? What is the harm other than the "psychic" injury of being subjected to disfavored treatment?

---

[154] The Court has recognized offense to sensibilities as being an injury sufficient to trigger standing in the cases dealing with the government's display of religious symbols. This harm, sometimes referred to as the alienation of outsiders, is discussed at notes 184–93 and accompanying text.

[155] *Larson*, 456 US at 231–32.

[156] Id at 269 (Rehnquist, J, dissenting).

[157] Id.

[158] Id at 270.

2. *The harms stemming from government coercion.* Another core concern of the Establishment Clause goal is preventing the state from coercing religious belief.[159] As the Court stated in *Lee v Weisman*,[160] "[i]t is beyond dispute that, at a minimum, the Constitution guarantees that government may not coerce anyone to support or participate in religion or its exercise, or otherwise act in a way which establishes a [state] religion or religious faith."[161]

The anti-coercion rationale could plausibly be interpreted narrowly. Dissenting in *Lee*, for example, Justice Scalia argued that coercion should be understood only as compelled support "of religious orthodoxy and of financial support by force of law and penalty."[162] But, with this narrow compass, the Establishment Clause adds little to the constitutional protections already found in the Free Exercise[163] and the Free Speech Clauses.[164]

For this reason, it is not surprising that the meaning of coercion has been drawn more broadly. In *Lee*, for example, the compulsion the Court found problematic was the psychological pressure placed upon students to "stand as a group or at least maintain respectful silence" during a religious invocation offered by a member of the clergy at a graduation exercise.[165] As the Court explained, the state-sponsored prayer created an atmosphere in which objecting students might feel obligated to hide their opposition in order to avoid jeopardizing relationships with their peers. This violated the Establishment Clause because "the government may no more use social pressure to enforce orthodoxy than it may use more direct means."[166]

As defined by *Lee*, then, the unconstitutional coercion substan-

---

[159] Michael W. McConnell, *Coercion: The Lost Element of Establishment*, 27 Wm & Mary L Rev 933, 939 (1986).

[160] 505 US 577 (1992).

[161] Id at 587, quoting *Lynch v Donnelly*, 465 US 668, 678 (1984).

[162] Id at 640 (Scalia, J, dissenting) (emphasis omitted).

[163] See *Employment Div., Dep't of Human Resources of Oregon v Smith*, 494 US 872, 877 (1990) ("The government may not compel affirmation of religious belief" under the Free Exercise Clause); Lupu and Tuttle, 2008 BYU L Rev at 135 (cited in note 75) ("State coercion of religious experience would seem to be a prima facie violation of the Free Exercise Clause.").

[164] *W. Va. State Bd. of Educ. v Barnette*, 319 US 624, 642 (1943) (holding that public school students could not be compelled to salute the flag over their conscientious objection).

[165] *Lee*, 505 US at 593.

[166] Id at 594.

tively proscribed by the Establishment Clause includes that which imposes only an intangible, psychic harm.[167] The litigants in *Lee* did not need to show that they were actually coerced in order to prove an Establishment Clause violation. They only needed to show that they suffered psychological pressure.

Lee's substantive account of what constitutes unconstitutional coercion under the Establishment Clause further underscores the weakness of demanding a showing of concrete, particularized injury as a standing requisite. Requiring concrete injury as a threshold for standing in Establishment Clause coercion cases means that the anti-coercion rationale will be underenforced because even persons who are unconstitutionally "coerced" will not have access to federal court to vindicate their claims.[168]

3. *The harms stemming from the "corruption" of religion fostered by dependence upon the state.* The Establishment Clause is also concerned with protecting religion from the corrupting influences of the state.[169] As the Court stated in *Engel v Vitale*,[170] "[t]he Establishment Clause . . . stands as an expression of principle on the part of the Founders of our Constitution that religion is too personal, too sacred, too holy, to permit its 'unhallowed perversion' by a civil magistrate."[171] This concern is deeply rooted. The early American evangelical position, for example, was that the separation of church and state was necessary to preserve religion's purity and integrity.[172] As Roger Williams and others maintained, state sup-

---

[167] Justice Scalia makes essentially this point in his *Lee* dissent. Id at 632 (Scalia, J, dissenting).

[168] To be sure, there may be substantive objections raised as to whether the Establishment Clause should be construed to prevent the type of coercion recognized in *Lee*. Certainly, Justice Scalia is not entirely wrong when he argues in his *Lee* dissent that the majority opinion presents a "boundless, and boundlessly manipulable, test of psychological coercion." Id at 632. Do prayers at city council meetings "coerce" dissenting council members into engaging in a religious exercise with which they disagree? Do they coerce citizens attending the meetings into participating in the same way students were ostensibly coerced in *Lee*? Do they coerce taxpayers who fund the cost of the meetings into financially supporting religious prayer? The point presented here, however, is that if preventing coercion, no matter how broadly or narrowly defined, is recognized as a legitimate Establishment Clause purpose, not granting standing to those who present such injuries undercuts the substantive concern.

[169] Koppelman, 50 Wm & Mary L Rev at 1831 (cited in note 142). See also *Zelman v Simmons-Harris*, 536 US 639, 711–12 (2002) (Souter, J, dissenting) (stating that the Establishment Clause was designed to save religion from its own corruption).

[170] 370 US 421 (1962).

[171] Id at 431–32.

[172] See Elwyn A. Smith, *Religious Liberty in the United States: The Development of Church-*

port of religion would weaken churches by fostering dependence on the state and subjecting them to "worldly corruptions."[173]

Who suffers injury, though, when religion is purportedly corrupted by state aid? The answer is potentially everyone. To the extent that religion is seen as a social good,[174] society as a whole suffers when religion is weakened. A citizen choosing to challenge a government action supporting religion on this basis, though, would likely be denied standing for asserting a generalized grievance.[175]

More particularized injuries, presumably, would accrue to the "benefited" religion. If state aid "corrupts" religion, then it is the "benefited" entity that is harmed. This means, paradoxically, that those who are most directly injured by the government action are those who have received the fruits of the government's largesse, an unlikely class of plaintiffs if there ever was one.[176] But what would happen if an insider did come forward and allege that government aid to his religion did cause the corruption injury? Justice Scalia, as it turns out, may have anticipated exactly this question in his opinion in *Salazar v Buono*.[177] In *Buono*, the plaintiff brought suit against the display of a cross on government property and then continued his action after the government transferred the property (with the cross) to the Veterans of Foreign Wars in an attempt to avoid the Establishment Clause challenge.[178] The plain-

State Thought Since the Revolutionary Era 15–26 (Fortress, 1972) (detailing the involvement of Isaac Backus, a New England pastor, in advocating the evangelical theory of separation of church and state). See also *Mitchell v Helms*, 530 US 793, 868 (2000) (Souter, J, dissenting) ("The establishment prohibition of government religious funding . . . is meant . . . to protect the integrity of religion against the corrosion of secular support. . . .").

[173] Mark DeWolfe Howe, *The Garden and the Wilderness* 6 (Chicago, 1965). See also Timothy L. Hall, *Roger Williams and the Foundations of Religious Liberty*, 71 BU L Rev 455, 469 (1991).

[174] Koppelman, 50 Wm & Mary L Rev at 1846 (cited in note 142) (the anti-corruption rationale rests on "the core assumption that religion is valuable.").

[175] See notes 200–205 and accompanying text (discussing possible Establishment Clause injuries that do not inflict personalized harm).

[176] Perhaps for this reason, the Court has rather illogically allowed opponents of parochial aid programs to raise the Establishment Clause claim that the integrity of religious schools is harmed by the receipt of state assistance. See *Lemon v Kurtzman*, 403 US 602, 623 (1971) (allowing standing to parochial aid opponents to challenge a parochial aid program on this ground). See also Esbeck, 84 Iowa L Rev at 39 (cited in note 115) (criticizing the Court for granting standing to parochial aid opponents to raise the contention that the aid would harm the religious integrity of the religious schools).

[177] 130 S Ct 1803 (2010).

[178] Id at 1811.

tiff was a Catholic who did not find the cross an affront to his religious belief.[179] He did, however, argue that government display of the cross was offensive. Although the majority did not reach the standing issue,[180] Justice Scalia stepped into the breach. Buono's alleged injury, he concluded, was not sufficient to establish standing:

> Buono has not alleged, much less established, that he will be harmed if the VFW does decide to keep the cross. To the contrary, his amended complaint averred that "he is deeply offended by the display of a Latin Cross on government-owned property" but "has no objection to Christian symbols on private property." In a subsequent deposition he agreed with the statement that "[t]he only thing that's offensive about this cross is that [he has] discovered that it's located on federal land." And in a signed declaration several months later, he reiterated that although the "presence of the cross on federally owned land in the Preserve deeply offends [him] and impairs [his] enjoyment of the Preserve," he "ha[s] no objection to Christian symbols on private property." In short, even assuming that being "deeply offended" by a religious display (and taking steps to avoid seeing it) constitutes a cognizable injury, Buono has made clear that *he* will not be offended.[181]

Justice Scalia's opinion, however, apparently overlooks the fact that Buono did not have to be offended by the religiosity of the display in order to sustain a cognizable Establishment Clause injury. Rather, his offense could be based on the anti-corruption rationale—from his belief that his own religion was being subverted by government support.[182] Nevertheless, given his opinion in *Hein*, it is unlikely that Justice Scalia would have been impressed by Buono's claim for standing on this basis.[183] After all, the injury suffered by the "corruption" of the believer's religion caused by reliance on state support is yet another form of psychic harm, stemming from a longed-for purity of religion in the mind of the adherent. But failing to allow standing to those who think that

---

[179] *Buono v Norton*, 212 F Supp 2d 1202, 2006 (CD Cal 2002).

[180] The Ninth Circuit had earlier ruled that Buono had standing when he sought and won an injunction to prevent the government from maintaining the cross on public land and the government did not appeal from this decision. The Court upheld the finding that Buono had standing to enforce that injunction when he later returned to court to contest the land transfer on grounds that a "party that obtains a judgment in its favor acquires a 'judicially cognizable' interest in ensuring compliance with that judgment." *Buono*, 130 S Ct at 1814–15.

[181] Id at 1826–27 (Scalia, J, concurring).

[182] To be sure, Buono did not articulate his objection on these grounds.

[183] *Hein*, 551 US at 619–20 (Scalia, J, concurring).

their religion is corrupted by state support, as Justice Scalia seems to suggests, would again undercut a foundational purpose of the Establishment Clause in an action brought by those most directly affected.

4. *The harm stemming from the alienation of outsiders.* Finally, the Establishment Clause has been construed as having the purpose of preventing the alienation harm of religious outsiders.[184] As Justice O'Connor has explained, government action that endorses religion violates the Establishment Clause, in part, because it "sends a message to non-adherents that they are outsiders, not full members of the political community."[185]

Feeling alienated is, of course, a classic, almost defining, form of psychic injury. It is also another Establishment Clause harm that, like coercion, can be drawn broadly or narrowly.[186] A citizen, for example, could complain, as in *Valley Forge Christian College v Americans United for Separation of Church and State*,[187] that she feels alienated when reading in the newspaper that the United States government is giving property to a religious school;[188] or when she learns, as in *Hein*, that the Executive Branch spends money to support faith-based organizations.[189] In *Winn* itself, the claim could be made that the Arizona taxpayers bringing suit were alienated by the state's use of money to support religious schools. The concept is, at the least, encompassing.[190]

But even if the injury is psychic and amorphous, the Court has

---

[184] Whether preventing the alienation of outsiders should be recognized as an Establishment Clause concern has been a matter of some debate. See Koppelman, 50 Wm & Mary L Rev at 1840 (cited in note 142) ("[I]n a pluralistic culture, alienation is inevitable"); Steven D. Smith, *Symbols, Perceptions, and Doctrinal Illusions: Establishment Neutrality and the "No Endorsement" Test*, 86 Mich L Rev 266, 307 (1987) (because not all beliefs can prevail in the political process, those whose positions are not accepted will necessarily feel like outsiders). But see, for example, Arnold H. Loewy, *Rethinking Government Neutrality Towards Religion Under the Establishment Clause: The Untapped Potential of Justice O'Connor's Insight*, 64 NC L Rev 1049, 1051 (1986) (arguing that the anti-alienation principle is "thoroughly consistent with our national heritage").

[185] *Lynch v Donnelly*, 465 US 668, 688 (1984) (O'Connor, J, concurring).

[186] See notes 162–67 and accompanying text.

[187] 454 US 464 (1982).

[188] Consider id at 469 (holding that citizens who read about the grant of real property by the federal government to a religious organization in a news release did not have standing to challenge the transaction).

[189] *Hein*, 551 US at 595.

[190] Consider *Lee*, 505 US at 632 (1992) (Scalia, J, dissenting) (coercion is "boundless, and boundlessly manipulable.").

readily conferred standing to plaintiffs raising anti-alienation claims in Establishment Clause challenges to government displays of religious symbols.[191] In this series of decisions, the Court has found that "observers" of the challenged display have standing to contest the government action.[192] "Observer" standing is thus one example of the Court's recognition of the need to allow intangible, widely shared injuries to trigger standing in order to enforce substantive Establishment Clause goals.

Whether the Court will continue to do so, however, is another matter. If *Winn* (along with *Hein*) signifies a continued move by the Court to cut back on standing not based on tangible injuries, observer standing could well be the next target. As Ira Lupu and Robert Tuttle have documented, the process of undercutting "observer" standing may have already begun, pre-*Winn*, in the lower courts.[193]

C. THE LIMITS OF PSYCHIC HARM AS A BASIS FOR STANDING IN ESTABLISHMENT CLAUSE CASES

The obvious concern with recognizing psychic harm as a basis for standing is that it is a concept which, if too broadly drawn, would effectively eliminate any constraints on litigants choosing to bring Establishment Clause challenges. A prospective plaintiff living in Oregon, for example, might read about a government's providing assistance to a religious organization somewhere in North Carolina and on that basis bring suit to redress the psychic harm she ostensibly suffered when learning about the purported Establishment Clause violation.[194] The Court, therefore, may be legitimately concerned with opening up the federal courts to suits in these circumstances. As the Court cautioned in *Winn*, federal

---

[191] *Lynch v Donnelly*, 465 US 668, 671–72 (1984); *County of Allegheny v ACLU Greater Pittsburgh Chapter*, 492 US 573, 578–79 (1989); *Van Orden v Perry*, 545 US 677, 681–82 (2005); *McCreary County, Ky. v ACLU of Ky.*, 545 US 844, 850 (2005).

[192] See Lupu and Tuttle, 2008 BYU L Rev at 158 (cited in note 75).

[193] Id at 158–64. Lupu and Tuttle specifically discuss Judge DeMoss's concurrence in *Doe v Tangipahoa Parish School District*, 494 F3d 494, 497–500 (5th Cir 2007), in which DeMoss contends that after *Hein*, observer standing should not be recognized.

[194] This fact pattern parallels the one that gave rise to the decision in *Valley Forge* where the plaintiffs in that case learned about the government's transfer of federally owned property to a religious organization through a news release. *Valley Forge*, 454 US at 757.

jurisdiction should not extend to "every question" under the Constitution.[195]

Understanding that the Establishment Clause protects against *specific* types of psychic injury, however, does not mean that there are no limits on standing to raise Establishment Clause claims. In order to satisfy standing, the plaintiff's claim cannot be merely that is she is upset that the government is not acting constitutionally. Rather, she must demonstrate that her psychic injury is one that the Establishment Clause was specifically designed to address. As suggested earlier, then, the Court may have it right in denying taxpayers the standing to challenge school prayer in the *Doremus* case because no government funds were used in support of the exercise.[196] In order to demonstrate taxpayer standing, a litigant must show that she has incurred taxpayer harm.[197] The same is true with plaintiffs alleging such injuries as disfavored sect treatment, coercion, corruption, or alienation. Plaintiffs seeking to establish standing on those grounds must demonstrate that they have suffered the pertinent injury.

Moreover, even beyond those circumstances when the plaintiff's injury and the constitutional violation are mismatched, as in *Doremus*, there are other factors that will limit the extent that psychic harm will suffice as a basis for standing. The Court, for example, has already adopted such a limitation in the religious symbol cases by requiring that, in order to satisfy standing requirements, the litigant must actually witness the challenged display.[198] This "proximity" requirement, as one commentator has explained, assures that the complainant's injury is "both direct and particularized" because "[t]hose nearest to the offending display are most likely to receive its message and thus to be uniquely affected by it."[199]

---

[195] *Winn*, 131 S Ct at 1442.

[196] See notes 130–32 and accompanying text.

[197] *Flast v Cohen*, 392 US 83, 102–03.

[198] See Lupu and Tuttle, 2008 BYU L Rev at 158 (cited in note 75), citing *ACLU v McCreary*, 96 F Supp 2d 679, 682 (ED Ky 2000), affirmed as modified, *McCreary County v ACLU of Ky.*, 545 US 844 (2005), and *Van Orden v Perry*, 545 US 677, 682 (2005).

[199] Note, *Expressive Harms and Standing*, 112 Harv L Rev 1313, 1329 (1999). As the Note also discusses, the Court has not confined its use of this physical proximity requirement to Establishment Clause cases. Id at 1327–28. The Court has also used proximity to identify who has standing to challenge racial gerrymandering. See *Shaw v Reno*, 509 US 630, 633 (1993) (granting standing to challenge racial electoral gerrymander to a plaintiff living in the gerrymandered district); *United States v Hays*, 515 US 737, 739 (1995) (denying standing to a plaintiff living outside the district).

The limitation thus serves justiciability interests without leaving Establishment Clause concerns underenforced.

Furthermore, Establishment Clause standing is also inherently confined because not every Establishment Clause claim gives rise to cognizable psychic harm.[200] Consider, for example, the Establishment Clause goal of reducing religious divisiveness.[201] Certainly, a person could claim that she is psychically distraught because the state has taken an action that is religiously divisive, such as, for example, adopting an official school prayer. But the psychic harm that stems from religious divisiveness, we suggest, is on a qualitatively different footing than the harms to taxpayers, outsiders, and coerced individuals previously discussed in this section. The Establishment Clause is specifically aimed at preventing these latter forms of personalized psychic harms. The anti-divisiveness interest, on the other hand, is directed at fostering a particular social good, not preventing personalized injury. A plaintiff who challenges a school prayer based only on the assertion that public prayers are divisive might, then, be appropriately denied recourse.[202]

---

[200] Of course some Establishment purposes, such as preventing religion from being corrupted by its dependence on the state, are aimed at both fostering a social good (religion) and preventing a widely shared, intangible yet personalized injury (the psychic harm of an adherent who believes her religion has been desecrated by state support). See notes 174–82 and accompanying text.

[201] *Lemon v Kurtzman*, 403 US 602, 622 (1971) ("[P]olitical debate and division . . . are normal and healthy manifestations of our democratic system of government, but political division along religious lines was one of the principal evils against which [the First Amendment's Religion Clauses were] . . . intended to protect."). See also *Zelman v Simmons-Harris*, 536 US 639, 718 (2002) (Breyer, J, concurring) (lessening divisiveness is a "basic First Amendment objective"); Richard Schragger, *The Relative Irrelevance of the Establishment Clause*, 89 Tex L Rev 583, 604 (2011) (identifying lessening divisiveness as an Establishment Clause concern); Michael E. Smith, *The Special Place of Religion in the Constitution*, 1983 Supreme Court Review 83, 95–98 (1983) (discussing the concern with religious strife as a justification for the Religion Clauses). But see Richard W. Garnett, *Religion, Division, and the First Amendment*, 94 Geo L J 1667, 1720 (2006) (contending that the concern with religious divisiveness is misplaced); Koppelman, 50 Wm & Mary L Rev at 1838 (cited in note 142) (arguing that anti-divisiveness has been recognized as an Establishment Clause rationale, but that it is not a persuasive justification).

[202] Similar to the anti-divisiveness rationale, in this respect, is the Establishment Clause purpose in preventing religion from using government imprimatur to establish its dominance. *Engel v Vitale*, 370 US 421, 429 (1962) (recognizing that "zealous religious groups [may] struggle with one another to obtain the Government's stamp of approval. . . ."). See also Gene R. Nichol, *Establishing Inequality*, 107 Mich L Rev 913, 930 (2009). See generally Martha Nussbaum, *Liberty of Conscience: In Defense of America's Tradition of Religious Equality* 224–305 (Basic, 2008). The general interest that society would be bettered if religion did not attempt to use the government to reinforce itself is again a claim of social betterment rather than an interest that accrues to an individual or any specific class

The Establishment Clause goal of guarding against excessive entanglement[203] between church and state is another example of the type of First Amendment interest whose violation does not implicate psychic harm. A religious school, for example, would likely have standing to bring a tangible nonentanglement action against a program that subjects it to significant regulatory burdens because it is concretely affected by the regulatory scheme.[204] But a plaintiff challenging the program who is not burdened by the regulations should not be able to gain standing solely on the grounds that she believes that church and the state are better served when confined to separate spheres. Though such a plaintiff may be personally upset by the purported entanglement, the Establishment Clause's purpose in promoting church-state separation, we suggest, is again better understood as promoting a social good rather than providing a specific protection against an individual's psychic injury.[205]

Finally, and perhaps most importantly, Establishment Clause standing will necessarily be confined by the substantive definition of the constitutional harm. A plaintiff who reads in a newspaper that a minister is going to lead the audience in prayer at a public school commencement may claim that she is being unconstitutionally coerced by the school's action, but she will not have standing to raise the claim if the substantive scope of improper coercion does not extend to those not personally exposed to the challenged activity. On the other hand, not allowing someone who fits within the scope of the substantive harm (e.g., a student attending the commencement[206]) to have standing because her injury is only an

of individuals. Of course, if a religious group did succeed in gaining the government's imprimatur, any resulting government action that granted that group special benefits or recognition could presumably be challenged as an improper denominational preference.

[203] See, for example, Paul Horwitz, *Churches as First Amendment Institutions: Of Sovereignty and Spheres*, 44 Harv CR-CL L Rev 79, 130 (2009); Esbeck, 84 Iowa L Rev at 2 (cited in note 115).

[204] See *NLRB v Catholic Bishop of Chicago*, 440 US 490, 507 (1979).

[205] We understand that some might consider these "fine distinctions" of Establishment Clause meaning. See *Walz v Tax Commission of City of New York*, 397 US 664, 679 (1970) (noting that Establishment Clause doctrine is marked by "fine distinctions"). But they recognize that it is possible for a constitutional provision to provide protection against some personally experienced, intangible, even psychic, broadly shared wounds, without opening the door to a wider and perhaps unmanageable regime in which anyone could literally make a federal case out of any asserted constitutional transgression.

[206] Justice Kennedy's majority opinion in *Lee v Weisman*, 505 US 577 (1992), of course, did not deny standing to a student challenging a commencement prayer in similar cir-

intangible, "psychic" harm, as the logic of *Winn* appears to suggest, illustrates exactly the problem inherent in the decision. Maintaining that the very injury that defines a substantive anti-establishment violation is not sufficient to confer standing means that the threshold necessary to trigger standing is higher, more imposing, than the threshold necessary to prove a constitutional violation. This approach makes no sense either as an interpretation of the Establishment Clause or as a measure of Article III.

III. CONCLUSION

Few areas of constitutional law are as difficult, or as frustrating, as standing.[207] The question of who is "injured" by an unconstitutional government action is extraordinarily amorphous and malleable. At the same time, the stakes are high. On one side is the need for constitutional enforcement and accountability.[208] On the other is the concern over an appropriate separation of powers—limiting the power of the judiciary to decide far-reaching and politically laden disputes without restraint.[209] The Establishment Clause terrain has proved to be equally hazy. In few areas has the Court so readily conceded its own lack of clarity,[210] and in few areas has the Court so often lived up to its acknowledged shortcomings.[211]

It might therefore be excusable if a judicial decision addressing

---

cumstances. Our point, however, is that the logic of denying standing to those presenting psychic claims leads to such a result.

[207] Erwin Chemerinsky, *Federal Jurisdiction* 57 (Aspen, 5th ed 2007).

[208] See Susan Bandes, *The Idea of a Case*, 42 Stan L Rev 227, 229 (1990).

[209] *Allen v Wright*, 468 US 737, 752 (1984).

[210] *Committee for Pub. Educ. and Religious Liberty v Regan*, 444 US 646, 662 (1980) (noting that in Establishment Clause cases the Court has frequently "sacrificed clarity and predictability for flexibility"). *Lee*, 505 US at 598 ("Our jurisprudence in this area is of necessity one of line-drawing.").

[211] See, for example, Jesse Hill, *Putting Religious Symbolism in Context: A Linguistic Critique of the Endorsement Test*, 104 Mich L Rev 491, 492 (2005) ("The treatment of Establishment Clause challenges to displays of religious symbolism by the Supreme Court and the lower courts is notoriously unpredictable."); see also Jessie Hill, *Of Christmas Trees and Corpus Christi: Ceremonial Deism and Change in Meaning Over Time*, 59 Duke L J 705, 727 (2010) (there is considerable confusion in the tests the Court applies in Establishment Clause cases); Kent Greenawalt, *Quo Vadis: The Status and Prospects of "Tests" Under the Religion Clauses*, 1995 Supreme Court Review 323, 323 (noting that the tests the courts apply in Religion Clause cases are in "nearly total disarray"); Daniel O. Conkle, *The Establishment Clause and Religious Expression in Governmental Settings: Four Variables in Search of a Standard*, 110 W Va L Rev 315, 315 (2007) ("Establishment Clause doctrine is a muddled mess. . . .").

both standing and the Establishment Clause did not turn out to be a model of lucidity. Still, the Court's decision in *Winn* disappoints even in this arena of low expectations. To begin with, it is internally incoherent. On the one hand, the Court rejects the notion that widely shared, intangible injuries may be sufficient to trigger standing. On the other, it reaffirms *Flast*, where standing was based precisely on such grounds.

The Court's distinction between the spending program in *Flast* and the tax credit in *Winn* is also not credible. There is no principled difference between the injuries a taxpayer incurs when she is required to subsidize religious schools and those she sustains when she is forced to subsidize the credits given to others to support religious schools.

Finally, and most importantly, *Winn* shortchanges both standing and the Establishment Clause. With respect to standing, *Winn* claims to adhere to a line between distinct, palpable, concrete harms and shared interests that is both incomprehensible and illegitimate. The line is incomprehensible because, as the Court's distinction between taxpayer challengers to the spending program in *Flast* and taxpayer challenges to the tax credit in *Winn* graphically demonstrates, the labeling methodology the Court deploys to separate who has standing and who does not is purely illusory. It is illegitimate because the Court relies on judicially fashioned barriers to jurisdiction that effectively negate norms of clear constitutional pedigree. It is difficult to see why an injury that is sufficient to demonstrate a substantive constitutional violation is somehow not sufficient to confer standing.

With respect to the Establishment Clause, the implications of *Winn* may be even more far-reaching. The Court's assumption that widely shared, intangible injuries such as psychic harm are not sufficient to confer standing conflicts with a large segment of Establishment Clause jurisprudence that identifies the prevention of such injuries as central First Amendment concerns. Failing to grant standing to those asserting these injuries means core Establishment Clause guarantees will be violated without judicial redress.

ERNEST A. YOUNG

"THE ORDINARY DIET OF THE LAW": THE PRESUMPTION AGAINST PREEMPTION IN THE ROBERTS COURT

In 2001, the Supreme Court decided a quiet little case about whether the beneficiary rules of a pension plan established under the federal Employee Retirement Income Security Act[1] (ERISA) trumped a Washington statute providing that designation of a spouse as a beneficiary of a nonprobate asset was automatically revoked upon divorce.[2] The majority held that it did. In dissent, Justice Breyer stepped back for a moment to discuss the broader importance of statutory preemption cases for federalism. He stressed "the practical importance of preserving local independence, at retail, that is, by applying pre-emption analysis with care, statute by statute, line by line, in order to determine how best to reconcile a federal statute's language and purpose with federalism's need to preserve state autonomy."[3] This task, Breyer suggested, is more consequential for federalism than "the occasional constitutional ef-

Ernest A. Young is Alston & Bird Professor, Duke Law School.

AUTHOR'S NOTE: I am grateful to Erin Blondel, Dennis Hutchinson, and Maggie Lemos for helpful comments on the manuscript and to Kate Dickinson-Varner for excellent research assistance. I am also indebted to the many lawyers and scholars that I have worked with on preemption-related projects over the years, especially Erin Busby, Brendan Crimmins, Melissa Davis, David Frederick, Michael Greve, and Garrick Pursley.

[1] 29 USC § 1001 et seq.

[2] *Egelhoff v Egelhoff*, 532 US 141 (2001).

[3] Id at 160 (Breyer, J, dissenting).

preemption cases, the different methodological commitments held by individual Justices have thus far prevented the Court from coalescing around a single theory. Textualists approach these cases differently from purposivists, and Justices willing to defer to administrative agencies will embrace distinct approaches from those who view the agencies with more skepticism. Without denying that preemption is a muddle, I hope to make the case that this muddle is fundamentally faithful to the statutory and methodological complexity that this area of the law presents.

That said, my normative project is to urge that preemption doctrine should align more closely to the broader imperatives of constitutional federalism doctrine in the post-New Deal era. Those imperatives, as I see them, can be captured in three broad propositions: First, national and state authority is largely concurrent, not limited by exclusive subject-matter spheres. Second, the limits of national authority stem primarily (although not exclusively) from the representation of the states in Congress and the Constitution's rigorous procedural constraints on federal lawmaking. And, third, it follows that the courts' role in protecting federalism should focus on facilitating and enhancing the operation of these political and procedural checks on national authority. These imperatives highlight the critical importance of the "presumption against preemption" developed in *Rice v Santa Fe Elevator Corp.*[12] and similar cases. My doctrinal focus here is thus to defend that presumption against its most prominent critics and to suggest how it might be applied more effectively going forward. I also suggest that tying preemption doctrine more firmly to the broader imperatives of federalism might help the Court transcend its current, more overtly political divisions over tort reform, aggregate litigation, immigration policy, and similar issues.

The analysis has four parts. Part I places preemption within its broader constitutional context, tracing the development of preemption doctrine alongside more general changes in the constitutional law of federalism. Part II then surveys the Court's five preemption cases decided in the 2010 Term. Although these cases cannot be said to present a coherent set of preemption principles, they do provide a window into the Court's evolving thinking on the underlying controversies of preemption doctrine. Part III fo-

---

[12] 331 US 218 (1947).

cuses on the debate concerning the legitimacy and scope of *Rice*'s anti-preemption presumption and underlying arguments about the original understanding of the Supremacy Clause. Part IV concludes with some comments on the politics of preemption in the Roberts Court.

I. Preemption Doctrine in Constitutional Context

It is only in the last few years that preemption cases have been considered constitutional cases at all. Although a preempted state law is technically unconstitutional under the Supremacy Clause, the cases are generally exercises in statutory construction. But the construction of federal statutes plays a critical role in our federal structure. Our founding document sketches only the barest outlines of our federalism, leaving the rest to be worked out through statutes, judicial decisions, executive branch regulations, and governmental practices.[13] Preemption cases thus significantly shape our federal balance, and preemption *doctrine* has been critically influenced by broader changes in constitutional law.

A. FROM DUAL FEDERALISM TO CONCURRENT JURISDICTION

For most of our history, federalism has been about drawing lines. For a century and a half between the Founding and the New Deal, judges, politicians, and scholars all understood the Constitution to mandate "two mutually exclusive, reciprocally limiting fields of power—that of the national government and of the States. The two authorities confront[ed] each other as equals across a precise constitutional line, defining their respective jurisdictions."[14] In this world of "dual federalism," challenges to state or federal measures required judges to determine whether the right government was acting within the right sphere: States were prohibited from acting on matters that were "in their nature national, or admit only of one uniform system,"[15] and the national government was fore-

---

[13] See generally Ernest A. Young, *The Constitution Outside the Constitution*, 117 Yale L J 408 (2007).

[14] Alpheus Thomas Mason, *The Role of the Court*, in Valerie A. Earle, ed, *Federalism: Infinite Variety in Theory and Practice* 8, 24–25 (1968); see also Anthony J. Bellia Jr., *Federalism* 183 (Aspen, 2011) ("The *dual federalism* paradigm understands federal and state governments to operate in different spheres of authority.").

[15] *Cooley v Board of Wardens of the Port of Philadelphia*, 53 US (12 How) 299, 319 (1852).

closed from regulating matters "essentially local."[16] Legislative and executive actors confronted similar choices: President Herbert Hoover, for example, rejected broad national action to ameliorate the effects of the Depression not because he was opposed to government economic intervention, but rather because he viewed it as predominantly a state responsibility.[17]

In practice, dual federalism was not always categorical. In *Cooley v Board of Wardens*, for instance, the Court distinguished between matters within Congress's commerce power, which required uniform national regulation and therefore excluded the states, and other matters that might be regulated by the states unless and until Congress chose to act.[18] The categories seemed to harden by the end of the nineteenth century.[19] In any event, dual federalism put a premium on line-drawing, and as the economy became more integrated and governments intervened in the market more frequently, the lines became increasingly difficult to draw.

The problem was not simply that the Court needed to know where to draw the lines, but also that the lines drawn needed to appear determinate—to be the product of objective "judgment" rather than judicial "will."[20] As conflict intensified over the reach of the New Deal into traditional spheres of state regulation, proponents of broader national authority pointed to plausible disagreements about the boundaries of national power as evidence that the Court was simply striking down laws that it opposed on policy grounds. President Franklin Roosevelt, for example, cited dissenting opinions in cases striking down New Deal legislation

---

[16] See id at 326 (Daniel, J, concurring in judgment); see also *United States v E. C. Knight Co.*, 156 US 1, 13–14 (1895) (rejecting national power to regulate local activities that affect interstate commerce).

[17] See, e.g., William J. Barber, *From New Era to New Deal: Herbert Hoover, the Economists, and American Economic Policy, 1921–1933* 98–99 (Cambridge, 1988) (observing that "Hoover insisted that no American should be allowed to go hungry or cold," but he believed that "[c]are for the needy was properly the responsibility of private organizations and of state and local officials").

[18] 53 US at 319.

[19] See *E. C. Knight Co.*, 156 US at 11 ("[T]he power of a State to protect the lives, health, and property of its citizens, and to preserve good order and the public morals . . . is a power originally and always belonging to the States . . . and essentially exclusive. . . . On the other hand, the power of Congress to regulate commerce among the several States is also exclusive.").

[20] See Federalist 78 (Hamilton) in Jacob E. Cooke, ed, *The Federalist* 521, 522–23 (Wesleyan, 1961); Ernest A. Young, *Making Federalism Doctrine: Fidelity, Institutional Competence, and Compensating Adjustments*, 46 Wm & Mary L Rev 1733, 1836–40 (2005) (discussing the judiciary's institutional need to decide according to determinate rules).

to say that "there is no basis for the claim made by some members of the Court that something in the Constitution has compelled them regretfully to thwart the will of the people."[21] Larry Lessig has thus argued that the indeterminacy problem ultimately helped undermine the legitimacy of the Court's stand against the New Deal.[22] After the Court's famous "switch in time" in 1937, it never again sought to draw such restrictive boundaries on national power, and it also significantly dialed back the rigor of its "dormant" Commerce Clause restrictions on state regulation.[23]

After the switch in time, the Court's federalism doctrine has generally abandoned dual federalism's notion of separate spheres in favor of a regime of *concurrent* jurisdiction.[24] The Court's new cases broadened Congress's Commerce Clause authority to reach all activity that "substantially affects" interstate commerce, and the Court expanded this category to include activities that were small in themselves but, in the aggregate, had substantial economic effects.[25] A national regulatory power this broad, however, could no longer be exclusive without wiping out virtually all state regulatory authority. Hence the Court shifted its dormant Commerce Clause jurisprudence from a rule categorically excluding state regulation wherever federal power could reach to a more modest antidiscrimination principle.[26] This meant that both state and national authorities have power to address most subjects of regulatory concern.

---

[21] Franklin Delano Roosevelt, Fireside Chat on Reorganization of the Judiciary, March 9, 1937, online at http://www.mhric.org/fdr/chat9.html (concluding that "[i]n the face of such dissenting opinions, it is perfectly clear that, as Chief Justice Hughes has said, 'We are under a Constitution, but the Constitution is what the judges say it is'").

[22] See Lawrence Lessig, *Translating Federalism: United States v Lopez*, 1995 Supreme Court Review 125, 176–80 ("[T]he retreat of the 'Old Court' tracks the collapse of what made it possible for the Court to sustain [formal legal distinctions] in the name of translating federalism. The formalisms themselves had been rendered political. They now seemed more the result of extra-judicial judgments than entailed by the legal material.").

[23] See *Wickard v Filburn*, 317 US 111 (1942); Stephen Gardbaum, *New Deal Constitutionalism and the Unshackling of the States*, 64 U Chi L Rev 483 (1997) (explaining how the New Deal revolution expanded the regulatory authority of *both* federal and state governments).

[24] See Corwin, 36 Va L Rev at 17–23 (cited in note 7) ("According to [the post-New Deal] conception, the National Government and the States are mutually complementary parts of a *single* governmental mechanism all of whose powers are intended to realize the current purposes of government according to their applicability to the problem in hand.").

[25] See *Wickard*, 317 US at 127–28.

[26] See, for example, *City of Philadelphia v New Jersey*, 437 US 617, 624 (1978) (stating that "[t]he crucial inquiry" is "whether [the state law] is basically a protectionist measure").

Vestiges of dual federalism remain. The Court often suggests that foreign relations is an exclusively federal field[27]—notwithstanding the myriad state activities that daily affect foreign relations and the inherent difficulty of drawing lines between "foreign" and "interstate" commerce in a globalized economy.[28] The Court's dormant Commerce Clause jurisprudence still forbids in principle—but only infrequently strikes down in practice—state actions that impose an excessive "burden" on interstate commerce, even absent discrimination against out-of-staters.[29] Since all economic regulation burdens commerce to some extent, this vestigial doctrine suggests that state regulation of interstate activity is somehow suspect. The Court's "intergovernmental immunity" jurisprudence likewise rests on dual-federalist premises,[30] although that doctrine has been narrowed significantly since the New Deal.[31] And the Court occasionally speaks in dual federalist terms in its affirmative Commerce Clause jurisprudence, suggesting that federal legislation is constitutionally suspect where it intrudes into areas of "traditional state regulation."[32] The confusion and criticism that each of these remnants has engendered,[33] however, tends

---

[27] See, for example, *Zschernig v Miller*, 389 US 429 (1968) (asserting that any state action that interferes with U.S. foreign relations is unconstitutional). For contemporary examples, see *American Insurance Assn. v Garamendi*, 537 US 1100 (2003) (holding state law preempted by implication from an executive agreement without any congressional action); *Crosby v National Foreign Trade Council*, 530 US 363 (2000) (finding preemption by federal statute more readily where foreign relations are at issue).

[28] See Ernest A. Young, *Dual Federalism, Concurrent Jurisdiction, and the Foreign Affairs Exception*, 69 Geo Wash L Rev 139, 178 (2001); Jack L. Goldsmith, *Federal Courts, Foreign Affairs, and Federalism*, 83 Va L Rev 1617, 1670–80 (1997).

[29] See, for example, *Kassel v Consolidated Freightways Corp. of Delaware*, 450 US 662 (1981) (striking down an Iowa law regulating the length of trucks); *Pike v Bruce Church, Inc.*, 397 US 137, 142 (1970) ("Where the statute regulates evenhandedly to effectuate a legitimate local public interest, and its effects on interstate commerce are only incidental, it will be upheld unless the burden imposed on such commerce is clearly excessive in relation to the putative local benefits.").

[30] See Laurence H. Tribe, 1 *American Constitutional Law* § 6-33 at 1221–22 n 4 (3d ed 2000).

[31] Compare *Penn Dairies, Inc. v Milk Control Commission of Pennsylvania*, 318 US 261, 270–71 (1943) (acknowledging that intergovernmental immunity doctrine must recognize the concurrent authority of state regulators), with *Hancock v Train*, 426 US 167 (1976) (continuing to state the doctrine in broad terms).

[32] See *United States v Lopez*, 514 US 549, 567–68 (1995) (insisting on the need to preserve "a distinction between what is truly national and what is truly local"); see also id at 580 (Kennedy, J, concurring) ("[W]e must inquire whether the exercise of national power seeks to intrude upon an area of traditional state concern.").

[33] See, for example, Neil S. Siegel, *Distinguishing the "Truly National" from the "Truly Local": Customary Allocation, Commercial Activity, and Collective Action*, 62 Duke L J (forth-

to confirm that the law of federalism has generally moved on to a concurrent model.

B. FROM JUDICIAL ENFORCEMENT TO POLITICAL AND PROCEDURAL SAFEGUARDS

The shift from dual federalism to concurrent state and national jurisdiction coincided with two additional changes in how we think about the division of authority between the state and national governments. Although it seems fair to say that these changes began in the New Deal period, they were not acknowledged by the Court until much later—primarily in its 1985 decision in *Garcia v San Antonio Metropolitan Transit Authority*.[34] The first change was from a federalism defined by hard jurisdictional boundaries to one maintained by political competition. Without dual federalism's sharp limits on Congress's power, state authority is maintained by a variety of political dynamics, including states' representation in Congress, underlying attachments of citizens to the state governments, bureaucratic resistance by state officials charged with implementing federal law, and federal governmental inertia induced by onerous constitutional procedures for making federal law.[35] Federalism becomes not so much a matter of drawing lines as one of calibrating incentives, enforcing procedural rules, and interpreting the output of the national political process in a way that respects the system's structural safeguards for states.

The second and related change concerned the role of the courts in enforcing federalism. As the post-New Deal Court largely gave up review of national legislation under the Commerce Clause and transformed its dormant Commerce Clause jurisprudence into a nondiscrimination principle, "the courts no longer played a central role in managing the relationship of the states and the federal government," and, in particular, "became much less active in pa-

coming 2012) (criticizing the effort to identify traditional subjects of state regulation as "indeterminate and thus unworkable").

[34] 469 US 528 (1985).

[35] See generally Herbert Wechsler, *The Political Safeguards of Federalism: The Rôle of the States in the Composition and Selection of the National Government*, 54 Colum L Rev 543 (1954) (political representation); Robert A. Mikos, *The Populist Safeguards of Federalism*, 68 Ohio St L J 1669 (2007) (popular attachments); Jessica Bulman-Pozen and Heather K. Gerken, *Uncooperative Federalism*, 118 Yale L J 1256 (2009) (bureaucratic resistance); Bradford R. Clark, *The Procedural Safeguards of Federalism*, 83 Notre Dame L Rev 1681 (2008) (procedural safeguards).

trolling the bounds of federal power."[36] The Court articulated the reasons for its retreat in *Garcia*, where it said that the Constitution's protection for federalism lies primarily in the states' representation in Congress—not in judicially enforceable boundaries for national power.[37] Consequently, as Herbert Wechsler argued, "the Court is on weakest ground when it opposes its interpretation of the Constitution to that of Congress in the interest of the states, whose representatives control the legislative process and, by hypothesis, have broadly acquiesced in sanctioning the challenged Act of Congress."[38] Although many observers viewed *Garcia* as an abdication of any judicial enforcement of limits on national power, it is better viewed as a shift from efforts to impose substantive limitations on national power to a focus on process.[39]

Preemption takes on particular importance in light of these shifts in our theory of federalism and the role of the courts. One reason has to do with the impact of preemption on a federal balance that is determined primarily by politics. *Garcia* built upon James Madison's much older theory of federalism as a competition between the national government and the states for the loyalty of their mutual citizens.[40] Notwithstanding the jurisdictional limitations that the Constitution placed on national power, Madison understood that the ultimate balance would be determined by politics—that is, by which level of government could best earn the electorate's trust by providing government services and ben-

---

[36] Schapiro, *From Dualism to Polyphony* at 40 (cited in note 8).

[37] See 469 US at 550–51.

[38] Wechsler, 54 Colum L Rev at 559 (cited in note 35). This "political safeguards" thesis is highly contested. See, for example, *Garcia*, 469 US at 574 n 17 (Powell, J, dissenting); Saikrishna B. Prakash and John C. Yoo, *The Puzzling Persistence of Process-Based Federalism Theories*, 79 Tex L Rev 1459 (2001); Lynn A. Baker, *Putting the Safeguards Back into the Political Safeguards of Federalism*, 46 Vill L Rev 951 (2001).

[39] Compare William W. Van Alstyne, *The Second Death of Federalism*, 83 Mich L Rev 1709, 1720 (1985) (seeing *Garcia* as the end of judicial enforcement of federalism) with Ernest A. Young, *Two Cheers for Process Federalism*, 46 Vill L Rev 1349, 1361–64 (2001) (finding a silver lining). To say that a "process federalism" model based on *Garcia* can actually go a long way toward promoting state autonomy is emphatically *not* to concede that substantive limits on national power are unnecessary or undesirable.

[40] See Federalist 45, 46 (Madison), in *The Federalist* at 308–23 (cited in note 20) (arguing that federal encroachment "will be easily defeated by the State Governments[,] who will be supported by the people"); see generally Todd E. Pettys, *Competing for the People's Affection: Federalism's Forgotten Marketplace*, 56 Vand L Rev 329 (2003) (discussing Madison's theory).

eficial regulation.[41] He thought the states would always have an advantage in this competition, however, because "[t]he powers reserved to the several States will extend to all the objects, which, in the ordinary course of affairs, concern the lives, liberties and properties of the people; and the internal order, improvement, and prosperity of the State."[42] The "political safeguards of federalism," in other words, depend on the states retaining important regulatory responsibilities and government functions that touch the daily lives of their citizens.[43]

Preemption, however, has the potential to alter these vital dynamics. As Garrick Pursley summarizes the argument, "[c]onstricting state regulatory authority reduces states' capacity to provide benefits to their citizens, which in turn diminishes states' effectiveness at checking national expansionism in the political process—a critical prerequisite for a functioning set of 'political process' safeguards for federalism."[44] Under dual federalism, preemption of state authority within areas delegated to national control could not unbalance the system, because the states retained their own realm of exclusive authority in which they could provide

----

[41] Federalist 46 (Madison), in *The Federalist* at 315–16 (cited in note 20). Madison reminded his readers that because "the ultimate authority . . . resides in the people alone," the question whether the states or the national government "will be able to enlarge its sphere of jurisdiction at the expense of the other" would ultimately "depend on the sentiments and sanction of their common constituents." Id. Madison's principle that governments compete by offering services and regulations to their constituents anticipated the contemporary economic theory of regulation. See Jonathan R. Macey, *Federal Deference to Local Regulators and the Economic Theory of Regulation: Toward a Public Choice Explanation of Federalism*, 76 Va L Rev 265 (1990).

[42] Federalist 45 (Madison), in *The Federalist* at 292–93 (cited in note 20). Hamilton similarly observed that because state governments "regulate all those personal interests and familiar concerns to which the sensibility of individuals is more immediately awake," the states are assured of possessing the "affection, esteem and reverence" of their citizens. Federalist 17 (Hamilton), in *The Federalist* at 107 (cited in note 20).

[43] I have developed this argument at greater length elsewhere. See generally Young, 46 Vill L Rev at 1349 (cited in note 39), and Ernest A. Young, *State Sovereign Immunity and the Future of Federalism*, 1999 Supreme Court Review 1, 43–47.

[44] Pursley, 71 Ohio St L J at 513 (cited in note 9). See also Ernest A. Young, *Federal Preemption and State Autonomy*, in Richard A. Epstein and Michael S. Greve, eds, *Federal Preemption: States' Powers, National Interests* 249, 252–54 (2007); Andrzej Rapaczynski, *From Sovereignty to Process: The Jurisprudence of Federalism after Garcia*, 1985 Supreme Court Review 341, 404 ("[T]he vitality of the participatory state institutions depends in part on the types of substantive decisions that are left for the states. Should the federal government preempt them from most fields that touch directly on the life of local communities, the states would become but empty shells within which no meaningful political activity could take place.").

government services and beneficial regulation to their citizens.[45] Preemption must be cabined more carefully, however, in a concurrent world where preemptive federal action threatens to cut off state access to the wellsprings of popular support.

Preemption's potential to undermine the structural safeguards of federalism also highlights the need for courts to play an independent role in this area. Our federalism has always relied on the courts to umpire the tug-of-war between national and state authority,[46] and while the nature of the courts' role has changed, its importance has not. Moreover, it has become clear that *Garcia*'s "process federalism"—that is, a constitutional model relying on the states' representation in the legislative process rather than on substantive limitations on national legislation—did leave a role for courts.[47] But that role consists in a John Hart Ely-esque form of "representation reinforcement"[48]—not the substantive line-drawing that prevailed under dual federalism.[49] *Garcia* said that the states' primary protection was "one of process rather than one of result,"[50] suggesting that judicial review should focus on ensuring that the political process did in fact operate to protect states' interests.

As the next section demonstrates, preemption doctrine fits readily within this process paradigm. In a world of concurrent power, federal legislation will frequently determine the actual allocation of responsibility between the federal and state authorities, and the courts are frequently called upon to interpret the allocation that

---

[45] Indeed, courts frequently invalidated state governmental activity within federal spheres, even in the absence of congressional action, under the dormant Commerce Clause and similar doctrines. See, for example, *Brown v Maryland*, 25 US (12 Wheat) 419 (1827).

[46] See John C. Yoo, *The Judicial Safeguards of Federalism*, 70 S Cal L Rev 1311 (1997); Young, 46 Wm & Mary L Rev at 1753 (cited in note 20) (noting that the Supreme Court has intervened to maintain balance in our federal system throughout our history); see also Brief of Constitutional Law Scholars as Amici Curiae in Support of Respondents, *Gonzales v Raich*, No 03-1454, *9-10 (US filed Oct 13, 2004) (collecting examples of other federal systems that rely on judicial review to resolve conflicts between subnational units and the central authority).

[47] See, for example, Rapaczynski, 1985 Supreme Court Review at 361 (cited in note 44) ("[T]he decision proposes to rely primarily on the political safeguards of federalism and to ground any future judicial intervention not in a defense of state sovereignty but in the idea of compensating for possible failings in the national political process." (footnote omitted)); Ernest A. Young, *The Rehnquist Court's Two Federalisms*, 83 Tex L Rev 1, 118–21 (2004) (discussing the process federalism strategies employed by the Rehnquist Court).

[48] See generally John Hart Ely, *Democracy and Distrust: A Theory of Judicial Review* (1980).

[49] See Young, 83 Tex L Rev at 15–16 (cited in note 47).

[50] 469 US at 554.

Congress has established. Preemption cases are the most significant category of these disputes, and the frequent ambiguities in Congress's preemptive intent afford the courts an opportunity to be more than just a mouthpiece for federal authority. As the next section recounts, the Court has developed doctrines for resolving preemption cases—in particular, the Court's "presumption against preemption" exemplified in *Rice v Santa Fe Elevator Corp.*[51]—that fit well within *Garcia*'s vision of process federalism. By requiring Congress to speak clearly in order to preempt state law, *Rice* ensures notice to legislative advocates of state interest that preemption is contemplated in proposed legislation, and it imposes an additional procedural hurdle to legislation that undermines state prerogatives.[52] Like other "clear statement rules" disfavoring legislation that alters the federal-state balance,[53] the *Rice* presumption operationalizes the political and procedural safeguards of federalism.[54]

C. THE DEVELOPMENT OF THE RICE PRESUMPTION

Stephen Gardbaum has written that "[t]he United States Supreme Court did not clearly and unequivocally recognize a congressional power of preemption until the beginning of the twentieth century."[55] In the nineteenth century, most cases that might raise preemption issues today would have been decided under the doctrine of dual federalism—that is, by determining whether a

---

[51] 331 US 218 (1947).

[52] See Young, 46 Vill L Rev at 1385 (cited in note 49); see also David L. Shapiro, *Continuity and Change in Statutory Interpretation*, 67 NYU L Rev 921, 944 (1992) (observing that interpretive canons disfavoring various kinds of change "increase the likelihood that a statute will not change existing arrangements and understandings unless the legislature—the politically accountable body—has faced the problem and decided that change is appropriate"); Matthew C. Stephenson, *The Price of Public Action: Constitutional Doctrine and the Judicial Manipulation of Legislative Enactment Costs*, 118 Yale L J 2, 40 (2008) (noting "that judicial demands for a clear congressional statement . . . can serve to increase legislative enactment costs for constitutionally problematic policies").

[53] See, for example, *Gregory v Ashcroft*, 501 US 452 (1991). For overviews of the debate about clear statement rules and their role in federalism doctrine, see William N. Eskridge Jr. and Philip P. Frickey, *Quasi-Constitutional Law: Clear Statement Rules as Constitutional Lawmaking*, 45 Vand L Rev 593 (1992); Ernest A. Young, *The Story of Gregory v. Ashcroft: Clear Statement Rules and the Statutory Constitution of American Federalism*, in William N. Eskridge Jr., Philip P. Frickey, and Elizabeth Garrett, eds, *Statutory Interpretation Stories* (Foundation, 2011).

[54] See, for example, Young, *The Story of Gregory v. Ashcroft* at 196 (cited in note 53).

[55] Stephen A. Gardbaum, *The Nature of Preemption*, 79 Cornell L Rev 767, 787 (1994). See also Lessig, 1995 Supreme Court Review at 166 (cited in note 22).

given exertion of regulatory authority fell within an area delegated to federal authority or the sphere reserved to the states.[56] The Court did recognize limited areas of concurrent authority, and in these areas federal law trumped state law in the event of a conflict, but these cases arose relatively infrequently.[57] As federal regulatory activity increased toward the end of the nineteenth century, however, the situation became more confused and pressure mounted to develop a coherent doctrine of preemption.[58]

The Court's first resolution of the matter was to establish a regime of automatic field preemption. As Professor Gardbaum explains, the Court applied a rule of "latent exclusivity" under which "preemption was an automatic consequence of congressional action in a given field."[59] In *Chicago, Rock Island & Pacific Railway Co. v Hardwick Farmers Elevator Co.*,[60] for example, the Court held that the federal Hepburn Act preempted state regulation of the delivery of interstate railroad cars. Chief Justice White argued that "it must follow in consequence of [the Hepburn Act] that the power of the State over the subject-matter ceased to exist from the moment that Congress exerted its paramount and all embracing authority over the subject. We say this because the elementary and long settled doctrine is that there can be no divided authority over interstate commerce and that the regulations of Congress on that subject are supreme."[61]

Some of the initial decisions laying out this position, like *Southern Railway v Reid*,[62] relied on actual conflict between state and federal law as an alternative ground. It did not take the Court long to make clear, however, that such conflicts were unnecessary. By 1915, Justice Holmes could dismiss arguments that there was

---

[56] See Gardbaum, 79 Cornell L Rev at 785–86 (cited in note 55).

[57] Id. Professor Gardbaum's account defines this species of preemption—federal law trumping state law in the event of a conflict—as "supremacy" and sharply distinguishes it from preemption, which he takes to mean federal ouster of even nonconflicting state law. See id at 771 ("Preemption . . . means (*a*) that states are deprived of their power to act *at all* in a given area, and (*b*) that this is so *whether or not* state law is in conflict with federal law.").

[58] See id at 795–800.

[59] Id at 801.

[60] 226 US 426 (1913).

[61] Id at 435. As Professor Gardbaum demonstrates, this principle was not in fact "long settled" but rather new law. See Gardbaum, 79 Cornell L Rev at 804–05 (cited in note 55).

[62] 222 US 424 (1912).

no actual conflict between state and federal law as "immaterial": "When Congress has taken the particular subject-matter in hand coincidence is as ineffective as opposition, and a state law is not to be declared a help because it attempts to go farther than Congress has seen fit to go."[63]

During and after the New Deal, however, the Court changed course. In 1933, *Mintz v Baldwin*[64] rejected an argument that the federal Cattle Contagious Diseases Acts preempted state efforts to deal with the same problem. Justice Butler wrote that "[t]he purpose of Congress to supersede or exclude state action against the ravages of the disease is not lightly to be inferred. The intention so to do must definitely and clearly appear."[65] *Rice v Santa Fe Elevator Corp.*,[66] which Professor Gardbaum describes as "the *locus classicus* of modern preemption doctrine,"[67] followed fourteen years later, on the other side of the Court's 1937 switch in time. The Court's narrowing of federal law's preemptive force in *Mintz*, *Rice*, and similar cases may seem inconsistent with its expansion of federal power in *NLRB v Jones & Laughlin Steel Corp.*[68] and *Wickard v Filburn*,[69] which it decided at roughly the same time. As Gardbaum explains, however, the two developments actually went hand-in-hand:

> In this context of a revolutionary extension of federal legislative competence, the consequence of the preexisting preemption doctrine (established while there were still significant areas of exclusive state jurisdiction) would have been to threaten vast areas of state regulation of seemingly local matters with extinction. Instead, the new constitutional strategy replaced a strict division of powers version of federalism

---

[63] *Charleston & Western Carolina Railway Co. v Varnville*, 237 US 597 (1915). See also Gardbaum, 79 Cornell L Rev at 805 (cited in note 55) (concluding, under prevailing doctrine in this period, "preemption eliminates the need to consider the content of state laws on the subject, to lay the two laws side by side to ascertain whether or not they conflict").

[64] 289 US 346 (1933).

[65] Id at 350.

[66] 331 US 218 (1947).

[67] Gardbaum, 79 Cornell L Rev at 807 (cited in note 55); see also Richard A. Epstein and Michael S. Greve, *Conclusion: Preemption Doctrine and Its Limits*, in Epstein and Greve, eds, *Federal Preemption* 309, 315 (cited in 44) (agreeing that "*Rice v Santa Fe Elevator* by all accounts offers the canonical statement of modern preemption doctrine").

[68] 301 US 1 (1937) (upholding the National Labor Relations Act and reversing the Court's prior tendency to construe the Commerce Clause narrowly).

[69] 317 US 111 (1942) (holding that the Commerce Power extended so far as to regulate individual growing decisions by small farmers).

with a new version embodying the presumption that state powers,
though no longer constitutionally guaranteed, survive unless clearly
ended by Congress.[70]

The old presumptive preemption regime, in other words, could
only work in a world still dominated by dual federalism. The *Rice*
presumption translated the Supremacy Clause into the post-1937
world of concurrent power. "At a time when the exercise of the
federal power is being rapidly expanded through Congressional
action," Justice Stone pointed out in 1941, "it is difficult to overstate the importance of safeguarding against such diminution of
state power by vague inferences as to what Congress might have
intended . . . or by reference to our own conceptions of a policy
which Congress has not expressed."[71]

Indeed, the shift in the Court's preemption jurisprudence may
have actually facilitated the expansion of Congress's legislative
role. David Shapiro has argued that canons of interpretation that
disfavor radical change help to overcome the ordinary risk aversion
of legislators. He points out that "the danger that any loose or
vague language will be broadly interpreted to favor change over
continuity may lead the drafters of legislation to be so fearful of
the consequences of their actions (and of the political ramifications
of those actions) that the process may become too cautious."[72] If
this is right, then "the most productive relationship between courts
and legislatures may well be one of providing some reassurance
that continuity will not be inadvertently sacrificed, absent sufficient evidence of legislative purpose to do so."[73] Applied to the
specific context of preemption, Professor Shapiro's point suggests
that courts might have eased congressional fears about intruding
on areas of traditional state regulatory authority by narrowing the
preemptive impact of new federal statutes.[74]

As I have already discussed, a second aspect of the post-New
Deal transformation had to do with the role and focus of judicial

---

[70] Gardbaum, 79 Cornell L Rev at 806 (cited in note 55); see also Lessig, 1995 Supreme
Court Review at 167 (cited in note 22) ("Just at the time the Court recognized the authority
of Congress to reach far more than before, it also transformed the significance of the
statutes that Congress had passed by radically cutting back on this automatic preemption.").

[71] *Hines v Davidowitz*, 312 US 52, 75 (1941) (Stone, J, dissenting).

[72] Shapiro, 67 NYU L Rev at 945 (cited in note 52).

[73] Id.

[74] By the same token, reining in the preemptive effect of federal statutes may have made
it easier for courts to accept the expansion of federal legislative authority.

review in federalism cases. The latent exclusivity of congressional power in pre-New Deal preemption doctrine was not a function of congressional intent; rather, it was intrinsic to the way that Congress's power worked. It was, as Professor Gardbaum has explained, derived from the "paramount" nature of Congress's power under the Supremacy Clause.[75] Early doctrine thus did not examine closely Congress's preemptive intent in particular statutes. *Mintz* and *Rice*, by contrast, turned the spotlight squarely on Congress's intentions concerning preemption,[76] and it is now settled doctrine that "'the purpose of Congress is the ultimate touchstone' in every pre-emption case."[77] Preemption doctrine thus fits the concurrent nature of state and federal power after the New Deal and reflects the essentially political structure of federalism safeguards in contemporary constitutional law.[78] The task of preemption doctrine, as the next section explores, is to make sure those safeguards are honored.

D. THE CURRENT DOCTRINE AND ITS TENSIONS

In a concurrent world, two levels of government operate within the same regulatory sphere, and the task of the law is to adjudicate conflicts between the two authorities. As Brad Clark has observed, "[t]o succeed, [a concurrent] system requires a means of deciding when federal law displaces state law."[79] Two sets of questions are particularly salient: What counts as preemption? And which institutions have the authority to preempt state law? Both issues

---

[75] Gardbaum, 79 Cornell L Rev at 801–02 (cited in note 55); see also id at 802 ("[Congressional] action itself was deemed to have automatic preemptive effect, rendering any determination of congressional intent irrelevant and unnecessary. Latent exclusivity was, therefore, understood more as a doctrine about the constitutional division of interstate commerce powers than as a general, discretionary power of Congress.").

[76] See id at 808 (describing the shift to "an intent-based test").

[77] *Medtronic, Inc. v Lohr*, 518 US 470, 485 (1996) (internal quotation marks omitted); see also *Wyeth*, 555 US at 565, quoting *Retail Clerks v Schermerhorn*, 375 US 96, 103 (1963).

[78] See generally Mary J. Davis, *Unmasking the Presumption in Favor of Preemption*, 53 SC L Rev 967, 971 (2002) ("[P]reemption doctrine . . . has evolved over the last century from one based on an assumption of congressional legislative exclusivity and almost certain preemption of state regulation to a doctrine, in the mid-part of the century, based on a search for congressional intent to preempt so that state laws, particularly those based on historical police powers, were not needlessly displaced.").

[79] Bradford R. Clark, *Process-Based Preemption*, in Buzbee, ed, *Preemption Choice* 192 (cited in note 8).

highlight the critical separation-of-powers dimension of federalism.

1. *What counts as preemption?* The first set of issues focuses on the relation between legislative and judicial power in statutory construction. Preemption cases do not typically involve the reach of congressional power; the question, rather, is whether Congress has in fact exercised its power to preempt state law. In recent years, the Court has grappled with a series of questions at increasing degrees of distance from Congress's direct intent: How should the courts construe ambiguous statutory language in express preemption cases? What sort of evidence can establish Congress's implicit intent to preempt a whole field of regulation? How much of a conflict between state and federal law should suffice for preemption? As Congress's intent becomes more difficult to ascertain, the question becomes not whether but *how* judges should fill in the gaps, either by establishing default rules of statutory construction (presumptions against, or sometimes in favor of, preemption), by pursuing increasingly attenuated evidence of Congress's preferences, or by making their own judgments about policy conflicts.

At the outset, it will help to be a little more specific about the difference between express and implied preemption, especially as it bears on the application of the *Rice* presumption. Preemption cases involve two distinct kinds of express provisions, and hence two corresponding kinds of implication. Some statutes have express *preemption* provisions—that is, clauses that purport to spell out the preemptive effect of the legislation on state law. Just about all statutes, however, have express *substantive* provisions,[80] and these provisions may have preemptive effect to the extent that they create conflicts with state law. "Express preemption," as that term is used in current doctrine, deals only with the former situation—that is, the construction of statutory provisions that expressly address the preemptive effect of federal law. Everything else is "implied" preemption, even though such cases may involve

---

[80] Not all, however. For example, the Labor Management Relations Act, 61 Stat 156, 18 USC § 185, and the First Judiciary Act, 1 Stat 76–77, current version codified at 28 USC § 1331(1), created federal judicial jurisdiction over collective bargaining and admiralty disputes, respectively. Neither provided substantive rules of decision, but courts have interpreted each as authorizing creation of federal common law that broadly preempts state law. See *Textile Workers Union of America v Lincoln Mills of Alabama*, 353 US 448 (1957) (LMRA); *Southern Pacific Co. v Jensen*, 244 US 205 (1917) (admiralty).

painstaking construction of a statute's express terms.

An interpretive presumption like the *Rice* canon generally "serves as a kind of burden allocator or tie-breaker . . . but allows the court to look to all relevant information and, if appropriate, to find an answer implicit in the statute despite the absence of express language."[81] On the other hand, "[c]lear-statement rules operate less to reveal *actual* congressional intent than to shield important values from an *insufficiently strong* legislative intent to displace them"; "such rules foreclose inquiry into extrinsic guides to interpretation and even compel courts to select less plausible candidates from within the range of permissible constructions."[82] Courts and scholars (including this one) sometimes lump these two categories together,[83] and much of the literature on "clear statement" requirements should be taken as encompassing both categories.[84] Each category, moreover, both blurs around the edges and encompasses meaningful differences in degree. A presumption, for example, might permit a court to canvass a broad range of sources of statutory meaning yet still impose a hefty burden of proof; similarly, even when a statute explicitly deals with a matter like preemption, the text may itself be far from clear. The scope of the inquiry, in other words, is analytically distinct from the weight of the burden of proof.

For present purposes, however, the distinction between presumptions and clear statement rules is helpful in pinning down the sources to which a court may look when it evaluates Congress's preemptive intent. The presumption against preemption has generally been just that—a *presumption*, not a clear statement rule.[85] If *Rice* were a strong clear statement rule, then there would only be "express" preemption cases—if Congress did not include a textual provision spelling out the preemptive effect of legislation,

---

[81] Shapiro, 67 NYU L Rev at 934 (cited in note 52) (footnote omitted).

[82] *EEOC v Arabian American Oil Co.*, 499 US 244, 262–63 (1991) (Marshall, J, dissenting).

[83] See, for example, id at 265 n 2 (noting prior cases in which the Court purported to apply a "clear-statement rule" but in fact "consulted the legislative history of the statutes at issue"); Young, *Gregory* (cited in note 53).

[84] See, for example, John F. Manning, *Clear Statement Rules and the Constitution*, 110 Colum L Rev 399, 407–08 (2010).

[85] See, for example, *Cipollone v Liggett Group, Inc.*, 505 US 504, 545 (1992) (Scalia, J, concurring in the judgment in part and dissenting in part) ("Though we generally 'assume that the historic police powers of the States [are] not to be superseded by . . . Federal Act unless that [is] the clear and manifest purpose of Congress,' we have traditionally not thought that to require express statutory text.") (quoting *Rice*, 331 US at 230).

then the required clear statement would be lacking. Such a rule would most likely be unmanageable, as Congress would have to anticipate all the possible ways in which state law might undermine federal legislation.[86] It seems inevitable that courts will sometimes have to evaluate implicit conflicts—that is, conflicts between the practical action of federal and state legal rules.

One could argue that an interpretive presumption like *Rice* should have no place in express preemption cases. After all, if Congress has included an express preemption clause, then the legislature has clearly stated its intent to preempt at least *some* state law. Justice Scalia has thus argued that any presumption against preemption "dissolves once there is conclusive evidence of intent to pre-empt in the express words of the statute itself, and the only remaining question is what the *scope* of that pre-emption is meant to be. Thereupon, I think, our responsibility is to apply to the text ordinary principles of statutory construction."[87]

Justice Scalia's approach seems overly simplistic, however. Consider a federal statute governing medical devices that clearly states Congress's intention to preempt negligent design claims, for example, but is ambiguous as to whether it preempts additional tort claims. The clarity of Congress's intentions with respect to negligent design hardly establishes that Congress also meant to preempt claims for negligent manufacture or failure to warn. It is unclear why the presumption against preemption should "dissolve," in Justice Scalia's terms, when we move from the first question to the second—that is, why the same concerns for state autonomy that raise the interpretive bar to find *any* preemption should not also weigh against interpreting the *scope* of preemption too broadly. After all, viewing the latter question as a subset of the first will generally be artificial. One might as well say that although Congress has manifested an intent to preempt claims relating to the design of a device, Congress has manifested no preemptive intent *at all* with respect to manufacturing or warning claims. Every federal statute clearly preempts *some* possible state

---

[86] Alternatively, Congress could simply state a broadly preemptive default rule in the statutory text. But that would simply substitute a problem of over-inclusion for one of under-inclusion. If we want preemption that is actually tailored to the interaction of federal and state laws in any sort of fine-grained way, courts will have to consider implied conflicts.

[87] *Cipollone*, 505 US at 545 (Scalia, J, concurring in part and dissenting in part).

laws, even if preemption is limited to a state statute directly coun-
termanding the federal provision.

Thus far, the Court has rejected Justice Scalia's position and
applied the presumption against preemption even where Congress
has included an express preemption clause in the relevant statute.
As Justice Blackmun said in *Cipollone*,

> The principles of federalism and respect for state sovereignty that un-
> derlie the Court's reluctance to find pre-emption where Congress has
> not spoken directly to the issue apply with equal force where Congress
> has spoken, though ambiguously. In such cases, the question is not
> *whether* Congress intended to pre-empt state regulation, but to what
> *extent*. We do not, absent unambiguous evidence, infer a scope of pre-
> emption beyond that which clearly is mandated by Congress' lan-
> guage.[88]

As I will discuss shortly, however, this point remains controversial.

When we move from express to implied or conflict preemption
cases,[89] we encounter a further distinction between those cases in
which the action of state and federal law creates "direct" or "actual" conflicts, and those cases in which state and federal law simply serve potentially contradictory purposes. The case law reflects
this distinction under the labels of "impossibility" and "obstacle"
preemption.[90] Traditionally, the Court has defined "impossibility"
very narrowly, limiting it to cases of "inevitable collision" between
state and federal law, where "compliance with both federal and
state [law] is a physical impossibility."[91] By contrast, the Court has
often defined "conflicting purposes" or "obstacle" preemption
quite broadly, holding state law preempted where it "stands as an

---

[88] Id at 533 (1992) (Blackmun, J, concurring in part, concurring in the judgment in
part, and dissenting in part); see id at 516–18 (majority opinion) (applying the *Rice* presumption in construing the statute's express preemption provisions).

[89] I do not consider field preemption as a distinct category here. A finding of field
preemption simply represents a judgment that *any* state intrusion in the field would conflict
with Congress's intent, because Congress meant for federal regulation in the field to be
exclusive. Field preemption may be express or implied, but in either case does not pose
any distinct problems for my purposes in this essay.

[90] See Richard H. Fallon Jr., John F. Manning, Daniel J. Meltzer, and David L. Shapiro,
Hart and Wechsler's The Federal Courts and the Federal System 646 (Foundation, 6th ed 2009)
("*Hart & Wechsler*").

[91] *Florida Lime & Avocado Growers, Inc. v Paul*, 373 US 132, 142–43 (1963); see also
Wyeth, 555 US at 573 (emphasizing that impossibility preemption "is a demanding defense"). The Court expanded this category somewhat last Term in *PLIVA, Inc. v Mensing*,
131 S Ct 2567 (2011). See Part II.B.

obstacle to the accomplishment and execution of the full purposes and objectives of Congress."[92]

It is not obvious how *Rice* should apply in conflict cases. Courts generally formulate the *Rice* presumption as a rule of statutory construction—that is, a tool for interpreting the legal import of ambiguous statutory language. In conflict preemption cases, courts have no text dealing with preemption to construe. Rather, two sorts of uncertainty may exist: The substantive content of the federal law may be ambiguous, such that it is unclear whether that law actually creates a conflict with state law, or the conflict in question may be so minor that a court is unsure whether Congress would prefer for state and federal law to operate side by side.[93] In the former case, one could argue that *Rice* should be reserved for interpreting express preemption provisions alone, so that "ordinary" rules of construction—whatever those are—should govern what the federal law actually does.[94] That such an approach is logically possible does not mean it makes sense, however. As Cathy Sharkey has noted, a one-time trend against applying *Rice* in implied conflict cases was "paradoxical because an interpretive default rule or 'thumb on the scale' would seem warranted, if at all, where there is no express statutory language."[95] In express preemption cases, the Court has said that in choosing between "plausible alternative reading[s]" of a federal statute, courts "have a duty to accept the reading that disfavors pre-emption."[96] Applying the

---

[92] *Hines v Davidowitz*, 312 US 52, 67 (1941), citing *Savage v Jones*, 225 US 501, 533 (1912) ("If the purpose of the act cannot otherwise be accomplished—if its operation within its chosen field else must be frustrated and its provisions be refused their natural effect—the state law must yield to the regulation of Congress within the sphere of its delegated power.").

[93] A third sort of uncertainty is possible, concerning the correct interpretation of *state* law. Federal courts, however, do not enjoy the same latitude in interpreting state law that they possess with regard to federal law. They are, first and foremost, obligated to apply state law as construed by the state's highest court. Even where the state courts have not definitively construed state law, federal courts are not generally free simply to set aside the most likely reading of state law in favor of one that would avoid preemption (unless, of course, that approach has itself been endorsed by the state's highest court).

[94] That position would be the inverse of Justice Scalia's in *Cipollone*, which was that *Rice* should apply *only* when there is no express preemption provision. Remarkably, Scalia has in fact joined at least one opinion arguing that *Rice* should not apply in implied conflict cases. See, for example, *Wyeth*, 555 US at 565 & n 14 (Alito, J, dissenting with Roberts and Scalia).

[95] Catherine M. Sharkey, *Products Liability Preemption: An Institutional Approach*, 76 Geo Wash L Rev 449, 458 n 34 (2008).

[96] *Bates v Dow Agrosciences, LLC*, 544 US 431 449 (2005).

same rule to construing federal law in conflicts cases would protect identical values of state autonomy.[97]

The second sort of ambiguity concerns the degree of tension between state law and congressional purpose. Almost any two laws will potentially undermine one another's purposes; indeed, in the Arizona immigration cases proponents of preemption have claimed that even state measures that precisely mirror federal requirements conflict with federal interests by adding a second and potentially contradictory level of enforcement.[98] The question in many conflict preemption cases is thus just how much conflict is tolerable.[99] Such an inquiry, practically speaking, is closer to a balancing of interests (the degree of impedance to national purpose versus the value of state autonomy) than to textual construction. In that context, *Rice*'s presumption becomes a "thumb on the scale" representing the value of state autonomy.

The Court has often seemed to say that the Supremacy Clause simply does not permit any such "balancing" of interests.[100] Generally speaking, as Mark Rosen has pointed out, "preemption is a 'unilateralist' doctrine that takes account of only one of the institutions whose interests are at stake: the federal government."[101] But the unilateralist character of preemption doctrine must be compromised once we recognize that virtually *all* preemption cases

---

[97] Indeed, the Court has frequently applied clear statement rules to limit the substantive sweep of federal law. See, for example, *Solid Waste Agency of Northern Cook County v United States Army Corps of Engineers*, 531 US 159 (2001); *United States v Jones*, 529 US 848 (2000); *Gregory v Ashcroft*, 501 US 452 (1991); *Will v Michigan Dept. of State Police*, 491 US 58 (1989).

[98] See *Chamber of Commerce v Whiting*, 131 S Ct 1968, 1990–91 (2011) (Breyer, J, dissenting).

[99] See, for example, *Crosby v National Foreign Trade Council*, 530 US 363, 373 (2000) (observing that "[w]hat is a sufficient obstacle is a matter of judgment, to be informed by examining the federal statute as a whole and identifying its purpose and intended effects").

[100] See, for example, *Gade v National Solid Wastes Management Association*, 505 US 88, 108 (1992) (observing that "under the Supremacy Clause . . . 'any state law, however clearly within a State's acknowledged power, which interferes with or is contrary to federal law, must yield'" and therefore rejecting "petitioner's argument that the State's interest in licensing various occupations can save from OSH Act pre-emption those provisions that directly and substantially affect workplace safety," quoting *Felder v Casey*, 487 US 131, 138 (1988)); *Fidelity Federal Savings & Loan Association v De La Cuesta*, 458 US 141, 153 (1982), quoting *Free v Bland*, 369 US 663, 666 (1962) ("The relative importance to the State of its own law is not material when there is a conflict with a valid federal law, for the Framers of our Constitution provided that the federal law must prevail.").

[101] Mark D. Rosen, *Contextualizing Preemption*, 102 Nw U L Rev 781, 785 (2008) (contrasting preemption with "multilateralist" doctrines that "ask[] the decisionmaker to take account of the concerns of all relevant institutions whose interests are implicated").

involve some degree of arguable conflict between state and federal law, and in some cases, the conflict between state and federal law is just not sufficiently serious to warrant preemption. Tom Merrill has noted, for instance, that preemption cases assess not simply whether "federal law . . . is in tension with state law" but also "whether this tension is sufficiently severe to warrant the displacement of state law."[102] Preemption doctrine thus cannot proceed without some standard for how much conflict is too much. If the Court were to reject *Rice*'s version of that standard, it would still have to come up with some other standard to replace it.

Rice survived an all-out assault from litigants in the Supreme Court in the 2008 Term.[103] In *Altria Group, Inc. v Good*,[104] the Court rejected a strong push from pro-preemption amici to eliminate the presumption in express preemption cases. And in *Wyeth v Levine*,[105] the Court turned back arguments that the presumption should not apply in implied preemption cases. *Altria* was a suit under the Maine Unfair Trade Practices Act by smokers of "light" cigarettes alleging that the cigarette manufacturers had fraudulently advertised that light cigarettes delivered less tar and nicotine than regular brands. The Court rejected both express and implied preemption arguments under the Federal Cigarette Labeling and Advertising Act and the Federal Trade Commission's regulatory activities, respectively. In the course of the express preemption argument, Justice Stevens's majority opinion reaffirmed that "[w]hen addressing questions of express or implied pre-emption, we begin our analysis 'with the assumption that the historic police powers of the States [are] not to be superseded by the Federal Act unless that was the clear and manifest purpose of Congress."[106] The Court explained, moreover, what this means in the express preemption context: "when the text of a pre-emption clause is

---

[102] Thomas W. Merrill, *Preemption and Institutional Choice*, 102 Nw U L Rev 727, 743 (2008); see also Untereiner, 84 Tulane L Rev at 1260 (cited in note 11) (observing that in conflict preemption cases, "courts make judgments about whether the degree of tension between federal and state laws rises to the level of an impermissible conflict under the Supremacy Clause").

[103] See generally Dan Schweitzer, *The Presumption Against Preemption Strikes Back: The Lessons of Altria Group v. Good and Wyeth v. Levine*, NAAGazette (2009), online at http://www.naag.org/the-presumption-against-preemption-strikes-back-the-lessons-of-altria-group-v.-good-and-wyeth-v.-levine.php.

[104] 555 US 70 (2008).

[105] 555 US 555 (2009).

[106] *Altria*, 555 US at 77, quoting *Rice*, 331 US at 230.

susceptible of more than one plausible reading, courts ordinarily 'accept the reading that disfavors pre-emption.'"[107] In a dissent joined by Chief Justice Roberts and Justices Scalia and Alito, Justice Thomas insisted that, in recent years, "the Court's reliance on the presumption against pre-emption has waned in the express pre-emption context."[108] Noting that "[t]he Court has invoked the presumption sporadically" and ignored it in a number of cases,[109] Thomas complained that the presumption results in "artificially narrow construction[s]" of preemption provisions that "distort the statutory text."[110]

Wyeth, on the other hand, focused on implied preemption. Diana Levine brought a Vermont common law tort claim against Wyeth, alleging that the drug manufacturer had failed to provide adequate warnings that its antinausea drug Phenergan could cause gangrene if administered by an "IV-push" method. The Court rejected claims that federal law made it impossible to comply with state tort rules that required a better warning and that state liability would interfere with Congress's purpose in entrusting a federal agency, the Food and Drug Administration, with authority to approve new drugs and drug labels. Echoing arguments by Wyeth's amici,[111] Justice Alito's dissent argued that the only question in conflict cases is "whether there is an 'actual conflict' between state and federal law; if so, then pre-emption follows automatically by operation of the Supremacy Clause."[112] That question left no room for any presumption against preemption, and Alito asserted that the Court had in fact not applied any such presumption in its previous conflict preemption cases.[113] Justice Stevens's majority

---

[107] *Altria*, 555 US at 77, quoting *Bates v Dow Agrosciences LLC*, 544 US 431, 449 (2005).

[108] *Altria*, 555 US at 98 (Thomas, J, dissenting).

[109] Id at 99.

[110] Id at 98, 101.

[111] See Brief of the Chamber of Commerce of the United States of America as Amicus Curiae in Support of Petitioner, *Wyeth v Levine*, No 06-1249, *27–28 (US filed June 3, 2008) (arguing that the federal courts should not apply a presumption against preemption); Brief of Amicus Curiae Products Liability Advisory Council, Inc., in Support of Petitioner, *Wyeth v Levine*, No 06-1249, *15–18 (US filed May 30, 2008) (arguing that the presumption against preemption does not apply to a conflicts preemption analysis).

[112] *Wyeth*, 555 US at 624 (Alito, J, dissenting). Chief Justice Roberts and Justice Scalia joined Justice Alito's dissent.

[113] Id at 624 n 14.

opinion, however, flatly rejected Alito's assertion, stating that "this Court has long held to the contrary."[114]

As a matter of current principle, then, *Rice* continues to apply in both express and implied preemption settings. Despite these express and recent reaffirmations of *Rice*, the Court frequently neglects to mention it. This occurs both in cases where the Court finds preemption and in cases where it does not. It thus seems fair to say that the legitimacy, strength, and scope of a presumption against preemption remains a live issue.

2. *Who can preempt state law?* The second set of issues implicates a distinct set of separation-of-powers concerns. Here the questions concern which branches of the federal government may preempt state law, and by what sorts of actions. The Supremacy Clause suggests that only Congress may preempt state law, by enacting "Laws of the United States made in Pursuance [of this Constitution]."[115] Nonetheless, the Court has said that federal administrative agencies, exercising authority delegated by Congress, may preempt state law in certain circumstances.[116] Likewise, federal courts may sometimes fashion federal common law rules that preempt state law.[117]

The limits of executive-agency and judicial preemption remain uncertain, however. Executive preemption occurs in a variety of scenarios, from an agency interpreting a statute to preempt state law to an independent preemptive action originating with the agency itself; such action, moreover, may take a range of forms from legislative rules promulgated after notice and comment to less formal agency actions.[118] When the agency interprets statutes as preempting state law, the issue becomes how much deference, if any, courts should accord to that judgment.[119] When the agency

---

[114] Id at 565 n 3 (majority opinion), citing *California v ARC America Corp.*, 490 US 93, 101–02 (1989); *Hillsborough County v Automated Medical Laboratories, Inc.*, 471 US 707, 716 (1985); and *Rush Prudential HMO, Inc. v Moran*, 536 US 355, 387 (2002).

[115] US Const, Art VI, § 2. The Supremacy Clause also indicates that the President and the Senate, by negotiating and ratifying self-executing treaties, can also preempt state law. Id.

[116] *Fidelity Savings & Loan v De La Cuesta*, 458 US 141 (1982).

[117] See, for example, *Southern Pacific Co. v Jensen*, 244 US 205 (1917) (holding that federal common law rules in admiralty preempt state law).

[118] See Ernest A. Young, *Executive Preemption*, 102 Nw U L Rev 869, 881–900 (2008).

[119] See Nina A. Mendelson, *Chevron and Preemption*, 102 Mich L Rev 737 (2004) (arguing that "political accountability . . . agency expertise, self-interest, and the prospect of increased arbitrariness in decisionmaking . . . all weigh against an across-the-board pre-

takes preemptive action on its own, the broader question is what sorts of acts can have preemptive effects. On the judicial side, federal common law jurisprudence remains murky as to the precise circumstances that warrant judicial lawmaking.[120]

The separation-of-powers issues raised by both sets of preemption cases have major implications for federalism. In recent years, a burgeoning literature has addressed the important ways in which the federal separation of powers protects the autonomy of the states.[121] Contemporary federalism jurisprudence emphasizes the states' representation in Congress as the primary safeguard of federalism; on this view, Congress is structured so as to take state regulatory interests into account before it acts.[122] Federal agencies, on the other hand, have no such incentives and can generally increase their own power by preempting state law. William Eskridge's survey of Supreme Court preemption cases involving federal administrative agencies between the 1984 and 2005 Terms found that "agencies pressed pro-preemption positions in two-thirds of the cases."[123] The only surprising thing about that number is that it is lower than one might expect.

Scholars have also emphasized how the procedural difficulty of enacting federal legislation, the multiple veto-gates that legislative proposals must navigate, and the limited nature of Congress's agenda ensure that *all* federal legislation—including, of course, preemptive legislation—will be relatively rare.[124] The difficulty of

---

sumption of deference to the agency"); Merrill, 102 Nw U L Rev at 769–79 (cited in note 102) (arguing that courts should defer to agency interpretations "only to the extent they are persuasive, thereby preserving judicial authority to maintain a uniform jurisprudence of preemption").

[120] Compare Louise Weinberg, *Federal Common Law*, 83 Nw U L Rev 805 (1989) (taking a very broad view), with Ernest A. Young, *Preemption and Federal Common Law*, 83 Notre Dame L Rev 1639, 1671–79 (2008) (considerably more skeptical).

[121] See, for example, Bradford R. Clark, *Separation of Powers as a Safeguard of Federalism*, 79 Tex L Rev 1321 (2001); Stuart M. Benjamin and Ernest A. Young, *Tennis with the Net Down: Administrative Federalism Without Congress*, 57 Duke L J 2111 (2008).

[122] See, for example, *Garcia v San Antonio Metropolitan Transit Authority*, 469 US 528, 550–51 (1985) (observing that "the composition of the Federal Government was designed in large part to protect the States from overreaching by Congress"); Wechsler, 54 Colum L Rev at 559 (cited in note 35) (arguing that states' representatives "control the legislative process and, by hypothesis, have broadly acquiesced in sanctioning the challenged Act of Congress").

[123] William N. Eskridge Jr., *Vetogates, Chevron, Preemption*, 83 Notre Dame L Rev 1441, 1484 (2008).

[124] See Clark, 83 Notre Dame L Rev at 1707 (cited in note 35) ("The federal government . . . may adopt 'the supreme Law of the Land' only by employing precise, constitutionally prescribed procedures."); Young, 46 Vill L Rev at 1363 (cited in note 39) ("Federal action

federal lawmaking, combined with at least some degree of congressional sympathy for state regulators, operates to ensure that federal law remains more interstitial than pervasive in nature[125]—although that arrangement is constantly eroding.[126]

From this standpoint, shifting preemptive authority away from Congress to judicial or executive institutions that do not represent the states and that can promulgate federal norms more easily than Congress amounts to a significant threat to state autonomy. When courts preempt state law based on implicit conflicts with federal policy or allow federal agencies to preempt state law by legislative fiat, they compound the central difficulty of contemporary federalism doctrine—that is, the Court's failure to articulate meaningful and sustainable limits on Congress's enumerated powers.[127] In this doctrinal landscape, it is critical that the Court fashion meaningful limits on the preemptive scope of the legislation that Congress does enact and on the ability of nonlegislative federal actors to extend that scope.

Of the two nonlegislative preemption problems, executive branch preemption is probably the more pressing. Preemption by administrative agency action became especially salient during the second Bush administration, which came to office with an extensive tort-reform agenda. When that agenda was largely stymied in Congress, the administration turned to the agencies, several of which issued broad interpretive "preambles" to federal regulations expressing the agency's judgment that federal regulatory decisions preempted further regulation—especially common law tort regulation—at the state level.[128] Similarly, the Bush administration

remains interstitial . . . not only because of political opposition from the states but because federal law is simply difficult to make." (footnote omitted)).

[125] See Henry Hart and Herbert L. Wechsler, *The Federal Courts and the Federal System* 435 (Foundation, 1st ed 1953).

[126] The current edition of *Hart & Wechsler*, for example, comments that "[i]n the more than fifty years since the First Edition was published, the expansion of federal legislation and administrative regulation . . . has accelerated; today one finds many more instances in which federal enactments supply both right and remedy in, or wholly occupy, a particular field." *Hart & Wechsler* at 459 (cited in note 90).

[127] See, for example, *Gonzales v Raich*, 545 US 1 (2005) (upholding Congress's authority to regulate medicinal use of homegrown marijuana); *South Dakota v Dole*, 483 US 203 (1987). See generally Ernest A. Young, *Popular Constitutionalism and the Underenforcement Problem: The Case of the National Healthcare Law*, 75 L & Contemp Probs no. 3, 157 (2012) (arguing that limits on the Commerce and Spending Powers are generally underenforced in contemporary federalism doctrine).

[128] See Thomas O. McGarity, *The Preemption War: When Federal Bureaucracies Trump Local Juries* 3–5 (Yale, 2008); Catherine M. Sharkey, *Preemption by Preamble: Federal Agencies*

resorted to agency action in an effort to overturn Oregon's "Death with Dignity Act" permitting physician-assisted suicide, after legislative efforts to preempt that law failed in Congress.[129] And the Obama administration has resorted to executive action—federal lawsuits alleging implied preemption claims—to combat restrictive state immigration policies, rather than pursuing legislative reform.[130]

Executive preemption has had a mixed reception in the Supreme Court. Professor Eskridge found that, in agency preemption cases between 1984 and 2006, "the Court rejected preemption claims in 47.3% (62/131 cases) of the cases and accepted preemption claims in 45.8% (60/131 cases), with 6.9% (9/131 cases) mixed," notwithstanding that the relevant agency favored preemption in two-thirds of the cases.[131] Six years ago, the Court rejected preemption in the Oregon case, emphasizing the states' traditional authority to regulate the medical profession.[132] In *Wyeth*, the Court refused to defer to an FDA preamble in construing the preemptive effect of federal law. The Court emphasized that while it has "given 'some weight' to an agency's views about the impact of tort law on federal objectives when 'the subject matter is technica[l] and the relevant history and background are complex and extensive,' . . . we have not deferred to an agency's *conclusion* that state law is pre-empted."[133] Justice Thomas made a similar point last Term in *PLIVA, Inc. v Mensing*, noting that "[a]lthough we defer to the agency's interpretation of its regulations, we do not defer to an agency's ultimate conclusion about whether state law should be pre-empted."[134] Nonetheless, it would be a stretch to say that the Court has come to rest on the complicated cluster of issues surrounding preemption by federal administrative agencies.

---

and the Federalization of Tort Law, 56 DePaul L Rev 227, 230–42 (2007) (reviewing the preemption preambles in rules promulgated by the Food and Drug Administration, the Consumer Product Safety Commission, and the National Highway Traffic Safety Administration).

[129] See *Gonzales v Oregon*, 546 US 243, 252–53 (2006) ("Members of Congress concerned about ODWDA invited the DEA to prosecute . . . Oregon physicians who assist suicide.").

[130] Jerry Markon, *Obama Administration Widens Challenges to State Immigration Laws*, Washington Post (Sept 29, 2011), online at http://www.washingtonpost.com/politics/obama-adminis tration-widens-challenges-to-state-immigration-laws/2011/09/28/gIQA8HgR7K_story.html.

[131] Eskridge, 83 Notre Dame L Rev at 1484 (cited in note 123).

[132] *Gonzales*, 546 US at 270.

[133] *Wyeth*, 555 US at 576–77, quoting *Geier*, 529 US at 883 (alteration in original).

[134] 131 S Ct at 2575 n 3, citing *Wyeth*, 555 US at 576.

Judicial preemption comes up somewhat less often than agency preemption, yet it remains important and in need of clarification by the Court. The critical decision here is, of course, *Erie Railroad Co. v Tompkins*,[135] which held that, in the absence of a federal statute or constitutional provision, federal courts may not ordinarily displace state law.[136] Notwithstanding *Erie*, federal courts have maintained their authority to formulate common law rules of decision in certain circumstances,[137] and unlike the "general" common law applied by federal courts in diversity cases prior to *Erie*, the "new federal common law" is "federal" within the meaning of the Supremacy Clause and therefore preempts state law.[138] Courts generally offer three distinct rationales in support of their authority to fashion federal common law: Much federal common lawmaking is interstitial, filling in "gaps" in federal statutes to achieve the ends intended by Congress;[139] sometimes Congress explicitly or (more often) implicitly delegates lawmaking authority to the courts;[140] and, finally, much federal common law rests on the asserted need to fashion a federal rule of decision to protect federal interests.[141]

This last category, which Tom Merrill has called "preemptive" lawmaking,[142] is the most troubling for preemption doctrine. Pre-

---

[135] 304 US 64 (1938).

[136] See id at 78 ("Except in matters governed by the Federal Constitution or by Acts of Congress, the law to be applied in any case is the law of the State. . . . There is no federal general common law.").

[137] We lack an agreed-upon definition of federal common law. See generally *Hart & Wechsler* at 607 & n 1 (cited in note 90) (comparing definitions and "us[ing] the term loosely to refer to federal rules of decision whose content cannot be traced directly by traditional methods of interpretation to federal statutory or constitutional commands").

[138] See generally Henry J. Friendly, *In Praise of Erie—and of the New Federal Common Law*, 39 NYU L Rev 383 (1964).

[139] See, for example, *D'Oench, Duhme & Co. v FDIC*, 315 US 447, 470 (1942) (Jackson, J, concurring) ("Were we bereft of the common law, our federal system would be impotent. This follows from the recognized futility of attempting all-complete statutory codes, and is apparent from the terms of the Constitution itself.").

[140] See, for example, FRE 501 (expressly delegating authority to the courts to formulate federal common law rules of privileges in federal question cases); *National Society of Professional Engineers v United States*, 435 US 679, 688 (1978) (interpreting the broad language of the Sherman Act as an implicit delegation of authority to courts to fashion a federal common law of antitrust).

[141] See, for example, *Banco Nacional de Cuba v Sabbatino*, 376 US 398 (1964) (formulating a federal common law "act of state" doctrine to protect federal interests in political branch control of foreign policy).

[142] Thomas W. Merrill, *The Common Law Powers of Federal Courts*, 52 U Chi L Rev 1, 36–39 (1985).

empting state law based on federal "interests"—not federal positive law, such as a statute or even an agency regulation—not only runs counter to the text of the Supremacy Clause but also end-runs the political and procedural safeguards at the center of contemporary federalism doctrine. I have argued elsewhere that this sort of federal common lawmaking, if it can be justified at all, should be viewed as a form of conflict preemption.[143] Preemptive common lawmaking thus occurs when state law would interfere with some federal regulatory scheme, but simply voiding the state law would leave an unacceptable gap. The court fills in the gap by fashioning a federal common law rule of decision, much as it might fill in an omission in an express statutory scheme, doing its best to conform that rule to Congress's overall intent in the field.[144] Perhaps recognizing that even this somewhat narrower view is tough to square with federalism doctrine, the Supreme Court has seemed to view preemptive federal common lawmaking with increasing skepticism in recent years.[145]

II. THE SUPREME COURT'S 2010 TERM PREEMPTION BONANZA

Preemption cases have not been scarce on the Court's docket in recent years, but last Term's output remains extraordinary by any measure. The Court issued five major decisions, addressing issues ranging from automobile and drug safety to class action litigation to the tug-of-war between the national and state governments over immigration policy. Factually speaking, several of these cases seemed to involve replays of recent important decisions, offering the Court a chance to define the limits of those earlier rulings. Moreover, the volume of preemption litigation— both last Term and in recent years—seems to be encouraging at least some of the Justices to think about preemption as a matter of general principle, rather than as a mass of largely unrelated issues of statutory construction arising under different regulatory regimes. That is not to say, however, that preemption battles can

---

[143] See Young, 83 Notre Dame L Rev at 1669–71 (cited in note 120).

[144] See id (analogizing to administrative law, where "the existence of a gap in a federal regulatory scheme is often construed as an implicit delegation by Congress to the agency that administers the statute of authority to make law that 'fills in' the gap" (footnote omitted)).

[145] See, for example, *Atherton v FDIC*, 519 US 213, 218 (1997); *Hart & Wechsler* 628–29 (cited in note 90).

ever fully transcend the statutory terrain on which they are fought; indeed, if there is any clear lesson from last Term's cases, it is that different statutes yield different results.

A. WILLIAMSON V MAZDA MOTOR

Williamson v Mazda Motor of America, Inc.,[146] involved the preemptive effect of Federal Motor Vehicle Safety Standard 208,[147] a Department of Transportation (DOT) safety regulation that required automobile manufacturers to install lap-and-shoulder seatbelts in the rear seats of passenger vehicles, but allowed those manufacturers the option of installing lap-only belts for rear inner seats. The case arose out of a tragic head-on collision between the Williamson family's Mazda minivan and another vehicle. Delbert Williamson and his daughter, Alexa, who were strapped in with lap-and-shoulder belts, survived the crash; Delbert's wife, Thanh, however, was wearing only a lap belt and died. The Williamsons sued Mazda on various state tort theories, all of which argued that the manufacturer should have provided a lap-and-shoulder belt for Thanh's rear interior seat as well. The case thus presented the question whether FMVSS 208, by allowing manufacturers a choice as to what sort of seatbelts to install in rear interior seats, preempted state common law actions that would effectively require the installation of lap-and-shoulder belts.

The California Court of Appeal thought that it had seen all this before, in the Supreme Court's 2000 ruling in *Geier v American Honda Motor Co.*[148] That case involved another provision in an earlier version of FMVSS 208 that required auto manufacturers to install passive restraints in cars, but left manufacturers a choice whether to use airbags, automatic seatbelts, or some other passive system. *Geier* held that FMVSS 208 preempted a state tort suit against Honda for failing to install a driver's side airbag that might have protected Alexis Geier from severe injuries in a crash.[149] Like many lower courts, the California appellate court in *Williamson* read *Geier* as holding that a federal regulatory decision to allow

---

[146] 131 S Ct 1131 (2011).

[147] Federal Motor Vehicle Safety Standards; Occupant Crash Protection, 54 Fed Reg 46257–46258 (1989).

[148] 529 US 861 (2000).

[149] Id at 874.

manufacturers a choice preempts state tort theories that would require them to adopt a particular form of equipment.[150]

The Supreme Court reversed the California court—somewhat remarkably without dissent. Writing for the Court as he had in *Geier*, Justice Breyer followed the earlier decision's roadmap but arrived at a different destination. The first two questions concerned the language of the National Traffic and Motor Vehicle Safety Act,[151] which includes both an express preemption clause and a savings clause. The preemption provision says that "no State" may "establish, or . . . continue in effect . . . any safety standard applicable to the same aspect of performance" of a motor vehicle or item of equipment "which is not identical to the Federal standard."[152] The savings clause, on the other hand, provides that "[c]ompliance with" a federal safety standard "does not exempt any person from any liability under common law."[153] *Geier* read the savings clause to make clear that state tort suits fall outside the scope of the preemption clause, and *Williamson* reaffirmed that reading.[154] As in *Geier*, however, the Court rejected the proposition that the savings clause immunized state tort suits not only from the effect of the preemption clause but also from principles of *conflict* preemption.[155]

Geier held state tort suits preempted on the ground that liability for failing to provide airbags would stand as an obstacle to the purpose of FMVSS 208, which was to give manufacturers a choice as to which passive restraint system to install.[156] In *Williamson*, Justice Breyer conceded "that the history of the regulation before us resembles the history of airbags to some degree."[157] Specifically, DOT had ordered manufacturers to install lap-and-shoulder belts in rear outer seats but decided to leave manufacturers a choice as to which kind of belt to install in rear inner seats. The Court

---

[150] 167 Cal App 4th 905, 914–17 (2008); see also *Carden v General Motors Corp.*, 509 F3d 227 (5th Cir 2007); *Griffith v General Motors Corp.*, 303 F3d 1276 (11th Cir 2002); *Heinricher v Volvo Car Corp.*, 809 NE2d 1094 (Mass App 2004).

[151] Pub L No 89-563, 80 Stat 718 (1966), codified as amended at 15 USC § 1381.

[152] 15 USC § 1392(d) (1988).

[153] 15 USC § 1397(k).

[154] See *Geier*, 529 US at 868; *Williamson*, 131 S Ct at 1135–36.

[155] *Williamson*, 131 S Ct at 1136.

[156] 529 US at 875–81.

[157] 131 S Ct at 1137.

determined, however, that manufacturer choice was not a "significant regulatory objective" of the seatbelt regulation in the way that it had been for the passive restraint regulation in *Geier*.[158] As Justice Breyer explained,

> DOT here was not concerned about consumer acceptance; it was convinced that lap-and-shoulder belts would increase safety; it did not fear additional safety risks arising from use of those belts; it had no interest in assuring a mix of devices; and, though it was concerned about additional costs, that concern was diminishing.[159]

As the last point indicates, the Court found no independent preemptive force in the agency's judgment that lap-and-shoulder belts in rear inner seats would not be cost effective. "[M]any, perhaps most, federal safety regulations embody some kind of cost-effectiveness judgment. While an agency could base a decision to preempt on its cost-effectiveness judgment, we are satisfied that the rulemaking record at issue here discloses no such pre-emptive intent."[160]

Finally, the Court accorded some degree of deference to the agency's view that FMVSS 208 did not preempt the state tort actions at issue. *Geier* had observed that "the agency's own views should make a difference,"[161] and *Williamson* reaffirmed that view, albeit without specifying exactly *how much* difference they should make. Justice Breyer did emphasize that the Solicitor General's position in the litigation was consistent with DOT's long-standing position on the matter.[162] The Court accordingly concluded that "even though the state tort suit may restrict the manufacturer's choice, it does not 'stan[d] as an obstacle to the accomplishment . . . of the full purposes and objectives' of federal law."[163]

All the sitting Justices except Justice Thomas joined Justice Breyer's opinion for the Court.[164] Justice Sotomayor wrote a short concurrence "only to emphasize the Court's rejection of an over-

---

[158] Id.

[159] Id at 1338. Each of these factors had been otherwise in *Geier*.

[160] Id. *Williamson*, 131 S Ct at 1139.

[161] 529 US at 883.

[162] 131 S Ct at 1139.

[163] Id at 1139–40, quoting *Hines v Davidowitz*, 312 US 52, 67 (1941) (alterations in original).

[164] Justice Kagan was recused on account of her role in the case as Solicitor General prior to joining the Court.

reading of *Geier* that has developed since that opinion was issued."[165] She stressed that *"Geier* does not stand . . . for the proposition that any time an agency gives manufacturers a choice between two or more options, a tort suit that imposes liability on
the basis of one of the options is an obstacle to the achievement
of a federal regulatory objective and may be pre-empted."[166]
Rather, "state tort suits are not obstacles" to federal law "[a]bsent
strong indications from the agency that it needs manufacturers to
have options in order to achieve a significant regulatory objective."[167]

Justice Thomas concurred only in the judgment, arguing that
the savings clause "speaks directly to the [preemption] question
and answers it."[168] As he had in *Geier*, Thomas maintained that
the statutory savings clause was not directed only at limiting the
scope of the express preemption clause, but rather independently
saved all state common-law claims.[169] Thomas spent the majority
of his concurrence criticizing the Court's reliance on "purposes-
and-objectives pre-emption," noting that he had rejected this approach to preemption "as inconsistent with the Constitution because it turns entirely on extratextual 'judicial suppositions.'"[170] As
Thomas put it, the majority's analysis asked "whether the regulators *really* wanted manufacturers to have a choice or did not
really want them to have a choice but gave them one anyway"—
a question that could be answered only by "a 'freewheeling, extratextual, and broad evaluatio[n] of the purposes and objectives'
of FMVSS 208."[171] He complained, moreover, that the fact "[t]hat
the Court in *Geier* reached an opposite conclusion reveals the
utterly unconstrained nature of purposes-and-objectives pre-emption"; after all, "the only difference" between *Williamson* and *Geier*

---

[165] 131 S Ct at 1140 (Sotomayor, J, concurring).

[166] Id (footnote omitted) (alteration in original).

[167] Id (internal quotation marks omitted). It was not completely clear from Justice Sotomayor's discussion whether this "strong indications" standard was a general judgment
about when state common law claims should be preempted or a product of the statutory
savings clause. See id at 1141 (indicating that respondents had not met the standard,
"[e]specially in light of" the savings clause).

[168] Id at 1141 (Thomas, J, concurring in the judgment).

[169] *Williamson*, 131 S Ct at 1141–42, citing *Geier*, 529 US at 896–98 (Stevens, J, dissenting). Justice Thomas had joined Justice Stevens's dissent in *Geier*.

[170] *Williamson*, 131 S Ct at 1142, citing *Wyeth*, 555 US at 603 (Thomas, J, concurring
in the judgment).

[171] *Williamson*, 131 S Ct at 1142.

"is the majority's 'psychoanalysis' of the regulators."[172]

B. PLIVA, INC. V MENSING

If *Williamson* seemed like a reprise of *Geier*, then *PLIVA, Inc. v Mensing*[173] arrived at the Court as an apparent rerun of *Wyeth v Levine*.[174] In *Wyeth*, the Court held that the federal Food and Drug Administration's (FDA) approval of a drug—and, in particular, of the warnings on the drug's label—did not preempt state tort suits for failure to warn of dangers associated with the drug's use.[175] *PLIVA* raised the same issue in the context of *generic* drugs. Under federal law, manufacturers of a new drug must obtain FDA approval by proving that the drug is safe and effective—an arduous and time-consuming process involving "costly and lengthy" clinical testing.[176] Although all drugs once had to go through this process, Congress amended the law in 1984 to provide an expedited approval process for "generic" forms of drugs that had already been approved by the FDA.[177] Such drugs must simply show "equivalence" to a "reference listed drug" that has already been approved.[178] Similar rules apply to the warnings on a drug's label. A new drug's manufacturer must show that the proposed label is accurate and adequate,[179] while a generic drug manufacturer must show simply that the "labeling proposed . . . is the same as the labeling approved for the listed drug."[180]

The defendants in *PLIVA* manufactured a generic form of the drug metoclopramide, a drug commonly used to treat digestive-tract disorders. The FDA approved metoclopramide in 1980 under the brand name "Reglan"; since that time, however, evidence emerged that the drug can cause a severe and often irreversible

---

[172] Id at 1143, quoting *United States v Public Utility Commission of California*, 345 US 295, 319 (1953) (Jackson, J, concurring).

[173] 131 S Ct 2567 (2011).

[174] 555 US 555 (2009).

[175] See id at 559.

[176] 131 S Ct at 2574; see also 21 USC §§ 355(b)(1), (d).

[177] This legislation, formally entitled the Drug Price Competition and Patent Term Restoration Act, Pub L No 98-417, 98 Stat 1585, is "commonly called the Hatch-Waxman Amendments." 131 S Ct at 2574.

[178] 21 USC § 355(j)(2)(A).

[179] See id §§ 355(d)(6), (7).

[180] Id § 355(j)(2)(A)(v).

neurological disorder called "tardive dyskinesia." Over the years, the FDA approved several changes to Reglan's labeling to increase the strength of its warnings about tardive dyskinesia, culminating in 2009 with a "black box" warning that "[t]reatment with metoclopramide for longer than 12 weeks should be avoided in all but rare cases."[181] Prior to the development of the stronger labels, physicians prescribed generic forms of metoclopramide to Gladys Mensing and Julie Demahy, who each developed tardive dyskinesia after taking the drug for several years.[182]

Both patients sued the drug's manufacturers, in separate lawsuits, claiming that the manufacturers had failed to change their warning labels "despite mounting evidence that long term metoclopramide use carries a risk of tardive dyskinesia far greater than that indicated on the label."[183] The manufacturers defended on preemption grounds, arguing that federal law's requirement that their warning labels be the same as the brand-name drug's label made it impossible for them to carry out any state tort-law duty to adopt a stronger warning. The Fifth and Eighth Circuits both rejected the preemption defense.[184]

A divided Supreme Court consolidated the two cases and reversed in each. Justice Thomas wrote for the majority, which also included Chief Justice Roberts and Justices Scalia, Kennedy, and Alito. Because the prescription drug statutes expressly save state regulation in the absence of a "direct and positive conflict" with federal law,[185] controversy focused on conflict preemption and, in particular, on the little-used doctrine of "impossibility."[186] Prior cases had confined that concept to cases where "compliance with both federal and state [law] is a physical impossibility."[187] *PLIVA* grappled with what that standard meant in a complex regulatory setting where a state-law defendant's actions are subject to federal regulatory approval. In so doing, the Court arguably expanded the "impossibility" category.

---

[181] 131 S Ct at 2573.

[182] Id.

[183] *Mensing v Wyeth, Inc.*, 588 F3d 603, 605 (8th Cir 2009).

[184] Id at 614; *Demahy v Actavis, Inc.*, 593 F3d 428, 449 (5th Cir 2010).

[185] See Drug Amendments of 1962, Pub L No 87-781 (1962), § 202, 76 Stat 780.

[186] The Court reserved the question "whether state and federal law 'directly conflict' in circumstances beyond 'impossibility.'" 131 S Ct at 2577 n 4.

[187] *Florida Lime & Avocado Growers, Inc. v Paul*, 373 US 132, 142–43 (1963).

The parties in *PLIVA* agreed that, taking the plaintiffs' factual allegations as true, "[s]tate law required the Manufacturers to use a different, safer label."[188] They disagreed, however, about the options that federal law left open for changing the label. Deferring to the FDA's view, the Court held that FDA regulations "prevented the Manufacturers from independently changing their generic drugs' safety labels."[189] It assumed for the sake of argument, however, that "federal law also required the Manufacturers to ask for FDA assistance in convincing the brand-name manufacturer to adopt a stronger label, so that all corresponding generic drug manufacturers could do so as well."[190] Even assuming that this requirement existed, however, the majority found impossibility preemption on the ground that "[i]t was not lawful under federal law for the Manufacturers to do what state law required of them [i.e., change the label]. And even if they had fulfilled their federal duty to ask for FDA assistance, they would not have satisfied the requirements of state law."[191]

The plaintiffs' argument against preemption asserted "that when a private party's ability to comply with state law depends on approval and assistance from the FDA, proving pre-emption requires that party to demonstrate that the FDA would not have allowed compliance with state law."[192] On this view, the manufacturers would have failed to establish preemption "because they did not even *try* to start the process that might ultimately have allowed them to use a safer label."[193] Justice Thomas reasoned that this approach "would render conflict pre-emption largely meaningless"; after all, even if federal law flatly prohibited compliance with state duties, defendants could have petitioned Congress to amend the law.[194] Instead, the majority concluded that "when a party cannot satisfy its state duties without the Federal Government's special permission and assistance, which is dependent on the exercise of judgment by a federal agency, that party cannot inde-

---

[188] 131 S Ct at 2574.

[189] Id at 2577.

[190] Id.

[191] Id at 2577–78.

[192] *PLIVA*, 131 S Ct at 2578–79.

[193] Id at 2579.

[194] Id.

pendently satisfy those state duties for pre-emption purposes."[195]

This conclusion required the Court to distinguish *Wyeth*, in which the plaintiff also contended that the defendant drug manufacturers' FDA-approved warning label was insufficient to satisfy the manufacturers' duty to warn under state law. Federal law permitted manufacturers of a brand-name drug, however, "to unilaterally strengthen its warning" without advance approval from the FDA.[196] This made it possible for a regulated entity to comply with state law duties, and it made no difference that the FDA retained authority to *dis*approve the new label after its adoption by the manufacturer: "[A]bsent clear evidence that the FDA would not have approved a change to Phenergan's label, we will not conclude that it was impossible to comply with both federal and state requirements."[197] As the *PLIVA* Court described its earlier holding, "the possibility of impossibility was not enough."[198]

The Court acknowledged that its reasoning in *PLIVA* produced some odd results. Justice Thomas recognized that, "[h]ad Mensing and Demahy taken Reglan, the brand-name drug prescribed by their doctors, *Wyeth* would control and their lawsuits would not be pre-empted."[199] The disparity arose, however, from the reality that the statutory regimes for brand-name and generic drugs "are meaningfully different."[200] "We will not distort the Supremacy Clause," the majority insisted, "in order to create similar preemption across a dissimilar statutory scheme."[201]

Justice Sotomayor dissented, joined by Justices Ginsburg, Breyer, and Kagan, and accused the majority of "dilut[ing] the impossibility standard."[202] In particular, she saw no meaningful distinction between *PLIVA* and *Wyeth*. Because federal law permitted the generic drug manufacturers to ask the FDA to initiate a label change, the possibility that the FDA would have refused to do so "demonstrated only 'a hypothetical or potential con-

---

[195] Id at 2581.

[196] *Wyeth*, 555 US at 73.

[197] Id at 571.

[198] 131 S Ct at 2581 n 8 (internal quotation marks omitted).

[199] Id at 2581.

[200] Id at 2582.

[201] Id.

[202] 131 S Ct at 2582 (Sotomayor, J, dissenting).

flict.'"[203] This possibility of adverse action by the federal regulators was no different from the possibility that the FDA would have vetoed a changed label in *Wyeth*—a possibility that the earlier court found insufficient for preemption. Emphasizing the Court's prior statements that "[i]mpossibility pre-emption . . . 'is a demanding defense,'" the dissenters insisted that in this case, as in *Wyeth*, "the mere possibility of impossibility is not enough."[204]

The dissent also emphasized the importance of generic drugs, noting that "[t]oday's decision affects 75 percent of all prescription drugs dispensed in this country."[205] This meant that the Court's preemption ruling would create a large class of consumers without recourse in the event of injury.[206] The dissenters likewise predicted that the decision would undermine drug safety. Noting that "[t]he FDA has limited resources to conduct postapproval monitoring of drug safety,"[207] Justice Sotomayor asserted that "[t]oday's decision eliminates the traditional state-law incentives for generic manufacturers to monitor and disclose safety risks."[208] Moreover, "brand-name manufacturers often leave the market once generic versions are available, meaning that there will be no manufacturer subject to failure-to-warn liability."[209] These factors, finally, might well discourage physicians from prescribing generic drugs and patients from accepting them.[210]

C. BRUESEWITZ V WYETH LLC

The Court confronted yet another drug statute in *Bruesewitz v Wyeth LLC*.[211] In the National Childhood Vaccine Injury Act of 1986 (NCVIA),[212] Congress took vaccines out of the traditional prescription drug regime construed in *Wyeth* and *PLIVA*. That traditional regime generally relies on federal premarket approval combined with back-end state tort regulation. The NCVIA instead

---

[203] Id at 2588, quoting *Rice v Norman Williams Co.*, 458 US 654, 659 (1982).

[204] 131 S Ct at 2587, quoting *Wyeth*, 555 US at 573 (Sotomayor, J, dissenting).

[205] Id at 2583.

[206] Id at 2592.

[207] Id at 2584

[208] Id at 2592 (Sotomayor, J, dissenting).

[209] Id at 2593 (citation omitted).

[210] Id.

[211] 131 S Ct 1068 (2011).

[212] Pub L No 99-660, 100 Stat 3758, codified as amended at 42 USC § 300aa et seq.

established "a no-fault compensation program" under which a person injured by a vaccine may seek compensation by filing a petition against the Secretary of Health and Human Services in the Court of Federal Claims. A special master reviews these petitions under the Court's supervision, after which a claimant may either accept the judgment or seek relief through the tort system.[213] This process affords compensation for a wide variety of medical expenses and injuries, including $250,000 for vaccine-related deaths, with awards paid out of a fund generated by an excise tax on vaccines.[214] As a "quid pro quo" for the establishment of this no-fault regime, however, the NCVIA provided "significant tort-liability protections for vaccine manufacturers."[215] These protections include immunity for failure to warn so long as manufacturers comply with regulatory requirements, a heightened standard of culpability for punitive damages, and elimination of liability "for a vaccine's unavoidable, adverse side effects."[216]

Hannah Bruesewitz was vaccinated for diphtheria, tetanus, and pertussis (DTP) in April 1992, when she was six months old. She experienced over 100 seizures, beginning within twenty-four hours of her vaccination. Hannah's parents filed a petition in the Court of Federal Claims in 1995, alleging that Hannah suffered from residual seizure disorder and encephalopathy injuries—disorders listed in the NCIVA's Vaccine Injury Table as compensable adverse side effects of the DTP vaccine. When a Special Master denied their claims, the Bruesewitzes filed a common law tort suit in Pennsylvania state court, alleging that the defective design of the DTP vaccine caused Hannah's injuries. Wyeth removed the case to federal court, which held the Bruesewitzes' claims preempted.[217]

Bruesewitz required the Court to decide whether the NCVIA's express preemption clause preempted state liability for defective design claims. The relevant provision of the NCVIA provides that

> No vaccine manufacturer shall be liable in a civil action for damages arising from a vaccine-related injury or death associated with the administration of a vaccine after October 1, 1988, if the injury or death resulted from side effects that were unavoidable even though the vaccine

---

[213] See 42 USC §§ 300aa-11(a)(1), 12(d), (e), & (g), 21(a).

[214] Id §§ 300aa-15(a), (i)(2); 26 USC §§ 4131, 9510.

[215] 131 S Ct at 1074.

[216] Id.

[217] See id at 1074–75.

was properly prepared and was accompanied by proper directions and warnings.[218]

Justice Scalia's majority opinion, joined by Chief Justice Roberts and Justices Kennedy, Thomas, Breyer, and Alito, construed the "even though" clause to "clarif[y] the word that precedes it"—that is, it "delineates the preventative measures that a vaccine manufacturer must have taken for a side-effect to be considered 'unavoidable' under the statute."[219] This meant that "[p]rovided that there was proper manufacture and warning, any remaining side effects, including those resulting from design defects, are deemed to have been unavoidable. State-law design-defect claims are therefore preempted."[220]

In dissent, Justice Sotomayor (joined by Justice Ginsburg) rejected this reading of the statute: "Given that the 'even though' clause requires the absence of manufacturing and labeling defects, the 'if' clause's reference to 'side effects that were unavoidable' must refer to side effects caused by something other than manufacturing and labeling defects."[221] She reasoned that "[t]he only remaining kind of product defect recognized under traditional products liability law is a design defect";[222] therefore, the statute's preemptive effect should be confined to a subset of design defects that are "unavoidable"—that is, "side effects stemming from the vaccine's design [that] could not have been prevented by a feasible alternative design that would have eliminated the adverse side effects without compromising the vaccine's cost and utility."[223]

The majority and dissent sparred at length over the proper application of grammatical rules to the statutory text and the relevance and import of the statute's legislative history. Justice Breyer wrote a separate concurrence to emphasize the importance of "other sources, including legislative history, statutory purpose, and the views of the federal administrative agency, here supported by expert medical opinion."[224] In particular, he emphasized the FDA's

---

[218] 42 USC § 300aa-22(b)(1).

[219] 131 S Ct at 1075.

[220] Id.

[221] Id at 1087 (Sotomayor, J, dissenting).

[222] Id.

[223] Id at 1093.

[224] Id at 1083 (Breyer, J, concurring). Justice Kagan took no part in the decision of the case.

view that the plaintiffs' claims were preempted; it was important, moreover, that "expert public health organizations support [the FDA's] views and the matter concerns a medical and scientific question of great importance."[225] Under these circumstances, Breyer suggested that deference was appropriate under *Skidmore v Swift & Co.*[226]

D. AT&T MOBILITY LLC V CONCEPCION

In *AT&T Mobility LLC v Concepcion*,[227] the Court considered whether the Federal Arbitration Act[228] (FAA) preempted a California rule that conditioned the enforceability of certain arbitration agreements on the availability of classwide arbitration procedures. Vincent and Liza Concepcion purchased AT&T cellphone service in 2002. Although AT&T had advertised that the service contract would include free phones, it charged them $30.22 in sales tax based on the phones' retail value. In 2006, the Concepcions sued AT&T for false advertising and fraud in the U.S. District Court for the Southern District of California. The district court later consolidated the Concepcions' suit with a putative class action making similar allegations. AT&T moved to compel arbitration under a provision of the service contract providing "for arbitration of all disputes between the parties, but requir[ing] that all claims be brought in the parties' 'individual capacity, and not as a plaintiff or class member in any purported class or representative proceeding.'"[229]

Section 2 of the FAA makes arbitration agreements "valid, irrevocable, and enforceable, save upon such grounds as exist at law or in equity for the revocation of any contract."[230] The provision preempts state efforts to limit arbitration outright; it saves from preemption "'generally applicable contract defenses, such as fraud, duress, or unconscionability,' but not . . . defenses that apply only

---

[225] Id at 1086.

[226] Id, citing 323 US 134 (1944). Although Justice Breyer cited *Skidmore*, he did not discuss why that level of deference was more appropriate than the more categorical deference accorded to agency views under *Chevron USA, Inc. v Natural Resources Defense Council*, 467 US 837 (1984).

[227] 131 S Ct 1740 (2011).

[228] 9 USC § 2.

[229] *AT&T*, 131 S Ct at 1744, quoting the contract.

[230] 9 USC § 2.

to arbitration or that derive their meaning from the fact that an agreement to arbitrate is at issue."[231] The question in *Concepcion* was on which side of this line to place California's doctrine of unconscionability, as applied to class-action waivers in *Discover Bank v Superior Court.*[232] That case found class-action waivers to be unconscionable "in a consumer contract of adhesion in a setting in which disputes between the contracting parties predictably involve small amounts of damages, and when it is alleged that the party with the superior bargaining power has carried out a scheme to deliberately cheat large numbers of consumers out of individually small sums of money."[233] In such circumstances, *Discover Bank* said, "the waiver becomes in practice the exemption of the party 'from responsibility for [its] own fraud, or willful injury to the person or property of another.'"[234]

Writing for the majority, Justice Scalia found that the *Discover Bank* rule "interferes with arbitration" and was therefore preempted under the FAA.[235] Although the majority acknowledged the existence of classwide arbitration procedures, it held that "the switch from bilateral to class arbitration sacrifices the principal advantage of arbitration—its informality—and makes the process slower, more costly, and more likely to generate procedural morass than final judgment."[236] Moreover, while "class arbitration greatly increases risks to defendants" in much the same way as class litigation (i.e., by aggregating claims), arbitration provides only extremely deferential judicial review for both certification decisions and final judgments.[237] "We find it hard to believe," Scalia wrote, "that defendants would bet the company with no effective means of review, and even harder to believe that Congress would have intended to allow state courts to force such a decision."[238] Hence, while parties remained free to agree to classwide arbitration, California's effort to require such procedures was preempted.

As he had in *Williamson,* Justice Thomas concurred to urge that

---

[231] 131 S Ct at 1746, quoting *Doctor's Associates, Inc. v Casarotto,* 517 US 681, 687 (1996).

[232] 113 P3d 1100 (Cal 2005).

[233] Id at 1110.

[234] Id, quoting Cal Civ Code § 1668 (West, 1984).

[235] 131 S Ct at 1750.

[236] Id at 1751.

[237] Id at 1752.

[238] Id.

preemption be grounded in the actual text of the statute rather than on a conflict between state and federal law. "As I would read it," he said, "the FAA requires that an agreement to arbitrate be enforced unless a party successfully challenges the formation of the arbitration agreement, such as by proving fraud or duress."[239] He acknowledged, however, that this reading rested on a "not obvious" distinction between "revocability" of a contract and challenges to a contract's "validity and enforceability"—a distinction, moreover, that "has not been fully developed by any party."[240] Noting that "when possible, it is important in interpreting statutes to give lower courts guidance from a majority of the Court," Thomas provided a fifth vote by "reluctantly join[ing] the Court's opinion" while "adher[ing] to my views on purposes-and-objectives pre-emption."[241]

Justice Breyer dissented in an opinion joined by the rest of the Court's liberal wing. He first insisted that the "[t]he *Discover Bank* rule is consistent with the federal Act's language" because it "'applies equally to class action litigation waivers in contracts without arbitration agreements as it does to class arbitration waivers in conctracts with such agreements.'"[242] He also argued that the California rule did not conflict with the FAA's purpose of "'ensur[ing] judicial enforcement' of arbitration agreements."[243] Debate centered on the extent to which class arbitration would, in fact, undermine the purposes of arbitration—especially that of reducing the cost and formality of litigation. The relevant comparison, Breyer suggested, was not between "the complexity of class arbitration [and] that of bilateral arbitration," but rather "between class arbitration and judicial class actions." Relying on American Arbitration Association statistics indicating that "'class arbitration proceedings take more time than the average commercial arbitration, but may take less time than the average class action in court,'" Breyer concluded that the *Discover Bank* rule's protection of class-wide procedures would not undermine the FAA's pro-arbitration policy.[244]

---

[239] Id at 1753 (Thomas, J, concurring).

[240] Id at 1754.

[241] Id.

[242] Id at 1757 (Breyer, J, dissenting), quoting *Discover Bank*, 113 P3d at 1112.

[243] 131 S Ct at 1757, quoting *Dean Witter Reynolds Inc. v Byrd*, 470 US 213, 219 (1985).

[244] 131 S Ct at 1759–60, quoting Brief of American Arbitration Association as Amicus

E. CHAMBER OF COMMERCE V WHITING

A final case, *Chamber of Commerce v Whiting*,[245] scrambled the voting alignments from the Court's other preemption decisions. Reflecting widespread dissatisfaction with the rigor of federal enforcement efforts under the nation's immigration laws, a number of states have enacted laws to supplement federal immigration enforcement.[246] Public controversy has centered around Arizona's Support Our Law Enforcement and Safe Neighborhoods Act (SB 1070),[247] which requires state and local officials to take various steps to enforce the national immigration laws, with the general import that those laws will be enforced more strictly in Arizona.[248] The United States has sued to challenge SB 1070 on preemption grounds, and the Supreme Court recently agreed to take up that case in the present Term.[249] *Whiting*, on the other hand, involved a lesser-known Arizona statute, the Legal Arizona Workers Act (LAWA),[250] which focuses on employers who hire unauthorized aliens. Although the relevant statutory regimes implicated by SB 1070 and the LAWA are meaningfully different, the Court's decision upholding the LAWA in *Whiting* may nonetheless foreshadow the Court's approach to SB 1070.

The LAWA, which the Arizona legislature enacted in 2007,

Curiae in Support of Neither Party, *Stolt-Nielson S.A. v AnimalFeeds International Corp.*, OT 2009 No 08-1198, *24 (US filed Sept 4, 2009).

[245] 131 S Ct 1968 (2011).

[246] See, for example, *United States v Arizona*, 703 F Supp 2d 980, 985 (D Ariz 2010) (citing "rampant illegal immigration, escalating drug and human trafficking crimes, and serious public safety concerns" as giving rise to state intervention). For examples of action by other states, see Beason-Hammon Alabama Taxpayer and Citizen Protection Act, 2011 Ala Acts 535, codified at Ala Code Ann §§ 31-13-1–30 (2011) (requiring officers to verify a person's immigration status during traffic stops or arrests if the officer has a reasonable suspicion that a person's presence is not lawful); Illegal Immigration Enforcement Act, 2011 Utah Laws Ch 21 (HB 497), codified at Utah Code Ann § 76-9-1001 et seq (2011) (requiring officers to verify the immigration status of persons arrested for certain misdemeanors and felonies, clarifying when an officer should question passengers about their immigration status, and giving grounds for a presumption of a person's lawful presence); Illegal Immigration Reform and Enforcement Act of 2011, Ga Laws 252 (HB 87), codified in various sections of Ga Code (authorizing officers to investigate a suspect's immigration status if the officer has probable cause).

[247] 2010 Ariz Legis Serv Ch 113 (West).

[248] SB 1070 also creates certain related crimes under state law, most importantly, a crime for an unauthorized alien to solicit, apply for, or perform work.

[249] See Lyle Denniston, *Another Landmark Ruling in the Offing* (SCOTUSblog, Dec 12, 2011), online at http://www.scotusblog.com/2011/12/another-landmark-ruling-in-the-offing/.

[250] Ariz Rev Stat Ann §§ 23-211 et seq.

"allows Arizona courts to suspend or revoke the licenses necessary to do business in the State if an employer knowingly or intentionally employs an unauthorized alien."[251] The law requires that state officials determine an individual's status by seeking federal verification of citizenship or immigration status, pursuant to federal law, and forbids any independent determination of that status. Likewise, employees may establish an affirmative defense by showing good-faith compliance with federal procedures for verifying an individual's eligibility for employment. Finally, state law requires all employers to verify an employee's eligibility by using the "E-Verify" system, an internet-based federal database.[252]

The Chamber of Commerce of the United States, along with various business and civil rights organizations, challenged the LAWA on preemption grounds. They argued, in particular, that the Arizona law was expressly preempted by the federal Immigration Reform and Control Act (IRCA),[253] which established extensive federal regulation of the employment of unauthorized aliens. The IRCA expressly preempts "any State or local law imposing civil or criminal sanctions (other than through licensing and similar laws) upon those who employ, or recruit or refer for a fee for employment, unauthorized aliens."[254] The primary question in *Whiting* was whether Arizona's law could escape express preemption by fitting into the category of "licensing and similar laws." The Chamber also argued that LAWA was impliedly preempted because it conflicted with IRCA's object and purpose, and in particular that federal law impliedly preempted Arizona's effort to mandate the use of the federal E-Verify program.

Writing for the Court,[255] Chief Justice Roberts began with the statutory text: "When a federal law contains an express preemption clause, we 'focus on the plain wording of the clause, which nec-

---

[251] 131 S Ct at 1976.

[252] See id at 1976–77 (summarizing the LAWA's provisions).

[253] Pub L No 99-603, 100 Stat 3359 (1986), codified as amended in scattered sections of 8 USC.

[254] 8 USC § 1324a(h)(2).

[255] Justices Scalia, Kennedy, and Alito joined the Chief's opinion in full. Justice Thomas joined all but the portions dealing with obstacle preemption—presumably because he has questioned the very legitimacy of obstacle preemption and thus wished to address only arguments based on the statutory text. See Part III.B. Although the Reporter described the Chief Justice's opinion on the obstacle preemption issues as not being "of the Court," it is worth noting that he still spoke for a 4–3 majority on those points because Justice Kagan was recused.

essarily contains the best evidence of Congress' preemptive intent.'"[256] "[O]n its face," he noted, the Arizona law "purports to impose sanctions through licensing laws," and Arizona's broad definition of license was consistent with dictionary definitions of the term, similar definitions in federal law, and the Court's own prior decisions.[257] The Court thus concluded that "Arizona's licensing law falls well within the confines of the authority Congress chose to leave to the States and therefore is not expressly preempted."[258]

The Chief Justice then turned to the implied preemption arguments. "At its broadest level," he said, "the Chamber's argument is that Congress 'intended the federal system to be exclusive,' and that any state system therefore necessarily conflicts with federal law."[259] That argument, the majority found, was inconsistent with the IRCA's explicit language saving state licensing regimes.[260] Moreover, the Chief Justice emphasized that "here Arizona went the extra mile in ensuring that its law closely tracks IRCA's provisions in all material respects."[261] The LAWA adopted the federal definition of unauthorized alien and required state investigators to verify the work authorization of allegedly unauthorized aliens with federal authorities; "[a]s a result, there can by definition be no conflict between state and federal law as to worker authorization, either at the investigatory or adjudicatory stage."[262] Likewise, the LAWA's prohibitions on employment of unauthorized aliens "trace the federal law" and provide employers "with the same affirmative defense for good-faith compliance with the I-9 process as does the federal law."[263]

---

[256] 131 S Ct at 1977, quoting *CSX Transportation, Inc. v Easterwood*, 507 US 658, 664 (1993).

[257] 131 S Ct at 1977. The Chief Justice noted, moreover, that "even if a law regulating articles of incorporation, partnership certificates, and the like is not itself a 'licensing law,' it is at the very least 'similar' to a licensing law, and therefore comfortably within the savings clause." Id at 1978.

[258] Id at 1981.

[259] Id, quoting Brief for the Petitioners, *Chamber of Commerce v Candelaria*, No 09-115, *39 (US filed Sept 1, 2010).

[260] 131 S Ct at 1981.

[261] Id.

[262] Id, citing Ariz Rev Stat Ann §§ 23-212(B), (H).

[263] 131 S Ct at 1982, citing Ariz Rev Stat Ann §§ 23-211(8), 212(J). Similarly, both the state and federal law allowed employers "a rebuttable presumption of compliance" when they use the E-Verify system. See 131 S Ct at 1982, citing Ariz Rev Stat Ann § 232-212(I).

Critically, the Court rejected the notion that "the law is pre-empted because it upsets the balance that Congress sought to strike" between "deterring unauthorized alien employment, avoiding burdens on employers, protecting employee privacy, and guarding against employment discrimination."[264] Cases finding such disruption, the Chief Justice observed, "all involve uniquely federal areas of regulation"—such as foreign affairs, maritime law, or fraud on a federal agency—while "[r]egulating in-state businesses through licensing laws has never been considered such an area of dominant federal concern."[265] Likewise, "all [the cases relied on by the Chamber] concern state actions that directly interfered with the operation of the federal program."[266] The present case, by contrast, involved no such interference, since Congress had specifically carved out a state role and Arizona law reinforced, rather than undermined, the IRCA's prohibitions on discrimination.[267] The Chief Justice emphasized that "[i]mplied preemption analysis does not justify a 'free-wheeling judicial inquiry into whether a state statute is in tension with federal objectives,'" and that "'a high threshold must be met if a state law is to be preempted for conflicting with the purposes of a federal Act.'"[268] "That threshold," the Court concluded, "is not met here."[269]

Justice Breyer (joined by Justice Ginsburg) and Justice Sotomayor both dissented. Breyer thought that while the Arizona law might fit dictionary definitions of a "licensing" scheme, it was inconsistent with the way that term was used in the IRCA: "ordinary corporate charters, certificates of partnership, and the like

---

[264] Id at 1983.

[265] Id (discussing *American Insurance Association v Garamendi*, 539 US 396 (2003); *Crosby v National Foreign Trade Council*, 530 US 363 (2000); *United States v Locke*, 529 US 89 (2000); *Buckman v Plaintiff's Legal Committee*, 531 US 341 (2001); and *Bonito Boats, Inc. v Thunder Craft Boats, Inc.*, 489 US 141 (1989)).

[266] 131 S Ct at 1983.

[267] Id at 1983–84.

[268] Id at 1985, quoting *Gade v National Solid Wastes Management Assn.*, 505 US 88, 110, 111 (1992) (Kennedy, J, concurring in part and in judgment).

[269] Id. The Chief Justice also rejected a narrower implied preemption argument, based on the fact that Arizona law requires employers to use the E-Verify system while federal law makes that system voluntary. He noted that the statute establishing E-Verify "contains no language circumscribing state action," id, and that "the Federal Government has consistently expanded and encouraged the use of E-Verify." Id at 1986. The Court rejected concerns about state-imposed burdens on the system and about the system's accuracy, noting that the United States had assured the Court of the system's adequacy on both counts. See id.

do not fall within the scope of the word 'licensing' as used in this federal exception."[270] Moreover, Breyer argued that the LAWA disrupted the balance Congress struck between the competing goals of federal immigration law. This was so because the state law increased the penalties for hiring an unauthorized alien in such a way as to outstrip federal penalties for discrimination, so that employers would have incentives to err on the side of not hiring "foreign-looking" persons.[271] The LAWA likewise "subjects lawful employers to increased burdens and risks of erroneous prosecution," particularly because of inaccuracies in the E-Verify system.[272] Breyer would thus have read the IRCA's "licensing" language more narrowly, "as limited in scope to laws licensing businesses that recruit or refer workers for employment."[273]

Also dissenting, Justice Sotomayor read the IRCA's saving language even more narrowly, "to preserve States' authority to impose licensing sanctions after a final *federal* determination that a person has violated IRCA by knowingly employing an unauthorized alien."[274] In other words, states may act only after federal authorities have determined that an employer is in violation of federal law. Although she read the savings clause differently than Justice Breyer, Sotomayor largely echoed his concerns that Arizona's scheme would undermine uniform federal enforcement of the immigration laws.[275]

F. AN INCOHERENT DOCTRINE?

At the end of his dissent in *Concepcion*, Justice Breyer harkened back to his admonition in *Egelhoff* that "the true test of federalist principle" occurs in preemption cases.[276] Implicitly invoking the conservative Justices' paeans to state sovereignty in cases like

---

[270] Id at 1988 (Breyer, J, dissenting).

[271] Id at 1990.

[272] Id at 1990–91.

[273] Id at 1995. Justice Breyer would likewise have held that the state law's mandate to use E-Verify was impliedly preempted. See id at 1995–97.

[274] Id at 1998 (Sotomayor, J, dissenting) (emphasis added).

[275] See id at 1999–2005. Justice Sotomayor likewise agreed with Justice Breyer that Arizona could not mandate the use of E-Verify. Id at 2005–07.

[276] See text accompanying note 6.

United States v Lopez and *Alden v Maine*,[277] Breyer noted that "federalism is as much a question of deeds as words. It often takes the form of a concrete decision by this Court that respects the legitimacy of a State's action in an individual case."[278] The Court's deeds in the 2010 Term, however, do not lend themselves to easy summation. This is true for a variety of reasons, some intrinsic to the nature of preemption cases and others contingent on the division of opinion on the current Court.

As Justice Breyer suggested in *Egelhoff*, preemption analysis occurs "at retail . . . statute by statute, line by line."[279] Sometimes Congress really does intend to preempt state law, and sometimes it doesn't; in the cases that reach the Supreme Court, typically by generating a split among the lower courts, Congress's intent is ambiguous almost by definition. If the Court were to impose very strong default rules—a super-strong version of the *Rice* presumption against preemption, for example—then we might expect all these intermediate cases to go one way or the other. But the default rules have never been *that* strong, nor is it clear that they should be. In the absence of heavy-handed defaults, any court deciding a series of preemption cases arising under a variety of different statutes that say different things and invoke different purposes is going to find preemption in some cases and reject it in others.[280] The different outcomes in *Wyeth* and *PLIVA*, for instance, reflect that the regulatory regimes for brand-name and generic drugs are meaningfully different in respects relevant to the preemption question.[281]

---

[277] See *United States v Lopez*, 514 US 549, 552 (1995) (citing as a constitutional "first principle[]" the need to maintain "a healthy balance of power between the States and the Federal Government"); *Alden v Maine*, 527 US 706, 713 (1999) (emphasizing "the vital role reserved to the States by the constitutional design").

[278] 131 S Ct at 1762 (Breyer, J, dissenting).

[279] 532 US at 160 (Breyer, J, dissenting).

[280] See Richard A. Epstein and Michael S. Greve, *Introduction: Preemption in Context* 1, 19, in Epstein and Greve, eds, *Federal Preemption* (cited in note 44), at 19 ("The congressional intent baseline raises the specter that preemption law can only be as coherent as the statutory universe on which it operates.").

[281] See, for example, *PLIVA*, 131 S Ct at 2582 ("It is beyond dispute that the federal statutes and regulations that apply to brand-name drug manufacturers are meaningfully different than those that apply to generic drug manufacturers."). Similarly, *Wyeth*'s decision that federal approval of a drug does not preempt state common law actions seems inconsistent with *Riegel v Medtronic*, 552 US 312 (2008), which held that federal approval of a medical *device* does preempt state tort suits. But as Justice Stevens explained in *Wyeth*, "when Congress enacted an express pre-emption provision for medical devices in 1976

The divergent outcomes in the Court's preemption cases last Term thus do not necessarily signify a jurisprudence that is incoherent, confused, or unprincipled.[282] To be sure, there are frustrating inconsistencies: In *Whiting*, for example, the politics of immigration may seem to have induced most of the Justices to reverse their usual stance on preemption matters. But politics does not tell the whole story.[283] Even where the divergent results cannot be traced, as in *PLIVA* and *Wyeth*, to the underlying statutes, it hardly follows that the Justices have thrown neutral principles out the window. Rather, multiple neutral principles—concerning both methodology and constitutional structure—may bear on preemption cases, and their relative importance plausibly may vary across cases. For the *Whiting* dissenters, for example, principles of avoiding discrimination based on ethnicity or preserving federal primacy in foreign affairs may have seemed more immediately at issue than principles of federalism. Each of these values is grounded in the Constitution, and each might plausibly be called upon to resolve a close case of statutory construction. To say that one could have weighed these principles differently—as the majority did in *Whiting*—is not to say that there was no principled basis for coming out where the dissenters did. And to say that we need a more foundational principle for choosing among competing values in such cases is simply to restate the fundamental problem of constitutional law.

As I have already discussed, the Justices find themselves divided on at least two sets of legal questions that arise in nearly all preemption cases: What counts as preemption? And who can preempt state law? Both sets of issues raise questions along three dimen-

---

. . . it declined to enact such a provision for prescription drugs." 555 US at 567. These statutory differences turn out to matter a great deal.

[282] See, for example, Ashutosh Bhagwat, *Wyeth v. Levine and Agency Preemption: More Muddle, or Creeping to Clarity?* 45 Tulsa L Rev 197, 197 (2000) ("The law of preemption . . . is infamous for its vagueness and unpredictability."); Pursley, 71 Ohio St L J at 515 (cited in note 9) ("Judicial preemption doctrine is thin and confusing."). Law professors love to say that this or that area of law is "incoherent" or "confused." See Young, 83 Tex L Rev at 11 n 41 (cited in note 47) (collecting citations to academics concluding that this or that field is "incoherent"). The fact that we say it so often, and about so many different doctrinal areas, suggests that a certain amount of disorder is inherent in any complex human construct like the law. In any event, there is no reason to believe that the Court's preemption jurisprudence is more confused than, say, its privacy or equal protection jurisprudence.

[283] For one thing, it is far from obvious what we mean by "politics" when we talk about judicial decisions. See Ernest A. Young, *Just Blowing Smoke? Politics, Doctrine, and the "Federalist Revival" after Gonzales v Raich*, 2005 Supreme Court Review 1, 18–20.

sions. The first dimension concerns the proper interpretation of the Supremacy Clause—in particular, the sort of conflict between state and federal law required before preemption must occur, and whether the Supremacy Clause forecloses a presumption against preemption. A second dimension is more methodological in nature, implicating broader debates about the relative importance in statutory construction of statutory text, legislative history, interpretive canons, the views of federal administrative agencies, and straight-up policy arguments. And, finally, the third dimension raises basic questions of separation of powers—not just which federal entities have the power to preempt state laws, but also whose views count as to whether preemption has occurred. These dimensions obviously overlap; the question of interpretive methodology, for example, implicates fundamental separation-of-powers concerns about the relationship between courts and other governmental actors. But distinguishing the broader dimensions of the Court's preemption disputes should spotlight the connection between those disputes and broader debates in public law.

Each individual Justice confronts these central questions of preemption doctrine, but the difficulty of developing coherent answers is compounded by the multimember nature of the Court. Some of the Justices have staked out clear positions on some of these issues, but not others, and other Justices remain uncommitted on most of them. For example, Justice Thomas has developed in recent years a distinctive and principled approach to preemption that stakes out a position on almost all of the relevant questions. Justice Breyer has likewise articulated a largely coherent theoretical position that, although allowing judges considerably more flexibility than Thomas's view, nonetheless at least has something to say about each of the relevant doctrinal and methodological issues. Outcomes in individual cases, however, are largely a function of where the less committed Justices fall. And even when these Justices sign on to a more theoretically ambitious opinion, they seem to feel relatively unconstrained to follow that theory in future cases. That is why, at least for now, preemption doctrine remains somewhat in flux.

It is not obvious that there *should* be a coherent body of "preemption doctrine"—that is, doctrine that is not a function of the particular regulatory field at issue. William Eskridge, for example, has argued that "the larger project of preemption jurisprudence is to develop area-specific precepts for calibrating the state-federal balance."[284] To some extent, area-specific doctrine is inevitable. Preemption stems from Congress's intent, which varies from statute to statute, and as the Court decides a series of cases under a particular statute, the Court will likely develop an area-specific picture of Congress's intent under that statute. The Court has thus interpreted the Federal Arbitration Act and the National Bank Act as broadly preempting state law,[285] while construing the regime governing new medical drugs as leaving an important role for state tort regulation.[286]

My own view, however, is that preemption questions are too critical to the overall balance of our federalism to leave them as matters of "ordinary" statutory construction, unconnected to the broader themes of national power and state autonomy. Our constitutional system has always left much, if not most, of the institutional architecture of federalism to be worked out through ordinary legislation; hence, federal statutes, administrative regulations, institutional practices, and judge-made doctrines play a greater role in defining the balance of state and federal power than do the entrenched provisions of the canonical constitution. As I have already discussed, the enumerated limits of Congress's powers now play an extremely limited role in preserving the federal balance, and preemption has become the central question of our federalism. It is critical to approach preemption questions in ways that cohere with the broader concerns of constitutional federalism doctrine.[287] The next part discusses the ways in which the Court has set about that task.

---

[284] Eskridge, 83 Notre Dame L Rev at 1485 (cited in note 123). For examples, see Thomas W. Merrill, *Preemption in Environmental Law: Formalism, Federalism Theory, and Default Rules*, in Epstein and Greve, eds, *Federal Preemption* at 166 (cited in note 44); Sharkey, 76 Geo Wash L Rev at 449 (cited in note 95).

[285] See *Moses H. Cone Memorial Hospital v Mercury Construction Corp.*, 460 US 1, 24–25 (1983) (stating that the FAA announces "a liberal federal policy favoring arbitration agreements, notwithstanding any state substantive or procedural policies to the contrary," and "create[s] a body of federal substantive law of arbitrability, applicable to any arbitration agreement within the coverage of the Act"); *Barnett Bank of Marion County, N.A. v Nelson*, 517 US 25, 32 (1996) (observing that, in the banking area, the Court's "history is one of interpreting grants of both enumerated and incidental 'powers' to national banks as grants of authority not normally limited by, but rather ordinarily pre-empting, contrary state law").

[286] See *Wyeth v Levine*, 555 US 555 (2009).

[287] See Ernest A. Young, *The Continuity of Statutory and Constitutional Interpretation: An Essay for Phil Frickey*, 98 Cal L Rev 1371 (2010) (arguing that because statutes flesh out the constitutional structure, constitutional values should inform statutory construction).

III. The Presumption Against Preemption

In theory, at least, the centerpiece of modern preemption doctrine remains the Court's statement in *Rice v Santa Fe Elevator Corp.*[288] that "we start with the assumption that the historic police powers of the States were not to be superseded by the Federal Act unless that was the clear and manifest purpose of Congress." Just three years ago, in *Wyeth*, the Court described the *Rice* presumption as a "cornerstone[] of our pre-emption jurisprudence."[289] Notwithstanding this and similar endorsements, many scholars have noted the Court's failure to consistently employ the *Rice* canon.[290] The 2010 Term was no exception to this tendency: The Justices ignored *Rice* in *Williamson* and *Concepcion* and invoked it only in dissent in *PLIVA* and *Bruesewitz*.[291] In *Whiting*, the majority looked only to the "plain wording" of the express preemption clause, but imposed a "high threshold" for finding *conflict* preemption.[292]

The unreliability of this presumption is nothing new: In *Rice* itself, the Court first articulated its strong anti-preemption presumption, but then went on to find *field* preemption based on a relatively weak showing of Congress's intent.[293] The presumption against preemption has become particularly controversial in recent years. On the one hand, some scholars (this one included) have developed theoretical accounts situating the *Rice* presumption within federalism doctrine as well as within the broader context

---

[288] 331 US 218, 230 (1947).

[289] 555 US at 565.

[290] See, for example, Merrill, 102 Nw U L Rev at 741 (cited in note 102) ("[T]he presumption against preemption is honored as much in the breach as in observance."); Rosen, 102 Nw U L Rev at 785 (cited in note 101) (observing that the presumption "is only inconsistently invoked and applied"). Some commentators go so far as to say that "the Supreme Court's recent preemption decisions . . . [have], in effect, created a presumption *in favor of* preemption." Davis, 53 SC L Rev at 971 (cited in note 78) (emphasis added).

[291] See *PLIVA*, 131 S Ct at 2586 (Sotomayor, J, dissenting); *Bruesewitz*, 131 S Ct at 1096 n 15 (Sotomayor, J, dissenting). *Williamson* is the most surprising, because the Court rejected preemption without invoking *Rice*. But the Court may have felt that the circumstances of the case were so close to *Geier* that the only issues concerned the differences between the regulations at issue in the two cases. It is plausible that general presumptions would have little impact on such a granular question.

[292] 131 S Ct at 1977, 1985.

[293] See 331 US at 232–36. Richard Epstein and Michael Greve are thus right to question whether *Rice* really did what it is generally cited for. See Epstein and Greve, *Conclusion* at 315 (cited in note 67). That hardly undermines the authority of subsequent decisions' application of a real presumption against preemption, however.

of statutory and constitutional interpretive methodology.[294] On the other hand, the presumption has also come under attack from litigants and academics. Parties and their amici before the Court have repeatedly called for the Court to abandon *Rice* explicitly, both in express and implied preemption cases,[295] and the Court's reaffirmation of *Rice* in *Altria* and *Wyeth* is unlikely to discourage further attacks for long.

One question that arises at the outset is what to make of the Court's failure to invoke *Rice* in many of the cases in which it might seem to apply. Dissenting Justices in *Altria* and *Wyeth* invoked these omissions to argue that *Rice* is no longer—if it ever was—good law.[296] To my mind, however, Justice Thomas himself provided the appropriate answer to this sort of argument in *Wyeth*, where he said that "[b]ecause it is evident from the text of the relevant federal statutes and regulations themselves that the state-law judgment below is not pre-empted, it is not necessary to decide whether, or to what extent, the presumption should apply in a case such as this one, where Congress has not enacted an express pre-emption clause."[297] In other words, when the Justices think that the preemption question is not a close one, they often choose not to invoke *Rice*'s tiebreaker rule. This is true both when the Court does and does not find preemption. The Court's approach

---

[294] See, for example, Young, 83 Tex L Rev at 130–34 (cited in note 47); Gardbaum, 79 Cornell L Rev at 767 (cited in note 55).

[295] See note 111; see also Viet D. Dinh, *Reassessing the Law of Preemption*, 88 Georgetown L J 2085, 2092 (2000) (attacking *Rice*); Untereiner, 84 Tulane L Rev 1265–68 (cited in note 11) (same).

[296] In *Altria*, for example, Justice Thomas cited the following express preemption cases that failed to refer to any presumption against preemption: *Sprietsma v Mercury Marine*, 537 US 51 (2002); *Rose v New Hampshire Motor Transport Association*, 552 US 364 (2008); *Engine Manufacturers Association v South Coast Air Quality Management Dist.*, 541 US 246 (2004); *Buckman Co. v Plaintiffs' Legal Commission*, 531 US 341 (2001); *United States v Locke*, 529 US 89 (2000); and *Geier v American Honda Motor Co.*, 529 US 861 (2000). He acknowledged that the Court had invoked it in *Medtronic, Inc. v Lohr*, 518 US 470 (1996); *Lorillard Tobacco Co. v Reilly*, 533 US 525 (2001); and *Bates v Dow Agrosciences LLC*, 544 US 431 (2005), but observed that *Lohr* was a "fractured decision," 555 US at 99, and asserted that *Lorillard* and *Bates* did not in fact rely on the presumption even though they found no preemption, id at 100–101. Most important, Thomas thought that *Riegel v Medtronic, Inc.*, 552 US 312 (2008), resolved any doubts: "[g]iven the [*Riegel*] dissent's clear call for the use of the presumption against pre-emption, the Court's decision not to invoke it was necessarily a rejection of any role for the presumption in construing the statute." 555 US at 102. See also *Wyeth*, 555 US at 623–24 (Alito, J, dissenting) (discussing *Geier* and *Buckman*).

[297] 555 US at 589 n 2 (Thomas, J, concurring in the judgment).

may well be a form of "incompletely theorized agreement"[298]—
after all, why undermine consensus on a result by invoking a pres-
ently controversial argument when one can resolve the case without it?[299] Just as William Eskridge and Lauren Baer have shown
that the Court frequently fails to invoke *Chevron* in cases in which
it might apply,[300] so too the Court's avoidance of *Rice* may signify
little about whether *Rice*'s interpretive presumption remains good
law.

It is not clear that the Court's stance on *Rice* represents a stable
equilibrium, however, and it is worth examining the arguments
advanced against a presumption against preemption and the extent
to which particular Justices have taken those arguments up. Much
of the debate about *Rice* is really a skirmish in the broader war
between reliance on the "plain meaning" of statutory text and
recourse to extrinsic tools like the canons of construction. What
Justice Scalia once said of *Chevron* is likely true of *Rice* as well: If
one generally believes that texts are clear, then one has less occasion to rely on interpretive rules and presumptions that aid in
construing ambiguous statutes.[301] One can read Scalia's unwillingness to invoke *Rice* in *Bruesewitz*, for example, as a rejection of
extrinsic sources of statutory meaning in general, not simply as
an attack on a particular rule of construction in preemption
cases.[302]

The 2010 Term also featured two more specific debates about
the standard for preemption, however. One concerned an academic
argument advanced by Caleb Nelson about the original under-

---

[298] See generally Cass R. Sunstein, *Incompletely Theorized Agreements*, 108 Harv L Rev
1733 (1995).

[299] See, for example, *Crosby v National Foreign Trade Council*, 530 US 363, 374 n 8 (2000)
(declining to address the controversial question whether *Rice* should apply in foreign
relations cases, stating that "[w]e leave for another day a consideration in this context of
a presumption against preemption").

[300] See William N. Eskridge Jr. and Lauren E. Baer, *The Continuum of Deference: Supreme
Court Treatment of Agency Statutory Interpretations from Chevron to Hamdan*, 96 Georgetown
L J 1083, 1090 (2008) (finding "that the Court usually does not apply *Chevron* to cases
that are, according to *Mead* and other opinions, *Chevron*-eligible"). Few seem to infer
from this that *Chevron* is no longer good law.

[301] See Antonin Scalia, *Judicial Deference to Administrative Interpretations of Law*, 1989
Duke L J 511, 521 ("One who finds *more* often (as I do) that the meaning of a statute is
apparent from its text and from its relationship with other laws, thereby finds *less* often
that the triggering requirement for *Chevron* deference exists.").

[302] See also *Cipollone*, 505 US at 544 (Scalia, J, concurring in part and dissenting in part)
("Under the Supremacy Clause, our job is to interpret Congress's decrees of pre-emption
neither narrowly nor broadly, but in accordance with their apparent meaning.").

standing of the Supremacy Clause,[303] which has important implications for both the *Rice* presumption and the proper approach to
conflict preemption. This argument has particularly influenced
Justice Thomas,[304] who has developed the most fully theorized
approach to preemption among the current Justices, as well as
prominent advocates of broad federal preemption.[305] The second
debate concerns the extent to which the Court should analyze
preemption differently in different regulatory fields—in particular,
whether the *Rice* presumption should be confined to fields of traditional state primacy, while other rules should govern areas like
immigration and foreign affairs where the national government
has taken a leading role. Sections A and B of this part address the
Nelson argument as it pertains to *Rice* and to conflict preemption,
respectively. Section C considers the subject-matter scope of the
presumption against preemption.

A. NON OBSTANTE, PART I — CHALLENGING RICE

In an important article published just over a decade ago,[306] Caleb
Nelson challenged much of contemporary preemption doctrine as
inconsistent with the original understanding of the Supremacy
Clause. That Clause provides that the Constitution, treaties, and
federal statutes "shall be the supreme Law of the Land; and the
Judges in every State shall be bound thereby, any Thing in the
Constitution or Laws of any State to the Contrary notwithstanding."[307] Professor Nelson argues that the last phrase would have
been understood by the Founding generation as a *non obstante*
clause. These clauses were frequently employed to overcome the
ordinary presumption against implied repeals of prior law.[308] He
asserts that *Rice*'s presumption against preemption is inconsistent
with this understanding: "A general rule that express preemption
clauses should be read 'narrowly' . . . is hard to square with the

---

[303] Caleb Nelson, *Preemption*, 86 Va L Rev 225 (2000).

[304] See, for example, 131 S Ct at 2579 (plurality opinion) (endorsing Nelson's view on
conflict preemption).

[305] See, for example, Untereiner, 84 Tulane L Rev at 1267–68 (cited in note 11) (endorsing Nelson's critique of *Rice*).

[306] See Nelson, 86 Va L Rev 225 (cited in note 303).

[307] US Const, Art VI, cl 2.

[308] Nelson, 86 Va L Rev at 237–44 (cited in note 303).

Supremacy Clause's non obstante provision."[309] Nelson's argument adds a valuable historical perspective to the preemption debate, and I embrace a number of his conclusions here. I do not believe, however, that he provides a persuasive argument for abandoning *Rice*.[310]

The Court did not confront Professor Nelson's argument against *Rice* directly in the 2010 Term. It did debate his claim that the Supremacy Clause must be read as a *non obstante* provision, but in the distinct context of *implied* preemption. And the Court's *express* preemption decision in *Bruesewitz* seemed to reflect some implicit skepticism about *Rice* by simply avoiding citing it. The remainder of this section addresses Nelson's argument against *Rice* on its merits, while Section B considers the likelihood that the Court will ultimately accept it.

1. *The strength and nature of the Rice presumption.* As an initial matter, it is not clear that Professor Nelson means to reject the presumption against preemption as the Court has actually applied it. He notes that "[o]ne should not take [his critique of *Rice*] too far,"[311] and he has no quarrel with the proposition that "judges should generally be 'reluctant to infer pre-emption.'"[312] Nelson's analysis thus provides no support for industry groups that have argued for "a presumption in favor of preemption."[313] It seems fair to read his argument as foreclosing only a strong clear statement requirement for preemption—a presumption that, as Judge Wald once put it, "Congress did not intend to interfere with the traditional power and authority of the states unless it signaled its intention in neon lights."[314]

Any such "neon lights" requirement would be far more rigid than the way the Court has traditionally applied *Rice*.[315] Professor

---

[309] Id at 293.

[310] My argument in this section relies substantially on points made in an amicus brief that I filed on behalf of a group of constitutional and administrative law scholars in *Wyeth v Levine*. Brief of Amicus Curiae Constitutional and Administrative Law Scholars in Support of Respondent, *Wyeth v Levine*, No 06-1249, *9–14 (US Aug 14, 2008).

[311] Nelson, 86 Va L Rev at 294 (cited in note 303).

[312] Id at 293, quoting *Exxon Corp. v Governor of Maryland*, 437 US 117, 132 (1978).

[313] Brief of Amicus Curiae Product Liability Advisory Council, Inc., in Support of Petitioner at *15 (cited in note 111).

[314] Patricia M. Wald, *Some Observations on the Use of Legislative History in the 1981 Supreme Court Term*, 68 Iowa L Rev 195, 209 (1983).

[315] See, for example, Karen Petroski, Comment, *Retheorizing the Presumption Against*

Nelson's point seems better read as a corrective to the danger, identified by Professor Shapiro, that any interpretive canon "will constitute both the starting and the ending point of analysis rather than serving as a helpful tool in resolving difficult cases."[316] But as long as courts do not apply *Rice* "in a way that subordinates other sources of information" about legislative intent—that is, so long as they do not transform it into a strong clear statement requirement—this danger does not arise.[317] None of last Term's preemption cases used *Rice* to exclude other sources of statutory meaning, and most of the cases ignored it entirely. The problem is that *Rice* is overlooked, not over-read.

At times, Professor Nelson seems to limit his anti-*Rice* argument to express preemption cases—that is, to cases in which Congress explicitly has dealt with the question of preemption.[318] It is fair to read his point as sweeping somewhat more broadly, however, to challenge any rule of construction that encourages courts to "strain the federal law's meaning in order to harmonize it with state law."[319] Nelson rejects the idea "that judges have a general

Implied Repeals, 92 Cal L Rev 487, 520 (2004) (noting that "the presumption against preemption does not enjoy the near-categorical status that the presumption against implied repeals currently does on the Supreme Court"). Professor Nelson also acknowledges that, given the placement of the semicolon in the Supremacy Clause, "the non obstante provision might have been directed especially at state judges," Nelson, 86 Va L Rev at 260 (cited in note 303)—not at the federal courts. But see id at 258–59 (arguing that the Framers played fast and loose with punctuation).

[316] Shapiro, 67 NYU L Rev at 956 (cited in note 52). Professor Nelson confirms this point when he acknowledges that "most of us view genuinely ambiguous statutory language as a delegation to the courts of authority to pick one interpretation from among the group of interpretations that are best," Nelson, 86 Va L Rev at 296 (cited in note 303), and that "[m]ost of the time, of course, Congress will leave courts free to take account of state interests when exercising their delegated authority," id at 298. He insists only that "courts [must] apply the presumption only *after* they have used whatever tools our theory of statutory interpretation permits," id at 296, and that "judges do not have complete discretion to base their selection [of an otherwise permissible interpretation] on whatever factors they like," id at 297. Nelson thus rejects only a categorical presumption that would "permit courts to base the decision *entirely* on [federalism] concerns," id at 298 (emphasis in original). I, for one, have never seen a Supreme Court decision that rested "entirely" on the *Rice* presumption.

[317] Shapiro, 67 NYU L Rev at 957–58 (cited in note 52); see also id at 958 (noting that strong "clear statement" rules "exclude the kind of purposive analysis that permits a court to find a result implicit in a statutory enactment"); see also Clark, *Process-Based Preemption*, in Buzbee, ed, *Preemption Choice* 208–09 (cited in note 8) (construing Professor Nelson's argument as objecting primarily to a strong clear statement approach to the presumption against preemption).

[318] See text accompanying note 309; see also Nelson, 86 Va L Rev at 292 (cited in note 303).

[319] Nelson, 86 Va L Rev at 255 (cited in note 303).

obligation to harmonize federal law with whatever state law happens to exist."[320] He targets cases like *Merrill Lynch, Pierce, Fenner & Smith v Ware*, which have stated that "the proper approach [in preemption cases] is to reconcile 'the operation of both statutory schemes with one another rather than holding one completely ousted.'"[321] In Nelson's view, "[u]nless there is some particular reason (over and above the general presumption against implied repeals) to believe that Congress meant to avoid such a contradiction, the Supremacy Clause indicates that the content of state law should not alter the meaning of federal law."[322]

This aspect of Professor Nelson's view seems to require little, if any, departure from current doctrine. In express preemption cases, preemption doctrine is, in Professor Rosen's terms, wholly "unilateralist"—courts construe what law Congress intended to preempt and do not place any countervailing value on state law.[323] And even in implied conflicts cases, where courts may deem some minor level of conflict tolerable for the sake of preserving state authority, courts do not generally "weigh" federal interests against state ones. Nor do they "harmonize" state and federal law in the sense of compromising each to attain some consensus norm.[324] The *Rice* presumption itself is a tool for discerning the content of *federal* law and whether that law conflicts with state regulation. As Louise Weinberg has said, we should not "suppos[e] that the presumption in favor of state law operates in cases of identified 'actual' federal-state conflict. Identification of a federal-state conflict-in-fact is, precisely, what overcomes the presumption."[325]

Congress's intent controls, however, as to the sorts of state regulation that conflict with the federal regulatory scheme. Many preemption decisions reflect the fact that Congress often intends for state and federal regulation to operate cooperatively within the same field—a possibility for which Nelson allows (as he must).

---

[320] Id at 292.

[321] 414 US 117, 127 & n 8 (1973), quoting *Silver v New York Stock Exchange*, 373 US 341, 357 (1963).

[322] Nelson, 86 Va L Rev at 256 (cited in note 303).

[323] Rosen, 102 Nw U L Rev at 785 (cited in note 101).

[324] See sources cited in note 100.

[325] Louise Weinberg, *The Federal-State Conflict of Laws: "Actual" Conflicts*, 70 Tex L Rev 1743, 1756 (1992).

The objectionable language in *Merrill Lynch*, for example, required the Court to "reconcile" state and federal law precisely because "Congress, in the securities field, has not adopted a regulation system wholly apart from and exclusive of state regulation. Instead, Congress intended to subject the exchanges to state regulation that is not inconsistent with the federal Act."[326]

One might go beyond *Merrill Lynch*'s specific-intent situation in two senses, however. The first would be to suggest that Congress should *always* be read as intending to preserve state regulatory authority, in the absence of some clear expression of intent to the contrary. Such a general presumption may be justifiable on purely descriptive grounds—that is, as the most likely description of Congress's *actual* intent.[327] Several commentators have observed that Congress's general tendency when it enters a regulatory field is to leave concurrent state regulatory authority in place.[328] Professor Nelson seems to accept this aspect of *Rice* when he allows that "judges should generally be 'reluctant to infer pre-emption.'"[329]

Justice Souter proposed a second and perhaps somewhat stronger version of *Rice* when he asserted that "[i]f the [federal] statute's terms can be read sensibly not to have a pre-emptive effect, the presumption controls and no pre-emption may be inferred."[330]

---

[326] 414 US at 137. Specifically, the Court noted that "Section 6(c), 15 U. S. C. § 78f (c), explicitly subjects exchange rules to a requirement of consistency with the Act 'and the applicable laws of the State in which [the exchange] is located.'" See also id at 138 n 16 (noting that "[t]he Act contains other provisions indicating the intent of Congress that state law continues to apply where the Act itself does not").

[327] See, for example, Stephen F. Ross, *Where Have You Gone, Karl Llewellyn? Should Congress Turn Its Lonely Eyes to You?* 45 Vand L Rev 562, 563 (1991) ("Descriptive canons are principles that involve predictions as to what the legislature must have meant, or probably meant, by employing particular statutory language. . . . In contrast, normative canons are principles . . . that do not purport to describe accurately what Congress actually intended or what the words of a statute mean, but rather direct courts to construe any ambiguity in a particular way in order to further some policy objective." (footnotes omitted)).

[328] See Schapiro, *From Dualism to Polyphony* at 41 (cited in note 8) ("Since 1937, overlapping state and federal regulation has become the norm for many, if not most, subjects."); Robert R. M. Verchick and Nina Mendelson, *Preemption and Theories of Federalism*, in Buzbee, ed, *Preemption Choice* 13, 15 (cited in note 8) ("Congress regularly legislates to share power or to preserve state authority.").

[329] Nelson, 86 Va L Rev at 293 (cited in note 303), quoting *Exxon Corp. v Governor of Maryland*, 437 US 117, 132 (1978).

[330] *Gade v National Solid Wastes Management Assn.*, 505 US 88, 116–17 (1992) (Souter, J, dissenting).

This view, which has not (to my knowledge) been embraced in so many words by a majority of the Court, requires a court to choose the interpretation of ambiguous federal laws that best accommodates state regulatory efforts. This is probably where Professor Nelson would jump off the train, arguing that the meaning of a *non obstante* clause is to foreclose this sort of harmonization. It is not clear, however, that Justice Souter's formulation of *Rice* is really much of a step. As I discuss in the next section, any interpretive presumption that is not simply ornamental will have this sort of effect.

2. *The Supremacy Clause and canonical construction.* Even a soft presumption like *Rice* is not simply a tool for divining Congress's intent. What Justice Marshall said of "[c]lear-statement rules"— that they "operate less to reveal *actual* congressional intent than to shield important values from an *insufficiently* strong legislative intent to displace them"[331]—is also true of *Rice*. Some critics of the Supreme Court's clear statement rules have suggested that it is illegitimate for courts to apply "normative" canons protecting state autonomy.[332] Viet Dinh has extended this complaint to the presumption against preemption, arguing that it encourages judges to "rewrite the laws enacted by Congress."[333] For Professor Dinh, any interpretive rule not designed simply "to discern what Congress has legislated and whether such legislation displaces concurrent state law," risks "an illegitimate expansion of the judicial function."[334] At times, Professor Nelson appears to echo this criticism. That critique, however, runs counter to established traditions in our law of statutory construction.

All interpretive presumptions require, to varying degrees, that courts set aside the interpretation of a statute that would otherwise

---

[331] *EEOC v Arabian American Oil Co.*, 499 US 244, 262 (1991) (Marshall, J, dissenting).

[332] See Eskridge and Frickey, 45 Vand L Rev at 593, 632–45 (cited in note 53) (arguing that "the Court . . . is creating a domain of 'quasi-constitutional law' in certain areas"); Manning, 110 Colum L Rev at 404 (cited in note 84) (arguing that the federalism canons depend on abstract values of federalism, but that "[v]alues such as federalism . . . do not exist in freestanding form" in the Constitution). Professor Manning's thoughtful critique of "freestanding federalism" is largely beyond the scope of this essay. I note only that it would call into question not only canons of statutory construction like the *Rice* presumption, but also other doctrines based on broad notions of federalism, such as the judicial abstention and anti-commandeering doctrines. It would also require rejecting many other principles predicated on freestanding structural values, such as federal sovereign immunity and functionalist doctrines of separation of powers.

[333] Dinh, 88 Georgetown L J at 2092 (cited in note 295).

[334] Id.

be most likely (in view of the other sources of statutory meaning) in favor of some less likely reading. Professor Nelson seems to suggest that *Rice* should control only where the court is in equipoise between two interpretations of a federal statute, only one of which would preempt state law.[335] But there are very few "ties" in statutory interpretation.[336] And assuming that the plausible interpretations are not actually *equal*, *Rice*'s presumption will matter only in those cases in which it prompts a court to choose the *less* likely reading; otherwise, the presumption does no independent work.[337] The function of an interpretive canon is thus to allow certain extrinsic elements—rules of linguistic usage, constitutional and subconstitutional values—to shape statutory construction. When Justice Souter says that *Rice* should counsel courts to choose nonpreemptive readings of federal statutes over preemptive ones, he is simply being specific about the traditional and utterly typical operation of interpretive presumptions.

The operation of such rules is foundational to the role of courts in statutory construction. Many commentators have pointed out that "[a]s applied to novel or unanticipated circumstances, all laws are more or less indeterminate," so that "courts necessarily engage in some degree of interstitial norm elaboration."[338] James Madison recognized as much in *The Federalist*:

---

[335] Nelson, 86 Va L Rev at 265 (cited in note 303); see also John F. Manning, *Textualism and the Equity of the Statute*, 101 Colum L Rev 1, 123 (2001) (criticizing clear statement rules to the extent that they "sometimes require judges to reject the most natural reading of a statute in favor of a plausible but less conventional interpretation").

[336] See, for example, Frederick Schauer, *Ashwander Revisited*, 1995 Supreme Court Review 71, 83 ("It is hard to imagine a case in which . . . there would be two identically plausible interpretations, such that . . . the rational judge would be reduced to something akin to tossing a coin."). Justice Scalia has said much the same thing about *Chevron*, observing that its interpretive rule "becomes virtually meaningless . . . if ambiguity exists only when the arguments for and against the various possible interpretations are in absolute equipoise. If nature knows of such equipoise in legal arguments, the courts at least do not." Scalia, 1989 Duke L J at 520 (cited in note 301). He concludes that "[i]f *Chevron* is to have any meaning, then, congressional intent must be regarded as 'ambiguous' not just when no interpretation is even marginally better than any other, but rather when two or more reasonable, though not necessarily equally valid, interpretations exist." Id.

[337] Justice Scalia and certain less august commentators have made a similar point about the constitutional avoidance canon. See *Almendarez-Torres v United States*, 523 US 224, 270 (1998) (Scalia, J, dissenting) (discussing the canon of constitutional avoidance); Ernest A. Young, *Constitutional Avoidance, Resistance Norms, and the Preservation of Judicial Review*, 78 Tex L Rev 1549, 1577–78 (2000) (same).

[338] Clark, *Process-Based Preemption* at 205 (cited in note 79); see also Amanda L. Tyler, *Continuity, Coherence, and the Canons*, 99 Nw U L Rev 1389, 1404 (2005) ("No one can debate seriously the need for some default rules in statutory construction. Indeed, courts consistently are called upon to make sense of ambiguous statutory language and to plug

> All new laws, though penned with the greatest technical skill and passed on the fullest and most mature deliberation, are considered as more or less obscure and equivocal, until their meaning be liquidated and ascertained by a series of particular discussions and adjudications.[339]

Eschewing the use of interpretive canons or presumptions in favor of relying on the "plain text"—as the majority purported to do last Term in *Bruesewitz*, for example[340]—thus risks submerging the courts' actual rationale for decision. If courts do not simply employ default rules without acknowledgment, they will need to recur either to increasingly attenuated sources of congressional intent or to their own policy judgments. Neither of those options is likely to appeal to textualists. The canons have at least the virtue of articulating the tiebreaker rules in play, so that they may be discussed and defended. As Amanda Tyler has recognized, "[t]he real question is what default rules we should have where the formal evidence of congressional purpose—i.e., statutory enactment— leaves us shorthanded."[341]

Professor Nelson concedes that the *non obstante* language in the Clause is directed only at the generic presumption against implied repeals. "While the *non obstante* provision tells courts not to apply the general presumption against implied repeals in preemption cases," he says, "it does not require them to discard their other tools of statutory interpretation."[342] Those tools include, as I have already suggested, an awareness that concurrent regulation—not wholesale ouster of the states—is the dominant pattern of contemporary national policy. They also include the basic proposition that "[n]ew statutes fit into the normal operation of the legal system unless the political branches provide otherwise"[343] and the concomitant role of the courts in harmonizing new enactments with preexisting law. David Shapiro has demonstrated that most of the canons serve "the essentially conservative role of the courts

---

statutory gaps. Congress does not and cannot necessarily contemplate every future application of a statute at the time of its drafting.").

[339] Federalist 37 (Madison), in *The Federalist* at 236 (cited in note 20).

[340] See 131 S Ct at 1081.

[341] Tyler, 99 Nw U L Rev at 1404 (cited in note 338).

[342] Nelson, 86 Va L Rev at 294 (cited in note 303).

[343] Frank H. Easterbrook, *The Case of the Speluncean Explorers: Revisited*, 112 Harv L Rev 1913, 1914 (1999); see also Stephen E. Sachs, *Constitutional Backdrops*, at 25–26 (unpublished manuscript on file with author) (explaining that new statutes are ordinarily "defeasible" by background principles of law even if the text does not refer to those principles).

. . . in the more moderate sense of accommodating change to the larger, essentially stable context in which it occurs."[344] One can agree with Nelson that courts should not distort the meaning of federal statutes in order to avoid preemption without accepting that the Framers of the Supremacy Clause meant courts to abandon this basic function.

Most importantly, the "other tools of statutory interpretation" have traditionally included a broad imperative to construe statutes in light of constitutional values, including our constitutional commitment to federalism. I have argued elsewhere that constitutional principles are often implemented through statutes and other forms of "ordinary" law.[345] This is particularly true of federalism, which has from the beginning been implemented not simply through Article I's division of powers but also through statutes allocating the division of labor between, and law applied in, the state and federal courts,[346] structuring state political processes and regulating the behavior of state officials,[347] and—especially in the modern era—delegating significant responsibilities to state governments within federal programs.[348] When statutes implement constitutional principles, statutory construction becomes a critical part of the "reasoned elaboration" of constitutional values.[349] As Henry Hart and Al Sacks wrote over a half century ago,

---

[344] Shapiro, 67 NYU L Rev at 925 (cited in note 52).

[345] See generally Young, 117 Yale L J at 408 (cited in note 13).

[346] See, for example, 28 USC §§ 1251, 1257 (giving the Supreme Court jurisdiction over "all controversies between two or more States" and "All controversies between the United States and a State," as well as the power to review the decisions of the states' highest courts); Anti-Injunction Act, 28 USC § 2283 (generally prohibiting federal courts from enjoining state-court proceedings); Rules of Decision Act, 28 USC § 1652 ("The laws of the several states, except where the Constitution or treaties of the United States or Acts of Congress otherwise require or provide, shall be regarded as rules of decision in civil actions in the courts of the United States, in cases where they apply.").

[347] See, for example, Voting Rights Act of 1965, Pub L No 89-110, Title 1, § 5, 79 Stat 439 (1965), codified as amended at 42 USC § 1973c; 42 USC § 1983; Equal Employment Opportunity Act of 1972, Pub L No 92-261, 86 Stat 103 (1972), codified as amended at 42 USC § 2000e(a) (extending Title VII of the 1964 Civil Rights Act to cover state governments).

[348] See, for example, Clean Air Act, 42 USC § 7401 et seq (regulating air emissions by, in part, establishing "National Ambient Air Quality Standards" for every state and requiring participating states to develop and enforce state implementation plans to reach those standards); Patient Protection and Affordable Care Act, Pub L No 111-148, 124 Stat 119 (2010), to be codified in scattered sections of 26, 42 USC) (using federal and state regulators to address health care reform). On the critical importance of such delegations to federalism, see, for example, Bulman-Pozen and Gerken, 118 Yale L J 1256 (cited in note 35).

[349] See Young, 98 Cal L Rev at 1384–86 (cited in note 287).

> Not only does every particular legal arrangement have its own particular purpose but that purpose is always a subordinate one in aid of the more general and thus more nearly ultimate purposes of the law. Doubts about the purposes of particular statutes or decisional doctrines, it would seem to follow, must be resolved, if possible, so as to harmonize them with more general principles and policies.[350]

Canons of statutory construction play a pivotal role in this effort. The "rule of lenity" harmonizes criminal statutes with broader principles of due process,[351] for example, and the canon of constitutional avoidance is best understood as a tool for protecting a variety of constitutional principles.[352]

Normative canons can play this role even when the underlying constitutional value might otherwise be extremely difficult for courts to enforce. Clear statement rules disfavoring restrictions on the jurisdiction of the federal courts, for example, may be the *only* viable way, in many instances, of protecting values of judicial independence grounded in Article III.[353] This is especially true of federalism, which has been underenforced at least since 1937, and many of the Court's pro-federalism clear statement rules predate the Rehnquist Court's "federalist revival."[354] As I have already discussed, the *Rice* presumption is an important aspect of this phenomenon.

If Professor Nelson's argument forbids reliance on *Rice*'s presumption against preemption, it is equally hostile to the Court's other pro-federalism clear statement rules. These include rules disfavoring interpretations of federal statutes that would impose conditions on states' acceptance of federal funds,[355] subject the

---

[350] Henry M. Hart Jr. and Albert M. Sacks, *The Legal Process: Basic Problems in the Making and Application of Law* 148 (William N. Eskridge Jr. & Philip P. Frickey, eds) (Foundation, 1994).

[351] See Cass R. Sunstein, *Nondelegation Canons*, 67 U Chi L Rev 315, 332 (2000) ("The rule of lenity is inspired by the due process constraint on conviction pursuant to open-ended or vague statutes.").

[352] See Young, 78 Tex L Rev at 1585 (cited in note 337); Philip P. Frickey, *Getting from Joe to Gene (McCarthy): The Avoidance Canon, Legal Process Theory, and Narrowing Statutory Interpretation in the Early Warren Court*, 93 Cal L Rev 397 (2005).

[353] See Young, 78 Tex L Rev at 1587 (cited in note 337).

[354] See, for example, *United States v Bass*, 404 US 336 (1971); *Murdoch v Memphis* 87 US (20 Wall) 590 (1875) (refusing to find that Congress intended to extend U.S. Supreme Court review to questions of state law on appeal from the state courts absent a clear statement of Congress's intent to that effect).

[355] *Arlington Central School District Board of Education v Murphy*, 548 US 291 (2006); *South Dakota v Dole*, 483 US 203 (1987).

states to statutory liability under federal law,[356] abrogate the states' sovereign immunity,[357] regulate the traditional functions of state government,[358] intrude on traditional concerns of state criminal law,[359] or regulate at the outer limits of Congress's Commerce Clause authority.[360] Each of these rules potentially alters the construction of federal statutes based on concern for state governmental autonomy; each, therefore, would seem to run afoul of the argument that the Supremacy Clause permits no presumption against "implied repeals" of state prerogatives. The ubiquity of these rules, however, and the decades of precedent behind many of them, emphasizes the radical change that a broad reading of Nelson's argument would impose on the federal law of statutory construction. One might thus apply the canon of avoidance to Nelson's argument itself, preferring a more modest reading that would leave this pervasive and traditional judicial function intact.

3. *Rice and the contemporary structure of federalism doctrine.* The *Rice* presumption rests not on the implied repeals canon but rather on the evolving structure of our federalism. The presumption, along with the Court's other federalism-based "clear statement" rules, developed long after the period examined by Professor Nelson. They developed for a reason: The Founders' initial institutional strategy for limiting national power and preserving state autonomy had failed. That strategy relied on the specific enumeration of national powers in Article I of the Constitution and the Tenth Amendment's corresponding reservation of all other powers to the states. As I described in Part I, this dual federalist regime ultimately collapsed as a result of the Court's difficulty in drawing determinate boundaries to cabin terms like "commerce among the several states" and "necessary and proper," as well as due to increasing pressure for national regulation in response to industrialization and economic crisis. Notwithstanding the Rehnquist Court's effort to retain *some* limits on the Commerce

---

[356] *Will v Michigan Dept. of State Police*, 491 US 58 (1989).

[357] *Atascadero State Hospital v Scanlon*, 473 US 234 (1985); see also *Chisholm v Georgia*, 2 US (2 Dall) 419, 429 (1793) (Iredell, J, dissenting).

[358] *Gregory v Ashcroft*, 501 US 452 (1991).

[359] *United States v Bass*, 404 US 336 (1971).

[360] *Solid Waste Agency of Northern Cook County v United States Army Corps of Engineers*, 531 US 159 (2001); *United States v Jones*, 529 US 848 (2000).

Power,[361] the principle of enumerated powers now offers relatively little constraint on national action.[362]

The expanding scope of potential federal regulatory authority in the mid-twentieth century transformed our federalism from a regime of separate spheres to one of concurrent powers. With few constitutional constraints on what Congress *can* do, the action shifts to what Congress *has* done. To the extent that the Court fashions doctrines to protect federalism in a concurrent regime, then, those doctrines must take a different form. As Louise Weinberg has observed, "the very absence of formal impediments to the erosion of dual federalism has elicited from the Supreme Court a variety of prudential means of shoring up state power."[363] These include judge-made abstention doctrines,[364] narrowing constructions of critical federal statutes,[365] and a variety of state-protective "clear statement" rules.[366] As the cases just cited demonstrate, this process of subconstitutional protection for federalism has been going on for a very long time. The *Rice* presumption is less mandatory than these other doctrines—it influences close cases of statutory construction, rather than requiring a particular result in all cases within its scope—but it is otherwise in the same vein.

Rice also responds to the parallel shift from relatively vigorous

---

[361] See *United States v Lopez*, 514 US 549 (1995) (holding that Congress did not have authority under the Commerce Clause to regulate guns in schools); *United States v Morrison*, 529 US 598 (2000) (holding that certain provisions of the Violence Against Women Act exceeded federal power).

[362] See, for example, *Gonzales v Raich*, 545 US 1 (2005) (holding that the Commerce Clause gives Congress authority to prohibit production and use of medical marijuana); Young, *Popular Constitutionalism* (cited in note 127) (arguing that enumerated limits on Congress's powers are "underenforced").

[363] Weinberg, 70 Tex L Rev at 1749 (cited in note 325).

[364] See, for example, *Younger v Harris*, 401 US 37 (1971) (requiring federal courts to abstain from enjoining pending state criminal proceedings); *Railroad Commission v Pullman Co.*, 312 US 496 (1941) (requiring federal courts to abstain in order to allow state courts to decide unresolved questions of state law that might permit federal court to avoid a federal constitutional question).

[365] See, for example, *Murdoch v City of Memphis*, 87 US 590 (1875) (construing the Judiciary Act to foreclose U.S. Supreme Court review of state court decisions on state law issues); *Wainwright v Sykes*, 433 US 72 (1977) (construing the *habeas* statute to disallow federal court review of federal claims not presented to the state courts unless the petitioner can show cause and prejudice for the default).

[366] See, for example, *Gregory v Ashcroft*, 501 US 452 (1991) (holding that Congress must clearly state its intent to regulate the traditional functions of state government); *Will v Michigan Dept. of State Police*, 491 US 58 (1989) (Congress must speak clearly in order to subject states to federal liability); *United States v Bass*, 404 US 336, 349 (1971) (Congress must speak clearly in order to intrude on state criminal jurisdiction).

judicial enforcement of constitutional boundaries to a primary reliance on political and procedural checks on national authority. Given that current federalism doctrine emphasizes the states' representation in Congress as the primary protection for federalism, "a presumption against preemption promotes legislative deliberation" about the implications of federal legislation for state autonomy.[367] Likewise, *Rice*'s presumption "may be used to implement constitutionally prescribed lawmaking procedures by ensuring that Congress and the president—rather than judges—make the crucial decision to override state law"; this is especially important because those procedures are "cumbersome and exclusive" by design.[368] As Justice O'Connor wrote in *Gregory*, "'to give the state-displacing weight of federal law to mere congressional *ambiguity* would evade the very procedure for lawmaking on which *Garcia* relied to protect states' interests.'"[369] The *Rice* presumption is thus consistent with contemporary federalism doctrine's emphasis on the political and procedural safeguards of federalism.

Professor Nelson asserts that "even though the political safeguards of federalism may affect Congress's policy choices, they do not compel any particular rules for construing the resulting statutes"; moreover, "[f]or courts always to adopt narrowing constructions of *the language that Congress enacts* would be to give the political safeguards of federalism a kind of double weight."[370] But even the *Garcia* Court did not say that the "political safeguards of federalism" (not to mention the *procedural* ones, which Nelson does not address) were never to be enforced by courts. The Court simply said that "the fundamental limitation that the constitutional scheme imposes on the Commerce Clause to protect the 'States as States' is one of process rather than one of result," and it suggested that any judicial doctrine limiting national power "must

---

[367] Verchick and Mendelson, *Preemption and Theories of Federalism* at 23 (cited in note 328).

[368] Clark, *Process-Based Preemption* at 213 (cited in note 79).

[369] *Gregory*, 501 US at 464, quoting Tribe, *American Constitutional Law* at § 6-25 (cited in note 30); see also Tribe, 1 *American Constitutional Law* at § 5-11 (cited in note 30) (explaining that *Gregory*'s clear statement rule "ensures the efficacy of the procedural political safeguards that were *Garcia*'s focus"). To say this is not necessarily to demand that Congress's preemptive intent must be explicit in the statutory text, as a clear statement rule would require. Rather, it is simply to ask that Congress's intent be clear based on the traditional sources by which courts generally determine that intent, including statutory structure, legislative history, and the like.

[370] Nelson, 86 Va L Rev at 299–300, 301 (cited in note 303) (emphasis in original).

find its justification in the procedural nature of this basic limitation."[371] Process-oriented judicial review, of course, can nonetheless be quite robust, as John Hart Ely's "representation reinforcement" approach to individual rights has famously demonstrated.[372] I have argued elsewhere that *Garcia* in fact supports a "Democracy and Distrust" approach to federalism, where the Court would emphasize process-oriented doctrines that would ensure that the political and procedural safeguards of federalism are respected and, where possible, enhance the operation of those safeguards.[373] Certainly the *Rice* presumption—which implements and enhances political and procedural checks on federal power but which imposes no substantive limits on congressional action—fits *Garcia*'s mandate that judicial review "must be tailored to compensate for possible failings in the national political process rather than to dictate a 'sacred province of state autonomy.'"[374]

Viewed in context, the *non obstante* aspect of the Supremacy Clause responded to a particular institutional relationship between state and federal law. In the early Republic, the new national government struggled to stake out a role in a political environment dominated by preexisting state governments.[375] In that circumstance, it made some sense to construe federal enactments broadly and subordinate concerns about preempting too much of the preexisting state legal background. But the world is very different now. As the current editors of the *Hart & Wechsler* casebook have pointed out, in the twentieth century "the expansion of federal legislation and administrative regulation . . . has accelerated. . . . [A]t present federal law appears to be more primary than interstitial in numerous areas."[376] And the norm in this denser regulatory environment is for state and federal legislation to coexist.[377] Indeed, the contemporary danger to our federal balance comes from the overexpansion of federal authority at the expense of state autonomy.[378]

---

[371] 469 US at 554.

[372] See Ely, *Democracy and Distrust* (cited in note 48).

[373] See sources cited in note 47.

[374] 469 US at 554, quoting *EEOC v Wyoming*, 460 US 226, 236 (1983).

[375] See generally Young, 46 Wm & Mary L Rev at 1751–52, 1775–76 (cited in note 20).

[376] *Hart & Wechsler* at 459 (cited in note 90).

[377] See sources cited in note 328.

[378] See Young, 46 Wm & Mary L Rev at 1806–09 (cited in note 20).

Under present circumstances, abandoning the *Rice* presumption would undermine an already weak set of constitutional safeguards for state autonomy. I have defended the presumption against preemption elsewhere as a necessary "compensating adjustment" to preserve the Constitution's commitment to federalism in an era when the courts no longer enforce strong substantive limits on Congress's enumerated powers and rely instead on political and procedural checks on federal legislative action.[379] To the extent that the Framers did intend a strong *non obstante* reading of the Supremacy Clause, they assumed it would operate in an institutional context defined by strong enumerated powers constraints on federal action, separation-of-powers constraints sharply limiting the production of federal law, and vigorous judicial enforcement of all those constraints. These assumptions no longer hold.[380] It makes little sense to apply a contemporary sense of the scope of Congress's regulatory authority and the role of judicial review in constitutional federalism cases but insist on a circa-1789 set of preemption rules.

One need not go so far, however, because courts can give effect to the Framers' original understanding of the Supremacy Clause as a *non obstante* provision without rejecting *Rice*. As I have already discussed, Professor Nelson's reading of the Clause may foreclose only weighing state interests against federal ones in preemption cases, "harmonizing" federal law with state law in ways that subvert the clear intent of Congress, or converting *Rice* into a strong clear statement rule that would disallow recourse to the traditional tools of statutory construction. The Supreme Court has applied *Rice*, however, as a "plus factor" for resolving close cases under ambiguous statutes. As the cases in the 2010 Term demonstrate, the problem with *Rice*'s presumption against preemption is not that it is inconsistent with the Supremacy Clause, but rather that it is too frequently ignored.

---

[379] See id at 1848–50. On compensating adjustments, see generally id at 1748–62; Adrian Vermeule, *Hume's Second-Best Constitutionalism*, 70 U Chi L Rev 421, 426 (2003). This approach is controversial. See, for example, John F. Manning, *Federalism and the Generality Problem in Constitutional Interpretation*, 122 Harv L Rev 2003 (2009); Michael J. Klarman, *Antifidelity*, 70 S Cal L Rev 381 (1997). That debate, which I have addressed in the earlier work cited above, is beyond the scope of the present essay.

[380] See, for example, Gary Lawson, *The Rise and Rise of the Administrative State*, 107 Harv L Rev 1231 (1994).

B. NON OBSTANTE, PART 2 — IMPLIED PREEMPTION

Professor Nelson's originalist reading of the Supremacy Clause has quite different implications for cases of *implied* preemption. Nelson argues that the Framers' understanding of the Supremacy Clause, within the context of a broader doctrine of repeals, compels a particular test for conflict preemption: state law is preempted only if there is a "logical contradiction" between state and federal law.[381] Under this approach, implied conflict preemption would generally be much narrower than the doctrine applied in many recent cases. Justice Thomas, for whom Nelson clerked in the 1994 Term, has adopted this argument in a series of separate opinions, and this body of opinions represents the most sustained effort by any Justice to develop a full-blown theory of preemption. Last Term, in *PLIVA*, he persuaded three other Justices—Roberts, Scalia, and Alito—to join that theory.[382] This section considers Professor Nelson's arguments about implied preemption, their contribution to Justice Thomas's emerging theory, and the implications of these arguments for future doctrine.

According to Professor Nelson, "the Supremacy Clause puts the doctrine of preemption within the same general framework as the traditional doctrine of repeals," which held that a later law superseded an earlier one only where the two provisions were "repugnant" to one another.[383] The Supremacy Clause established a rule of federal priority rather than a temporal one, but "the Supremacy Clause's rule of priority matters only when state law is 'repugnant to' valid federal law; the rule of priority comes into play only when courts cannot apply *both* state law *and* federal law, but instead must choose between them."[384] Under this "logical-contradiction test," broad notions of obstacle preemption are unconstitutional.[385] Nelson concludes that, under this view, "courts could no longer find preemption simply because they think that

---

[381] Nelson, 86 Va L Rev at 260 (cited in note 303).

[382] 131 S Ct at 2579–80 (plurality opinion). Justice Kennedy, who provided the fifth vote for the remainder of Thomas's *PLIVA* opinion, did not join the *non obstante* section.

[383] Nelson, 86 Va L Rev at 236, 245–46 (cited in note 303), quoting William Blackstone, 1 *Commentaries* 59 (1765).

[384] Nelson, 86 Va L Rev at 251 (cited in note 303).

[385] Id at 260, 265–90.

state law hinders accomplishment of the 'full purposes and objectives' behind a federal statute."[386]

Justice Thomas adopted some of this reasoning three Terms
ago, in his separate concurrence in *Wyeth*. There, Thomas announced that "I have become increasingly skeptical of this Court's
'purposes and objectives' pre-emption jurisprudence," which "routinely invalidates state laws based on perceived conflicts with broad
federal policy objectives, legislative history, or generalized notions
of congressional purposes that are not embodied within the text
of federal law."[387] These "implied pre-emption doctrines that wan-
der far from the statutory text," he concluded, "are inconsistent
with the Constitution."[388] Thomas's argument in *Wyeth* rested
primarily on two grounds: First, he read the Supremacy Clause
to require "that pre-emptive effect be given only to those federal
standards and policies that are set forth in, or necessarily follow
from, the statutory text that was produced through the constitutionally required bicameral and presentment procedures."[389]
This "structural limitation" preludes implied preemption "based
on [the Court's] interpretation of broad federal policy objectives,
legislative history, or generalized notions of congressional purposes that are not contained within the text of federal law."[390]
Second, Thomas emphasized the incompatibility of obstacle preemption with judicial restraint. "[T]his brand of the Court's preemption jurisprudence," he said, "facilitates freewheeling, extratextual, and broad evaluations of the 'purposes and objectives'
embodied within federal law," leading to "decisions giving improperly broad pre-emptive effect to judicially manufactured policies, rather than to the statutory text enacted by Congress."[391]
Wyeth cited Professor Nelson's work and suggested that Nelson's
"logical contradiction" test might provide a superior approach to
conflict preemption questions.[392]

Justice Thomas's opinion last Term in *PLIVA* went further, explicitly adopting Professor Nelson's reading that "[t]he phrase 'any

---

[386] Id at 304.
[387] 555 US at 583 (Thomas, J, concurring in the judgment).
[388] Id.
[389] Id at 586.
[390] Id at 586, 587.
[391] 555 US at 604.
[392] Id at 590.

[state law] to the Contrary notwithstanding' [in the Supremacy Clause] is a non obstante provision."[393] This aspect of the Clause "therefore suggests that federal law should be understood to impliedly repeal conflicting state law"; moreover, it also "suggests that courts should not strain to find ways to reconcile federal law with seemingly conflicting state law."[394] Justice Kennedy declined to join this section of the opinion, and Justice Sotomayor's dissent criticized the plurality for "adopt[ing] the novel theory that the Framers intended for the Supremacy Clause to operate as a so-called non obstante provision."[395] According to Sotomayor, "[t]he plurality's new theory of the Supremacy Clause is a direct assault" on *Rice* and many other precedents "presum[ing] that federal law does not pre-empt, or repeal, state law."[396]

It is easy to see the reasons for Justice Sotomayor's concern. As she noted, "whereas [the Court has] long required evidence of a 'clear and manifest' purpose to pre-empt, the plurality now instructs courts to 'look no further than the ordinary meaning of federal law' before concluding that Congress must have intended to cast aside state law."[397] The implications of Justice Thomas's approach are complex, however. As Sotomayor acknowledged, "[t]he plurality . . . carefully avoid[ed] discussing the ramifications of its new theory for the longstanding presumption against preemption";[398] instead, Justice Thomas invoked the *non obstante* argument as part of the Court's most sophisticated discussion to date of *impossibility* preemption. The upshot of *PLIVA* was to make impossibility preemption somewhat easier to establish. The Court held that manufacturers of generic drugs had made out a case of impossibility preemption because the manufacturers could not comply with state-law labeling requirements without seeking prior federal approval—even though that approval might well have been forthcoming if they had sought it.[399]

It is critical to remember, however, that for *PLIVA*'s author,

---

[393] 131 S Ct at 2579 (plurality opinion), citing Nelson, 86 Va L Rev at 238–40 (cited in note 303).

[394] 131 S Ct at 2580.

[395] Id at 2590 (Sotomayor, J, dissenting).

[396] Id at 2591.

[397] Id (citation omitted).

[398] Id at 2591 n 14.

[399] See Part II.B (discussing *PLIVA*, 131 S Ct 2567 (2010)).

impossibility is the *only* kind of conflict preemption; in *Wyeth*, after all, Thomas rejected "obstacle" preemption as unconstitutional. Taking the two positions together—a loosening of impossibility preemption in *PLIVA*, and a rejection of obstacle preemption in *Wyeth*—the result is surely a net gain for preemption opponents. *PLIVA*'s significance is limited to contexts in which the source of impossibility is a need for government approval to take an action required by state law, and it is also cabined by *Wyeth* itself, which held that a regulated entity can *not* establish impossibility simply by showing that a step required by state law would ultimately be subject to a federal regulatory veto.[400] On the other hand, there are hordes of obstacle preemption claims out there, and eliminating this whole category of preemption would significantly limit the preemptive impact of federal law.

There is, of course, one rather large fly in this ointment. Justice Thomas's expansion of impossibility preemption was for a majority of the Court (even if he did not get five for the *non obstante* aspect of his argument), while his rejection of obstacle preemption remains a dissenting position. Worse, he has not thus far been able to persuade *any* other Justices to join him in rejecting "purposes and objectives" preemption. If the Court lowers the bar to impossibility preemption while maintaining a broad view of obstacle preemption, that would hardly be good for state autonomy.

Last Term's cases did, however, provide some evidence that the Court is raising the overall bar for conflict preemption. The Court rejected a strong obstacle preemption argument in *Whiting*, and while the majority did not invoke *Rice* per se, Chief Justice Roberts's opinion did insist that "[o]ur precedents 'establish that a high threshold must be met if a state law is to be pre-empted for conflicting with the purposes of a federal Act.'"[401] The Chief echoed Justice Thomas's call for judicial restraint in *Wyeth* when he said that "[i]mplied preemption analysis does not justify a 'freewheeling judicial inquiry into whether a state statute is in tension

---

[400] See Part II.C. But see James M. Beck, *Top Ten Best Prescription Drug/Medical Device Decisions of 2011*, Drug and Device Law (Dec 30, 2011), online at http://druganddevicelaw.blogspot .com/2011/12/top-ten-best-prescription-drugmedical.html (predicting that *PLIVA*'s holding is "usable elsewhere . . . [considering] how that test might play in the context of, say, black box warnings, design defect claims (both drugs and non-PMA devices), Dear Doctor letters, and any other situation where our clients are required to get the FDA's (or some other federal agency's) sign off before doing this or that").

[401] 131 S Ct at 1985, quoting *Gade*, 505 US at 110 (Kennedy, J, concurring in part and in the judgment).

with federal objectives'; such an endeavor 'would undercut the principle that it is Congress rather than the courts that preempts state law.'"[402]

Perhaps equally significant, a unanimous Court in *Williamson* made a critical point about the preemptive effects of federal cost/benefit analyses. Although the federal agency had determined that requiring lap-and-shoulder belts in rear interior seats would not be cost effective, the Court rejected the notion that a contrary judgment under state law would pose an obstacle to federal policy. Justice Breyer explained:

> [M]any, perhaps most, federal safety regulations embody some kind of cost-effectiveness judgment. . . . [T]o infer from the mere existence of such a cost-effectiveness judgment that the federal agency intends to bar States from imposing stricter standards would treat all such federal standards as if they were *maximum* standards, eliminating the possibility that the federal agency seeks only to set forth a *minimum* standard potentially supplemented through state tort law. We cannot reconcile this consequence with a statutory saving clause that foresees the likelihood of a continued meaningful role for state tort law.[403]

Given *Geier*'s holding that the mere existence of such a savings clause does not foreclose obstacle preemption arguments,[404] *Williamson*'s statement seems generalizable to most obstacle preemption contexts: A federal agency's decision not to impose a regulatory requirement based on a cost/benefit calculus will not, without more, necessarily preempt a state-law judgment that such a requirement *is* cost effective. Many preemption arguments take just this form, and *Williamson* should make that sort of argument much harder to win.

Finally, even *Bruesewitz* may contain some good news for opponents of obstacle preemption. *Bruesewitz* was an express preemption case, and it ruled in favor of preemption. But the opinions featured a key methodological disagreement between Justice Scalia's majority opinion, with its somewhat remarkable unwillingness to consider arguments outside the text of the statute, and the concurrence and dissent, respectively, of Justices Breyer and Sotomayor. Although they disagreed as to outcome, both Breyer

---

[402] 131 S Ct at 1985, quoting *Gade*, 505 US at 111 (Kennedy, J, concurring in part and in the judgment).

[403] 131 S Ct at 1139.

[404] See 529 US at 869 ("We now conclude that the saving clause . . . does *not* bar the ordinary working of conflict pre-emption principles.").

and Sotomayor were willing to consider a much broader universe of agency positions and policy arguments to resolve what otherwise seemed a close case on the text alone.[405] Obstacle preemption arguments, of course, tend to rely heavily on precisely these sorts of arguments, and the determination of a majority of the Court to stick close to the text—if it holds in other contexts—may well cut against obstacle preemption more often than not. However, *Bruesewitz* also highlights one of the obstacles, if you will, to adoption of Thomas's position by a majority of the Court. At least some of the Court's liberal wing, who generally tend to vote against preemption, are methodologically attached either to policy arguments generally (Sotomayor) or to both policy arguments and agency views (Breyer).[406] Breyer, after all, was the author of *Geier*, which found obstacle preemption in the teeth of an express savings clause for state common law claims.[407] Those methodological commitments will make it difficult for the liberals to abandon obstacle preemption altogether, although they may take a narrower view of it than some of their more conservative colleagues.

It thus seems possible that Justice Thomas will influence some of his conservative colleagues to take a narrower view of obstacle preemption, but consensus on that point seems likely to remain elusive. The other obvious question concerns the implications of these arguments about implied preemption for the *Rice* presumption. After all, Professor Nelson framed his attack on broad notions of implied preemption and his critique of the *Rice* presumption as two sides of the same coin. One observer has noted that "*Mensing* . . . reveals a Court that is about as evenly split as it is possible to be on the presumption against preemption, with four Justices saying no, four saying yes, and Justice Kennedy (who else on this Court?) supporting preemption without feeling the need to address that issue."[408] And Justice Stevens—the author of both *Altria* and *Wyeth* and the Court's most consistently anti-preemption Jus-

---

[405] See notes 221–26 and accompanying text.

[406] See generally Stephen G. Breyer, *Active Liberty: Interpreting Our Democratic Constitution* (Vintage, 2005).

[407] 529 US at 869–74. Justice Thomas wrote separately in *Williamson* primarily to express his continuing dissent from that approach. See 131 S Ct at 1141–42 (Thomas, J, concurring in the judgment).

[408] Beck, *Top Ten Best Decisions* (cited in note 400).

tice during his long tenure[409]—is no longer on the Court.

The Court's failure to invoke *Rice* as part of a majority holding in any of the five cases last Term may provide some evidence that the presumption against preemption is in trouble, notwithstanding the reasons already given not to take that failure too seriously. And Justice Thomas (joined by the Chief and Justices Scalia and Alito) signaled his opposition to applying *Rice* to express preemption in his *Altria* dissent three years ago.[410] It is not clear, however, that Thomas's emerging position ought to foreclose a presumption against preemption. First, the Nelson/Thomas position on conflict preemption, functionally speaking, *is* a form of *Rice*. By ruling out obstacle preemption and requiring a "direct" conflict or "logical contradiction" between federal and state law, Thomas would raise the bar—quite substantially—for conflict preemption. That result would strengthen *Rice*'s presumption against preemption in conflict cases.

Nor is it clear that Justice Thomas's rejection of *Rice* for *express* preemption in his *Altria* dissent follows from the other positions he has taken. In particular, Thomas's separate opinion in *Wyeth* emphasized the procedural safeguards of federalism: obstacle preemption based on extratextual evidence of Congress's broad purpose, he argued, contravened the Supremacy Clause's command that only textual mandates that have run Article I's legislative gauntlet can supersede state law.[411] The *Rice* presumption in express cases rests on similar arguments. I have argued that the presumption against preemption is designed to ensure that Congress deliberates about preemption and that preemption does not occur unless its proponents have surmounted the procedural obstacles to federal lawmaking.[412] And as Brad Clark has suggested, inferring preemption from ambiguous language "risk[s] circumventing the political and procedural safeguards of federalism built into the Supremacy Clause."[413] There is no obvious reason, in other words, why Justice Thomas's reasoning in *Wyeth* should not have applied in *Altria* as well.

---

[409] See Young, 46 Vill L Rev at 1380–95 (cited in note 39) (discussing Justice Stevens's leadership on preemption issues).

[410] See text accompanying notes 108–10.

[411] See 555 US at 586–88 (Thomas, J, concurring in the judgment).

[412] See notes 121–27 and accompanying text.

[413] Clark, *Process-Based Preemption* at 209 (cited in note 79).

Finally, Professor Nelson has acknowledged that it makes no sense to reject *Rice* in express preemption cases unless one also adopts his position barring obstacle preemption:

> To be sure, [the *Rice*] presumption makes some sense within the Framework that the Supreme Court has developed for preemption cases. . . . By telling judges to approach federal statutes with "the starting presumption that Congress does not intend to supplant state law," the Supreme Court offsets its own expansive formulations of "implied" preemption. The presumption thus operates as an artificial way to bring the courts' results closer to Congress's probable "pre-emptive intent."[414]

To be sure, Nelson views *Rice* as "a second-best alternative to a broader overhaul of the Court's doctrine."[415] But until Justice Thomas succeeds in persuading his colleagues to undertake a "broader overhaul" of conflict preemption,[416] he and others sympathetic to Nelson's argument should hesitate to reconsider *Rice*. Nelson's historical research provides no support for doing the latter without the former.

C. TRADITIONAL SPHERES AND THE VESTIGES OF DUAL FEDERALISM

The other salient question concerning *Rice*'s presumption against preemption concerns its subject-matter scope. Although the presumption is sometimes framed as a general one,[417] courts frequently purport to limit it to fields of traditional state authority. The latter approach, however, reintroduces the same confusion that led to the demise of dual federalism in the first place.

The most prominent recent example of the bounded approach to *Rice* is the Court's 2000 decision in *United States v Locke*.[418] That decision held that federal laws regulating the safety of oil tankers preempted measures enacted by the state of Washington, in the wake of the *Exxon Valdez* oil spill, imposing more rigorous pre-

---

[414] Nelson, 86 Va L Rev at 290–91 (cited in note 303).

[415] Id at 291.

[416] For a skeptical view, see Michael C. Dorf, *The Most Confusing Branch*, 45 Tulsa L Rev 191, 193 (2009) (suggesting that "given Justice Thomas's willingness to express idiosyncratic views on a range of issues—including federalism—one cannot be very optimistic about the prospect of his inspiring a wholesale doctrinal reformulation in this area").

[417] See, for example, *Building & Construction Trades Council v Associated Builders & Contractors*, 507 US 218, 224 (1993) ("We are reluctant to infer pre-emption."); *Maryland v Louisiana*, 451 US 725, 746 (1981) ("Consideration under the Supremacy Clause starts with the basic assumption that Congress did not intend to displace state law.").

[418] 529 US 89 (2000).

cautions on tankers operating in state waters. Prior precedent on this question had applied *Rice*'s presumption against preemption,[419] but the Court rejected that approach in *Locke*. Emphasizing *Rice*'s observation that "Congress legislated here in a field which the States have traditionally occupied,"[420] Justice Kennedy's opinion for the Court in *Locke* reasoned that "an 'assumption' of nonpreemption is not triggered when the State regulates in an area where there has been a history of significant federal presence."[421] Observing that "[t]he state laws now in question bear upon national and international maritime commerce"—a field in which "Congress has legislated . . . from the earliest days of the Republic"— Kennedy concluded that "in this area there is no beginning assumption that concurrent regulation by the State is a valid exercise of its police powers."[422]

This rejection of *Rice*'s interpretive presumption mattered in *Locke*. Not only did the Court not resolve doubts about the federal regulatory measures at issue against preemption, it also narrowly construed express savings clauses in the federal Oil Pollution Act that preserved state authority to regulate risks relating to oil spills.[423] "Limiting the saving clauses as we have determined," Justice Kennedy said, "respects the established federal-state balance in matters of maritime commerce between the subjects as to which the States retain concurrent powers and those over which the federal authority displaces state control."[424] More fundamentally, the statutory construction issues in *Locke* were quite close, as illustrated both by the Court's contrary conclusions about the interaction of similar statutory schemes in *Ray* twelve years earlier[425] and the *Locke* Court's decision to remand several of the preemption issues to the lower courts for further consideration.[426]

Although the Court was unanimous in *Locke*, subsequent decisions have not consistently adhered to its restriction of *Rice* to

---

[419] See *Ray v Atlantic Richfield Co.*, 435 US 151, 157 (1978), quoting *Rice*, 331 US at 230.

[420] 331 US at 230.

[421] 529 US at 108.

[422] Id.

[423] 33 USC §§ 2718(a), (c).

[424] 529 US at 106.

[425] *Ray*, 435 US at 157.

[426] 529 US at 116–17.

certain subject-matter spheres. Just as *Locke* ignored the Court's statement four years earlier that *Rice* applies "[i]n all cases,"[427] subsequent cases have occasionally ignored *Locke* and reaffirmed *Rice*'s general applicability.[428] This sort of flip-flopping may illustrate a broader phenomenon. The Justices evidently consider themselves bound to prior results and specific statutory interpretations arrived at in preemption opinions they have joined, but they often seem to treat discussions of interpretive methodology in those prior cases as something like dictum. A Justice may not feel the need to refuse to join, much less dissent from, a statement applying or refusing to apply an interpretive presumption, so long as she thinks the ultimate interpretation of the statute is correct. This phenomenon may simply reflect the necessities of peaceful coexistence on a multimember court,[429] and as such it is not necessarily a bad thing. On the other hand, it is not exactly conducive to clarity in the Court's preemption jurisprudence.

There is another ambiguity in the Court's approach in *Locke* and similar decisions. In *Rice*, the presumption against preemption was triggered by a history of *state* regulation in the relevant field—as Justice Douglas put it, the fact that "Congress legislated here in a field which the States have traditionally occupied."[430] Most of the other cases that tie *Rice* to specific regulatory fields use similar language.[431] Justice Kennedy's opinion in *Locke*, however, switched the relevant actors, inquiring whether "the *State* regulates in an area where there has been a history of significant *federal* presence."[432] This bit of slippage matters, because the truth is that most regulatory fields have a history of concurrent federal and state presence. That is especially true from the New Deal onward, but there are many significant examples dating to the dawn of the

---

[427] *Medtronic, Inc. v Lohr*, 518 US 470, 485 (1996).

[428] See, for example, *Wyeth*, 555 US at 565.

[429] See note 298 and accompanying text (suggesting that such practices are a form of "incompletely theorized agreement").

[430] 331 US at 230.

[431] See, for example, *Jones v Rath Packing Co.*, 430 US 519, 525 (1977) (applying *Rice* "[w]here, as here, the field which Congress is said to have pre-empted has been traditionally occupied by the States"); *Hillsborough County v Automated Medical Laboratories, Inc.*, 471 US 707, 715 (1985) (same); *Medtronic*, 518 US at 485 (stating that *Rice* applies "[i]n all pre-emption cases, and particularly in those in which Congress has 'legislated . . . in a field which the States have traditionally occupied,'" quoting *Rice*). This remains true after *Locke*. See, for example, *Wyeth*, 555 US at 565, quoting the language from *Medtronic* above.

[432] 529 US at 108 (emphasis added).

Republic. Consider, for example, the field at issue in *Locke*—maritime commerce and safety. Federal law and (more importantly) federal *courts* have long had a significant role in maritime matters, but the First Judiciary Act's "Savings to Suitors" Clause guaranteed state courts and state law a role in maritime disputes,[433] and Chief Justice Marshall acknowledged in *Gibbons v Ogden*[434] that state governments have legitimate police power grounds to regulate commerce on navigable waters.[435] In other words, Justice Kennedy is plainly correct to say that maritime commerce has "a history of significant federal presence," but he would also be correct to say maritime commerce has a history of significant *state* presence. The answer to *Rice*'s applicability, in other words, will frequently depend on which way one asks the question.

The more fundamental problem, however, is the indeterminacy of any approach that tries to divide up the world into spheres of state and federal primacy.[436] One might avoid the *Locke* problem simply by asking whether state or federal law *predominates* in a given area—a question that *Locke* arguably got right with respect to maritime commerce.[437] But in most areas where preemption litigation arises, this predominance problem will be considerably less clear. Consider last Term's drug safety decisions in *Bruesewitz* and *PLIVA*, or the auto safety decision in *Williamson*. Each area is marked by a mix of state and federal regulation. Federal law tends to set standards for and approve products on the front end, before they are marketed to consumers; state products liability law, on the other hand, provides incentives to identify and correct unforeseen dangers in approved products and compensates victims when products do harm. Both forms of regulation have been

---

[433] Judiciary Act of 1789, ch 20, 9(a), 1 Stat 77. The current version is 28 USC § 1333.

[434] 22 US (9 Wheat) 1, 21–22 (1824). See also *Cooley v Board of Wardens of Port of Philadelphia*, 53 US (12 How) 299 (1852) (upholding state regulation of maritime commerce where it was necessarily adapted to local conditions).

[435] See generally David W. Robertson, *Admiralty and Federalism: History and Analysis of Problems of Federal-State Relations in the Maritime Law of the United States* (Foundation, 1970) (surveying the complicated interplay of federal and state law in maritime matters); Ernest A. Young, *Preemption at Sea*, 67 Geo Wash L Rev 273 (1999) (sailing in Professor Robertson's wake).

[436] See *Garcia*, 469 US at 546 (rejecting "as unsound in principle and workable in practice, a rule of state immunity . . . that turns on a judicial appraisal of whether a particular governmental function is 'integral' or 'traditional'").

[437] Some difficult people might quibble even here, arguing that for most of our history, maritime law was considered neither state nor federal in character. See Young, 67 Geo Wash L Rev at 293 (cited in note 435).

around for a relatively long time, and both are plainly important. But it is hard to know how one would go about determining which level of regulation "predominates." Would one measure the number of government officials at each level involved in regulation? Assess the relative costs imposed by each? Count the number of government enforcement actions? The more specific one gets about methods of measurement, the more nonsensical the enterprise seems. But as things stand, it is hard not to conclude that courts are simply making off-the-cuff intuitive judgments.

A related difficulty compounds the problem: In most cases, the relevant "field" can be characterized in multiple ways.[438] Fields can, for instance, be characterized at different levels of generality. Was *Bruesewitz* a case about vaccines—a matter on which federal law has taken the lead? Was it a case about medical safety—which features divided responsibility between federal premarket approval of drugs and devices and state postmarket regulation through the tort system? Or was it, even more broadly, simply a products liability case—a field of traditional state regulation? There is also a problem of overlap. *Concepcion*, for instance, was an arbitration case, and federal law has traditionally dominated that field. But it was also an important case about consumer protection, a traditional state field. Similarly, *Whiting* could easily be characterized as an immigration case, and therefore a state intrusion into a field that many view as *exclusively* federal. But Chief Justice Roberts dismissed this argument by pointing out that "[r]egulating in-state businesses through licensing laws has never been considered such an area of dominant federal concern."[439]

These characterization games are great fun for law professors but not necessarily good for the law. They are reminiscent of the difficulties that plagued and ultimately hastened the end of the Court's "dual federalism" regime—in particular, the Court's inability to draw determinate lines.[440] To be sure, the stakes are lower in the current context, because the Court is not assessing whether Congress or a state government has the power to legislate *at all*, but rather which interpretive rules to apply in construing Con-

---

[438] See Daryl J. Levinson, *Framing Transactions in Constitutional law*, 111 Yale L J 1311 (2002) (noting the indeterminacy problems that arise from different ways of framing the same transaction).

[439] 131 S Ct at 1983.

[440] See Part I.A.

gress's intent. Nonetheless, as Trevor Morrison has pointed out, the "problem with both the presumption against preemption and federalism-enforcing clear statement rules, at least as they are currently formulated," is that "[t]hey are all structured around substantive triggers that require courts to identify and attach great consequence to the 'historic' functions of the states."[441] Similarly, Robert Schapiro has noted that "current federal preemption doctrine at times manifests a . . . dualist spirit."[442]

To some extent, some differentiation of preemption doctrine by subject matter may be inevitable. Congress's purpose remains the "ultimate touchstone" in preemption cases,[443] and that intent varies by regulatory field. Over time, the Court develops an interpretive tradition, if you will, in particular regulatory areas. In the banking field, for instance, the Court's "history is one of interpreting grants of both enumerated and incidental 'powers' to national banks as grants of authority not normally limited by, but rather ordinarily pre-empting, contrary state law."[444] This history does not mean that preemption claims always win in banking cases,[445] but it does mean that the Court employs a somewhat different set of interpretive assumptions in that area. Problems may arise when regulatory schemes intersect; *Barnett Bank*, for example, could have been characterized as an insurance case—and therefore part of a regulatory tradition considerably more favorable to state law—rather than a banking case.[446] But while such cases may raise difficult questions of statutory construction, they are hardly intractable and stem directly from the Court's obligation to determine Congress's will.

It may also be possible to characterize the contexts in which

---

[441] Trevor W. Morrison, *The State Attorney General and Preemption*, in Buzbee, ed, *Preemption Choice* at 81, 91 (cited in note 8). See also Pursley, 71 Ohio St L J at 515 n 5 (cited in note 9) (noting that even if one reads recent decisions as clarifying that *Rice* applies in all cases, "the Court has retained the most confusing element of the doctrine—the need to identify areas of 'traditional' state authority—by suggesting gradations in the 'force' of the presumption based on whether the potentially preempted state law occupies such an area," citing *Altria*, 555 US· at 77).

[442] Schapiro, *From Dualism to Polyphony* at 48 (cited in note 8).

[443] *Medtronic*, 518 US at 486.

[444] *Barnett Bank of Marion County, N.A. v Nelson*, 517 US 25, 32 (1996).

[445] See *Cuomo v Clearing House Association, LLC*, 129 S Ct 2710 (2009) (holding that federal banking laws did not preempt the states' authority to enforce state banking laws against national banks).

[446] See 517 US at 37–41.

the Court views preemption more favorably in a nonarbitrary way. Rick Hills has suggested that the Court finds preemption more readily in "commercial" cases involving laws "defining the rules for bargaining and remedies for breach of bargains," than in "regulatory" cases "involv[ing] state and federal laws defining the baseline entitlements over which the parties bargain."[447] For Professor Hills, this explains the Court's willingness to construe the Federal Arbitration Act broadly in *Concepcion*, while approaching preemption more cautiously in an auto-safety case like *Williamson*. The availability of arbitration, after all, is part of the remedies for breach of bargains, while products liability cases like *Williamson* involve substantive safety requirements.[448]

However useful Professor Hills's distinction between commercial and regulatory cases is as a descriptive matter, I doubt that it provides a useful principle to *guide* the Court in deciding hard cases going forward.[449] One problem is that the distinction is hardly crisp. As Hills acknowledges,[450] questions of remedy are not unrelated to regulatory matters—the availability of class actions, for instance, significantly increases the deterrent effect of state consumer protection rules.[451] And it is possible to frame the issues in some of the "regulatory" drug cases as "commercial" questions about the forum for and nature of available remedies. *Bruesewitz*, for example, concerned whether persons injured by federally approved vaccines could seek compensation through the state tort system or must rely on a federal procedure through the Court of Claims.[452] Moreover, converting the commercial/regulatory distinction into a normative principle would require some argument for grounding it in the Constitution, rather than in a policy argument about what state and national decision makers do

---

[447] Roderick M. Hills Jr., *Preemption Doctrine in the Roberts Court: Constitutional Dual Federalism by Another Name?* (unpublished manuscript at 1) (Oct 12, 2011) (on file with author). Professor Hills explains that "[t]he 'mailbox rule' defining when a contract is accepted is an example of a 'commercial' law, while a prohibition on filling a wetlands or building a cement plant in a residential zone are examples of 'regulatory' laws." Id.

[448] See Id. To be sure, *Bruesewitz* and *PLIVA*—also "regulatory" cases—nonetheless found preemption. But it does seem fair to say that the Court's overall record in arbitration cases is more strongly preemptive than in its drug and medical device safety cases.

[449] Professor Hills makes clear that his argument is meant to be primarily descriptive. See Hills, *Preemption Doctrine in the Roberts Court* (cited in note 447).

[450] Id.

[451] See *Concepcion*, 131 S Ct at 1752.

[452] See Part II.C.

best.[453] For that reason, it compares unfavorably with process federalism rules like the presumption against preemption, which can be grounded in the political and procedural checks built into the constitutional structure of federal lawmaking.[454]

Controversy over the scope of *Rice* seems likely to increase in the 2011 Term, when the Court will hear *Arizona v United States*.[455] That case is the Justice Department's challenge to Arizona's SB 1070, which provides for broad state enforcement of federal immigration laws and extends beyond the employment context considered in *Whiting*. As Rick Hills has noted, "[t]he surprising aspect of *Whiting* . . . is that the Roberts Court's analysis of preemption was so conventional"; the Court "brushed aside the idea that Arizona encroached on a forbidden federal field of foreign relations law."[456] That argument will return with a vengeance in *Arizona*, as it formed a critical theme in the Ninth Circuit's decision striking down SB 1070. Judge Paez's opinion for the court of appeals held that "[t]he states have not traditionally occupied the field of identifying immigration violations so we apply no presumption against preemption."[457] As the Court did in *Locke*, the Ninth Circuit read a savings clause in the federal immigration statutes narrowly, and it gave effect not only to the preemptive choices of Congress but also to the enforcement discretion of the national Executive.[458] Finally, the Court of Appeals gave independent preemptive force to its judgment that the Arizona law intruded on the national government's power over foreign relations,[459] a theme that Judge Noonan posted in neon lights in his separate concurrence.[460]

---

[453] See Hills, *Preemption Doctrine in the Roberts Court* (cited in note 447) (approving the distinction primarily on policy grounds).

[454] See text accompanying notes 44–54.

[455] 132 S Ct 845 (2011).

[456] Hills, *Preemption Doctrine in the Roberts Court* (cited in note 447).

[457] *United States v Arizona*, 641 F3d 349, 348 (9th Cir 2011).

[458] See id at 349, 351–52.

[459] Id at 352–53 & n 12 (observing that "[t]he Court's decision in [*Hines v Davidowitz*, 312 US 52 (1941)] demonstrates that the Court has long been wary of state statutes which may interfere with foreign relations").

[460] See *Arizona*, 641 F3d at 368 (Noonan concurring) ("The foreign policy of the United States preempts the field entered by Arizona. Foreign policy is not and cannot be determined by the several states. Foreign policy is determined by the nation as the nation interacts with other nations. Whatever in any substantial degree attempts to express a policy by a single state or by several states toward other nations enters an exclusively federal field.").

I have argued elsewhere that foreign relations law is the last bastion of the dual federalism that the Court generally abandoned in 1937.[461] At the height of the Cold War, the Court purported to set foreign relations aside as an exclusively federal sphere, so that state action touching that field would be preempted even in the absence of action by Congress.[462] That doctrine largely withered on the vine, however, because a virtually infinite variety of actions by state governments in fact affect foreign relations. The Court has repeatedly refused to interfere with the power of state governments to execute foreign nationals for murders committed within the state, notwithstanding vociferous protests by the relevant foreign governments and, in some cases, attempts by the national executive to intervene.[463] The truth is that, in our constitutional system of both horizontal and vertical separation of powers, it is virtually impossible for the United States actually to speak "with one voice"—in foreign relations or otherwise.[464]

Arizona v United States thus provides the Court with an opportunity to state more explicitly what it implicitly established in *Whiting*: That dual federalism is dead, and that concurrent regulation is the norm even in fields like immigration that impact foreign relations. After all, if foreign affairs cannot be cordoned off as a separate sphere of federal primacy, then it is hard to think of any other fields that can be. Adopting one set of interpretive rules that applies to all preemption cases regardless of the underlying substance of the case would go a long way toward rationalizing the Court's preemption jurisprudence.

IV. The Politics of Preemption Doctrine in the Roberts Court

One observer recently asserted that "Chief Justice John

---

[461] Young, 69 Geo Wash L Rev at 177–80 (cited in note 28).

[462] *Zschernig v Miller*, 389 US 429 (1968).

[463] See, for example, *Medellin v Texas*, 552 US 491 (2008) (holding that neither the President nor the International Court of Justice had the power to prevent Texas from executing a Mexican national, notwithstanding Texas's alleged violation of the Vienna Convention on Consular Relations); *Breard v Greene*, 523 US 371 (1998) (rejecting suit by Paraguay seeking to stop Virginia's execution of a Paraguayan national, allegedly in violation of the Vienna Convention on Consular Relations).

[464] See, for example, Sarah H. Cleveland, *Crosby and the "One Voice" Myth in U.S. Foreign Relations*, 46 Vill L Rev 975 (2001) (arguing that neither the Constitution nor U.S. history supports the claim that the President speaks for the nation with one voice).

Roberts has an opportunity to add his name to the . . . exclusive list of those—like John Marshall, Roger Taney and Earl Warren—whose leadership of the Court has marked a shift in Court history and a new era of constitutional doctrine."[465] All three of the potential blockbuster cases cited in support of this prediction—the Arizona immigration case, the Texas redistricting case, and the challenge to the national healthcare law—raise significant issues of federalism.[466] And while only one of them—the Arizona case—is explicitly framed as a preemption issue, the other two have significant preemption implications.[467] It is too early, in my view, to say that this Court will usher in "a new era of constitutional doctrine." The Roberts Court's record to date does strongly suggest, however, that preemption will be an important part of its doctrinal legacy.

One might think that the Supreme Court's conservative wing—which has generally pushed for broader constitutional limits on federal power, albeit with only limited success—would be enthusiastic about limiting the scope of federal preemption. The actual pattern, however, has been considerably more complex. While some of the conservative Justices, especially Justice Thomas, have been willing to restrict preemption, most of them have tended to favor broad preemption of state law. The Court's more liberal wing, by contrast, has tended to limit preemption notwithstanding those Justices' aversion to constitutional limits on federal authority.[468] Prior to his retirement, John Paul Stevens was the Court's

---

[465] Todd Brewster, *Will the Supreme Court Take a Historic Turn in 2012?* Constitution Daily (Dec 19, 2011), online at http://blog.constitutioncenter.org/will-the-supreme-court -take-a-historic-turn-in-2012/. On the other hand, Chief Justice Roberts turned fifty-seven this year, and by all indications he will be Chief Justice for a long time to come. It is worth remembering, then, that the Roberts Court's legacy may well be defined by issues that are not even on the radar screen at this early date in the Chief's tenure.

[466] See Lyle Denniston, *Political Trouble Ahead for the Supreme Court*, Constitution Daily (Dec 13, 2011), online at http://blog.constitutioncenter.org/political-trouble-ahead-for -the-supreme-court/) (agreeing that these are the 2011 Term's blockbusters, and observing that "[w]hat those three controversies have most in common is this: every one of them involves the fundamental constitutional question of how governmental power is to be divided up between Washington and the states"); *Arizona, Texas and Healthcare Reform* (UPI.com, Dec 18, 2011), online at http://www.upi.com/Top_News/US/2011/12/18/Under-the-US-Supreme-Court-Arizona-Texas-and-healthcare-reform/UPI-80901324197000/.

[467] The Voting Rights Act, after all, preempts state authority to draw congressional districts in certain circumstances. And although the national healthcare law permits certain waivers in order to allow state policy experimentation, it also supplants state regulatory authority in innumerable ways.

[468] See generally Young, 83 Tex L Rev 1 (cited in note 47) (documenting and discussing

most consistently anti-preemption Justice, notwithstanding his consistent dissents in the Rehnquist Court's landmark cases expanding constitutional protections for state sovereignty.[469]

This pattern arises because preemption cases implicate a number of cross-cutting ideological and methodological conflicts on the Court. Federal preemption is generally deregulatory—that is, preemption cases typically arise only where a state government has regulated more strictly than has the national government. In *Wyeth v Levine*,[470] for example, the Court considered whether state tort law could impose liability for failure to warn even where a drug's warning label had been approved by federal regulators. Preemption cases thus pit the deregulatory impulses of conservative Justices against their sympathy for the states; likewise, liberals find themselves torn between their nationalism and their pro-regulatory views.[471] Put another way, preemption calls into conflict a *libertarian* form of federalism that sees federalism as a way of limiting national regulatory power and promoting competition among the states, with a *checks-and-balances* view that emphasizes the role of states in diffusing power.[472] The latter view is largely indifferent to how states actually use their autonomy—that is, whether they choose to regulate or deregulate.

Libertarian federalism has an honorable pedigree. It finds its roots in Madison's desire for a federal "negative" on unwise state laws—a veto that, in the hands of Federalists like Madison, would have been used to undo excessive state intervention such as the debtor relief legislation adopted by the populist Pennsylvania legislature.[473] Its modern advocates stress the market-based benefits

this pattern); Richard H. Fallon Jr., *The Conservative Paths of the Rehnquist Court's Federalism Decisions*, 69 U Chi L Rev 429 (2002); Daniel J. Meltzer, *The Supreme Court's Judicial Passivity*, 2002 Supreme Court Review 343.

[469] See, for example, *Lorillard Tobacco Co. v Reilly*, 533 US 525, 598 n 8 (Stevens, J, concurring in part and dissenting in part) (pointing out the irony that the five conservative Justices who formed the majority in *United States v Lopez* were willing to hold that federal law preempted state authority to regulate tobacco advertising within 1,000 feet of a school).

[470] 555 US 555 (2009).

[471] See, for example, Gregory M. Dickinson, *An Empirical Study of Obstacle Preemption in the Supreme Court*, 89 Neb L Rev 682, 682 (2011) ("Preemption defies traditional conservative-liberal alignment, as conservatives are torn between support of federalism and capitalist efficiency, and liberals are torn between support of strong national governance and multiplicity of legal remedies.").

[472] *See* Young, *Federal Preemption and State Autonomy* at 255–57 (cited in note 44) (describing and critiquing the libertarian model).

[473] See, for example, Epstein and Greve, *Introduction* 6–8 (cited in note 280) (discussing Madison's negative).

of competition among states to develop the most attractive policies, benefits to business of avoiding excessive or conflicting regulation, as well as the more fundamental benefit of limiting national power to intrude on the lives of individuals.[474] For libertarian federalists, however, state autonomy has no inherent value apart from these benefits, and that autonomy can be readily sacrificed in circumstances where national regulation is less intrusive on economic liberty than is state policy.[475]

My own view is that the Court should resist allowing a preference for deregulatory results to influence its resolution of preemption disputes. Our Constitution created an institutional structure of checks and balances; with certain relatively narrow exceptions, it did not incorporate an inherent preference for deregulation.[476] Moreover, it is not at all clear that courts are institutionally suited to administer a preemption doctrine predicated on a self-conscious effort to promote economic efficiency.[477] Such judgments are likely to seem—and have seemed—to outside observers as though the Justices are simply enforcing their own policy preferences. In *Whiting*, for example, it was hardly edifying to see the conservative Justices who so frequently vote for preemption switching places with the nationalists who most often oppose it, to all appearances simply because both sides have more specific preferences about immigration policy.

More fundamentally, even libertarian federalism ultimately presupposes strong, vital state governments. Competition cannot exist without competitors, and enfeebled states with few significant responsibilities are unlikely to produce the sorts of innovative choices for businesses and individuals that libertarian federalists seek. Nor are weak states likely to check efforts to expand the reach of federal regulation that intrudes on the autonomy of individuals, as several states have sought to do in the current healthcare litigation.[478] Some attention must be paid, in other words, to the institutional health of the states as states. And post-New Deal

---

[474] See, for example, Untereiner, 84 Tulane L Rev at 1261–63 (cited in note 11).

[475] For an incisive statement of this view, see Michael S. Greve, *The Upside-Down Constitution* 7–8 (Harvard, 2012).

[476] Consider *Lochner v New York*, 198 US 45, 75 (1905) (Holmes, J, dissenting).

[477] See Young, *Federal Preemption and State Autonomy* at 255–56 (cited in note 44).

[478] See Young, *Popular Constitutionalism* (cited in note 127) (discussing how federalism-based limits on Congress's power provide breathing space for more expansive views of economic liberty that current federal constitutional doctrine may not support).

constitutional doctrine is quickly running out of options for protecting federalism. The Commerce Clause is largely dead, the Spending Clause is practically nonjusticiable, the Eleventh Amendment is generally unhelpful to state autonomy, and the anticommandeering doctrine is very narrow and subject to ready circumvention under the Spending Clause. In other words, the presumption against preemption may be the last best hope for preserving a meaningful measure of state autonomy in our constitutional system.

The preemption cases of the 2010 Term reveal a Court that has still not made up its mind about preemption but perhaps one that is asking increasingly basic questions about preemption and its relation to other constitutional issues. The more that the Justices see preemption cases as not simply disputes about the scope of federal and state regulation under specific regulatory statutes, but rather as raising fundamental questions of federalism, the more likely they are to transcend the current divide between proponents and opponents of regulation. Their ability to do so will be, in Justice Breyer's phrase, "the true test of federalist principle."[479]

---

[479] *Egelhoff v Egelhoff*, 532 US 141, 160–61 (2001).

JUSTIN DRIVER

THE SIGNIFICANCE OF THE FRONTIER
IN AMERICAN CONSTITUTIONAL LAW

I. Introduction

On the evening of July 12, 1893, at the American Historical Association's annual conference, an unknown thirty-one-year-old history professor from the University of Wisconsin named Frederick Jackson Turner delivered his first academic paper.[1] As occurs with most professorial debuts, nothing about the audience's immediate reaction suggested that the occasion would eventually prove momentous. Far from it: Turner's fellow historians greeted him with the yawning indifference typically accorded novice professors from the provinces.[2] The paper received a similarly bleak reception from the leading scholarly journals, which all but ignored Turner and his ideas for three full years following the presentation.[3] From these humble academic origins, it must have appeared implausible

Justin Driver is Assistant Professor, University of Texas School of Law.

AUTHOR'S NOTE: I received particularly helpful feedback on earlier drafts from Laura Ferry, William Forbath, Jacob Gersen, Dennis Hutchinson, Jennifer Laurin, Sanford Levinson, Charles Mackel, Lucas Powe, and David Strauss. I also benefited from excellent research assistance provided by Andrew Clearfield, Parth Gejji, Corbin Page, Michael Raupp, and Lauren Ross.

[1] See John Mack Faragher, *Introduction: "A Nation Thrown Back Upon Itself": Frederick Jackson Turner and the Frontier*, in John Mack Faragher, ed, *Rereading Frederick Jackson Turner: "The Significance of the Frontier in American History" and Other Essays* 1, 2 (Yale, 1998); Ray Allen Billington, *Frederick Jackson Turner: Historian, Scholar, Teacher* 5 (Oxford, 1973).

[2] See Billington, *Frederick Jackson Turner* at 129 (cited in note 1).

[3] See id at 184.

that Charles Beard would one day declare that Turner's seemingly ill-starred entry into academia was in fact "destined to have a more profound influence on thought about American history than any other essay or volume ever written on the subject."[4]

Turner entitled his essay "The Significance of the Frontier in American History."[5] He argued that, in order to understand why a democratic political culture flourished in the United States, the nation's settlement of the West must be placed in the historical foreground. "American social development has been continually beginning over again on the frontier," Turner wrote. "This perennial rebirth, this fluidity of American life, this expansion westward with its new opportunities, its continuous touch with the simplicity of primitive society, furnish the forces dominating American character."[6] According to Turner, the frontier—which he identified as western expansion's "outer edge," where wilderness meets civilization—inherently promoted individualism, and that individualism, in turn, promoted democracy.[7] "What the Mediterranean Sea was to the Greeks, breaking the bond of custom, offering new experiences, calling out new institutions and activities, that, and more, the ever retreating frontier has been to the United States . . . ," Turner contended.[8]

Among U.S. historians, it is virtually impossible to overstate the influence of Turner's article.[9] Writing in the *New York Times* in 1935, Francis Brown observed that the essay "set the style for a whole generation of historians" and that "so many men have utilized the Turner thesis that it is probably the most generally approved approach to historical writing."[10] Predictably, this first wave of unadulterated admiration gave way to wary revision. In 1969, Richard Hofstadter noted that Turner's sanguine depiction of westward ex-

---

[4] Charles A. Beard, *Turner's "The Frontier in American History,"* in Malcolm Cowley and Bernard Smith, eds, *Books That Changed Our Minds* 61, 61 (Kelmscott, 1939).

[5] See Frederick Jackson Turner, *The Significance of the Frontier in American History*, in Faragher, ed, *Rereading Frederick Jackson Turner* 31, 31 (cited in note 1).

[6] Id at 32.

[7] See id at 32, 53.

[8] Id at 59–60.

[9] See Richard Hofstadter, *The Progressive Historians: Turner, Beard, Parrington* 164 (Knopf, 1969) ("Among all the historians of the United States it was Turner alone of whom we can now say with certainty that he opened a controversy that was large enough to command the attention of his peers for four generations.").

[10] Francis Brown, *Frederick Jackson Turner and the Frontier's Influence*, NY Times BR4 (June 30, 1935).

pansion overlooked its pernicious consequences. "[W]hile Turner was moved, and rightly so, by a feeling for the achievement of America, he had little countervailing response to the shame of it . . . ," Hofstadter wrote.[11] Such critiques have only hardened over the ensuing decades, as scholars have increasingly dedicated energy to exploring not the magnificence of American settlement, but the people whom settlement displaced.[12]

In contrast to the long shadow that Turner casts over historians, his influence on legal scholars is slight.[13] The modest figure that he cuts among law professors may be at least somewhat surprising because Turner offered an extremely early articulation of a central idea in American constitutional thought. In a course called "Constitutional History" that he taught during the early 1890s, Turner reportedly offered his students an unconventional understanding of the nation's founding document that was rooted in his fascination with the frontier:

> To Turner the Constitution was no sacred document, handed down by a benevolent deity, but the product of social and economic forces operating through the colonial era. "The constitutional convention of 1787," he told his class, "was only one stage, not an abrupt unconnected beginning." Nor had its evolution ended with its adoption. "It was still played upon by all the vital forces of American growth and adapted itself to them," particularly to "the needs of the wonderful expansion which is the dominant fact of American history."[14]

In emphasizing to his students how changed conditions have resulted in changed constitutional understandings, Turner was, of course, advancing a notion that would become widely known as the living Constitution.[15]

---

[11] Hofstadter, *The Progressive Historians* at 104 (cited in note 9).

[12] See Alan Brinkley, *The Western Historians: Don't Fence Them In*, NY Times BR1 (Sept 20, 1992). For prominent examples of such historical revision, see generally Patricia Nelson Limerick, *The Legacy of Conquest: The Unbroken Past of the American West* (Norton, 1987); Richard White, *"It's Your Misfortune and None of My Own": A History of the American West* (Oklahoma, 1991).

[13] Slight, not nonexistent. Legal scholarship that mentions Turner's work, however, overwhelmingly does so in passing. See, for example, John Fabian Witt, *Speedy Fred Taylor and the Ironies of Enterprise Liability*, 103 Colum L Rev 1, 16 (2003) (briefly mentioning Turner); G. Edward White, *The Arrival of History in Constitutional Scholarship*, 88 Va L Rev 485, 502 (2002) (same).

[14] Billington, *Frederick Jackson Turner* at 94 (cited in note 1).

[15] In 1908, Roscoe Pound appears to have been the first legal scholar to use the term "living constitution." See Roscoe Pound, *Mechanical Jurisprudence*, 8 Colum L Rev 605, 615 (1908) (stating that Chief Justice Marshall gave the nation "a living constitution by

More than one century after Turner initially gestured toward the concept, times have grown grim for living constitutionalism. Although Justice Antonin Scalia recently informed the Senate Judiciary Committee that he was "hoping the living Constitution will die,"[16] one might be forgiven for wondering whether Scalia simply missed the funeral. After all, the *National Review* announced the living Constitution's death several years ago, when Democratic Senators declined to press Judge John Roberts on the concept during his hearings to become Chief Justice.[17]

More telling than the conservative attacks on the living Constitution, however, is that legal liberals both within the judiciary and beyond now eschew such terminology. Although even then-Justice William Rehnquist embraced one conception of living constitutionalism during the 1970s,[18] no current Supreme Court Justices embrace that term to describe their judicial approaches. Recently, three left-leaning legal scholars—Goodwin Liu, Pamela Karlan, and Christopher H. Schroeder—jointly authored a book making explicit what had long remained tacit: liberal law professors now overwhelmingly reject the living Constitution, or at least the label. "[T]he claim that ours is a 'living Constitution' has been vulnerable to the criticism that our Constitution is a written document and, as such, does not grow or evolve except by formal amendment," the trio wrote two years ago. "The metaphor of a 'living Constitution' misleadingly suggests that the Constitution itself is the primary site of legal evolution in response to societal change. . . . Describing our Constitution as a 'living' document unduly minimizes the fixed and enduring character of its text and principles."[19]

---

judicial interpretation"). Two decades later, Howard Lee McBain of Columbia University used the phrase for a book title. See generally Howard Lee McBain, *The Living Constitution: A Consideration of the Realities and Legends of Our Fundamental Law* (Macmillian, 1928).

[16] David G. Savage, *Justice Scalia: Americans "Should Learn to Love Gridlock,"* LA Times (Oct 5, 2011), online at http://articles.latimes.com/2011/oct/05/news/la-pn-scalia-testifies-20111005.

[17] See Curt Levey, *Living Constitution, R.I.P.,* Natl Rev (Sept 30, 2005), online at old.nationalreview.com/comment/levey200509301609.asp.

[18] See William H. Rehnquist, *The Notion of a Living Constitution,* 54 Tex L Rev 693, 694 (1976) (contending that Justice Holmes's espousal of living constitutionalism in *Missouri v Holland,* 252 US 416 (1920), was one "with which scarcely anyone would disagree.").

[19] Goodwin Liu, Pamela S. Karlan, and Christopher H. Schroeder, *Keeping Faith with the Constitution* 31 (Oxford, 2010). See also James E. Ryan, *Laying Claim to the Constitution: The Promise of New Textualism,* 97 Va L Rev 1523, 1524 (2011) ("Living constitutionalism is largely dead."); Robert C. Post and Reva B. Siegel, *Democratic Constitutionalism,* in Jack M. Balkin and Reva B. Siegel, eds, *The Constitution in 2020* at 25, 25 (Oxford, 2009) ("Progressives *used to* conceptualize the Constitution as 'living law,' as a 'living charter'

One of the few remaining stalwarts of living constitutionalism is Professor David A. Strauss. Two years ago, in a book called simply *The Living Constitution*, Strauss set forth what has quickly become the theory's leading account.[20] Professor Adrian Vermeule has, for instance, praised Strauss for providing "the most promising version of living constitutionalism by far."[21] Strauss's book, which is a distillation of his major scholarly contributions from the preceding fifteen years,[22] emphasizes the role that tradition and precedent play in constitutional adjudication, and likens constitutional decision making to the common law method of judging. The volume contains much to recommend it—not the least of which is Strauss's devastating assault on a prominent version of originalism.[23]

Yet for all of the volume's considerable virtues, it would be misguided to permit Strauss's version of living constitutionalism to dominate the field. Some distinguished scholars have criticized Strauss's conception of living constitutionalism for providing what they deem a myopic focus on judges; constitutional change, these scholars urge, generally arises from the streets, not the courts.[24] Such critiques, however, tend to overlook the weaknesses of Strauss's theory even taken on its own terms, namely, as a theory of judging. Those weaknesses should be taken seriously, as Strauss's precedent-centric model unduly diminishes living constitutionalism's greatest virtue: its capacity for judicial innovation. Most no-

---

'capable of growth'" (emphasis added) (footnotes omitted)); id ("[M]any on the left are intimidated by the charge that a living Constitution expresses political preferences instead of law.").

[20] See generally David A. Strauss, *The Living Constitution* (Oxford, 2010).

[21] See Adrian Vermeule, *Living It Up*, New Republic (Aug 2, 2010), online at http://www.tnr.com/book/review/living-it.

[22] See generally David A. Strauss, *Common Law Constitutional Interpretation*, 63 U Chi L Rev 877 (1996); David A. Strauss, *The Irrelevance of Constitutional Amendments*, 114 Harv L Rev 1457 (2001); David A. Strauss, *Freedom of Speech and the Common-Law Constitution*, in Lee C. Bollinger and Geoffrey R. Stone, eds, *Eternally Vigilant: Free Speech in the Modern Era* 33 (Chicago, 2002); David A. Strauss, *Common Law, Common Ground, and Jefferson's Principle*, 112 Yale L J 1717 (2003); David A. Strauss, *The Common Law Genius of the Warren Court*, 49 Wm & Mary L Rev 845 (2007).

[23] See Strauss, *Living Constitution* at 7–31 (cited in note 20).

[24] See Jack M. Balkin, *Living Originalism* 278 (Belknap, 2011) (asserting that "a theory of living constitutionalism that focuses primarily on what judges should do is at odds with the very assumptions behind the idea of a living Constitution. To rethink living constitutionalism, then, we have to begin by jettisoning the idea that it is primarily a theory about good judging."); Bruce Ackerman, *2006 Oliver Wendell Holmes Lectures: The Living Constitution*, 120 Harv L Rev 1737, 1801 (2007) (contending that "[t]he common law tradition was created by judges for judges," and that "its judge-centered character slights the central importance of popular sovereignty").

tably, Strauss's model—which portrays judges as subconsciously abandoning doctrine in the course of issuing decisions that hollow out existing law—distorts the historical record by minimizing the groundbreaking nature of opinions where the judiciary has afforded legal protections to previously marginalized groups. But Strauss's model not only contains descriptive inaccuracies. The model also leads to normatively unattractive judicial decisions. Indeed, if judges internalized Strauss's excessively backward-looking conception of adjudication, it seems doubtful that they would actually issue opinions that bring legally subordinated groups into the constitutional fold. Professor Strauss's version of living constitutionalism, in other words, risks draining the very life from living constitutionalism.

Because the ranks of living constitutionalists have grown so thin, it may appear churlish or foolish (or maybe both) for one avowed living constitutionalist to challenge the account of another.[25] Now, it might be suggested, is the time for closing ranks, not for intramural squabbling. After the common foe of originalism has been vanquished, there will be ample time for sorting out the differences among living constitutionalists of various stripes.[26] It is nevertheless imperative that living constitutionalists initiate an internal conversation regarding the judiciary's appropriate role in constitutional interpretation.

My aim here is to begin the process of reviving a more robust conception of the living Constitution by providing a detailed critique of Strauss's framework and its attendant frailties. This historically-grounded critique will emphasize particular instances in which Supreme Court Justices have placed themselves at the frontier of constitutional law—that is, when the Justices decide to back away from precedents, and move the law in a new direction in order to embrace new understandings. I do not endeavor here to articulate anything so elaborate as a fully unified theory of living constitutionalism. Yet in underscoring the significance of the constitutional frontier to America's expanding conception of democracy, I nevertheless attempt to supply an indispensable element for any compelling theory of living constitutionalism, an element that the dom-

---

[25] For an earlier assertion of my own living constitutionalist bona fides, see Justin Driver, *It's Alive*, New Republic 10–12 (July 8, 2010).

[26] Professor Balkin has argued, of course, that originalism and living constitutionalism, properly understood, should be conceived of as complementary rather than competing ideas. See generally Balkin, *Living Originalism* (cited in note 24).

inant conception mistakenly disregards. Contrary to a central pillar of Strauss's theory, judges typically have not stumbled away from the precedents that they and their predecessors have built up over time without realizing they are doing so. Rather, judges must generally make affirmative choices to distance themselves from the framework of prior judicial decisions before setting out in a fresh jurisprudential direction, venturing into uncharted judicial territory. Judges on the constitutional frontier by no means necessarily depart from precedent knowing a particular doctrinal destination in advance; judges do realize, though, that they have departed from the established order.

The existence of the constitutional frontier does not mean that judges have carte blanche to impose any decision that simply strikes their collective fancy. As Turner's essay emphasized in terms that have strong applicability to the constitutional domain, even the freedom associated with the wide-open frontier was not wholly uncabined. On the frontier, Turner wrote, "[t]here is not *tabula rasa*. The stubborn American environment is there with its imperious summons to accept its conditions; the inherited ways of doing things are also there. . . ."[27] So, too, with judges and the legal landscapes arrayed before them. But while judges cannot do anything they wish regarding constitutional law, they do possess greater flexibility to reject outmoded precedents than the dominant understanding of living constitutionalism allows. This phenomenon is particularly important to emphasize and preserve where judges believe, however tentatively, that prior judicial decisions may have failed to afford marginalized groups the constitutional protections they are due. "[I]n spite of environment," Turner wrote, "and in spite of custom, each frontier did indeed furnish a new field of opportunity, a gate of escape from the bondage of the past; and freshness, and confidence, and scorn of older society, impatience of its restraints and its ideas, and indifference to its lessons, have accompanied the frontier."[28] It would be absurd to think such anti-establishment sentiments figure prominently in a typical Term of the United States Supreme Court. Such sentiments do, however, enjoy an underappreciated role in the history of living constitutionalism. It is necessary to recover that legacy because, without it, the Supreme Court

---

[27] Turner, *Significance of the Frontier* at 59 (cited in note 5).
[28] Id.

may in the future unnecessarily decline to extend constitutional protections to marginalized groups who do not currently receive constitutional protections. Such decisions, which occur on the constitutional frontier, are nothing less than essential, serving as a form of renewal for our nation's founding charter.

Some readers will surely contend that the only thing less desirable than defending the concept of a living Constitution is attempting to layer an additional metaphor—like the frontier—on top of that already metaphorical concept.[29] This objection admits of at least two central responses. First, one of the most esteemed and innovative judges of the twentieth century, Chief Justice Roger Traynor of the California Supreme Court, employed the frontier metaphor to describe the experience of issuing constitutional decisions that lack a firm foundation in existing case law. Among his many decisions that contributed to his sterling judicial reputation,[30] Traynor wrote an opinion invalidating California's antimiscegenation law in 1948, nearly two decades before the Supreme Court got around to issuing *Loving v Virginia*.[31] In a law review article called "Law and Social Change in a Democratic Society," Traynor urged in 1956 that judges must "be aware of the signs that we may cross new frontiers in constitutional law" because "[i]n no other area has there been such a dramatic interrelation between law and social change."[32] Traynor would, moreover, repeatedly invoke this concept of the constitutional frontier in his extrajudicial writings.[33] That a leading progressive judge deemed the frontier metaphor useful in illuminating the enterprise of judging suggests that the concept should not be dismissed quite so readily.

---

[29] Consider Rehnquist, 54 Tex L Rev at 693 (cited in note 18) (contending that "the phrase 'living Constitution' has about it a teasing imprecision that makes it a coat of many colors").

[30] See, for example, G. Edward White, *The American Judicial Tradition: Profiles of Leading American Judges* 243–66 (Oxford, 3d ed 2007) (analyzing and assessing Traynor's contributions to American jurisprudence); Mathew O. Tobriner, *Chief Justice Roger Traynor*, 83 Harv L Rev 1769 (1970) (praising Traynor's capacities).

[31] Compare *Perez v Sharp*, 198 P2d 17 (Cal 1948), with *Loving v Virginia*, 388 US 1 (1966).

[32] See Roger J. Traynor, *Law and Social Change in a Democratic Society*, 1956 U Ill L F 230, 237. Judge Richard Posner has, without directly invoking the word "frontier," set forth a similar notion when he recently noted that law often leaves "an open area in which judges have decisional discretion—a blank slate on which to inscribe their decisions— rather than being compelled to a particular decision by 'the law.'" Richard A. Posner, *How Judges Think* 9 (Harvard, 2008).

[33] See text accompanying notes 32, 238.

Second, although metaphors necessarily contain a considerable degree of indeterminacy, they also have proven extraordinarily important—and often invaluable—in shaping American attitudes about the law. Contemplate, for instance, one of constitutional law's most enduring metaphors and the ongoing role it plays in resolving current legal disputes: Even many nonlawyers realize that the Supreme Court's freedom of speech jurisprudence has been molded by viewing society as a "marketplace of ideas."[34] In his essay on living constitutionalism, furthermore, then-Justice Rehnquist recognized the power contained in metaphors that do not necessarily relate to particular legal doctrines. "While it is undoubtedly true, as Mr. Justice Holmes said, that 'general propositions do not decide concrete cases,' general phrases such as [the living Constitution] have a way of subtly coloring the way we think about concrete cases," Rehnquist wrote.[35] By identifying the phenomenon when judges consciously (if silently) decide to turn their backs on precedents as occurring on constitutional law's frontier, I hope to relegitimate a judicial practice that history demonstrates has proven essential to the development of living constitutionalism, but now risks falling into disrepute.

II. One Life of the Living Constitution

Professor Strauss has articulated the leading theory of living constitutionalism. To understand how that theory overly constrains the judicial role and thereby obscures constitutional law's frontier, it is first necessary to explicate the theory's central elements. Understood at its broadest level, Strauss's book admirably aims to close the gap between how constitutional law works as an abstraction and how constitutional law actually works in practice. It may be tempting for the uninitiated to believe that the Constitution's text plays a starring role in resolving most constitutional law disputes. But it comes closer to the mark, Strauss observes, to say that constitutional text typically plays a bit part. In many First Amendment cases, for instance, the opinion will—generally near the outset—dutifully re-

---

[34] *Lamont v Postmaster General*, 381 US 301, 308 (1965) (Brennan, J, concurring). For an adumbration of this idea, see *Abrams v United States*, 250 US 616, 630 (1919) (Holmes, J, dissenting) (contending that "the best test of truth is the power of the thought to get itself accepted in the competition of the market").

[35] Rehnquist, 54 Tex L Rev at 693 (cited in note 18), quoting *Lochner v New York*, 198 US 45, 76 (1905) (Holmes, J, dissenting).

cite: "Congress shall make no law . . . abridging the freedom of speech."[36] Such ritualized incantations, however, provide mere prelude to the main event. Strauss notes that in most constitutional law opinions judges do not expend much effort either examining the relevant constitutional text, or attempting to discern that text's original public meaning. Rather, the real action in constitutional decisions occurs when judges turn their attention toward parsing prior judicial decisions.

In the land of Strauss's living constitutionalism, precedent is indisputably king.[37] Strauss usefully defines a living Constitution as "one that evolves, changes over time, and adapts to new circumstances, without formally being amended."[38] The method by which constitutional evolution and adaptation have occurred in the United States, Strauss argues, is best understood as a type of common law adjudication whose touchstone is prior judicial decisions. "The common law is a system built not on an authoritative, foundational, quasi-sacred text like the Constitution," Strauss writes. "Rather, the common law is built out of precedents and traditions that accumulate over time. Those precedents allow room for adaptation and change, but only within certain limits and *only in ways that are rooted in the past*."[39] Strauss repeatedly emphasizes the constraints that bind judges within his understanding of living constitutionalism: "A common law constitution is a 'living' constitution, but . . . it is not one that judges (or anyone else) can simply manipulate to fit their own ideas."[40]

Strauss's great emphasis on precedent is not, of course, wholly unprecedented. Indeed, it comes as little surprise to learn that the patron saint of Strauss's precedent-based living constitutionalism is

---

[36] US Const, Amend I.

[37] Strauss, *Living Constitution* at 34 (cited in note 20) ("On a day-to-day basis, American constitutional law is about precedents. . . .").

[38] Id at 1.

[39] Id at 3 (emphasis added). Earlier versions of Professor Strauss's work on constitutional interpretation have afforded greater freedom for the legitimacy of judicial innovation. See, for example, Strauss, 63 U Chi L Rev at 895 (cited in note 22) ("If one has a great deal of confidence in an abstraction, it can override the presumption normally given to things that have worked well enough for a long time."). But, in the book, that space appears severely constrained.

[40] Strauss, *Living Constitution* at 3 (cited in note 20); see id at 45 (contending that, while "[t]he common law approach explicitly envisions that judges will be influenced by their own views, . . ." "[t]his doesn't mean that judges can do what they want").

Edmund Burke.[41] From Burke, Strauss derives his theory's two foundational pillars, which he calls the "attitudes of humility and cautious empiricism."[42] First, Strauss suggests that judges in a common law system must demonstrate humility about the limitations of their own individual capacities to reason. "It is a bad idea to try to resolve a problem on your own, without referring to the collective wisdom of other people who have tried to solve the same problem. That is why it makes sense to follow precedent . . . ," Strauss writes. "It is an act of intellectual hubris to think that you know better than that accumulated wisdom."[43] Second, Strauss contends that cautious empiricism requires judges to "distrust . . . abstractions when those abstractions call for casting aside arrangements that have been satisfactory in practice, even if the arrangements cannot be fully justified in abstract terms."[44] Burke, as Strauss notes, initially expressed this notion with a vivid metaphor: "[I]t is with infinite caution that any man ought to venture upon pulling down an edifice which has answered in any tolerable degree for ages the common purposes of society. . . ."[45]

Precedent occupies such exalted status in Strauss's account that he contends judges seldom have meaningful decisions to make, even when they issue a decision. "A judge who is faced with a difficult issue looks to how earlier courts decided that issue, or similar issues," Strauss explains. "The judge starts by assuming that she will do the same thing in the case before her that the earlier court did in similar cases. Sometimes—almost always, in fact—the precedents will be clear, and there will be no room for reasonable disagreement

---

[41] See generally Edmund Burke, *Reflections on the Revolution in France* (Oxford, 2009) (L. G. Mitchell, ed). For earlier explorations of Burke's theories and their applications to constitutional law, see generally Thomas W. Merrill, *Bork v. Burke*, 19 Harv J L & Pub Pol 509 (1996); Ernest Young, *Rediscovering Conservatism: Burkean Political Theory and Constitutional Interpretation*, 72 NC L Rev 619 (1994). For a claim that Burke's thought has been misrepresented as being more conservative than his record actually warrants, see generally Carl T. Bogus, *Rescuing Burke*, 72 Mo L Rev 387 (2007).

[42] Strauss, *Living Constitution* at 40 (cited in note 20).

[43] Id at 41. The familiar Burke quotation from which Strauss draws inspiration follows: "We are afraid to put men to live and trade each on his own private stock of reason; because we suspect that this stock in each man is small, and that the individuals would be better to avail themselves of the general bank and capital of nations, and of ages." Burke, *Reflections on the Revolution in France* at 87 (cited in note 41). Under the common law, Strauss concludes: "The accumulated precedents are 'the general bank and capital.'" Strauss, *Living Constitution* at 41 (cited in note 20).

[44] Strauss, *Living Constitution* at 41 (cited in note 20).

[45] Burke, *Reflections on the Revolution in France* at 61 (cited in note 41).

about what the precedents dictate."[46] In the lion's share of cases, then, judges simply implement the result that the precedents demand. On rare occasions, Strauss allows that "the earlier cases will not dictate a result. The earlier cases may not resemble the present case closely enough. Or there may be earlier cases that point in different directions, suggesting opposite outcomes in the case before the judge. *Then the judge has to decide what to do.*"[47] That last sentence is a remarkable one. It is, apparently, only when confronted with ambiguous or nonexistent precedential authority that judicial discretion enters Strauss's conception of living constitutionalism. "At that point—when the precedents are not clear—a variety of technical issues can enter into the picture," Strauss writes. "But often, when the precedents are not clear, the judge will decide the case before her on the basis of her views about which decision will be more fair or is more in keeping with good social policy."[48]

The effort to elevate precedent and diminish judicial discretion can, at times, make Strauss's living constitutionalism sound less like a theory of judging and more like a description of a naturally occurring scientific phenomenon. On this telling, judges do not so much issue decisions that craft legal doctrine; rather, "the living Constitution develops through the accumulation and evolution of precedents. . . ."[49] On a similar note, Strauss elsewhere explains: "Characteristically, the law emerges from this evolutionary process through the development of a body of precedents."[50] It is no accident that the actors primarily responsible for law's "development" and its "emerge[nce]" are missing in action here. Strauss's emphasis on the incremental evolution of the law, a process that generally unfolds over the course of decades, renders the identity of particular judges relatively insignificant. "[L]aw can be like a custom in important ways," Strauss explains. "It can develop over time, not at a single moment; it can be the evolutionary product of many people, in many generations. There does not have to be one entity who commanded the law in a discrete act at a particular time."[51]

Despite his veneration of precedent, Strauss does acknowledge

---

[46] Strauss, *Living Constitution* at 38 (cited in note 20).

[47] Id (emphasis added).

[48] Id.

[49] Id at 35.

[50] Id at 38.

[51] Id at 37.

the existence of a narrow band of instances where judges may disavow prior judicial decisions while remaining firmly within the common law tradition. "The working presumption in a common law system is that judges should follow precedent," Strauss explains. "But this is not an inflexible rule; in a common law system, judges sometimes may overrule precedents."[52] This acknowledgment forms an integral part of Strauss's living constitutionalism because, in its absence, his theory would be inextricably yoked to the past in a way that bears an uncomfortable resemblance to original expected application originalism. The role that such originalists assign to the framers would—without the ability to overrule precedents—instead be fulfilled by the judges with precedential authority who initially resolved any given legal dispute.[53]

If judges may reject precedents, the key question becomes: *when* may they legitimately do so? Strauss answers this question by way of inductive reasoning. He carefully walks readers through two canonical lines of cases in order to offer instances of judges legitimately overruling precedents within the common law tradition. Then, he draws back to extract broader principles from those instances. Given the centrality of these exemplars to Strauss's depiction of legitimate precedential overruling and the way that they obscure the judicial frontier, it is necessary to recount his treatment in some detail.[54]

Strauss's central focus in his examination of judicial innovation within living constitutionalism is *Brown v Board of Education*.[55] As

---

[52] Id at 40.

[53] Consider Saikrishna Prakash, *Radicals in Tweed Jackets: Why Extreme Left-Wing Law Professors Are Wrong for America*, 106 Colum L Rev 2207, 2213 (2006) ("[M]inimalism is a backwards-looking theory. New cases are to be decided as prior cases were resolved. Although Sunstein criticizes originalism's dead hand problem and its obsession with history, his brand of minimalism ironically has the same features.").

[54] Strauss is uncharacteristically cagey in his exploration of when it is permissible to overrule precedents while staying within the common law constitutional tradition. "When can a judge properly [overrule precedent]?" Strauss writes. Strauss, *Living Constitution* at 40 (cited in note 20). "The answer is complex—I will describe one such example in chapter 4. . . ." Id. It seems incumbent upon Strauss to delve further into the "complex[ity]" of permissible overruling than simply recounting instances that fall well within the ambit of common law constitutionalism. Although Strauss's formulation allows some space for painstaking readers to conclude that his account of permissible overruling is nonexhaustive, many readers seem likely to miss that subtlety. In all events, Strauss abandons readers to their own devices to contemplate instances of overruling that approach—and perhaps even exceed—the common law's outer reaches.

[55] 347 US 483 (1954). Chapter 4 of *The Living Constitution* is "*Brown v. Board of Education* and Innovation in the Living Constitution (with a Note on *Roe v. Wade*)." Strauss, *Living Constitution* at 77 (cited in note 20).

has often been remarked, *Brown* has become a litmus test for theories of constitutional interpretation, as any theory worth its salt must accommodate the decision.[56] No evidence better indicates that constitutional theories must pledge allegiance to *Brown* than the heroic, if ultimately unpersuasive, efforts of originalists to explain how the Equal Protection Clause's original meaning supports the judicial invalidation of racial segregation in public schools.[57] Yet even if *Brown* cannot be squared with originalism, Strauss urges that does not mean the decision must be deemed "a kind of mini coup d'état" or "a lawless act"—a morally honorable, but extralegal usurpation by the Warren Court.[58] "*Brown* didn't come out of the text and the original understandings, but it also didn't come out of nowhere," Strauss explains. "The common law . . . does not treat precedents as untouchable. . . . Once we understand that our Constitution is not just the text, and not just the original understandings—but is a living constitution that evolves as the common law does—*Brown* begins to look, if not routine, unquestionably lawful."[59]

Before launching headlong into a defense of *Brown*'s constitutional common law origins, Strauss pivots to examine how common law innovation has transpired in "its native habitat."[60] Here, Strauss highlights the familiar line of manufacturer liability cases that culminated in 1916 with Judge Benjamin Cardozo's celebrated opinion for the Court of Appeals of New York in *MacPherson v Buick Motor Co.*[61] In *MacPherson*, an automobile purchaser suffered an injury as a result of Buick's defective wheel production. *MacPherson* is remembered today for its articulation of a new rule declaring that a

---

[56] See, for example, Richard A. Posner, *Bork and Beethoven*, 42 Stan L Rev 1365, 1374 (1990) ("No constitutional theory that implies that *Brown v. Board of Education* . . . was decided incorrectly will receive a fair hearing nowadays. . . .").

[57] See Michael W. McConnell, *Originalism and the Desegregation Decisions*, 81 Va L Rev 947, 953 (1995) (arguing that originalism can account for *Brown*). For a powerful critique of McConnell's claim, see Michael J. Klarman, *Brown, Originalism, and Constitutional Theory: A Response to Professor McConnell*, 81 Va L Rev 1881, 1883 (1995).

[58] Strauss, *Living Constitution* at 79, 85 (cited in note 20).

[59] Id at 79–80. Professor Cass Sunstein has espoused a similar line on *Brown*. See Cass R. Sunstein, *One Case at a Time: Judicial Minimalism on the Supreme Court* 38 (Harvard, 1999) (contending that *Brown* "did not come like a thunderbolt from the sky," but rather "had been presaged by a long series of cases testing the proposition that 'separate' was 'equal,' and testing that proposition in such a way as to lead nearly inevitably to the suggestion that 'separate' could not be 'equal'").

[60] Strauss, *Living Constitution* at 80 (cited in note 20).

[61] 111 NE 1050 (NY 1916).

manufacturer may be held liable for harm suffered by individuals who were foreseeably injured by manufacturer negligence. This new foreseeability rule meant, at bottom, that Mrs. MacPherson could attempt to receive compensation for her injuries from Buick. Prior to *MacPherson*, her ability to sue Buick would have been deeply uncertain because of the then-prevailing privity-of-contract requirement, which generally prohibited negligent manufacturers from being held liable by parties with whom they had not contracted. As a practical matter, this privity regime typically prevented consumers from holding negligent manufacturers liable because manufacturers usually distribute goods to retailers, who in turn sell those goods to consumers.

Although Cardozo's notions of fairness suggested to him that the privity requirement should be abandoned in favor of the foreseeability rule, Strauss indicates that two additional factors, each rooted in the past, allow *MacPherson* to fit comfortably within the common law tradition. First, Strauss notes that Cardozo's opinion abandoning the privity requirement did not drop from the clear blue sky: many prior decisions, including some that predated the Civil War, had succeeded in slowly undermining the privity regime. New York courts had long acknowledged an exception to the privity requirement for manufacturers of "inherently dangerous" goods. But by the time of *MacPherson*, the New York judiciary had invoked the concept so often that it effectively allowed the "inherently dangerous" exception to swallow the privity rule. With decisions in the early 1900s finding that seemingly innocuous items (including a large coffee urn and a bottle of aerated water) were in fact "inherently dangerous," Cardozo could declare that the privity regime had been corroded.[62]

Second, Strauss suggests that it is crucial that this corrosion occurred in an organic fashion, as judges seemed to act unwittingly in abandoning privity and embracing foreseeability. "[W]hile the courts were purporting to apply the privity regime—and no doubt generally believed that they were, to the best of their ability, applying the privity regime—they were, quite possibly without knowing it, gravitating to a new rule," Strauss explains.[63] These two features reveal that *MacPherson* was not some sort of judicial frolic,

---

[62] See Strauss, *Living Constitution* at 83 (cited in note 20) ("[T]he earlier cases had demonstrated that the privity regime was no longer workable.").

[63] Id at 84.

with Cardozo unilaterally reading his idiosyncratic views into law. Instead, *MacPherson*'s conclusion "was, in a sense, not just Cardozo's alone," Strauss writes. "It was a conclusion that the earlier judges had also gradually reached, over several decades, even though those judges did not acknowledge the evolution in the law. Cardozo's innovation consisted of making that conclusion, reached inexplicitly in fits and starts, fully explicit."[64]

With *MacPherson*'s common law lineage firmly established, Strauss turns his attention to detailing how *Brown* should be understood as constitutionally legitimate because it emerged from a markedly similar incremental series of decisions. It may seem as though in *Brown*, the Supreme Court, in a singular act, tore down the edifice of Jim Crow that it had propped up in *Plessy v Ferguson*.[65] But that appearance is woefully misleading, Strauss suggests, because it disregards the Supreme Court's many decisions prior to 1954 undermining *Plessy*'s determination that racially separate railroad cars could in fact be equal for purposes of the Fourteenth Amendment. "The cases leading up to *Brown* . . . had already left 'separate but equal' in a shambles," Strauss writes. "*Brown* was the completion of an evolutionary, common law process, not an isolated, pathbreaking act."[66]

Recovering the Court's gradual erosion of *Plessy* is essential, Strauss suggests, because doing so belies the notion that *Brown* was unlawful. Accordingly, while Strauss acknowledges in passing that the Court endorsed segregated education in the period following *Plessy*, he then emphasizes that the Court simultaneously began "sow[ing] some of the seeds of the common law demise of separate but equal" during the 1910s.[67] In 1914, the Court in *McCabe v Atchison, Topeka & Santa Fe Railway*[68] questioned an Oklahoma stat-

---

[64] Id at 84–85. It merits noting that—in some tension with Professor Strauss's account—scholars have suggested that Judge Cardozo in fact played a far more significant role in *MacPherson* than simply announcing a rule that other judges had already been implicitly implementing. See, for example, Richard A. Posner, *Cardozo: A Study in Reputation* 109 (Chicago, 1990) ("Carefully qualified though it was, modest though it was in pretending to be restating rather than changing the law of New York, reticent as it was about the policy considerations relevant to the change it made, the opinion nevertheless managed to change profoundly the climate of opinion regarding privity of contract."); id at 126 ("The vast majority of [Cardozo's] opinions apply established principles without altering them. *MacPherson* is a notable exception. . . .").

[65] See *Plessy v Ferguson*, 163 US 537 (1896).

[66] Strauss, *Living Constitution* at 85 (cited in note 20).

[67] Id at 86.

[68] 235 US 151 (1914).

ute that permitted railroads to provide upmarket accommodations for white passengers (such as sleeping cars), but not for black passengers.[69] Although Oklahoma contended that an insufficient number of black passengers sought such services, *McCabe* deemed the overall black demand for such services irrelevant because the arrangement denied at least some black individuals the equality they were owed under separate but equal. "Arguably," Strauss contends, "the Court even cut back on the segregationist logic of separate but equal."[70] Three years after *McCabe*, the Court in *Buchanan v Warley*[71] rejected a housing ordinance from Louisville, Kentucky, that was designed to promote racial segregation by preventing people from occupying a home on a block where the majority of the homes were occupied by members of a different race.[72] Although "[t]he Court's reasoning emphasized the seller's right to dispose of his property as he saw fit," Strauss writes, "*Buchanan*, too, can be seen as undermining, however subtly, the logic of *Plessy* and separate but equal."[73]

Strauss contends that in 1938, with the Supreme Court's decision in *Missouri ex rel Gaines v Canada*,[74] "the seeds that were arguably sown in *McCabe* and *Buchanan* bore fruit."[75] Rather than either admitting black students to the state's law school or establishing a law school for blacks, Missouri made arrangements for them to attend law schools in surrounding states and paid their tuition fees. Even though Lloyd Gaines appears to have been the first black applicant to the University of Missouri Law School, the Court nevertheless struck down the measure, relying in part upon *McCabe*'s holding that modest black demand did not absolve states from providing equal facilities for blacks.[76] Strauss contends that building a separate law school for blacks would not have been economically viable in most states. "Realistically, *Gaines*—while not questioning the principle of separate but equal—left many states with no choice but to admit blacks to the same graduate schools that whites at-

---

[69] Id at 158, 161.

[70] Strauss, *Living Constitution* at 86 (cited in note 20).

[71] 245 US 60 (1917).

[72] Id at 82.

[73] Strauss, *Living Constitution* at 86–87 (cited in note 20).

[74] 305 US 337 (1938).

[75] Strauss, *Living Constitution* at 87 (cited in note 20).

[76] *Gaines*, 305 US at 350–52.

tended," Strauss writes.[77] This absence of meaningful choice inspires Strauss to conclude: "There is a direct line from *McCabe*, decided in 1914, to *Gaines*, decided in 1938, and a direct line from *Gaines* to *Brown*."[78]

The Supreme Court's steady erosion of *Plessy* only intensified after *Gaines*. Among the most important opinions during this onslaught of Jim Crow were *Shelley v Kraemer*,[79] finding that the judiciary may not enforce racially restrictive covenants without violating the Fourteenth Amendment;[80] *McLaurin v Oklahoma State Regents for Higher Education*,[81] prohibiting states from keeping black students separated from their white classmates within a historically white graduate school;[82] and *Sweatt v Painter*,[83] prohibiting states from establishing racially separate graduate schools for blacks if those schools do not equal their white counterparts in both tangible and intangible terms.[84] "*Plessy* had upheld separate but equal, and that technically remained the law until *Brown*," Strauss writes. But surveying "the legal landscape . . . when *Brown* came before the Supreme Court" leaves no doubt "that this progression of precedents had left separate but equal hanging by a thread."[85]

Stepping back to place these two lines of cases in perspective, Strauss concludes that "*Brown* is strikingly parallel to *MacPherson*."[86] The opinions by Chief Justice Warren and Judge Cardozo both announced the rejection of an established legal doctrine, but those announcements arrived only after numerous decisions by numerous judges had slowly, almost imperceptibly, eroded the doctrine. Strauss contends that the decisions in both *Brown* and *MacPherson* could accurately state that they were "just making explicit the con-

---

[77] Strauss, *Living Constitution* at 88 (cited in note 20).

[78] Id.

[79] 334 US 1 (1948).

[80] Id at 20–21.

[81] 339 US 637 (1950).

[82] Id at 642.

[83] 339 US 629 (1950).

[84] Id at 633–36. As Strauss acknowledged in his law review article articulating common law constitutionalism, the argument that Supreme Court doctrine had by the 1950s hollowed out *Plessy*'s rule can be traced back to Professor Louis Michael Seidman's scholarship. Strauss, 63 U Chi L Rev at 902 n 61 (cited in note 22). See also Louis Michael Seidman, *Brown and Miranda*, 80 Cal L Rev 673, 708 (1992) ("Given what came before, the real question is why *Brown* needed to be decided at all.").

[85] Strauss, *Living Constitution* at 90 (cited in note 20).

[86] Id at 91.

clusions that the earlier decisions had arrived at in fact, but had not acknowledged in name: there was no distinct category of inherently dangerous products, and there was no such thing as facilities that were segregated but equal."[87] Just as *MacPherson* grew partly out of Cardozo's concerns regarding the fairness of the privity requirement, Strauss notes, the Court in *Brown* was surely driven in part by its viewing segregation as morally suspect. But moral sentiment alone did not account for *Brown*. Instead, Strauss notes, the moral sentiment of those judges was "buttressed by the lessons of the past," in keeping with the common law tradition.[88] "Earlier Courts, trying to apply separate but equal, kept coming to the conclusion that the particular separate facilities before them were not equal," Strauss writes. "In concluding that separate could never be equal, the Court in *Brown* was taking one further step in a well-established progression. It was acting not as the interpreter of the views of mid-nineteenth-century politicians, but as a court with responsibility for the evolution—in a properly restrained, common law fashion—of the living Constitution."[89]

III. THE LIVING CONSTITUTION: A COUNTER-LIFE

Professor Strauss's theory of living constitutionalism suffers from two principal weaknesses. First, as a descriptive matter, Strauss's living constitutionalism elides the deep uncertainties and anxieties that afflict judges when they contemplate issuing decisions that break with existing traditions, particularly at the initial point of departure. Strauss advances orderly narratives of judicial incrementalism that begin with the culmination of particular doctrinal developments and then look backward to identify decisions prefiguring those developments. On this telling, judges subconsciously gravitate from one legal position to another after a sufficient body of precedent has quietly accumulated demonstrating that the old position has proven unworkable. These stylized accounts fail to capture the realities of constitutional innovation. Living constitutionalism, instead, should attempt to recreate the concrete set of choices and obstacles that confront judges in each step of their decision making. Second, as a normative matter, judges who inter-

---

[87] Id at 91–92.

[88] Id at 92.

[89] Id.

nalize Strauss's living constitutionalism may find themselves overly inhibited from issuing decisions that they deem constitutionally appropriate, but garner little or no support from existing judicial decisions. Consequently, judges who are theoretically committed to interpreting the Constitution in a dynamic manner could find themselves in practice advocating static constitutional interpretation—even in cases that they believe, as a first-order matter, demand constitutional dynamism.

Rather than merely articulating those shortcomings in the abstract, this section instead illuminates those shortcomings by offering a counter-narrative of crucial opinions on the Supreme Court's road to reversing *Plessy*. In doing so, this counter-narrative aims to provide a more accurate, historically grounded account of living constitutionalism at work. Rather than taking the Court's ultimate destination as prearranged and then examining the earlier cases through that prism, this counter-narrative attempts to sketch the legal and precedential backdrop as it would have appeared to judges charged with deciding cases during particular historical moments. The following counter-life of living constitutionalism emphasizes how before *Brown* judges repeatedly issued decisions that placed themselves on the constitutional frontier. Had the Justices employed the precedent-centric approach to judging and demonstrated an aversion to abstractions, it seems highly implausible that the Supreme Court's decisions expanding conceptions of equality would ever have been issued in the first instance.

A. DEPARTURE

Nowhere is the need for a richer account of living constitutionalism more apparent than in the initial moment when judges depart from precedent. It is crucial to capture that moment vividly because it is at that time that judges must typically either confront precedential authority that points in the opposite direction, sidestep that authority with an effort to distinguish it, or simply ignore it altogether. It strains credulity to believe that at this decisive moment members of the legal community—including the judges responsible for issuing those decisions—are unaware that alterations in legal doctrine are afoot. That statement carries particular force when the judicial departure involves protecting the rights of marginalized minorities who have previously been denied judicial protection. Rather than depicting judges as unwittingly and subconsciously gravitating toward a new understanding of whose rights deserve protection, it seems more plausible to describe judges as keenly aware of the instances when decisions first afford groups even modest amounts of judicial protection. Indeed, what in hindsight may be described as an opinion that is merely an incremental step can—at the time it is issued—seem like an enormous stride.

It is helpful, here, to recover the legal community's understanding of *Plessy* during the late 1890s and early twentieth century, as that understanding differs from today's common understanding. Rather than fixating on the notorious language from the Louisiana statute mandating "'equal but separate accommodations,'"[90] many lawyers instead concentrated on *Plessy*'s extremely forgiving language determining that racial classifications would be upheld provided that they were merely reasonable. "So far . . . as a conflict with the Fourteenth Amendment is concerned, the case reduces itself to the question whether the statute of Louisiana is a reasonable regulation, and with respect to this there must necessarily be a large discretion on the part of the legislature," Justice Brown wrote in *Plessy*.[91] When the legislature enacts racial classifications, *Plessy* made clear, it does so reasonably when it acts "with reference to the established usages, customs and traditions of the people, and with a view to the promotion of their comfort, and the preservation of the public peace and good order."[92] Assessed against this lax standard of reasonableness, the Court concluded that it could not find that Louisiana's segregated railcars were "unreasonable, or more obnoxious to the Fourteenth Amendment than" laws requiring segregated schools.[93]

With this understanding of the breadth of *Plessy*'s holding in mind, it becomes possible to see that the first meaningful moment of departure from *Plessy* occurred not (as Strauss posits) in 1914 with *McCabe*, but three years later with its decision invalidating segregated housing ordinances in *Buchanan*. *McCabe*—which suggested states must provide upscale train accommodations for black and white passengers alike—is more persuasively conceived as strictly enforcing "separate but equal" rather than undercutting

---

[90] *Plessy*, 163 US at 540, quoting Separate Car Act, 1890 La Acts 152 (1890).

[91] Id at 550.

[92] Id.

[93] Id at 551.

it.[94] *Buchanan*, in contrast, represented a true departure from *Plessy*, as Justices who conceived of their jobs as simply applying precedent would have viewed segregation ordinances as raising a laughably easy question.

The accuracy of that statement is made clear by examining how thoroughly the legal community's expectations were turned upside down by the Court's decision in *Buchanan*. Before the Court decided *Buchanan*, commentary in law reviews uniformly predicted that the Court would uphold segregated housing ordinances.[95] Predictably, *Plessy*'s reasonableness standard often loomed large in their assessments. Warren Hunting, writing in the *Columbia Law Review* six years before *Buchanan*, was typical in advancing the idea that segregation ordinances helped to preserve the racial peace: "If there is a mutual repugnance between the races, is it not reasonable to separate them in their dwellings when it is remembered that neither the whites' nor the negroes' right to live where they will is curtailed any more than is absolutely necessary to secure the desired separation?"[96] In 1911, Hunting's rhetorical question virtually seemed to answer itself. "Under the reasoning of *Plessy v. Ferguson* it could hardly be said to be unreasonable," he concluded.[97] Four years later, T. B. Benson similarly concluded that "[t]he bona fides of these ordinances can not be made a serious

---

[94] See Michael J. Klarman, *Race and the Court in the Progressive Era*, 51 Vand L Rev 881, 932 (1998) (contending it would be incorrect to view *McCabe* as "a significant departure"). In contrast to the firestorm that *Buchanan* generated in law reviews, *McCabe* apparently received only three contemporaneous notices. See generally *Oklahoma's Separate Coach Law*, 80 Central L J 43 (1915); Editorial, 20 Va L Reg 781 (1915); Note, *Statutory Discriminations Against Negroes with Reference to Pullman Cars*, 28 Harv L Rev 417 (1915). Those three notices, moreover, contained nothing like the vitriol directed at *Buchanan*. Portraying *McCabe* as creating a fissure in the wall of Jim Crow, as Professor Randall Kennedy has urged, "reads into *McCabe* too much subsequent history" and "give[s the decision] a meaning that it simply did not have in its own historical context." Randall Kennedy, *Race Relations Law and the Tradition of Celebration: The Case of Professor Schmidt*, 86 Colum L Rev 1622, 1646 (1986). *McCabe* itself, moreover, did not even mandate relief for the plaintiffs who filed suit. *McCabe*, 235 US at 163.

[95] See David E. Bernstein, *Rehabilitating Lochner: Defending Individual Rights against Progressive Reform* 84 (Chicago, 2011) (observing that "pre-*Buchanan* law review commentary . . . universally argued that residential segregation laws were constitutional"). For pieces condemning *Buchanan*, see, for example, James F. Minor, *Constitutionality of Segregation Ordinances*, 18 Va L Reg 561, 572 (1912) (contending that segregated-housing ordinances passed constitutional muster); Note, *Constitutional Law—Segregation Ordinance*, 63 U Pa L Rev 895, 897 (1915) (contending "[i]t is hard to see . . . how [a segregation ordinance] could be construed to be a denial of the equal protection of the laws").

[96] Warren B. Hunting, *The Constitutionality of Race Distinctions and the Baltimore Negro Segregation Ordinance*, 11 Colum L Rev 24, 31–32 (1911).

[97] Id at 29.

question in law," as "[a] reasonable necessity for segregation arises from the ill-effect of a too close commingling of the two races, which is of ill effect to both. . . ."[98]

Such views were far from confined to the corridors of legal academia. Indeed, the lower courts consistently found no constitutional fault with properly drafted segregation ordinances prior to *Buchanan*.[99] In *Harden v City of Atlanta*,[100] the Georgia Supreme Court reasoned that the constitutionality of segregated schools—something that *Plessy* had treated as bedrock[101]—necessarily meant that housing ordinances were constitutionally legitimate. Policies in both arenas, *Harden* underlined, were driven by antimiscegenation sentiment. "If it be justifiable to separate the races in the public schools in recognition of the peril to race integrity, induced by mere race association, then we cannot see why the same public policy cannot be invoked to prohibit the black and white races from living side by side," *Harden* observed. "Segregation is not imposed as a stigma upon either race, but in order to uphold the integrity of each race and to prevent conflicts between them resulting from close association."[102] In the case that would become known as *Buchanan* when it reached the Supreme Court, the Kentucky Court of Appeals similarly upheld Louisville's segregation ordinance on the public welfare grounds that the law had been enacted: "[1] in order to prevent . . . racial discord consequent upon the close association of the races, and [2] in order that the solidarity of the races may be preserved. . . ."[103]

Even after the Court invalidated segregation ordinances in *Buch-*

---

[98] T. B. Benson, *Segregation Ordinances*, 1 Va L Reg, NS 330, 330, 354 (1915).

[99] See, for example, *Harris v City of Louisville*, 177 SW 472 (Ky 1915) (validating segregation ordinance); *Hopkins v City of Richmond*, 86 SE 139 (Va 1915) (same); *Harden v City of Atlanta*, 93 SE 401 (Ga 1917) (same). The Georgia Supreme Court's decision in *Harden* effectively overruled its earlier decision invalidating a housing ordinance that did not include an exemption for property acquired before the ordinance's enactment. See *Carey v City of Atlanta*, 84 SE 456 (Ga 1915). Although *Buchanan* cites *Carey* for support, it completely ignores the Georgia Supreme Court's subsequent decision validating the properly drawn segregation ordinance. The failure to include such an exemption also prompted the Maryland Court of Appeals to invalidate a housing ordinance. See *State v Gurry*, 88 A 546 (Md Ct App 1913). The pattern seems clear: when states and localities drew up segregation ordinances with exemptions for existing property arrangements, lower courts upheld those ordinances.

[100] 93 SE 401 (Ga 1917).

[101] See *Plessy*, 163 US at 544–45.

[102] *Harden*, 93 SE at 402–03.

[103] *Harris*, 177 SW at 477.

anan, legal commentators nevertheless overwhelmingly denounced the decision as lawless and as an unwarranted break with tradition.[104] Writing in the *Michigan Law Review*, a student captured the sentiments of many within the legal community in expressing outrage that *Buchanan* flouted not only relevant Supreme Court precedent, but several state court opinions that were directly on point. "After all this direct and emphatic expression of opinion that the ordinance was reasonably necessary and conducive to public welfare it is surprising that the Supreme Court should have declared it unreasonable and, therefore, unconstitutional," the author complained. "In declaring the ordinance void without such obvious reasonableness, the court has exceeded the limits of its privilege as fixed by judicial declaration ever since the right of review has been exercised."[105]

Tellingly, one of the few legal commentators who expressed some sympathy for *Buchanan*'s outcome nevertheless felt compelled to concede that the decision exceeded the proper bounds of judicial authority. This piece, written by a student for the *Harvard Law Review*, merits examination because it vividly illustrates how even people who held relatively advanced understandings of racial equality during the 1910s had difficulty believing that those views could find legitimate expression in the form of constitutional interpretation. "Doubtless this is a desirable result to reach. . . . Be that as it may, it is difficult to feel convinced that the result has been reached by sound canons of judicial review," the note concluded.[106] The frontier of constitutional law often witnesses legal commentators bemoaning the distance between their understandings of the constitutional *is* and the policy *ought*. *Buchanan*,

---

[104] For a mere sampling of the negative commentary, see generally Note, *Race Segregation Ordinance Invalid*, 31 Harv L Rev 475 (1917); Note, *Constitutionality of Segregation Ordinances*, 16 Mich L Rev 109 (1917); S. S. Field, *The Constitutionality of Segregation Ordinances*, 5 Va L Rev 81, 89 (1917); W. F. Chapman, Note, *Segregation Ordinances*, 3 Cornell L Q 133 (1918); Comment, *Unconstitutionality of Segregation Ordinances*, 27 Yale L J 393 (1918). Despite the substantial amount of law review commentary that *Buchanan* generated, only one favorable response can be found in that first wave. See David E. Bernstein, *Philip Sober Controlling Philip Drunk: Buchanan v. Warley in Historical Perspective*, 51 Vand L Rev 797, 856 (1998) (noting, with the exception of one law review note, "all other law review commentary was hostile to" *Buchanan*). Predictably, the lone law review comment that praised the Court for *Buchanan* did not contend that the decision was in any way required by precedents. See Note, *Constitutionality of Race Segregation*, 18 Colum L Rev 147, 152 (1918).

[105] Note, 16 Mich L Rev at 111 (cited in note 104).

[106] Note, 31 Harv L Rev at 476 (cited in note 104).

the author suggested, was driven by the latter consideration when it should have been limited to the former. Instead of adhering to Supreme Court precedents, the decision appeared motivated by extralegal desires. "While opinions may well differ as to the efficacy and ultimate consequences of such [segregation ordinances], can it be said that there is no reasonable and appropriate relation between the end sought and the means adopted?" the author asked rhetorically. "The Supreme Court of the United States must find it difficult to say there is no such relation, for it had already sustained state legislation requiring railway companies to provide . . . equal, but separate, accommodations for the two races, and a state statute requiring the separation of the races in schools."[107]

Even many years after the Court had invalidated segregation ordinances, some legal commentators continued to find *Buchanan* constitutionally dubious.[108] In 1934, some seventeen years after *Buchanan*, Professor Arthur Martin could still be found complaining in the *Michigan Law Review* that the decision lacked proper legal foundation. "There are no legal doctrines or case precedents which required these segregation ordinances to be held unconstitutional," Martin wrote. "Inasmuch as public welfare was the criterion of validity there should have been some conscious appraisal of the social desirability of segregation by legal device."[109]

The foregoing assessments of segregation ordinances demonstrate that *Buchanan* cannot convincingly be portrayed as providing mere subtle erosion of *Plessy* in the manner typically associated with common law constitutionalism. Rather, contemporaneous legal observers—almost without exception—viewed *Buchanan* as representing a sharp (and unwelcome) break with the prevailing legal order. Commentators repeatedly and vehemently asserted that *Buchanan* found no grounding in either the nation's legal traditions or in the Supreme Court's precedents. Such assertions, moreover, proved remarkably durable.

---

[107] Id at 478 (citing *Plessy* and *Berea College*).

[108] See George D. Hott, Note, *Constitutionality of Municipal Zoning and Segregation Ordinances*, 33 W Va L Q 332, 349 (1927) ("If a municipality can prevent the establishment of a 'Piggly-Wiggly' store in a residential section, without violating any of the constitutional prohibitions, it should follow that an ordinance, excluding negroes from a 'white' zone and vice versa, should, in the absence of infringement of existing property rights, be constitutional.").

[109] Arthur T. Martin, *Segregation of Residences of Negroes*, 32 Mich L Rev 721, 730–31 (1934).

It seems deeply implausible that the Supreme Court Justices could—on such a pressing and prominent legal question—issue a decision thoroughly upending the legal community's settled expectations without consciously understanding that they were about to do so. Modern legal scholars have often contended that property rights, not civil rights, motivated the Court's decision in *Buchanan*.[110] Some of the Court's language in *Buchanan*, coupled with the fact that the notoriously racist Justice McReynolds failed to file a dissenting opinion, undeniably lend support to this idea.[111] Nevertheless, it is extremely difficult to read Justice Day's opinion for the Court in *Buchanan* without appreciating that the opinion advanced a conception of race that stands in clear tension with the one embodied in *Plessy*. It is equally difficult to read *Buchanan* and believe that its author was simply unaware of this tension.

Although Louisville justified its segregation ordinance on the usual grounds of attempting to avoid racial conflict, *Buchanan* subjected those reasons to considerable scrutiny and refused—as was the order of the day—merely to rubberstamp them as reasonable. The Court declined, for instance, to uphold the statute even though Louisville asserted that the ordinance was necessary to prevent miscegenation—an assertion that then typically acted as a legal trump card. "Such action is said to be essential to the maintenance of the purity of the races," Justice Day wrote, "although it is to be noted in the ordinance under consideration that the employment of colored servants in white families is permitted, and nearby residences of colored persons not coming within the

---

[110] See, for example, Lucas A. Powe, Jr., *The Supreme Court and the American Elite, 1789–2008* at 189 (Harvard, 2009) (suggesting that *Buchanan* should not be viewed as "a true civil rights case"); Michael J. Klarman, *From Jim Crow to Civil Rights: The Supreme Court and the Struggle for Racial Equality* 80 (Oxford, 2004) (contending that the decision "was not a significant departure with regard to *race. Buchanan* was decided . . . when the justices were most committed to protecting property rights."). Some scholars have periodically attempted to dislodge the notion that *Buchanan* was driven primarily by property considerations rather than racial considerations. See Alexander M. Bickel and Benno C. Schmidt, Jr., *The Judiciary and Responsible Government 1910–1921* at 810–17 (Cambridge, 2007); Bernstein, *Rehabilitating Lochner* at 81–85 (cited in note 95); Jack M. Balkin, *Plessy, Brown, and Grutter: A Play in Three Acts*, 26 Cardozo L Rev 1689, 1704 (2005). But the conventional perception of *Buchanan* stubbornly persists.

[111] See *Buchanan*, 245 US at 74 (construing the Fourteenth Amendment as involving property rights outside of *Buchanan*'s particular racialized context). For an intimate account of Justice McReynolds's racism offered by one of his law clerks, see generally John Knox, *The Forgotten Memoir of John Knox: A Year in the Life of a Supreme Court Clerk in FDR's Washington* (Chicago, 2002) (Dennis J. Hutchinson and David J. Garrow, eds).

blocks, as defined in the ordinance, are not prohibited."[112] Turning to Louisville's claim that blacks living in white neighborhoods would decrease property values, *Buchanan* took the then-unusual step of drawing a cross-racial comparison, noting that "property may [also] be acquired by undesirable white neighbors."[113] Such analyses may not seem to articulate especially enlightened racial attitudes today. Pointing out that whites have black servants and that not every white person makes a delightful neighbor would not, it seems clear, suffice to get one shortlisted for an NAACP Image Award. Nevertheless, *Buchanan* established for the first time in the twentieth century that judges would no longer automatically allow the quest to preserve racial segregation to defeat all other considerations. "That there exists a serious and difficult problem arising from a feeling of race hostility which the law is powerless to control, and to which it must give a measure of consideration, may be freely admitted," Justice Day noted. "But its solution cannot be promoted by depriving citizens of their constitutional rights and privileges."[114]

The conclusion that the Court's decision in *Buchanan* represented a conscious departure from *Plessy*'s rationale is perhaps most apparent in Justice Day's utterly unsatisfying attempt to distinguish the earlier case.[115] Here, in its entirety, is Justice Day's effort to explain why a law requiring segregated housing was impermissible, but a law requiring segregated traveling was permissible:

> It is to be observed that in [*Plessy*] there was no attempt to deprive persons of color of transportation in the coaches of the public carrier, and the express requirements were for equal though separate accommodations for the white and colored races. In *Plessy v. Ferguson*, classification of accommodations was permitted upon the basis of equality for both races.[116]

---

[112] *Buchanan*, 245 US at 81.

[113] Id at 82.

[114] Id at 80–81.

[115] As a technical matter, the Supreme Court decided *Buchanan* under the Fourteenth Amendment's Due Process Clause, not the Equal Protection Clause. See id at 82 (indicating that the ordinance "is in direct violation of the fundamental law enacted in the Fourteenth Amendment of the Constitution preventing state interference with property rights except by due process of law"). I am in agreement with Professor Strauss's tacit view, however, that this technical hook does not substantially alter the Court's analysis. Indeed, *Buchanan* is far from precise about keeping its analyses of the two clauses distinct—a feature of the case demonstrated by its perceived need to distinguish *Plessy*.

[116] Id at 79.

One may inspect every page of the U.S. Reports without being able to locate a better example of an ipse dixit.[117] After all, the segregation ordinances did not aim to deprive black citizens from living in homes altogether. Rather, they were prohibited only from living in homes in certain blocks, just as the statute at issue in *Plessy* prohibited black passengers from riding in certain railcars. If, as *Plessy* instructed, black railcars did not violate "separate but equal," it is far from clear what required a different rule to govern black neighborhoods. Indeed, to the extent that one took anti-miscegenation sentiments seriously, it is challenging to articulate why the need to keep the races separated was not more pressing in the context of living arrangements than in the context of traveling arrangements.[118] Supreme Court Justices, like the larger legal community, must have understood that *Buchanan* simply asserted rather than demonstrated a meaningful distinction with *Plessy*.

It is important, however, not to overstate *Buchanan*'s meaning. That opinion should in no way be understood as indicating that it was only a matter of time before the Court issued *Brown*. Topping the lengthy list of reasons that such an interpretation would be absurd is that during the 1950s, some four decades after *Buchanan*, many Supreme Court Justices continued to view school segregation as presenting an exceedingly close constitutional question.[119] To that end, it would be sorely mistaken to view *Buchanan* as accomplishing everything. But it would also be mistaken to view *Buchanan* as accomplishing nothing. When the Supreme Court invalidated segregation ordinances in *Buchanan*, the Court made its first unmistakable break with the logic of *Plessy*. Had the Court in 1917 feared articulating constitutional understandings that lacked support in existing legal materials, that barrier would almost certainly have remained unbroken.

---

[117] Consider Bickel and Schmidt, *The Judiciary and Responsible Government* at 813 (cited in note 110) (noting "the opinion makes no serious effort to reconcile its holding with *Plessy*").

[118] See Field, 5 Va L Rev at 88 (cited in note 104) ("People travel on railway trains only occasionally—they live in their homes all the time.").

[119] See Klarman, *From Jim Crow to Civil Rights* at 293 (cited in note 110) (noting that "many of the Justices found *Brown* difficult" and that "the outcome was uncertain"); Dennis J. Hutchinson, *Unanimity and Desegregation: Decisionmaking in the Supreme Court, 1948–1958*, 68 Georgetown L J 1, 3 (1979) ("Although Mr. Justice Fortas suggested a few years ago that the 1950 decisions made *Brown* inevitable, the eventual result in *Brown* was not a foregone conclusion in 1950." (quotation marks and citation omitted)).

B. EXPLORATION

The Supreme Court's decision in *Gaines* should similarly be understood as an instance where the Justices deliberately chose to turn their backs on the most closely related precedents in order to place themselves once again on the constitutional frontier. Had the Supreme Court focused primarily on precedent when it decided *Gaines*, the Justices almost certainly would have felt they had precious little choice other than to uphold Missouri's scheme for educating black law students. Rather than stretching to locate a favorable proposition in *McCabe*—a case that involved upmarket train accommodations, after all—it seems more probable that a precedent-focused Court would instead have examined cases far more clearly resembling the matter at hand. The Supreme Court had already issued three decisions involving education in the Jim Crow context when it considered *Gaines* in 1938. In each of those three cases, the Supreme Court declined to interfere with the states' educational choices. There is little reason to believe that Missouri's tuition-subsidy program treated black citizens more harshly than the other three programs upon which the Court had already placed its imprimatur; indeed, of the four regimes, *Gaines*—as a practical matter—appears to have involved the least objectionable treatment of blacks that the Court confronted.

The Supreme Court decided its first case involving education and race in *Cumming v County Board of Education*[120] in 1899, just three years after *Plessy*. In *Cumming*, black plaintiffs complained that, despite their paying an educational tax, a Georgia county had closed the high school for black children even as it continued to operate the high school for white children.[121] In a unanimous opinion by Justice Harlan, the Court ignored *Plessy* altogether and refused to declare that even this avowedly unequal arrangement violated the Fourteenth Amendment. "[T]he education of the people in schools maintained by state taxation is a matter belonging to the respective states," Justice Harlan reasoned, "and any interference on the part of Federal authority with the management of such schools cannot be justified except in the case of a clear and unmistakable disregard of rights secured by the supreme law of

---

[120] 175 US 528 (1899).
[121] Id at 529–31.

the land."[122] *Cumming*, in the Court's eyes, presented no such case.[123]

The next Supreme Court case involving race and education took place, as *Gaines* eventually would, in the field of higher learning. In *Berea College v Kentucky*,[124] the Supreme Court in 1908 considered whether a private institution that accepted both white and black undergraduates must abide by a Kentucky law prohibiting integrated education.[125] *Berea College* potentially raised some thorny legal issues for segregationists, most prominently whether the state law permissibly regulated interracial contact when such contact could easily be construed as both private and consensual. Nevertheless, the Court seized upon the fact that the college was a state-chartered corporation to find that it must adhere to Kentucky's law and abandon its experiment in educational integration.[126]

Finally, the Supreme Court decided *Gong Lum v Rice*[127] in 1927, just eleven years before the Court decided *Gaines*. *Gong Lum* involved a challenge to a Mississippi school district's decision prohibiting a Chinese American girl from attending the local school for white children, but leaving her free to attend the school for black children.[128] In an opinion written by Chief Justice Taft, the Supreme Court simplified the case by essentially treating it as only the latest in a long series of lawsuits contesting racial segregation in public schools. "Were this a new question," Chief Justice Taft wrote, "it would call for very full argument and consideration; but we think that it is the same question which has been many times decided to be within the constitutional power of the state Legislature to settle, without intervention, of the federal courts under the federal Constitution."[129] In reaching this conclusion, *Gong Lum* expressly relied upon dicta in *Plessy*—a case that raised, in Taft's view, "a more difficult question than this"—indicating that seg-

---

[122] Id at 545.

[123] Id.

[124] 211 US 45 (1908).

[125] Id at 46.

[126] Id at 54–58.

[127] 275 US 78 (1927).

[128] Id at 79–80, 82.

[129] Id at 85–86.

regated schools stood on firm constitutional footing.[130] That this particular lawsuit was brought on behalf of a pupil of the "yellow race[]" rather than a "black pupil[]" made no difference, according to the Court.[131]

By foregrounding these three precedents, it becomes easier to grasp the Missouri Supreme Court's decision finding that the state's tuition program did not violate the Constitution.[132] In its equal protection analysis, the Missouri Supreme Court placed particular emphasis on *Plessy*'s dicta blessing segregated schools and *Gong Lum*'s somewhat exasperated observation that courts had repeatedly found that such schools passed constitutional muster.[133] "Since it is settled law that the mere separation of the races for the purpose of education deprives neither of any rights," the Missouri Supreme Court reasoned, "the remaining question is whether or not the advantages for higher education offered to the negroes of the state are substantially equal to the advantages furnished white students."[134] The Missouri Supreme Court answered that question in the affirmative, finding that the law schools in Kansas, Nebraska, Iowa, and Illinois would furnish Gaines with a legal education "as sound, comprehensive, [and] valuable" as he would acquire at the University of Missouri.[135]

Law review commentators praised the Missouri Supreme Court's decision, noting that it rested on a firm precedential foundation. "The decision by the Missouri Court is clearly in line with the established holdings on this question," Harry Bitner wrote in the *Kansas City Law Review*.[136] Professor Solbert Wasserstrom, writing in the *Missouri Law Review*, echoed Bitner's assessment: "This ruling follows well established precedent."[137]

After the Supreme Court decided *Gaines*, the response among legal journals—while dramatically more favorable than that received by *Buchanan*—was nevertheless mixed. Among the law review commentators who praised *Gaines*, they did not typically de-

---

[130] Id at 86.

[131] Id at 87.

[132] See *State ex rel Gaines v Canada*, 113 SW2d 783 (Mo 1937).

[133] See id at 788.

[134] Id at 789.

[135] Id.

[136] Harry Bitner, *Recent Decisions*, 6 Kan City L Rev 154, 156 (1938).

[137] Solbert M. Wasserstrom, *Constitutional Law*, 3 Mo L Rev 355, 359 (1938).

pict the decision as a logical outgrowth of precedents.[138] Indeed, the reaction among the pro-*Gaines* contingent was closer to the opposite, viewing the decision as a welcome but hardly anticipated development. As a student writing in the *University of Chicago Law Review* commented: "In view of the traditional delicacy with which the Court has handled the problem of southern race relations, the instant decision represents a bold and laudable affirmation of Negro rights."[139] Whatever common law constitutionalism's many virtues, "bold[ness]" is not usually considered among them.

Not surprisingly, the negative reaction to *Gaines* was most pronounced in law reviews in the southern and border states.[140] But the phenomenon was not limited regionally, as law reviews based in the North also sounded skeptical notes about the decision.[141] An observer writing in the *Temple Law Quarterly*, for instance, warned about the dangers of addressing problems by "legal fiat."[142] A student note appearing in the *Fordham Law Review* criticized *Gaines* for taking what it viewed as an insufficiently pragmatic view of Missouri's program. "In these days of facility of locomotion no valid objection lies against distances to be traveled merely because a state border line must be crossed," the author chided. "[M]any a white student has elected to leave the state of his residence and seek legal education in another state. If he must travel to get to school what substantial difference could the *direction* of his travel make to any negro seeking a legal education in good faith?"[143]

Intriguingly, the Court's alleged elevation of abstract ideals over

---

[138] For some of the commentary praising *Gaines* as a welcome decision, see Willis David Curtiss, Jr., Note, 24 Cornell L Q 419, 421 (1939); Note, *The Negro Citizen in the Supreme Court*, 52 Harv L Rev 823, 830–31 (1939).

[139] Recent Case, 6 U Chi L Rev 301, 305 (1939).

[140] See, for example, Frank Thomas Miller, Jr., Recent Case, 17 NC L Rev 280, 284–85 (1939) (offering criticism of *Gaines*); Note, 13 Tulane L Rev 465, 466 (1939) (same).

[141] See Recent Cases, 13 Temple L Q 254, 256 (1939); Recent Decisions, *Refusal to Admit Negro to State Law School*, 8 Fordham L Rev 260, 260, 263 (1939). For an argument contending that constitutional scholars have often overstated regional differences regarding attitudes toward racial integration, see Justin Driver, *The Consensus Constitution*, 89 Tex L Rev 755, 803–25 (2011).

[142] Recent Cases, 13 Temple L Q at 256 (cited in note 141).

[143] Recent Decisions, *Refusal to Admit Negro*, 8 Fordham L Rev at 263 (cited in note 141). Professor Mark Tushnet has commented that the analysis contained in this note "is persuasive and suggests that *Gaines* had the potential to undermine the idea that separate facilities within a state were constitutional. The Supreme Court's willingness to invalidate Missouri's system by pinning its decision to an irrelevancy suggested that its real motivation was hostility to segregation." Mark V. Tushnet, *The NAACP's Legal Strategy against Segregated Education, 1925–1950* at 76 (North Carolina, 1987).

practical realities figured prominently in the contemporaneous critiques of *Gaines*. Some of the decision's detractors drew inspiration along these lines from Justice McReynolds's dissenting opinion in the decision. "The problem presented obviously is a difficult and highly practical one," McReynolds explained. "A fair effort to solve it has been made by offering adequate opportunity for study when sought in good faith. The State should not be unduly hampered through theorization inadequately restrained by experience."[144] A note appearing in the *North Carolina Law Review* concurred with Justice McReynolds's assessment that the issue "presents problems of great practical difficulty to those states which seek to segregate the races for the purpose of higher education."[145] John Breckinridge, writing in the *Kentucky Law Journal*, similarly explained: "To the crusader, acceptance of [Missouri's program] may seem a flagrant violation of the 'equal protection' guaranteed citizens under the Federal Constitution, but to one more concerned about the best interests of the colored race, the solution suggests itself as a sane and acceptable answer to a difficult question."[146] Wariness of the abstract commitment to equality evinced in *Gaines* even appeared in newspaper coverage. As the *St. Louis Post-Dispatch* editorial commented: "The United States Supreme Court brushed aside the more realistic approach of the Missouri Supreme Court, deciding the issue on a basis of pure logic."[147]

These negative reactions to *Gaines* vividly illustrate how living constitutionalism has periodically thrived on judicial commitments that are derided as insufficiently engaged with the real world. Indeed, judges have often traveled the path toward expanded conceptions of legal equality along an abstract plane. Constitutional theories that embrace the Burkean disdain for abstractions may have the effect of stifling innovative constitutional interpretations. Whereas Burkeans continually elevate what has worked, abstract commitments sometimes usefully reveal how what has worked is no longer workable.

---

[144] *Gaines*, 305 US at 354 (McReynolds, J, dissenting).

[145] See Miller, 17 NC L Rev at 285 (cited in note 140).

[146] John B. Breckinridge, Case Comment, 27 Ky L J 335, 338 (1939). Consider *Negroes in Law Schools*, 43 L Notes 1, 6 (1939) ("It is unfortunate that some cannot realize they injure only themselves and the cause they seek to further when they insist upon immediate reformations.").

[147] Quoted in *Press Comment on the Gaines Case*, Crisis 52 (Feb 1939).

But perhaps the clearest indication that the Court placed itself on the constitutional frontier in invalidating Missouri's program can be witnessed in the governmental reception that greeted *Gaines*. Rather than admitting blacks to the state's law school, Missouri simply opted to establish a slapdash law school for blacks within its own borders.[148] The University of Missouri, moreover, treated *Gaines* as though its logic applied exclusively to law school. As NAACP Legal Defense and Education Fund attorney Jack Greenberg would later recount: "A subsequent case had to be filed to secure admission of blacks to the Missouri School of Journalism."[149] More significantly, outside of Missouri, *Gaines* elicited not merely resistance but outright defiance. Only four other states had passed tuition subsidy laws similar to Missouri's when the Court outlawed such schemes in 1938. Ten years later, however, seventeen states had adopted such programs.[150] Although most of Strauss's account of living constitutionalism seems hermetically sealed from the real world ramifications of judicial decisions,[151] it seems safe to assume that actual judges are at least somewhat aware when they issue decisions that encounter substantial resistance. Such resistance matters, of course, because its existence may cause judges to refrain from issuing a decision otherwise seemingly required by precedential logic.

Turning to the Supreme Court's decision in *Gaines*, the opinion written by Chief Justice Hughes is perhaps most remarkable for how little effort it dedicates to asserting that its result finds much support in Supreme Court precedents. Early in the opinion, Chief Justice Hughes acknowledges: "The State has sought to fulfill [its] obligation by furnishing equal facilities in separate schools, a method the validity of which has been sustained by our decisions."[152] To support this proposition, *Gaines* cites four decisions:

---

[148] See Klarman, *From Jim Crow to Civil Rights* at 161 (cited in note 110) ("Missouri responded to *Gaines* by establishing a separate but obviously inferior law school for blacks."). Three months after the decision, Lloyd Gaines himself disappeared into thin air before he ever had an opportunity to enroll. See David Stout, *A Supreme Triumph, Then Into the Shadows*, NY Times A19 (July 11, 2009).

[149] Jack Greenberg, *Brown v. Board of Education: An Axe in the Frozen Sea of Racism*, 48 SLU L J 869, 881 (2004).

[150] See Klarman, *From Jim Crow to Civil Rights* at 161 (cited in note 110).

[151] A stark exception to Strauss's usual practice occurs in his analysis of *Roe v Wade*. See Strauss, *Living Constitution* at 92–97 (cited in note 20) (analyzing *Roe*'s legitimacy principally in light of its public acceptance).

[152] *Gaines*, 305 US at 344.

Plessy, McCabe, Gong Lum, and *Cumming*.[153] But, with the exception of *McCabe,* Chief Justice Hughes fails to cite any of those cases throughout the remainder of the opinion, never even attempting to explain how those decisions might be reconciled with the Court's conclusion in *Gaines.*

Admittedly, *Gaines* does cite *McCabe* in support of its conclusion, a point that Professor Strauss underlines. But it seems doubtful that *McCabe,* which cast doubt on a law permitting railways to provide upscale accommodations for white passengers but not black passengers, was actually vital to the Court's decision to invalidate Missouri's program. *Gaines* drew upon *McCabe* to support its conclusion that the small number of blacks seeking legal education in no way relieved the state of its obligations. But if precedent played a major role in *Gaines,* one would think that the Court would have grappled with its own precedents involving education. That it declined to do so speaks volumes about *Gaines's* regard for precedent. Professor Randall Kennedy pressed a similar point twenty-five years ago: "[E]ven without *McCabe* there is little doubt that *Gaines* would have been decided the same way for the same underlying reasons—reasons that had little to do with doctrinal seeds planted in 1914 and much more to do with the pressures of 1938."[154]

In addition, the most critical juncture of *Gaines*—which declares that states must provide in-state educational facilities for their own residents—fails to cite any Supreme Court precedents whatsoever. Instead, the Court simply announces the principle by suggesting that its newly articulated rule is somehow self-evident. "*Manifestly,* the obligation of the State to give the protection of equal laws can be performed only where its laws operate, that is, within its own jurisdiction," Chief Justice Hughes wrote. "It is there that the equality of legal right must be maintained."[155] But there is nothing self-evident about the rule articulated in *Gaines.* That rule stands in rather sharp contrast to the Court's earlier rule, which consistently found that the federal courts should not interfere with how states saw fit to educate, or—in the case of *Cumming*—not to educate their citizens.[156]

---

[153] See id. The Court's decision in *Berea College* goes wholly unmentioned.

[154] See Kennedy, 86 Colum L Rev at 1646 (cited in note 94).

[155] *Gaines,* 305 US at 350 (emphasis added).

[156] See text accompanying notes 120–31.

The manner in which Chief Justice Hughes constructed *Gaines*, in sum, strongly suggests that the Court was not sincerely attempting to apply *Plessy* and its progeny involving Jim Crow in the educational sphere. Rather than subconsciously drifting away from *Plessy*, the Court in *Gaines* appears to have been fully aware that its decision fit uncomfortably alongside existing Court precedents. *Gaines* nevertheless departed from those precedents, and demonstrated a new willingness to rein in state educational practices in the name of racial equality.

C. UNEASY ARRIVAL

The Supreme Court's decision in *Brown v Board of Education* reveals that the Justices who issued that decision did not view themselves as merely taking the final step in an orderly common law procession that slowly unfolded during a period spanning several decades. Even though the Justices who considered *Brown* could conceivably have claimed that the Court's prior decisions had completely eroded *Plessy*, the Justices generally viewed *Brown* as abandoning precedents, not extending them. *Brown* thus usefully illustrates that judges sometimes experience the constitutional terrain as rocky even if lawyers in subsequent years can identify certain precedents as having cleared the path. A theory of living constitutionalism that fails to capture how judges go about reaching decisions during the moments they actually reach those decisions risks stunting constitutional development.

Professor Strauss, to his credit, correctly acknowledges that "[t]he justices themselves apparently did not think of *Brown*" "[a]t the time . . . as merely the inevitable culmination of a common law evolution."[157] If anything, though, this statement errs in understating how the Justices generally interpreted the Court's precedents. Chief Justice Warren's replacement of Chief Justice Vinson in 1953 meant that ten Justices participated in the Court's internal deliberations on *Brown*. Of those ten Justices, the notes from conference discussions about the case suggest that only two Justices—Harold Burton and Sherman Minton—mentioned any of the Court's prior decisions as indicating that segregation should be

---

[157] Strauss, *Living Constitution* at 91 (cited in note 20).

deemed unconstitutional.[158] Neither Justice Burton nor Justice Minton, moreover, mentioned any Supreme Court decision that was decided before 1948.[159]

The eight remaining Justices expressed a wide range of views regarding the constitutionality of segregated schools during the conferences. With the exception of Justice Douglas—who found segregated schools to be plainly unconstitutional, but in no way suggested that precedent led him to that conclusion[160]—every other Justice interpreted the Court's precedents as supporting, rather than undermining, segregation in public schools.[161] Chief Justice Fred Vinson's opening comments during the Court's deliberations noted that "[t]here is a [b]ody of law [in] back of us on separate but equal."[162] Similarly, Justice Felix Frankfurter contended that invalidating school segregation would amount to declaring "this court has long misread the Constitution."[163] Justice Robert Jackson echoed this sentiment, saying: "[There is] nothing in the opinions of the courts that says it's unconstitutional. Nothing in the history of the 14th amendment [says it's unconstitu-

---

[158] Justice Burton contended: "*Sipuel* [and *Sweatt*] crossed the threshold of these cases. Education is more than building and facilities. It's a habit of mind." Klarman, *From Jim Crow to Civil Rights* at 297 (cited in note 110) (quotation marks and citations omitted). Justice Minton stated: "[A] body of law has laid down [the] separate but equal doctrine. That however has been whittled away in these cases [referring to *Sweatt* and *McLaurin*]." Id (quotation marks and citations omitted).

[159] Id.

[160] Justice Douglas stated that "[s]egregation is an easy problem" and that "[n]o classifications on the basis of race can be made." Id at 296 (quotation marks and citations omitted).

[161] Justice Black stated that he would likely find "segregation per se is bad *unless* the long line of decisions bars that construction of the amendment." Id at 294 (quotation marks and citations omitted). Justice Clark suggested that the Court's precedents "had led the states on to think segregation is OK" and that the Court should "let them work it out." Id at 297 (quotation marks and citations omitted). Justice Reed pressed the familiar line from the Court's education cases that "states should be left to work out the problem for themselves." Id at 295 (quotation marks and citations omitted). Along similar lines, John W. Davis—widely thought to be among the finest lawyers of his day—claimed in 1953 that the Court's many decisions affirming the constitutionality of segregated schools effectively eliminated the Court's ability to deem the practice unconstitutional. Arguing in the Supreme Court on behalf of South Carolina's schools, Davis contended: "[S]omewhere, sometime, to every principle comes a moment of repose when it has been so often announced, so confidently relied upon, so long continued, that it passes the limits of judicial discretion and disturbance." William H. Harbaugh, *Lawyer's Lawyer: The Life of John W. Davis* 514 (Oxford, 1973) (quotation marks and citations omitted).

[162] Klarman, *From Jim Crow to Civil Rights* at 294 (cited in note 110) (quotation marks and citations omitted).

[163] Id at 295 (quotation marks and citations omitted).

tional]. On [the] basis of precedent [I] would have to say segregation is ok."[164] In a separate opinion that Justice Jackson drafted in *Brown* but ultimately opted against publishing, he communicated this idea with his characteristic eloquence: "Almost a century of decisional law rendered by judges, many of whom risked their lives for the cause that produced these Amendments, is almost unanimous in the view that the Amendment tolerated segregation by state action."[165]

Chief Justice Warren's authorship of *Brown* lends his approach to the case particular salience. According to his comments at conference, the Court's precedents seem to have played an insignificant role in motivating his assessment that segregation was impermissible in public schools. Early in his remarks, Warren acknowledged concern about reversing the Court's precedents that had long affirmed the constitutionality of segregated schooling.[166] "But the more I've read and heard and thought," Chief Justice Warren explained, "the more I've come to conclude that the basis of segregation and 'separate but equal' rests upon a concept of the inherent inferiority of the colored race. I don't see how *Plessy* and the cases following it can be sustained on any other theory."[167] In order to bolster this conclusion, Chief Justice Warren cited the Reconstruction Amendments, but he pitched them at an extremely abstract level of generality.[168] Permitting school segregation, Chief Justice Warren contended, "would be contrary to the Thirteenth, Fourteenth, and Fifteenth Amendments. They were intended to make the slaves equal with all others."[169] Rather than contending that a decision striking down segregated schools was somehow rooted in judicial decisions from the past, Chief Justice Warren repeatedly emphasized to his colleagues that modernity required abandoning the racial attitudes of yesteryear. "I don't see how in

---

[164] Id at 296 (quotation marks and citations omitted).

[165] Id at 306 (quotation marks and citations omitted).

[166] See Bernard Schwartz, *Super Chief: Earl Warren and His Supreme Court—A Judicial Biography* 86 (NYU, 1983) (quotation marks and citations omitted).

[167] Id (quotation marks and citations omitted).

[168] Chief Justice Warren's intuition to make that analytical move was sound. See Laurence H. Tribe and Michael C. Dorf, *Levels of Generality in the Definition of Rights*, 57 U Chi L Rev 1057, 1058 (1990) ("The more abstractly one states the already-protected right, the more likely it becomes that the claimed right will fall within its protection.").

[169] Schwartz, *Super Chief* at 86 (cited in note 166) (quotation marks and citations omitted).

this day and age we can set any group apart from the rest and say that they are not entitled to exactly the same treatment as all others," Warren wrote. "Personally, I can't see how today we can justify segregation based solely on race."[170]

Warren's opinion for the Court in *Brown* elaborated upon this idea that racial segregation, whatever may have been appropriate during a bygone era, had become incompatible with modern understandings. "In approaching this problem, we cannot turn the clock back to 1868 when the [Fourteenth] Amendment was adopted, or even to 1896 when *Plessy v. Ferguson* was written," Warren wrote. "We must consider public education in the light of its full development and its present place in American life throughout the Nation."[171] Warren contended that it had become evident that the *Plessy* regime had grown antiquated along two different dimensions: the educational and the racial. In one of *Brown*'s most celebrated passages, Warren repeatedly proclaimed that the decision was rooted in contemporary notions regarding the value of education. "*Today*, education is perhaps the most important function of state and local governments. . . . *Today* it is a principal instrument in awakening the child to cultural values. . . . *In these days*, it is doubtful that any child may reasonably be expected to succeed in life if he is denied the opportunity of an education."[172] In perhaps *Brown*'s most controversial passage, Warren contended that contemporary understandings regarding race allowed society to appreciate the damage that segregated schooling inflicted upon black schoolchildren. In the sentence appended to *Brown*'s eleventh footnote, Warren wrote: "Whatever may have been the extent of psychological knowledge at the time of *Plessy v. Ferguson*, this finding is amply supported by modern authority."[173]

Warren's opinion in *Brown*, admittedly, drew some support from the Court's two most recent cases invalidating Jim Crow practices in graduate schools. Both *Sweatt* and *McLaurin*, Warren noted, hinged on "intangible considerations," which Warren cited in or-

---

[170] Id (quotation marks and citations omitted).

[171] *Brown*, 347 US at 492–93.

[172] Id at 493 (emphasis added).

[173] Id at 494. See id at 494 n 11 (citing, inter alia, Kenneth B. Clark, *Effect of Prejudice and Discrimination on Personality Development* (1950); Gunnar Myrdal, *An American Dilemma* (Harper, 1944)).

der to support his exploration of segregation's psychic tolls.[174] But the role of precedent in *Brown* is quite modest; Warren quickly cycled through the prior cases before making clear that they will not much inform the Court's analysis because *Brown*, unlike the precedents, squarely presented the constitutionality of separate but equal.[175]

That the Supreme Court in *Brown* did not avail itself of Strauss's conception of common law constitutionalism to explain that *Plessy* had already undergone gradual deterioration raises fundamental questions concerning the precedent-centric version of living constitutionalism. A theory of judging does not seem to provide much help if it fails to comport with how judges themselves understand their own actions in deciding cases at the time of the decisions. Originalists, no doubt in good faith, have sometimes seemed to engage in such ex post jurisprudential reasoning, offering explanations for how their theories can accommodate cases a few decades after they were initially decided, and, not coincidentally, well after those decisions have become canonical.[176] The problem with such enterprises, of course, is that judges employing these methods would have been unable to reach the now-venerated results in the first instance. And that, of course, is the instance that counts.[177] A robust theory of living constitutionalism must be able to account for how judges approach pathbreaking cases during the particular moments that they are actually deciding them, rather than merely offer justifications to prop them up decades after the fact. But without some conception of the constitutional frontier, living con-

---

[174] *Brown*, 347 US at 493; see id at 494 ("Such [intangible] considerations apply with added force to children in grade and high schools. To separate them from others of similar age and qualifications solely because of their race generates a feeling of inferiority . . . that may affect their hearts and minds in a way unlikely ever to be undone.").

[175] See id at 492 (stating that "[i]n the instant cases . . . [the separate but equal] question is directly presented").

[176] See, for example, McConnell, 81 Va L Rev at 1131–34 (cited in note 57) (arguing that originalism can account for *Brown*); Steven G. Calabresi and Julia T. Rickert, *Originalism and Sex Discrimination*, 90 Tex L Rev 1, 2 (2011) (arguing that originalism can account for the Court's sex equality cases).

[177] Notably, Professor Strauss has himself advanced this critique of originalism with particular force. See Strauss, 63 U Chi L Rev at 931 n 122 (cited in note 22) ("Even if Professor McConnell is right, and there is an originalist defense of *Brown*, it is surely a major difficulty with originalism as an approach to constitutional interpretation that no one was able to discover that defense for forty years—even though the advocates (and the Justices and law clerks) at the time of *Brown* had the strongest incentives to do so."). Yet Strauss's conception of living constitutionalism appears to suffer from precisely this weakness.

stitutionalism may be rendered stagnant, preventing decisions that would have eventually become revered from ever even getting on the books.

IV. The Living Constitution in Modern Life

The ongoing significance of the constitutional frontier, and the judges' affirmative role in that arena, can perhaps most clearly be glimpsed by examining a pressing legal issue from the modern era: the question of gay equality. Only fifteen years after the Supreme Court issued its first major decision vindicating the constitutional rights of gays and lesbians, it now seems nearly inevitable that the Court was bound to do so. But that was far from the case at the time. Indeed, the Court's initial foray into this arena set off no trivial amount of anxiety regarding the boundaries of judicial propriety. That anxiety extended even to people who, at least as a policy matter, supported the gay rights cause. Recovering that anxiety—along with the doctrinal innovation that was required to overcome it—is crucial, as doing so helps to belie the idea that marginalized groups acquire constitutional protections because judges somehow subconsciously gravitate away from permitting subordination and toward requiring equality. Rather than viewing themselves as participating in the orderly elaboration of common law constitutionalism, judges seem more likely to view themselves as consciously issuing decisions from the constitutional frontier at each step along the way. That lesson contains considerable timeliness, of course, because the Supreme Court may soon find itself in a position to breach the largest remaining legal barrier to gay equality.

The Supreme Court issued *Romer v Evans*[178] in 1996. In response to antidiscrimination laws based on sexual orientation that several Colorado localities had enacted, voters passed a statewide referendum adopting "Amendment 2" to the state constitution. Amendment 2 sought to prohibit state entities from treating gays, lesbians, and bisexuals as members of a protected class.[179] The Supreme Court, in a 6–3 opinion written by Justice Kennedy, invalidated Amendment 2 for violating the Equal Protection

---

[178] 517 US 620 (1996).

[179] Colo Const, Art II, § 30b (superseded 1996).

Clause. *Romer*, it appears safe to say, shocked the legal community.[180]

The shock stemmed principally, of course, from the existence of *Bowers v Hardwick*.[181] Only ten years before *Romer*, the Supreme Court had declared in *Bowers* that states could—without violating the Due Process Clause—criminally punish consenting adults for privately engaging in sodomy. In reaching that decision, the Court bitterly divided 5–4. It is hardly incidental that the central fault line separating the Justices in the *Bowers* majority from those in the dissent ran along the grounds of tradition. Justice White justified the result in his opinion for the Court mainly by citing a desire to avoid breaking with a practice that extended back into a distant age. Justice White's initial framing of the legal stakes at issue in *Bowers* reveals a pronounced concern with the august lineage of antisodomy provisions: "The issue presented is whether the Federal Constitution confers a fundamental right upon homosexuals to engage in sodomy and hence invalidates the laws of the many States that still make such conduct illegal and have done so for a very long time."[182] Given that antisodomy laws enjoy "ancient roots" and that "[s]odomy was a criminal offense at common law and was forbidden by the laws of the original thirteen States when they ratified the Bill of Rights," Justice White concluded that "to claim that a right to engage in such conduct is 'deeply rooted in this Nation's history and tradition' or 'implicit in the concept of ordered liberty' is, at best, facetious."[183] Chief Justice Burger's concurring opinion revealed a similarly reverential attitude toward tradition. In a dizzying historical display, Burger characterized in rapid succession negative attitudes toward homosexuality as they appeared in "the history of Western civilization," "Judeo-Christian moral and ethical standards," "Roman law," "the King's Courts," "the common law of England," and— almost inexorably—Blackstone.[184]

Conversely, the dissenting Justices in *Bowers* demonstrated a marked willingness to reject the constraints of traditional attitudes

---

[180] See, for example, Jeffrey Toobin, *Supreme Sacrifice*, New Yorker 44 (July 8, 1996) (calling *Romer* "the most surprising decision of this term").

[181] 478 US 186 (1986).

[182] Id at 190.

[183] Id at 192–94.

[184] Id at 196–97 (Burger, CJ, concurring).

toward homosexuality. Justice Blackmun—writing on behalf of Justices Brennan, Marshall, and Stevens—contended in his dissent that the extended existence of antisodomy laws did not establish they were constitutionally valid. "I cannot agree that . . . the length of time a majority has held its convictions . . . can withdraw legislation from this Court's scrutiny," Justice Blackmun reasoned.[185] "Like Justice Holmes, I believe that '[i]t is revolting to have no better reason for a rule of law than that so it was laid down in the time of Henry IV. It is still more revolting if the grounds upon which it was laid down have vanished long since, and the rule simply persists from blind imitation of the past.'"[186] Unlike his colleagues in the *Bowers* majority, Justice Blackmun did not fear suggesting that the Court's modern constitutional interpretations should reflect the modern world. "Despite historical views of homosexuality," Justice Blackmun wrote, "it is no longer viewed by mental health professionals as a 'disease' or disorder."[187] Justice Stevens's dissent in *Bowers* also demonstrated a strong willingness to abandon customs that had outlived their utility: "[T]he fact that the governing majority in a State has traditionally viewed a particular practice as immoral is not a sufficient reason for upholding a law prohibiting the practice; neither history nor tradition could save a law prohibiting miscegenation from constitutional attack."[188]

The fallout from *Bowers* in the lower courts vividly illustrates the perils of judges simply applying the closest available precedent without independently assessing whether a prior decision is constitutionally sound. In 1987, just one year after *Bowers*, the D.C. Circuit held in *Padula v Webster*[189] that the Federal Bureau of Investigation's alleged refusal to hire a lesbian on account of her sexual orientation did not violate the equal protection principles. Although *Bowers* was decided under the Due Process Clause, the D.C. Circuit reasoned, it effectively precluded courts from affording homosexuality heightened scrutiny under equal protection analysis. "If the Court was unwilling to object to state laws that

---

[185] *Bowers*, 478 US at 210 (Blackmun, J, dissenting).

[186] Id at 199 (Blackmun, J, dissenting), quoting Oliver Wendell Holmes, *The Path of the Law*, 10 Harv L Rev 457, 469 (1897).

[187] *Bowers*, 478 US at 202 n 2 (Blackmun, J, dissenting).

[188] Id at 216 (Stevens, J, dissenting).

[189] 822 F2d 97 (DC Cir 1987).

criminalize the behavior that defines the class, it is hardly open
. . . to conclude that state sponsored discrimination against the
class is invidious," *Padula* reasoned. "After all, there can hardly be
more palpable discrimination against a class than making the conduct that defines the class criminal."[190] Two years later, in *Wood-
ward v United States*,[191] the Federal Circuit employed this same
greater-includes-the-lesser reasoning when it weighed the Navy's
discharge of a gay reservist because of his sexual orientation. In
determining that the Navy's actions did not violate the Constitution, the Federal Circuit relied on *Padula* and explained: "After
Hardwick it cannot logically be asserted that discrimination against
homosexuals is constitutionally infirm."[192] Prior to *Romer*, the federal circuit courts routinely and overwhelmingly employed this
analysis in the course of denying constitutional protections to gays
and lesbians.[193]

With *Bowers* and its progeny firmly in mind, it becomes easy to
understand why the legal community during the mid-1990s generally thought that the Supreme Court in *Romer* had little choice
other than to uphold Amendment 2's legitimacy.[194] As Professor
Ronald Dworkin noted: "Many lawyers were . . . fearful . . . that
even if a majority of the justices wanted to strike down Amendment
2, they would not find room to do so within the network of doctrine and precedents they had themselves constructed."[195] If Georgia can declare that gay sex is illegal, such precedent-centered
thinking ran, Colorado can surely declare that sexual orientation
is an impermissible category for antidiscrimination law.

In the period leading up to *Romer*, some legal commentators

---

[190] Id at 103.

[191] 871 F2d 1068 (Fed Cir 1989).

[192] Id at 1076.

[193] See, for example, *Ben-Shalom v Marsh*, 881 F2d 454, 464 (7th Cir 1989) ("If homosexual conduct may constitutionally be criminalized, then homosexuals do not constitute
a suspect or quasi-suspect class entitled to greater than rational basis scrutiny for equal
protection purposes."); *Equality Foundation of Greater Cincinnati v City of Cincinnati*, 54
F3d 261, 268 (6th Cir 1995) (contending "*Bowers v. Hardwick* and its progeny command
that, as a matter of law, gays, lesbians, and bisexuals cannot constitute either a 'suspect
class' or a 'quasi-suspect class'. . . .").

[194] See David G. Savage, *Gay Rights at Stake in High Court Case*, LA Times A1 (Oct 9,
1995) ("Most constitutional lawyers say the Supreme Court is likely to . . . uphold Amendment 2 as constitutional"); Ronald Dworkin, *Sex, Death, and the Courts*, NY Rev Books
44 (Aug 8, 1996) ("[T]he experts were doubtful that the Supreme Court would invalidate
what Colorado had done.").

[195] Dworkin, NY Rev Books at 49 (cited in note 194).

with clear commitments to gay equality had difficulty believing that the Court would invalidate Amendment 2. Matthew Coles, director of the ACLU's Lesbian and Gay Rights Project, no doubt articulated the fears of many: "In my heart, I can't believe the Supreme Court would say it's OK to have two sets of rules—one for gays and one for everyone else. But the lawyer in me is a lot more worried than that."[196] Professor Jeffrey Rosen took that idea one step further, suggesting not only as a descriptive matter that the Court would likely validate Amendment 2, but as a normative matter that it would be correct to do so. Rosen's disdain for Colorado's law was palpable, as he called it "a stark and public insult to the dignity and equality of homosexual citizens," one that demeans them "based on their deepest personal characteristics."[197] Rosen nevertheless stated: "I'd gladly vote against the anti-gay rights initiative as a citizen of Colorado, but that's not the same as saying it's unconstitutional."[198] Characterizing himself as a "reluctant[] defend[er]" of Amendment 2's constitutionality, Rosen contended that invalidating the measure would amount to "judicial fiat," and furthermore that "striking down Amendment 2 as entirely irrational would be a very aggressive position for a judge to take."[199]

After the Supreme Court adopted precisely this very aggressive position in *Romer* by finding that the Colorado law did not pass even rational basis scrutiny,[200] prominent legal conservatives roundly denounced the decision as an improper judicial usurpation. Professor Lino Graglia, for instance, called *Romer* "[t]he operation of judicial policymaking in the name of the Constitution."[201] In addition to claiming that *Romer* exceeded the bounds

---

[196] Savage, LA Times at A1 (cited in note 194).

[197] Jeffrey Rosen, *Disoriented*, New Republic 26 (Oct 23, 1995).

[198] Id at 24.

[199] Id at 25–26.

[200] See *Romer*, 517 US at 632 ("[Amendment 2's] sheer breadth is so discontinuous with the reasons offered for it that the amendment seems inexplicable by anything but animus toward the class it affects; it lacks a rational relationship to legitimate state interests.").

[201] Lino A. Graglia, *Romer v. Evans: The People Foiled Again by the Constitution*, 68 U Colo L Rev 409, 412 (1997). See Linda Greenhouse, *Colorado Law Void*, NY Times A1, A20 (May 21, 1996) (quoting Gary L. Bauer as contending that *Romer* "should send chills down the back of anyone who cares whether the people of this nation any longer have the power of self-rule" and that the decision came from "an out-of-control unelected judiciary") (quotation marks omitted); Robert H. Bork, *Federalist Society Symposium Tenth Anniversary Banquet Speech*, 13 J L & Pol 513, 513 (1997) (suggesting that in *Romer* the Court "legislated special protections for homosexuals").

of judicial propriety, conservatives further charged that the opinion failed as a matter of judicial craft, not only ignoring precedent but also inadequately explaining its legal reasoning.[202] Professor Douglas Kmiec put the point concisely. "The court had only assertion on its side," he wrote.[203]

Skeptical evaluations of *Romer* were far from limited to arch conservatives. Indeed, reporters writing in mainstream periodicals also cast grave doubt on *Romer*'s constitutional legitimacy. Writing in *Newsweek*, David Kaplan and Daniel Kleidman acerbically observed: "The majority opinion of Justice Anthony Kennedy . . . is emotional and grand. . . . The problem is that Kennedy's opinion reads more like a political manifesto than a piece of judicial reasoning."[204] In particular, *Newsweek* faulted Justice Kennedy for writing a decision that "offered no explanation in terms of constitutional history or theory."[205] Pressing this same criticism, journalist Stuart Taylor commented: "Justice Kennedy's majority opinion conspicuously failed to articulate a principled justification. His opinion was rooted neither in original meaning nor in precedent, and provided little guidance for future controversies."[206]

Romer also inspired widespread teeth gnashing among liberal law professors—the group who would have been most expected to greet warmly a Supreme Court decision advancing gay equality. When prominent legal academics aired doubts about *Brown v Board of Education*'s constitutional legitimacy, Professor Charles Black wrote a celebrated defense called simply "The Lawfulness of the Segregation Decisions."[207] Four decades later, Professor H. Jefferson Powell dusted off the formulation in defending "The

---

[202] See Steven G. Calabresi, *Textualism and the Countermajoritarian Difficulty*, 66 Geo Wash L Rev 1373, 1381 (1998) (calling *Romer* "cryptic"); Jay S. Bybee, *The Equal Process Clause: A Note on the (Non)Relationship between Romer v. Evans and Hunter v. Erickson*, 6 Wm & Mary Bill Rts J 201, 203, 225 (1997) (same). Consider Bork, 13 J L & Pol at 513 (cited in note 201) ("It is hard to tell what the *Romer* decision means, because it is basically incomprehensible.").

[203] Douglas W. Kmiec, *Irrationality Prevails in Gay Rights Ruling*, LA Times B9 (May 22, 1996).

[204] David A. Kaplan and Daniel Kleidman, *A Battle, Not the War*, Newsweek 24, 30 (June 3, 1996).

[205] Id.

[206] Stuart Taylor, Jr., *Is Judicial Restraint Dead?* Legal Times S25, S27 (July 29, 1996).

[207] Charles L. Black, Jr., *The Lawfulness of the Segregation Decisions*, 69 Yale L J 421, 421 (1960).

Lawfulness of *Romer v. Evans.*[208] As Powell explained, "[T]here is considerable sentiment for the proposition that *Romer* is difficult to justify on conventional terms or that it must rest on some basis not easily reconciled with the opinion of the Court itself."[209] Even among academics who ultimately embraced *Romer*, many of them allowed that they initially found the decision perplexing and difficult to reconcile as legitimate. As Professor Akhil Amar noted, "I must confess that before I read Justice Kennedy's opinion . . . I too had great difficulty in seeing how the Colorado referendum was unconstitutional. . . . It is hard to see how, under existing equal protection doctrine, a simple declaration that 'sexual orientation is not just like race' is unconstitutional."[210] Relatedly, Professor Lynn Baker indicated that her "initial reaction . . . to the Supreme Court's decision . . . was deeply ambivalent" and stated that she "was troubled by the Court's opinion."[211] Amplifying these concerns, Marc Larkins contended: "Although the Court may be correct that laws of this nature are morally deplorable, it appears clear that the Court should have found more substantial judicial precedent in which to base its opinion."[212] But the difficulty, of course, was not an insufficient effort to locate supporting precedential authority; such authority simply did not exist to be found.

Romer's most ardent supporters extolled the decision not for its careful parsing of precedents, but for its willingness to cast off prevailing doctrinal paradigms. Dworkin welcomed *Romer* as a "surprisingly bold" decision in its approach toward the Equal Protection Clause.[213] Writing in these pages one year after the decision, Professor Louis Michael Seidman contended that *Romer* harkened back to the Warren Court's style of judicial decision

---

[208] See H. Jefferson Powell, *The Lawfulness of Romer v. Evans*, 77 NC L Rev 241, 241 (1998). Consider Andrew Koppleman, *Romer v. Evans and Invidious Intent*, 6 Wm & Mary Bill Rts J 89, 93 (1997) (contending *Romer* was a lawful decision driven by a concern regarding "impermissible purpose").

[209] Powell, 77 NC L Rev at 242 (cited in note 208). See Daniel Farber and Suzanna Sherry, *The Pariah Principle*, 13 Const Comm 257, 262 (1996) (noting that *Romer* has elicited "puzzlement [from] legal commentators").

[210] Akhil Reed Amar, *Attainder and Amendment 2: Romer's Rightness*, 95 Mich L Rev 203, 204 (1996).

[211] See Lynn A. Baker, *The Missing Pages of the Majority Opinion in Romer v. Evans*, 68 U Colo L Rev 387, 387 (1997).

[212] Marc D. Larkins, Case Note, 7 Seton Hall Const L J 987, 1008 (1997).

[213] Dworkin, NY Rev Books at 49 (cited in note 194).

making with its "casual attitude" toward prior opinions.[214] "In place of technical discussion of precedent and doctrine, Kennedy relies upon sweeping moral generalities—some might say bromides," Seidman wrote.[215] Despite the opinion's frailties owed to the lack of existing legal authorities, Seidman nevertheless applauded *Romer* for its advancement of gay equality. "By handing gay people their first major Supreme Court victory in the history of the republic," Seidman noted, "the opinion substantially alters the legal landscape."[216]

The Supreme Court's reliance in *Romer* on an unusual amicus brief written by Professor Laurence Tribe usefully illustrates how the decision stemmed from the constitutional frontier.[217] Rather than assembling precedents and making them march in syllogistic splendor toward a seemingly inescapable legal destination, Professor Tribe eschewed the standard brief-writing practice and instead began with something close to first principles.[218] Tribe's brief—which weighed in at a lean thirteen pages and cited only a small handful of precedents—amounted to an exercise in defamiliarization. "No extrapolation from precedents dealing with racial or other minorities, or from precedents dealing with rights of political or legal participation, is needed to conclude that this selective preclusion of claims of discrimination violates the Equal Protection Clause," he wrote.[219] Tribe contended that Colorado's law was extremely unusual and that the Court need not resort to its ready-made tiers of scrutiny: "Amendment 2 is a rare example of a *per se* violation of the Equal Protection Clause."[220] In subsequently explaining how he arrived at the brief's argument, Tribe revealed a willingness to adopt a fresh approach to legal questions

---

[214] Louis Michael Seidman, *Romer's Radicalism: The Unexpected Revival of Warren Court Activism*, 1996 Supreme Court Review 67, 69.

[215] Id at 69.

[216] Id at 67–68.

[217] See Brief of Laurence H. Tribe, John Hart Ely, Gerald Gunther, Philip B. Kurland, and Kathleen M. Sullivan, as Amici Curiae in Support of Respondents, *Romer v Evans*, No 94-1039, *4 (filed June 9, 1995) ("Tribe Brief") (available on Westlaw at 1995 WL 17008432). The Court's reliance may have occurred sub silentio, but it nevertheless seems unmistakable. See Greenhouse, NY Times at A1, A20 (cited in note 201) (noting the close resemblance between Tribe's brief and *Romer's* analysis).

[218] I owe the phrase "syllogistic splendor" to Professor Charles Alan Wright. See Charles Alan Wright, *"How I Write" Essays*, 4 Scribes: J Legal Writing 87, 90 (1993).

[219] Tribe Brief at *4.

[220] Id at *3.

and ignore the prior decisions that the Supreme Court had amassed over the years. "I really started with the words of the Constitution—'equal protection of the laws,'" Tribe explained. "The law protects people by giving them remedies when they've been wronged. What Amendment 2 did was say that some people can't get the same protections as others. The protection is not equal. It sounds like third-grade reasoning, but that's how I came to it."[221] It should come as little surprise that some liberal legal commentators viewed Tribe's brief as hopelessly abstract with little chance of gaining traction in the real world.[222]

Abstractions, as it turned out, were precisely what Justice Kennedy relied upon to support the Court's decision in *Romer*. The very first sentence of Justice Kennedy's opinion made clear that the decision would examine the Equal Protection Clause's implications for Amendment 2 at an extraordinarily high level of generality. Rather than pitching the decision as one involving gay rights, Justice Kennedy instead began with Justice Harlan's dissent in *Plessy*, suggesting that Amendment 2 was but a recent instantiation of a long, dishonorable legacy of American exclusion. "One century ago, the first Justice Harlan admonished this Court that the Constitution 'neither knows nor tolerates classes among citizens,'" Justice Kennedy began.[223] With an implicit nod toward Professor Tribe's brief, Justice Kennedy conceived of Amendment 2 as falling outside of the typical Equal Protection Clause rubrics. "A law declaring that in general it shall be more difficult for one group of citizens than for all others to seek aid from the government is itself a denial of equal protection of the laws in the most literal sense," Justice Kennedy wrote.[224] As to the question of how to distinguish *Bowers*—a precedent that many observers viewed as an insurmountable obstacle to the Court issuing a decision invalidating Amendment 2[225]—Justice Kennedy's opinion in *Romer*

---

[221] Toobin, New Yorker at 43, 44 (cited in note 180).

[222] Professor Rosen stated at the time: "The weakness of Tribe's elegant argument is that it relies on an unusually abstract definition of 'discrimination.'" Rosen, New Republic at 26 (cited in note 197). Rosen further argued, "By defining the wrong of 'discrimination' so abstractly, Tribe elides the difference between forms of discrimination that are and are not wrongful and illegal under state and federal law." Id.

[223] *Romer*, 517 US at 623, quoting *Plessy*, 163 US at 559 (Harlan, J, dissenting).

[224] Id at 633.

[225] See Seidman, 1996 Supreme Court Review at 69 (cited in note 214) (observing that *Romer* "fails so much as to mention *Bowers v Hardwick*, which many had thought dispositive").

simply turned a blind eye to the Court's most prominent decision involving homosexuality. During the decade between 1986 and 1996, the Supreme Court issued no opinions in any way suggesting that it had become impermissible to treat gays and lesbians as criminals and pariahs. But *Romer*, thanks to its bold willingness to abandon precedent, suddenly made clear that the days of such treatment were limited.[226]

Justice Scalia's dissent in *Romer*, predictably, excoriated the Court for its shabby treatment of tradition and precedent. Scalia contended that the Court had "take[n] sides in this culture war" about homosexuality "not only by inventing a novel and extravagant constitutional doctrine to take the victory away from traditional forces, but even by verbally disparaging as bigotry adherence to traditional attitudes."[227] Scalia further complained: "Today's opinion has no foundation in American constitutional law, and barely pretends to."[228] The novelty of the Court's approach, Justice Scalia commented, helped to explain why *Romer* ran "so long on emotive utterance and so short on relevant legal citation."[229] The citation most conspicuous in its absence did not, of course, escape Justice Scalia's notice. "In *Bowers v. Hardwick*, we held that the Constitution does not prohibit what virtually all States had done from the founding of the Republic until very recent years—making homosexual conduct a crime," Justice Scalia wrote. "That holding is unassailable, except by those who think that the Constitution changes to suit current fashions."[230]

Many observers believe that current attitudes will soon motivate the Supreme Court to acknowledge a constitutional right to same-sex marriage.[231] Should the Supreme Court issue such a decision, the opinion will almost certainly cite the judiciary's expanding conception of gay rights, and may even intimate that precedents

---

[226] See Dworkin, NY Rev Books at 50 (cited in note 194) ("Scalia was right, in his biting dissent, that the combination of the result in *Evans* and the result in *Bowers* is ludicrous. . . .").

[227] *Romer*, 517 US at 652 (Scalia, J, dissenting).

[228] Id at 653 (Scalia, J, dissenting).

[229] Id at 639 (Scalia, J, dissenting).

[230] Id at 640–41 (Scalia, J, dissenting).

[231] Since Judge Vaughn Walker issued a decision validating the right to same-sex marriage on August 4, 2010, that case has been—haltingly—making its way to the Court. See *Perry v Schwarzenegger*, 704 F Supp 2d 921 (ND Cal 2010). The Ninth Circuit affirmed Judge Walker's opinion. See *Perry v Brown*, 2012 WL 372713.

like *Romer* and *Lawrence v Texas*[232] (and perhaps an invalidation of the Defense of Marriage Act,[233] too) have foreordained it. But should a decision recognizing marital equality arrive, it will not be because the Justices look up only to realize that they must take one final, modest step along a path that has been laid out for them by their predecessors. Rather, just as the Court in *Romer* required Justices who were willing to repudiate traditional attitudes toward homosexuality, and just as *Lawrence* required the same, a Supreme Court opinion announcing a constitutional right to same-sex unions will require Justices who knowingly reject conventional attitudes toward marriage. Preserving the tradition of robust living constitutionalism, in sum, requires Justices who are willing to buck tradition.

V. Conclusion

Frederick Jackson Turner opened his address in 1893 by observing that the American frontier had closed.[234] Citing a bulletin from the Superintendent of the Census, Turner noted that the United States government had recently declared that it would no longer track the frontier in its reports because the nation's western settlement had succeeded in eliminating the existence of wide-open expanses of land. Turner commented, "This brief official statement marks the closing of a great historic movement. Up to our own day American history has been in a large degree the history of the colonization of the Great West."[235] From that point of departure, Turner launched into his argument pressing the frontier's centrality in the forging of American democracy and, indeed, in the creation of American identity. But, at the very end of his essay, Turner circled back to where he began and concluded with a dramatic flourish. Given how the preceding remarks ele-

---

[232] 539 US 558 (2003).

[233] The federal cases decided by Judge Tauro in July 2010 involving challenges to the Defense of Marriage Act, 1 USC § 7 and 28 USC § 1738c (2006) (DOMA), potentially raise a narrower set of issues than those raised by lawsuits directly challenging state prohibitions on same-sex marriage. See *Gill v Office of Personnel Management*, 699 F Supp 2d 374 (D Mass 2010) (holding that DOMA violated the equal protection principles embodied in the Fifth Amendment); *Massachusetts v United States Department of Health & Human Services*, 698 F Supp 2d 234 (D Mass 2010) (holding that DOMA exceeded Congress's power under the Spending Clause and violated the Tenth Amendment).

[234] Turner, *Significance of the Frontier* at 31 (cited in note 5).

[235] Id.

vated the frontier and equated it with nothing less than the national character, the final sentence assumes the form of a eulogy. "[N]ow," Turner wrote, "four centuries from the discovery of America, at the end of a hundred years of life under the Constitution, the frontier has gone, and with its going has closed the first period of American history."[236]

Whatever the precise relationship between the geographical frontier and American history, it is quite distinct from the relationship between the conceptual frontier and American constitutional law in at least one substantial respect: No governmental entity will soon issue a bulletin announcing that the Constitution's conceptual frontier has closed. Unlike an amount of land, which is necessarily limited, the possibilities contained in constitutional interpretation are virtually limitless.[237] Writing in 1968, at the twilight of the Warren Court, Justice Traynor put this point memorably. "A modern judge has the last word in a steadily widening area of unprecedented controversies," Traynor noted. "Spectacular examples of new frontiers indicate that there are no last frontiers in the law."[238]

Many modern legal liberals would hasten to qualify, though, that it is no longer 1968. During the intervening four decades, the nation in general and the Supreme Court in particular have become dramatically more conservative. Accordingly, these legal liberals would argue, it is unwise to acknowledge, let alone emphasize, the wide-ranging possibilities that exist in constitutional interpretation. Liberals are unlikely to find attractive the jurisprudential structures that the current Supreme Court would erect in its newly discovered frontiers anyway. Picking up on this theme, some legal scholars have suggested that liberals currently venerate precedent-based approaches to judicial decision making not as a first-order preference; rather, liberals extol prior judicial decisions as a method of both preserving victories that have already been

---

[236] Id at 60.

[237] But see generally Sanford Levinson, *Our Undemocratic Constitution: Where the Constitution Goes Wrong (and How We the People Can Correct It)* (Oxford, 2006) (emphasizing the severe constraints imposed by constitutional structure).

[238] Roger J. Traynor, *Statutes Revolving in Common-Law Orbits*, 17 Catholic U L Rev 401, 401 (1968).

won, and forestalling conservative defeats that would otherwise loom on the horizon.[239]

To the extent that this critique accurately captures the motivation of precedent-centric liberal legal scholars, it suffers from two primary problems. First, the current Supreme Court has given little indication that it requires permission from liberal law professors before moving constitutional law in newly conservative directions. During the course of a single Term, the Roberts Court engineered dramatic overhauls of existing liberal precedents in several key areas, including campaign financing,[240] taxpayer standing in the Establishment Clause setting,[241] and racial classifications to achieve meaningfully integrated educational environments.[242] This deluge prompted Ronald Dworkin to complain: "The revolution that many commentators predicted when President Bush appointed two ultra-right-wing Supreme Court justices is proceeding with breathtaking impatience, and it is a revolution Jacobin in its disdain for tradition and precedent."[243] Those remarks preceded the Supreme Court's decision discarding a nearly seventy-year-old precedent in *District of Columbia v Heller*,[244] where the Court discovered that the Second Amendment protects an individual's right to bear firearms for purposes of self-defense.[245] While the old adage holding that it is best to let sleeping dogs lie may well be true, the current Supreme Court can hardly be accused of napping.

Second, in addition to overstating the benefits that flow from exalting stare decisis to conservatives, the theory may also underestimate the costs that such an approach inflicts on liberal jurists faced with determining whether to bring marginalized groups into the constitutional fold. Deeming legal opinions "lawless" because they cannot find close links to prior judicial decisions risks

---

[239] See, for example, Prakash, 106 Colum L Rev at 2214 (cited in note 53) ("Sunstein's minimalism is a defense of the doctrinal status quo. Cynics might say that the minimalist defense of current doctrine is the best that liberals currently can hope to achieve. On this view, minimalism is a rear-guard action designed to fend off the supposed conservative trajectory of the law. . . .").

[240] *Federal Election Commission v Wisconsin Right to Life*, 551 US 449 (2007).

[241] *Hein v Freedom from Religion Foundation, Inc.*, 551 US 587 (2007).

[242] *Parents Involved in Community Schools v Seattle School District No. 1*, 551 US 701 (2007).

[243] Ronald Dworkin, *The Supreme Court Phalanx*, NY Rev Books 92 (Sept 27, 2007).

[244] 554 US 570 (2008).

[245] Id at 635–36.

motivating even liberally inclined judges to offer stifled conceptions of the nation's constitutional commitments. One danger of
shouting the importance of precedent from the rooftops is that
doing so may inadvertently inspire left-leaning judges to shrink
from issuing decisions that they believe are compatible with the
Constitution, but find no clear analog in prior case law. Sometimes,
no matter how closely a judge scrutinizes the legal past, history
may lack decisions paving the way for opinions that sustain the
modern constitutional order. The absence of such prior judicial
authority does not mean, however, that judges should either refrain
from issuing progressive constitutional interpretations, or feel that
they are acting lawlessly if they do so. Some of our most cherished
constitutional decisions have come about precisely because judges
decide—consciously—to cast aside their predecessors' outmoded
thinking, and place themselves on the constitutional frontier. Any
theory of constitutional interpretation that even implicitly suggests
that judges who participated in those decisions somehow fell down
on the job should similarly be cast aside.

   Living constitutionalism, properly conceived, must create significant leeway for judicial interpretations that deviate from even
well-settled precedents. Without that leeway, it will prove extremely difficult, if not impossible, to expand constitutional visions
in ways that are not already accommodated, in at least some ger-
minal sense, by prevailing constitutional interpretations. That is
a recipe for constitutional stasis. Such a backward-looking view
of constitutional interpretation fits at best awkwardly within the
American tradition of liberal legal thought, as it effectively forecloses the constitutional frontier. A living constitutionalism that
accounts for periodic breaks with the past, in contrast, presents a
living constitutionalism liberals can live with.